HANGING ON IN PARADISE

HANGING ON IN PARADISE

FRED LAWRENCE GUILES

SELECTED FILMOGRAPHIES BY JOHN E. SCHULTHEISS

McGraw-Hill Book Company

New York   St. Louis   San Francisco   Toronto

Book Design by Marcy J. Katz

123456789KPKP798765

Library of Congress Cataloging in Publication Data

Guiles, Fred Lawrence.
    Hanging on in paradise.

    1.   Moving-picture industry—California—Hollywood.
I.   Title.
PN1993.5.U65G84   338.4′7′791430973   74-18394
ISBN 0-07-025118-5

The author is grateful to the following for permission to quote passages
from copyrighted material:

Avon Books/Discus and Richard Corliss for *The Hollywood Screenwriters*,
     copyright © 1972.
Columbia Pictures and Charles Lederer for material from *His Girl Friday*,
     © 1940.
Crown Publishers, Inc., John Gassner, and Dudley Nichols for the Preface
     to "Wilson," from Best Filmplays 1943–1944, copyright © 1945,
     1972.
Dell Publishing Company, Inc./Delacorte Press and Sara Mayfield for *The
     Constant Circle: H. L. Mencken and His Friends*, copyright © 1968.
Doubleday & Company and Will H. Hays for *The Memoirs of Will H.
     Hays*, copyright © 1955.
Doubleday & Company and Anthony Glyn for *Elinor Glyn*, copyright ©
     1955.
E. P. Dutton & Co., Inc., and Herman G. Weinberg for *The Lubitsch
     Touch*, copyright © 1968.
Esquire magazine for Ben Hecht, "Elegy for Wonderland," © 1959 by
     Esquire, Inc.
Faber and Faber and Elsa Lanchester for *Charles Laughton and I*, copyright
     © 1938.
Bernard Geis Associates, Inc., Harpo Marx, and Rowland Barber for *Harpo
     Speaks!*, copyright © 1961.
Harper & Row, Publishers, Inc., and John Mason Brown for *The Worlds of
     Robert E. Sherwood: Mirror to His Times*, copyright © 1965.
Harper & Row, Publishers, Inc., and Grover Smith for *Letters of Aldous
     Huxley*, copyright © 1969.
Hill & Wang and John Howard Lawson for *Film: The Creative Process*,
     copyright © 1964.

(continued on page 396)

TO MY FATHER
(1884–1950)

Also by Fred Lawrence Guiles

NORMA JEAN: The Life of Marilyn Monroe
MARION DAVIES

A NOTE OF ACKNOWLEDGMENT

I owe a large debt to screenwriter Charles Lederer for giving so much of his time and vitality. Charlie saw to it that the shark I was pursuing did not turn out to be a whale.

While in progress, this book resembled a film in production. There were whole chapters processed down to the last draft and later discarded as of only peripheral interest. Anecdotes that had no direct relationship to the main narrative were eliminated; thus, we have very little about the brilliant Harry Kurnitz, since none of the anecdotes about him seemed central to the story. Furthermore, I interviewed half a dozen contemporary Hollywood figures who were not writers simply for background on the current scene there. I am sorry indeed that quotations from them have been used so sparingly, if at all, but they contributed to my understanding in ways I hope are visible.

Many thanks to Billy Wilder and Joseph L. Mankiewicz for allowing me inside their working areas (Wilder on the set and Mankiewicz in his Eastern study where he was in the midst of the first draft of a new movie) to discuss the problems of the filmwriter. My most profound appreciation, too, must go to authors John Howard Lawson, Christopher Isherwood, Nunnally Johnson, George Oppenheimer, Miss Anita Loos, Wells Root, Allen Rivkin, Frances Goodrich and Albert Hackett,

Abraham Polonsky, Albert Maltz and Wyatt Cooper; and to Miss Helen Hayes (Mrs. Charles MacArthur), Miss Geraldine Fitzgerald, the late Veronica Lake, Mrs. Anne Shirley Lederer, and Mrs. Beatrice Ames for allowing me to intrude, discreetly I hope, into relatively private corners of their lives; to James Powers of the American Film Institute for giving me access to transcriptions of oral film history; to Joseph J. Cohn, former Metro-Goldwyn-Mayer production supervisor, and Elihu Winer, of the Writer's Guild of America, East; to Professor Matthew Bruccoli for discussing all phases of Fitzgerald's career with me; to Fouad Said of Cinemobile, Richard Berg of Metromedia, Herb Steinberg of Universal Pictures, and producer Martin Manulis for giving me their views of contemporary Hollywood; and to the Librarians of the Academy of Motion Picture Arts and Sciences, the American Film Institute, and the Lincoln Center Library of the Performing Arts. Acknowledgment is made here and elsewhere to Professor John Schultheiss for his brilliant Filmographies; they appear in the back of this book.

Additionally, I wish to thank Mrs. Barbara Jackson and Miss Lily Shohan for helping to type the final manuscript, and last, but surely not least, Albert Leventhal, whose enthusiasm for this project kept it from becoming an orphan.

Fred Lawrence Guiles
New York City, November 1974

CONTENTS

picture sections appear following pages 96, 190, and 280

They are gone.

New geniuses have muscled in to replace them. New producers, stars, directors, writers, fill the empty shoes. They have the look to me of a second team taking over. Not that there is less talent in them, less know-how, or even less ego. But there is small mania in them.

The mania that kept the first and second flowering of moviemakers working till they dropped; that turned every dinner party, drinking bout, and love hegira into a story conference; that gave no hoot for politics, patriotism, global disturbances, or anything else on earth except the making of a knockout movie; the mania that believed in movies as if God had sent them; that put the movies unblushingly beside Shakespeare, Shaw, Dostoevsky, and Euripides; that regarded New York, Paris, and London as bourgeois suburbs of Hollywood; the mania that buttonholed a billion of the earth's inhabitants and held them spellbound with the zaniest, goriest, and most swivel-headed swarm of humpty-dumpty fables ever loosed on mankind—that mania is almost gone out of today's moviemakers.

Ben Hecht, 1960

Hang there like fruit, my soul,
Till the tree die!

POSTHUMUS in *Cymbeline*

PART ONE
REQUIEM

1.

First of all, let us concede that Hollywood as "a dream factory" has passed into history. This story, then, of writers in Hollywood confines itself to that era when the film community not only was alive but harbored many of the most creative talents anywhere: the best writers, directors, cinematographers, set and costume designers, editors, and performers—although the studios did create a breed of star personalities who never did anything but slight variations of themselves.

Illusion was the coin of the realm in Hollywood. It was, for the most part, *a sanitized illusion* if one accepts the bloody sadism of Cecil B. De Mille's Biblical dramas as pure in intent (a very difficult thing to do, but which was managed neatly by every Christian church in this country and abroad). Illusion was something that went onto celluloid and in some instances was carried home to the good life in Benedict Canyon.

But disillusion was always a threat, rather like a subterranean fault running below Sunset Boulevard. It was a sinking feeling in the pit of the stomach when a picture failed; when your wife turned out to be a hustler who left you for a producer; when an option was dropped. It was a great breach of local mores to concede that there were miasmic swamps just beyond your doorstep (perhaps that is why there are no sidewalks in Bel Air or Beverly Hills above Sunset). Disillusion quietly stained the souls of handsome kids suddenly turned gas jockeys or waitresses when they found themselves on the bottom rung of the economic ladder. Their seductive blue eyes and flirty smiles could have won them easy advancement back home. Here in southern California, they faded into the tall, blondish, tanned multitudes.

Today, it is no longer possible to conceal the generalized malaise and melancholy that have seeped into the corners of the place. Newcomers are shaken by the discovery that it is no longer a movie center; that most of the features being shot are made on modest budgets for a quick return on television. And yet the old myth prevails enough to draw most of the rock stars and some of the new film personalities to make their homes in the hills or at the beach. It appears to satisfy something that their mothers have taught them—that success in show business means either Hollywood or Broadway. Rock stars especially are more tuned in to California ways than Eastern ones. Conversation is spare, near cabalistic.

Among the old-timers, those who remember when Hollywood was more than just a town full of movie studios and stars, when it was a force in the world, hard times have sealed their lips. It is as though they fear that the curse that has befallen them will become more terrible and lasting if they breach the silence. There is a sense of mortuary rectitude in their responses.

In old Hollywood today, that geographical section of Los Angeles whose outer boundaries appear to be Doheny Drive on its western edge and Vermont Avenue to the east, the numerous "For Rent" signs suggest that the town is well on its way to becoming another Virginia City, the difference being that an army of carny men has invaded the Sunset Strip to generate some human excitement on the lowest level. For the rest—cut-rate stores, super markets, used-car lots, and gas stations—it is no more an outrage to the sensibilities than, say, Pittsburgh. And some peculiarly Hollywood customs persist. If there are weeds in some front yards of untenanted houses and plywood over a few cracked windows, this seaminess disappears at night when the neighboring houses turn on their palm tree floodlights. It has the chromatic appeal of Las Vegas after dark.

The film moguls, like the Comstock millionaires several generations earlier, left plaster and stucco ghost mansions behind them. Those Italianate and Spanish villas are comfortable to look at. They are unique examples of a bastard form of architecture that suited their time and place perfectly. They suggest an opulence that is gone but that was much more civilized and less *kitsch* than Hollywood's historians have indicated (a great deal of snobbery has gone into Hollywood chronicles). Nearly all built when a free imagination was rampant in the colony and touched everything (including a number of movies made then), these mansions have defied time; their landscaping has flourished and, as much as anything, they sustain the illusive hope that a few *Godfathers* will bring it all to life again.

It is significant that the Founding Fathers of American films came to California and stayed. If they had settled in Long Island, as they did early in this century, American movies would have taken a different turn. But that sense of impermanence, that tinge of unreality, which pervades the atmosphere in southern California, gave the big studios' product an identifiable, "Hollywood" stamp.

Swanson and Negri and wild Clara Bow with her red chow dog in her Kissel will never be seen again on their way to Paramount Studios down on Marathon Street. Blithe and handsome Dorothy Mackaill, a transitional figure who began in silents as the blind girl in *Tol'able David,* no longer seethes in her dressing room at Warner Brothers–First National over Jack Warner's abuse of her considerable talents. Ernst Lubitsch, more than anyone the personification of the European filmmaker in Hollywood—undersized, wearing knickers, a cigar perpetually clenched between his teeth—gone.

There was a time when none of them believed in the impermanence of that world. Perhaps one had the breath of a suspicion. Clara's laughter was said to have been a little shrill.

Rita Hayworth and other surviving legends living quiet, very private lives in a perpetual morning-after, as well as landladies of those half-empty apartment houses whose fa-

çades have a Christmasy glow at night, all insist that nothing
has changed. Multimedia men heavily into television will
agree like party faithful and speak of the "rebirth" of Hollywood as a world film center.

The old studio lots should have landmark status. There are
few theatrical film features being shot on them. Space is leased
there for television productions. There are the exceptions, but
a major film being shot in what remains of the physical
facilities of Twentieth Century-Fox spilled out over the entire
premises, even encompassing the company headquarters
building, which was given a "nineties" appearance. Century
City, a complex of high-rise office buildings, hotels and
theaters, had absorbed much of Fox's back lot—at a huge
profit to the studio's stockholders. Real estate had become
more valuable than production space. If there are as many as
two theatrical film features being shot at Universal Studios,
the lot is considered to be "humming." Universal became a
subsidiary of the largest of the talent agencies, MCA, and
is chiefly concerned with television series and studio tours
(for which the place has been restyled with something of
the look of Knott's Berry Farm, a tourist attraction below
Los Angeles where the pioneer West has been reproduced;
sittable, shootable, and walk-throughable, "for the entire
family to enjoy").

Thus Hollywood in the year 1974. The technicians have
taken over, explaining much about the strange dead weight of
such recent major successes as *2001,* and we might as well be
in Wilkes-Barre. Sammy Glick stands a foot taller and he may
be blond or, worse, blondined. His confreres are a little too
bronzed and white-toothed. Their ethics may be the same as
Sammy's, but their performance in the art of stealing has been
refined. There is a premium on originality but not too many of
the television networks, who seem to like the climate here, or
the sponsors are willing to pay it. A few independent
filmmakers scrounge around and come up with the backing for

a *Bang the Drum Slowly* and it comes, surprisingly, from nonmovie people and companies as often as it does from a major distributor. Writers and directors seek "angels" just as they did back on Broadway, and even friends contribute to the backing of movies. As for the big majors, a builder of bridges is quite likely to own a movie firm.

Since this book was begun, the largest and most prestigious movie company, Metro-Goldwyn-Mayer, has ceased to exist as a maker of films. If one of its Presidents (they say the last was a mortician), was the inspiration for a best-selling *roman à clef* unrapturously entitled *The Love Machine*, then his technical proficiency in the boudoir (if we accept the book as rooted in fact) and his success in doing in the largest of the majors would chillingly suggest that Hollywood has fallen into the hands of front-office types whose amours and dispassionate souls were once kept safely a continent's expanse away from movies' creators.

There was more than one top executive nibbling away at Hollywood's foundations, but the collapse of Metro served notice to the world that an age of protean splendor and peculiar, spellbinding fantasy was over. Unlike its flesh-and-blood sibling in the East—the American theater, which has had its Lazarus recall to life every couple of years—Hollywood films had been in a death agony for a decade or more. American movies are now, truly, in the hands of the independents, many of them young, a number of them brave, and an encouraging platoon of them outrageous. They shoot their films in Pittsburgh, New York, Seattle, San Francisco, or Miami. They have turned up in Des Moines and Kansas City. They go where the action in the script tells them to go.

2.

Not only illusion but perpetual adolescence played a large role in the making of Hollywood films. There was a disregard for

reality that led to an often absurd emphasis on the fantasies of
youth. Death and poverty in *most* Hollywood films were
nearly always tinged with romanticism. It was a nice conta-
gion that infected almost everyone upon their arrival in the
film community. Some came with their arms exposed for the
humbug to bite them.

This is not to suggest that these fantasies were spun out by
amateurs. They were hand-crafted in the big studios by the
best talent around. And talent was a purchasable commodity
in Hollywood of the 1930s and on every level. It was a
common assumption that every mortal being had his price. It
didn't necessarily follow that your celebrity was involved with
show business. If you were a public figure and were accessible
(reachable by Western Union), you could expect an invitation
from Thalberg, Wanger, Goldwyn, or Warner. It is believed
that Albert Einstein and Calvin Coolidge were both approached. In his mind's eye, some producer or studio head
saw "Starring Albert Einstein" blazoned across a marquee and
a telegram was dispatched.

This urge—to put the famed and exalted on display—is as
old as the carnival or the fair. At the height of his enormous
fame in the twenties, Charles E. Lindbergh was given the sort
of Hollywood reception reserved for heads of state. He
doubtless was swayed for a moment. Half a million dollars—
the gilt-edged offer served up with the caviar and Mary
Pickford (as his dancing partner, of course)—could have
financed a great many aerial explorations. Aviatrix Ruth Elder
was given a screen contract and appeared briefly, flickeringly
one might say, with one expression—dark eyes blazing furi-
ously. It was difficult to determine whether she was vamp or
heroine.

For a time, it seemed that nearly everyone in the world of
letters could be bought. But there were a few authors who
spurned Hollywood. One was the celebrated novelist Willa

Cather,* perhaps America's most significant Midwestern writer, who was to include a provision in her will insisting that none of her novels (*A Lost Lady, Death Comes for the Archbishop, Sapphira and the Slave Girl*, and *One of Ours*, to name the most successful of them) ever would be sold to the movies, a provision still in force although she died in 1947. Another was playwright Philip Barry, who refused a dozen times to write for the movies but allowed all of his plays (*Holiday, The Animal Kingdom*, and *The Philadelphia Story*, among others) to be purchased. Possibly to make Mr. Barry seem to have made a substantial contribution to Hollywood, most of his work has been filmed twice.

One wonders just why Robert E. Sherwood, whose plays helped keep Broadway alive throughout the Depression, could be tempted by Thalberg or Sam Goldwyn to spend weeks and often months in a community so alien to his spirit. By the time of his second and longest visit there in 1931, half a dozen major plays had placed him on a level with Sidney Howard and Maxwell Anderson and only a little below O'Neill. But Howard was already there and Anderson would follow shortly (O'Neill routinely turned down movie jobs but, like Barry, allowed his dramas to be filmed without his participation).

Some writers' egos are more visible than others', and we always have had our colorful exceptions—Sinclair Lewis, Ernest Hemingway, Gertrude Stein, the early Scott Fitzgerald—but imagine the outrageous damper stifling Sherwood on

---

*A Lost Lady was bought by Hollywood soon after its publication in 1923 and a movie was made. According to William A. Koshland, speaking for her publisher, Alfred A. Knopf: "Miss Cather felt that the resulting picture did violence to the novel and her concept of the story and resolved never to permit anything of hers ever to be filmed, performed, or whatever." The provision in her will enjoins her executors from leasing, licensing, or otherwise disposing of the following rights: "dramatization, whether for the purpose of spoken stage presentation or otherwise, motion picture, radio broadcasting, television, and rights to mechanical reproduction, whether by means now in existence or which hereafter may be discovered or perfected."

his Hollywood assignments! His fame and prestige and that of Sidney Howard's and Maxwell Anderson's were overlooked by their studio bosses for as long as they remained in the West! Routinely, they would be summoned to story conferences, not as major dramatists but as hirelings, and they came meekly and they were not on equal terms with their producers or the head of the studio.

Lillian Hellman, who suggests in the last volume of her memoirs (*Pentimento*) that she swaggered around Hollywood with considerable incaution, writes of a story conference with director Sidney Franklin, a session known to every screenwriter as an effort to get at the essence of the movie to come, to "break the back" of the story.

> That is, indeed, an accurate description. We, a nice English playwright called Mordaunt Shairp* and I, would arrive at Franklin's house each morning at ten, have a refined health lunch a few hours later, and leave at five. The next day whatever we had decided would sometimes be altered and sometimes be scrapped because Franklin had consulted a friend the night before or discussed our decisions with his bridge partners. After six or seven weeks of this, Franklin said it was rude of me to lie all day on his couch with my back turned to him, napping. I left his house saying I was sorry, it was rude, but I couldn't go on that way. I took the night plane to New York, locked myself in with some books, and the first telephone call I answered two days later was from Mr. Goldwyn. . . .

She was offered a room to herself, a raise, but Miss Hellman declined and went to Paris. Goldwyn was a stubborn man in his pursuit of talent and found her there a week later, where she was tendered a long-term contract to do nothing but movies she liked and when she liked. She thought she had

---

*Author of *The Green Bay Tree*, a Broadway success that introduced Laurence Olivier to New York audiences in 1933.

become valuable to Goldwyn because she had abandoned him or fled for reasons he didn't understand. Actually, Goldwyn considered Miss Hellman a writer who knew how to put a drama together—no small accomplishment in the theater or in Hollywood.

Other authors, less addicted to nose-thumbing and rebellion, would be asked to work on stories written by story craftsmen such as Frances Marion, who was Metro's Scheherazade,* or often lesser talents. They would tell you that they came for the cash, and the payroll at Metro alone was between $60,000 and $100,000 a week for writers; less at the Goldwyn Studio, since he produced far fewer films, but usually paid higher salaries per man.

Some came for the rent. In 1934, John O'Hara, whose first novel, *Appointment in Samarra,* was sent in proof form to Paramount, did not sell his novel to them but they wanted his person as a screenwriter. Despite his rave reviews, he still had to buy his first new Ford phaeton on the installment plan. He settled into an apartment on North Rossmore Avenue, an elegant residential area near the Wilshire district and close to Paramount, an "Eastern-styled" neighborhood where the landscaping was very un-Californian, with privet, towering oaks and maples, and huge expanses of neatly trimmed grass.

O'Hara was excited by the prospect but was soon disappointed in the system—which brought promising authors West to sit out their contract time awaiting an assignment. It wasn't until his second Hollywood summons in 1935 that he was to become known as a "dialogue rewrite specialist," working for nearly all of the major studios. On that occasion

---

*Frances Marion was the highest-paid woman screenwriter of all time. She possessed a hair-trigger mind and was widely respected within the film colony. She had a tough exterior, a gravelly voice from too many cigarettes and too much Scotch; it is said that she thought like a man and, indeed, from personal observation, I found her to have very few obvious feminine traits. But she was an accomplished portraitist (a large oil study of Zasu Pitts captured that brilliant, droll lady perfectly), and, progressively, wife, mother, and grandmother.

the presence of Bob Benchley and Dorothy Parker helped to lessen his feeling that he was misplaced.

Broadway had been reduced by the Depression to less than thirty productions running at any one time. Financial backing had all but disappeared. Even the Shuberts had sought governmental aid. *Strike Me Pink,* starring Jimmy Durante, Hope Williams, and Lupe Velez, had been backed by gang-land money, but was a financial disaster and, luckily for the theater, the mobsters never again invaded the precincts of Max Gordon and the Theatre Guild. Then there was Hollywood itself in one of its more self-destructive moods. It had robbed Broadway of more than half its playwrights, cutting off part of a major source of new screen material. Still, with a kind of blood loyalty, the half dozen box-office playwrights: Sherwood, Marc Connelly, Maxwell Anderson, S. N. Behrman, Sidney Howard, and, later, Clifford Odets, would fly or train East with their annual contribution to the theater or their own professional reputations. Moss Hart and George S. Kaufman, as well as Noel Coward, were too busy writing for the stage to accept anything but occasional Hollywood assignments (Coward never did spend any appreciable time in California), although nearly all of their work eventually reached the screen. And there would be a major contribution by Eugene O'Neill every couple of years (in 1933, it was *Ah, Wilderness!*), whose indifference to Hollywood went much farther than Philip Barry's. The closest he was ever to come to the place itself was at an estate in the San Francisco area, where he and wife Carlotta lived for a time.

But crippled as it was and even though the Shuberts discouraged anything experimental, the American theater was to spring into a kind of glory, still remembered, during the risky thirties.

There was the Federal Theatre Project, launched in the darkest heart of the Depression by Harry Hopkins, head of the Works Progress Administration, and headed by Hallie Flanagan Davis, then director of the Experimental Theatre at Vassar College.

The country was divided into large regional areas; its aim, to keep the darkened theaters of the nation open and the thousands of unemployed actors, directors and set designers working. Elmer Rice, in charge of the New York Region, issued a statement to ensure that those theater people too proud to apply for "charity" would participate:

> The Federal Theatre Project has been created for the purpose of providing worthwhile employment for professional theatre workers. Please bear in mind that you are not being offered relief or charity but WORK . . . Our object . . . to set up so high a standard of professional excellence in these projects that they will be able to continue on their own momentum after the Federal program is completed.

The price of admission to these plays and the "Living Newspaper" productions was minimal and competitive, in most instances, with the movies' admission scale.

One of the most exciting groups within the project was the Negro Theatre, directed by John Houseman and Orson Welles, both of whom later made the transition to commercial Broadway productions with their Mercury Theatre. They leased Harlem's Lafayette Theatre and staged there a most original *Macbeth*, which they set in nineteenth-century Martinique. There were witches performing voodoo rites, among other innovations.

Then there was the Group Theatre, composed of thirty-one promising newcomers whose writing, directing, and performing had not been afforded a Broadway showcase. The Group began a long-term alternative to the entrenched George Kaufmans and Cohans, the vehicles for Helen Hayes and Katherine Cornell, and the sensation for the folks from

Altoona, i.e., *Tobacco Road.* With Harold Clurman and Lee Strasberg directing and Cheryl Crawford producing, and an acting company that included Franchot Tone, John Garfield, Frances Farmer, Stella and Luther Adler, and Elia Kazan, it got the radical theater that was exciting Germany onto a paying footing in the United States.

By 1930, the Germans were aware that dramatist Bertolt Brecht was no longer serving "culinary theater" (entertainment served up like so many soufflés). To its audience, it was a provocation. "The bourgeois heaven was being torn apart by sacrilegious hands," so Brecht's American biographer Frederic Ewen informs us, "and its inner emptiness exposed." In *The Rise and Fall of the City Mahagonny,* Brecht presupposes a knowledge not only of what is happening on the stage but what the audience is thinking about it and even what is occurring in the world beyond the exit doors. He looked upon his audience as both "productive" and transformed. He saw it as formerly

> Rushing out of the subway stations, eager to be turned into putty at the hands of magicians—grown men, tried and tested in the struggle for existence, scurry to the box-office. There they check their hats, and along with those, their customary habits, their normal attitude of everyday life. Once outside the cloak-room, they take their seats with the bearing of kings. . . . Let us go into one of these theatres and observe the effect which it has on the spectators. When we look around, we see somewhat motionless figures in a peculiar state: They seem to be tensing their muscles strenuously, unless they are enervated and exhausted. They scarcely communicate with one another—their association here is like that of sleepers—but sleepers who dream incessantly. . . . True, their eyes are open, but they see not—they stare. They hear not—but listen. . . . These people seem relieved of all activity and like men to whom something is being done.

We could just as easily substitute a Hollywood movie audience for Brecht's pre-epic theater audience. His aim was to make them as much a part of the play as the text or the actors.

The Group Theatre did not take the radical German theater quite as far as this. In fact, its strenuous efforts to shake up an audience make much of the drama created for it seem dated today. Beginning in 1931 with Paul Green's *The House of Connelly*, which had its roots in Chekhov rather than Brecht, it moved on to John Howard Lawson's *Success Story* (with capitalism as a believable villain), reaching its apogee, critically and financially, with Clifford Odets's *Waiting for Lefty* and, a little later, *Awake and Sing*.

Odets was hailed by Brooks Atkinson in *The New York Times* as "our most promising new dramatist," but the irony of this movement and Odets's personal success was that by the mid-thirties they would succumb from an astonishing malady in that lean decade—prosperity. The movies would snatch actors Kazan (who later became a leading director), Frances Farmer, John Garfield, and Tone. With the exception of Kazan, who was wiry and indestructible, all of their Hollywood years would be marked by rebellion, restlessness, and, finally, early deaths; Miss Farmer's after years in a madhouse* and Tone's after losing his puckish handsomeness and maturing into a brief career as a character actor.

Even playwright Odets, stormer of the capitalistic barricades, spokesman for the casualties of the crack-up of our economic system, would be unable to resist. He would remain in the West for more than five years and marry an Academy Award-winning star, Luise Rainer.

---

*Before her death, Miss Farmer was to write a harrowing autobiography, *Will There Really Be a Morning?*, documenting her rise and fall in films and her long ordeal in mental institutions. It is especially recommended to anyone contemplating an acting career.

Perhaps the glamour of being in the same town and often under the same roof with Garbo, Rainer, Dietrich, and Chaplin was part of the lure for writers. Many of them had been film fans in their youth. Christopher Isherwood began going to the movies at around ten years of age. It was one of the earliest passions of his life and he wanted to get out to California just as quickly as possible and see it all. He was to become very fond of many of the stars and was himself a famed author and sought out by them. He never would put them down, as some writers are inclined to do, and would say, "You know the great thing about actors and actresses is that they know they are a little vain sometimes, but there's one thing you can say about them that you can't say about an awful lot of people—they are out to give pleasure. And there's something in them, this desire to please . . . which is good. It's a great, great virtue. It's very precious."

But this admiration was not always returned. It will become increasingly evident as this chronicle of the Hollywood writer proceeds that he was very nearly a shunned creature and always had been. On the set, it was often worse. Film writers, if not banned from the set, were taught to be invisible. Nunnally Johnson, assigned to his first film for Darryl Zanuck's newly formed Twentieth Century Pictures, *Moulin Rouge* (not to be confused with John Huston's later film biography of Toulouse-Lautrec), remembers venturing cautiously onto the set. He found leading lady Constance Bennett in conference with director Sidney Lanfield. Johnson remained in the shadows, unsure of whether the author of the screenplay had a right to be on the sound stage, but he was curious about what they were doing with his script. Lanfield was remonstrating with Miss Bennett: "But, Connie," he said, "this is what the writer said." "*The hell with the writer!*" the leading lady shouted. Miss Bennett probably did not realize that she was delivering The Credo of the Industry in dealing with that peculiar but necessary creature, the author.

3.

Writers were often thought to be amusing companions and it was not unusual for bachelor George Oppenheimer to be invited at the last moment to fill in at a supper party, and at least once Joan Crawford phoned him and said she was alone and needed company on a Saturday night. He went, unshaven and in the old clothes he usually wore at home. They sat in Miss Crawford's kitchen and talked until early morning. On another occasion, long before she became a comedienne, Lucille Ball drove onto the Sam Goldwyn lot and honked noisily until Goldwyn himself appeared at a window, wondering what the racket was all about. "Mr. Goldwyn," Miss Ball implored a little wistfully, "Can George Oppenheimer come out and play?"

And there were nearly a dozen more formal salons, at most of which you dressed for dinner. There were the Arthur Sheekmans' (she was horror films' favorite victim Gloria Stuart) colorful dinner parties; Marion Davies's beachhouse and costume parties and castle weekends; the King Vidors' "do's," not given often but events to which everyone of importance came; the Samuel Goldwyns' formal very British dinners where the service was so grand one forgot Goldwyn's bad grammar; the informal gatherings of Salka Viertel, whose guests included many refugees from Hitler's Europe, more interesting than glamorous with Brecht, Isherwood, Huxley, the Mann brothers and occasionally Garbo in the same room together, and Anita Loos's Sunday brunches in Santa Monica, where not only Huxley and Isherwood were regulars, but Charlie Chaplin, the astronomer Edwin Hubbell and Lord and Lady Mendl (Elsie de Wolfe). "We were a little snooty," Anita confessed. "We weren't interested in actors. That was Frances Marion's chief amusement, spending a lot of time with Harlow and Marie Dressler and the others. Our little group never invited any of them except Chaplin. We

only wanted amusing people around with wit and intelligence." So Anita pursued the most original minds in town
and nearly all of them were delighted to join the company of
her friends. Always on the move, she knew everyone atop the
literary heights on the coast, in New York, and in London and
Paris. At one point or another her name creeps into nearly all
of their memoirs. A typical example was her contribution to
the welcome of Joseph Hergesheimer, as recorded by Sara
Mayfield, a lifelong friend of the H. L. Menckens:

> When the *City of Angels* roared into the station with
> Hergesheimer aboard, Mencken met him with a battery
> of ten movie cameras. After he had embraced Joe,
> bussing him on both cheeks, Continental fashion, Aileen
> Pringle (*who, according to Hollywood myth, was always sent to
> greet authors by Louis B. Mayer because she was thought to be
> the most literate of his stable of stars*) draped a garland of roses
> around the novelist's neck and presented him with an
> immense papier-mâché domino as a souvenir of the
> games they'd played at the Dower House. The camera-
> men moved in as Mencken took a stance with an
> American flag in his hand and his foot on the domino.
> Then Aileen Pringle and Anita Loos linked arms with
> Hergesheimer and escorted him to a white Rolls-Royce,
> borrowed from Tom Mix for the occasion.

Only Dorothy Parker seemed immune to Anita's elfin
charms. Mrs. Parker knew of Anita's collection of the literary
elite but said, "She was all out to improve herself." This
remark, naturally, got back to Anita and she is today rather
bitter toward Mrs. Parker's memory. But no one was spared
during Mrs. Parker's lifetime. During the last year or so of her
life, she said that "Lily" (Lillian Hellman) had been in and out
of analysis for eleven years. "She thought she was cured," said
Mrs. Parker. "Well, I've never seen a cure. . . . Heywood
Broun went in and out like a revolving door."

Beyond the whimsey, the good conversation, and the

money, many of the world's playwrights and novelists were drawn to Hollywood in the early thirties because, in less than six years, talking pictures had grown up. *Trouble in Paradise*, a sleek, sophisticated and even raffish film, was released in 1932. Critics saw at once that Ernst Lubitsch, its producer and director, had liberated not only movie dialogue but the sound camera as well, and it roamed freely up and down stairs, in and around buildings and streets (one suspects that the more mobile silent camera was utilized here). This was no Marx Brothers farce that even the kiddies could enjoy. This was adult entertainment with the suavest thieves in Europe triumphant at the fade-out.

The "Lubitsch touch" was never more visible than in this chronicle of two sneak thieves and confidence artists (a man, played by Herbert Marshall, and a woman, played with a joyous bitchiness by Miriam Hopkins) as they endeavor to steal nearly a million francs from a ravishing Parisian widow (Kay Francis), who has inherited the largest Parfumerie in France. They are constantly imperiled by the widow's numerous suitors, her huge staff, and a cagy old Chairman of the Board of her firm (C. Aubrey Smith), who, Marshall insists, is "robbing her blind."

When one of her suitors (Edward Everett Horton) recognizes Marshall as the man who once entered his Venice hotel suite disguised as a doctor "to look at my tonsils, which had nothing wrong with them, mind you," then mugged him and disappeared, the jig is up. Lily (Miss Hopkins) paces a nearby hotel room (Marshall has moved into the widow's townhouse and just about taken over her life), waiting for her lover-accomplice to join her in flight, while Marshall is kissing his employer good-bye.

Now everything so carefully planned by the thieving couple begins unraveling. Widow Colet discovers her housemoney (100,000 francs) is gone and her lover wrecks their romantic farewell embrace by confessing his true identity. The widow plays her role of the wronged benefactress well until Marshall mentions the Board Chairman's perfidy. He takes careful note of the fear it arouses in her and is not surprised when she tosses in her best string of pearls "as a gift to Lily."

In a taxi, the pair silently hurry to their train to Berlin as Marshall searches his pockets for the pearls. They are missing and Lily cheerfully pulls them from her blouse. She also has the widow's expensive handbag, from which she extracts Marshall's wallet. But he has the last laugh; he has the 100,000 francs it contained.

Amoral, of course. Evil triumphant, not in this context. This film and a number of others by Lubitsch that preceded and followed it were as authentically European as anything by Pabst, Clair, Feyder, or Renoir. They were an ocean and a civilization removed from American humor, but Americans were titillated. It was naughty but no one was hurt. (They still react the same way to suave knavery; witness their reaction to the Clifford Irving hoax.)

Hollywood's maturity was further evidenced by the contrast between this screenplay, written by Samson Raphaelson, and *The Jazz Singer*, that screenwriter's—or anybody's—first sound film, which was sentimental, maudlin, and, today, unintentionally laughable from beginning to end except for Jolson's songs. Given a better play to draw upon (*The Honest Finder* by Laszlo Aladar as adapted by Grover Jones), Raphaelson proved to be one of Lubitsch's most deft collaborators. Ahead of them were *The Shop Around the Corner* and *Heaven Can Wait*. Raphaelson, in an interview with Herman G. Weinberg, gives us a glimpse of the way Lubitsch worked:

> I think almost every writer who ever worked with him wrote his best. Lubitsch didn't necessarily make him write like Lubitsch; but he brought out what the fellow had. . . . To a remarkable extent, the film was in the script. Lubitsch prepared a foolproof script that you'd say

almost any director could direct. That's not true, of course, but it's comparatively true. Seventy-five percent of his work was done when that script was done. And he already had the performances in mind and they weren't just performances that he knew those actors could give. And very rarely did any actor fail to give his best performance with Lubitsch, and that's why they loved working with him.

An Aside—Kay Francis

Catherine Gibbs Francis was the perfect Lubitsch heroine. Born in 1905 in Oklahoma City, by eighteen she was in Paris living at the Vendôme (around the corner from the Ritz). She had been sent there by her family to get her out of range of Harry Crocker, a Hearst aide as well as an assistant to Chaplin at various times, who had been pursuing Kay for months.

Although she had a slight lisp, she spoke in a hushed contralto and her voice was seductive even when she was out shopping for a new necklace or a handbag. Her dark hair, so in contrast with the numerous blondes populating the screen in the early thirties, was usually swept back, revealing a "widow's peak." She had enormous, faintly mocking eyes and a long, regal neck—later she would be the ideal *Cynara*.

There are some in Hollywood who say that she married Dwight Francis, of an old Massachusetts family, simply to take his name, but the truth was that she married this playboy when she was playing quite a lot of the time herself. When it seemed obvious to everyone that marriage to Kay would not be the making of him, Dwight's aunt told her, "Kay, if you keep the family name, I will take you to Paris where you will receive your divorce." Kay always was a lady who liked big decisions made for her and Paris was her spiritual hometown. She didn't need the gift of the trip since she was already a star, but when you are making $12,000 a week sometimes it's nice for someone to give you something.

In Paris, she picked up a slight friendship she had had with

Maurice Chevalier back in Hollywood and soon it ignited into what she thought was a serious romance. Chevalier was already more celebrated around the world than Kay, having made *The Innocents of Paris, The Love Parade,* and *The Big Pond* in America as well as a dozen films in his native France. His income was larger than Kay's as he had recordings and music hall concerts, but he had a flaw in his character, at least at that point, and while Kay overlooked it, her friends did not. Dorothy Taylor (the Countess di Frasso), Jessica Barthelmess (Mrs. Richard), and Beatrice Ames Stewart (Mrs. Donald Ogden) urged her to give up the affair. "You simply can't afford it," Beatrice told her. And she couldn't, for despite her huge income in that day of low taxes, she and Chevalier were going out on the town nearly every evening and he was allowing her to pick up the tab. Kay listened and came home to marry Kenneth MacKenna, a studio story editor, less ardent and certainly less colorful but with an engaging modesty and, especially endearing to her, great generosity both in spirit and in purse.

Kay Francis, like others before and after her, was a victim of her own success. She played slightly tarnished but oh-so-ladylike heroines so very well, film men would say this is a "Kay Francis type" and soon these "types" were playing the roles she could have done much better. She lived well into her sixty-fourth year, dying in 1968.

Lubitsch, free in that day and given full authority over his work on B. P. Schulberg's Paramount lot, was soon to be crippled by restrictive forces. The guardians of American morality, including both the Catholic Church and the Motion Picture Production Code, began to see what he and others were doing. After they recovered from shock, hysteria, and Mae West, the Production Code began to be enforced. Supervising its enforcement was Will H. Hays, a former Postmaster General (under Harding) who headed up the

Motion Picture Producers and Distributers of America, a self-censoring body. Their premise was that films should not be "cut to ribbons" by the various local and state censoring boards. Their goal was to send out inoffensive, morally uplifting movies, and there would be a long list of prohibitions governing the content of films.

The Code was a challenge to Lubitsch, but in his old *Mittel*-European wisdom, caution began to dim his delightfully cynical vision. His screen version of Noel Coward's *Design for Living* (1933) was the first major casualty.* Much of the charm of this free-wheeling race through unconventional sexual byways was lost in one of Ben Hecht's least successful scripts. Hecht later insisted that the fault was Lubitsch's, that the director had picked up on a blast of Coward by critic George Jean Nathan and insisted that Coward "writes like a cheap vaudevillian." Hecht's claim was that he had cribbed some of the dialogue from two earlier Coward plays, *Hay Fever* and *The Vortex*, leaving in only one of Coward's original lines ("Good for our immortal souls!")

Little wonder then that Shirley Temple began her rise that year and that Will Rogers would have kept American film humor on a folksy level precisely to Will Hays's taste had he not died in a plane crash in 1935. Rogers† was mourned throughout the land, but the death of a free American screen was not.

---

*The film version of Coward's comedy was by no means a failure at the box office, however. Its three stars, Gary Cooper, Miriam Hopkins, and Fredric March, were all leading performers of some magnitude, and even Mordaunt Hall in *The New York Times*, while conceding that the movie was only "a skeleton of the parent work," said it had the "same familiar rattle" of the original, and Lubitsch's "own sly humor" in place of Coward's. It was an assumption on the part of nearly all playwrights and novelists dealing in delicate or amoral subject matter that a sale to the movies meant that, in all probability, the film would retain only the title and, if you were lucky, part of the original theme.

---

†Rogers, whose off-screen journalism was tart and deservedly embarrassing to highly placed functionaries, had completed his first serious role in *Steamboat 'Round the Bend* at the time of his death. It is likely that he would have evolved into a homespun star much like Walter Brennan, had he not died at the height of his popularity.

4.

There was a certain Mlle. Perrier, a lady of French birth, living on the island of Guernsey in 1899. She had a sleek bull terrier who followed her everywhere and even slept with her—in the slang idiom of our own day.

There also was a constable in the town who had small use for Mlle. Perrier, perhaps because she was extraordinarily attractive and all but ignored him. It was he, peeking through her bedroom windows at night, who saw the unusual bedmates for the first time. He could not wait to pass along his version of the sight to the authorities.

Mlle. Perrier was arrested and her dog was imprisoned in the town pound. Guernsey, then as now, being a part of the Channel Islands, is under the direct jurisdiction of the Crown and not the British Empire (as it was respectfully known then). Its people are governed by the Code of Rollo, an eleventh-century nobleman. When the local authorities searched the Code for a precedent to follow, they discovered that the penalty for such a "crime" was death by burning. There was no alternative.

And so Mlle. Perrier was summarily tried for sleeping with her bull terrier and sentenced to death by burning. She appealed at once to the French Ambassador to intervene, and he immediately got in touch with the British Home Secretary and said, "This is ridiculous. Mlle. Perrier did nothing to warrant such a barbaric sentence." The Home Secretary cabled the authorities on Guernsey to do nothing to Mlle. Perrier and await further instructions.

The Governor of the island resented this cable intensely. He knew that Guernsey was not part of the British Empire and he was not about to take orders from the Home Secretary. His rage was so explosive, Mlle. Perrier in her cell was afraid that the sentence would be carried out simply to put the Home Secretary in his place. And she pined for her dog.

But the Governor was in a dilemma. He felt that he could not take the matter up with the Queen because it was too indelicate. He had never been confronted before with such a perplexing legal problem. So he shot off a rudely worded cable to the Home Secretary and if the language had not been so offensive, the Home Secretary might have guessed that the authorities on Guernsey were not about to burn Mlle. Perrier.

The Home Secretary went into a fury, then a panic. He suggested that a Cabinet meeting be called, which was done quickly. The Cabinet decided that a British battleship should land two companies of marines on Guernsey, pick up Mlle. Perrier and her bull terrier, and transport them to LeHavre, where they were to be released. This was accomplished without bloodshed.

Whereupon, Guernsey declared war on England. They also filed a suit in the British courts for invasion. It was then decided by British authorities that, for the sake of the record, Mlle. Perrier and her dog should be made parties to the case so that the "indelicate" matter could be disposed of for all time. A British Lord was assigned to represent the Crown and defend Mlle. Perrier. He lost the case but the judgment was one shilling damages.

This, insisted Aldous Huxley, who came to Hollywood in 1937, is a true story. And it is also true that Huxley was heard to remark, "Wouldn't this make a good movie?"

Huxley collected animal stories of this nature, and some others were dillies, too. He was probably innocent of any knowledge of the movie Code, drawn up under Will Hays and then being administered by Joseph Breen. Among the Code's "don'ts" was one that would cover Mlle. Perrier and her bull terrier rather specifically.

Perhaps somewhere in Huxley's innocence and the fact that he was placed under contract by Metro-Goldwyn-Mayer as a screenwriter (and highly regarded there because of his fame and literary reputation) lies the secret of the wild scramble for talent and the weird amalgam of those talents that made the films of the late thirties and most of the forties what they were.

When amorality was banned from the screen and thieves no longer could rejoice at the end and adultery could not remain unpunished and killers were always gunned down at fade-out, glamour and fantasy became the first resort of most film makers.

Glamour, described as long ago as 1840 as "a delusive or alluring charm," already had become part of Hollywood's alchemy. While it was not a word anyone would associate with either Shirley Temple, then ascendant, or Mary Pickford, then in decline, certainly the way Miss Pickford lived was glamorous. And there were the stars—Garbo, Dietrich, Francis, del Rio, who had been groomed for the haunting, commanding close-up, as well as a new kind of beauty— Lombard, Hopkins, and Colbert—who could look sultry in the close-up and crack wise in the two-shot.

If the world could not be shown as it really was, then make it beautiful or amusing—or both. That appeared to be the philosophy behind Irving Thalberg's success at Metro-Goldwyn-Mayer. The emphasis was altogether on the star, although a great deal of Metro's money went for properties for them, often diluted or rendered unrecognizable, but always done with "class." Metro under Thalberg inspired an entire social structure in the film capital. If you were a Metro star, director, producer, or writer, you were given the sort of snob status accorded a Vanderbilt or a Van Rensselaer in New York society.

A star groomed for bigger things under Thalberg and Louis B. Mayer, who supervised the entire operation in Culver City, was not allowed to live his or her own life away from the camera. There were no rebels, for this was the heart and soul of the Hollywood Establishment. Lucky for Bette Davis and

Lauren Bacall that they were never under contract to Mayer. Unlucky for Judy Garland that she was. If a human error or crime was committed, there was Howard Strickling, director of press relations, to mop everything up. He had the unique job of minimizing or erasing all evidence of any breach of decorum short of a capital offense committed by a Metro personality.

So the faint glow of iridescence was forged into the contract players there from the beginning. Directors at Metro knew that they could not tamper with the merchandise, these super personalities, starlets, and character actors. The studio's most successful directors were those who followed the blueprint— Clarence Brown, Victor Fleming, Sidney Franklin, and Edmund Goulding. Even George Cukor, whose major screen credits are more extensive than any other director's and who has *endured* through a dozen changes in Hollywood filmmaking, admitted to Gavin Lambert, in a dialogue with Cukor published in 1972, that he "never played any politics. . . . Once I wanted to do a story called *Escape,* an anti-Nazi thing. I proposed myself but they'd assigned it to someone else. . . . They cast directors, you know, like actors. Frank Borzage did *Seventh Heaven* and they labeled him a romantic director. My first film at Metro was *Dinner at Eight,* so they pegged me as a New York wise guy. Then, when I made *David Copperfield* for them, I found myself in a costume period. I had to pull myself out of that. (Today, I suppose, I have to pull myself out of being 'establishment.')" King Vidor attempted to persuade Irving Thalberg to produce *Our Daily Bread,* but failed. There was no glamour in this vivid and moving drama of the Depression. Eventually, the film was done by Vidor himself and released through United Artists (1934).

It is a matter of some astonishment that so many important writers of the day came to Metro, since it typified the fakery of Hollywood and it rarely violated the Code. All of them had seen at least some of Metro's films and they knew that they would have to write in a way to make even poverty give off a glow and look attractive. If the movie were set in a hovel, it would have to be such a charming hovel the audience would envy those who lived there. Part of it was a matter of emphasis and a great deal was a matter of photography. Each and every scene in a Metro film, from Garbo's *Queen Christina* to *Love Finds Andy Hardy* was lighted with all the exquisite care of a Clarence Bull portrait. Anything that appeared to be fake (a painted flat, for example) was reshot even though the final product could not have been more artificial.

But like nearly all sophisticated filmgoers, Donald Ogden Stewart, F. Scott Fitzgerald, John Howard Lawson, Ernst Vajda, Charles MacArthur, and other Metro writers had come to admire Hollywood's (and Metro's) product because the Code had forced the American screen into something quite different from novels or the stage, where freedom of expression still existed. Hollywood had met that challenge with a world of its own making and, unfailingly in the last reel, the Hays office would pluck at all the plot strings.

Sir Howard Shortt, President of the British Board of Film Censors, made a sensible observation about movies, but his comment, when applied to Hollywood productions of the thirties and forties, gives them a disturbing dimension:

> I cannot believe that any *single* film can have any lasting effect on the public, but the result of the same theme *repeated over and over again,* might be most undesirable.

The Code was ensuring that good always triumphed, while abroad Hitler was proving just the opposite as he tightened his grip on Germany and began his sanctions against the Jews. In the context of Hollywood and the countries where its films were appreciated and absorbed into the culture, Hitler's ranting was not a serious threat to the world. The business of race extermination was a good half decade away.

So the world's best writers continued to come in a steady stream, and they learned their craft for the most part from those professional screenwriters already established. In the long view, theirs was the film that kept the American screen going, that even shaped it—Herman Mankiewicz, Charles Lederer, Jo Swerling, Sonya Levien, Jules Furthman, Anita Loos, Francis Goodrich and Albert Hackett, John Lee Mahin, Robert Riskin, Norman Krasna, Billy Wilder, Dudley Nichols, Charles Brackett, and the rest. The eminent authors were invited because of their reputations and whatever strength they might bring to the creation of a film story was secondary. But Hollywood executives were errant hosts. Once their illustrious guests arrived, they were either ignored or patronized.

A few came prepared to write "in another gear" in order to subsidize their more serious work. But the great majority realized that while they might be turning out trash, the fault for a bad script often was theirs. Samuel Goldwyn believed almost to the end of his long career that writers' talents could be compartmentalized and he would speak of a writer being "a good constructionist." In actual fact, unless a writer had "a good ear for dialogue" and some sense of the screen possibilities of a story, he was not worth very much as a specialist. The warp could not be separated from the woof.

Sometimes a large literary reputation could excuse innate failings which no amount of time in the studios could remedy. Dorothy Parker could inject wit and bright dialogue into a script only if it already had been pulled together on paper by her husband, Alan Campbell. And yet she was the reason they were desirable. This was blatantly obvious when Alan Campbell failed to find screen work during their divorce. He was bluntly told by a Fox executive that he should "talk her into getting together again. Then we'll rehire you as a team, just like before." They did remarry and they did collaborate again, almost immediately.

5.

When sound first came in, knowledgeable studio chiefs believed that a literary success qualified an author to write for the screen. They concluded that talking pictures needed more literacy than the old scenarists and title writers could provide. But even so they kept a tight grip on Laurence Stallings, Anita Loos, Herman Mankiewicz, and the other reliable screenwriters of the day.

The film moguls' belief that the movies, with the advent of talkies, now rivaled and even surpassed the stage emboldened them to consider hiring George Bernard Shaw. He declined, telling Samuel Goldwyn (by way of publicist Howard Dietz), "The trouble, Mr. Goldwyn, is that you are only interested in art, and I am only interested in money." He would be captured later by the British cinema. Then they lowered their sights slightly and there were few famed authors outside the Orient, Africa, and Russia who were not queried on their interest.

It was not an especially new idea. Soon after World War I a number of important authors were called to Hollywood; Rupert Hughes, Elinor Glyn, Edna Ferber, Elmer Rice, Cosmo Hamilton, Maurice Maeterlinck, Mary Roberts Rinehart, Edward Knoblock, Michael Arlen, Somerset Maugham, and Gertrude Atherton. More than half of them failed to grasp the demands of the medium—the necessity for action whenever possible; a flowing movement rather than static "scenes"; and the trick of never revealing too much.

An exception was Mrs. Glyn, whose novels were brisk and artificial enough to serve as models for a whole string of "flaming flapper" movies and who even was asked by Metro to supervise the filming of her book *Three Weeks*. Her nephew Anthony, in his biography of her, describes her as "caring terribly that *Three Weeks* should be worthily produced and several times she had scenes, which still dissatisfied her, reshot at her own expense."

Mrs. Glyn was deferred to constantly and even was asked to stage one of the scenes since it proved beyond the resources of the studio's continuity writer to describe:

> For the scene in the Queen's boudoir in Lucerne where she lies on the tiger skin, quivering with emotion and passion, he wrote, a little helplessly:
> SCENE 137 CLOSE-UP INTERIOR THE LADY'S SUITE
> Better than describe this scene, I will simply mention that Mrs. Glyn will enact it for Mr. Crossland (the director) on the set. . . .

Foolish films, nearly all of them, but successes in their day and written by a woman whose themes seemed permissive in a day of relaxed morals. Other writers equally exotic did not fare as well. Maeterlinck came and went very quickly but was given a second try by Samuel Goldwyn in the thirties, sending the veteran studio head reeling into the sunlight shouting dazedly, "The hero is a bee!"

The hiring process itself was not much more successful in the 1930s than in Mrs. Rinehart's day—there was the same number of failures, but films by now had become such an enormous and profitable industry, the misfits weren't very conspicuous. Options were discreetly dropped. It often took longer to determine just who was cut out for film writing and who was not. But dropped they were if they could neither come up with a viable treatment or adaptation, screenplay, or playable dialogue. And there were the successes, the big ones like Nunnally Johnson, Ben Hecht, Sidney Howard, who became allied with the men who were forging the new Hollywood, the Hollywood that was going to nearly put the legitimate theater out of business—Darryl Zanuck, David O. Selznick, and Sam Goldwyn. A number of the less flashy talents stayed on and learned the craft, or at least enough of it to warrant a credit. (The matter of credits remains controversial ground. F. Scott Fitzgerald worked on approximately twenty scripts and emerged with one screen credit.) Playwright George Oppenheimer was used mostly as a "play doctor" to ailing scripts; Dorothy Parker's wit was laced through nearly a dozen comedies and dramas; Thornton Wilder's humanity brought some soul into half a dozen saccharine melodramas; Bertolt Brecht's personal hatred for the Nazis enabled him to set down for all time the violent story of the butcher Heydrich in his single but eloquent screenplay *Hangmen Also Die*.

But some never did find a niche and yet clung to the notion that *movies* now emerging as the most vital of the arts were a challenge they had to meet with some success. The myth that all writers of consequence consider their Hollywood writing "hackwork" may as well be laid to rest here and now and by the writers themselves. In the words of Christopher Isherwood: "It's really almost impossible for anybody who has the right to call himself an artist to do second-rate work deliberately. People who do that kind of thing are really not professionals. They're just amateurs and then they moan over it and say, 'I'm a whore' or something. I have no time for that. Why don't you just get on with the job? If you get good money, why you give value for it, and if they don't see the value, well, that's their loss and not yours.

Of another mind entirely was Nathanael West. He never used the word "hack" and it probably does not apply to his screen work, despite his disclaimers. He came to town in 1933 and it was his announced intention to have his filmwriting for Columbia Pictures underwrite his fiction. He was hired by several studios, including Republic, where he stayed longest, wrote twenty scripts, and achieved a certain competence—one of them more than that, *I Stole a Million*—but West seemed to prove the theory. He attempted another gear of writing on his films and his talent really only shows in his four novels, one of them the bitterest satire of Hollywood ever written, *The Day of the Locust*.

West quickly attracted supportive friends within the writing fraternity who saw the importance of what he was doing—established filmwriter Wells Root (who adapted Selznick's *The Prisoner of Zenda*), West's brother-in-law S. J. Perelman, and Scott Fitzgerald. William Faulkner went hunting with him at least once. He finally cut down on the number of invitations he and his wife, Eileen (immortalized by her sister Ruth McKenny in *My Sister Eileen*), would accept. She was an almost perfect partner, anticipating his moods, which were wide-swinging and which often only Eileen could read.

While he admittedly shifted gears "way down" for his film work and had small respect for the "junk" that he had to write, West understood movies—they were a product from which money could be made. He worked hard and did his best toiling on the "junkpile." He was not kidding himself, as some writers did in his position in Hollywood, turning out programmers. Their egos would not permit most of them to face the fact that they were writing trash (and therefore had to blow it up into something more significant). It is regrettable that West never was given more important screen properties to work on, but it is highly probable that his frustrations as a screenwriter created the flood of bile and mordant humors that set his work apart from every other California novelist of the time. A central symbol in *The Day of the Locust* is a panoramic painting, "The Burning of Los Angeles." Its central situation is the attempt of its hero to persuade an unsuccessful actress to sleep with him or become his "steady." Faye is filled with pretensions. Her airs are not merely assumed; they are lacquered on along with her false fingernails. The reader is so annoyed with the young man's dogged pursuit of this sad-sack female, less than halfway through the book one begins to hope ardently that the painting is a portent of some early annihilation of Faye Greener.

This was West's forte—novels about failures (whose schemes are often grandiose), always exaggerated, but not too remote from the substrata of outcasts attracted to Hollywood.

Filmwriting for him was a way of survival. He rarely discussed film as art. He had tried writing for *Field & Stream* because he loved the out-of-doors so much, but that had not worked out.

We are dealing mostly then with a group of misfits and misplaced talents, trying their damndest to succeed at writing movies, and the wonder is that they stayed as long as they did; that a number of them wrote some memorable films, classics such as *A Star Is Born, Three Comrades, Gone with the Wind, Dodsworth, Camille, The Grapes of Wrath, Dead End,* and *Body and Soul.*

They settled in the California hills or the flatlands of Beverly or the canyons of Santa Monica and attempted to sing away their disillusion with wassails old and dear from Manhattan. Dorothy Parker was once seen weeping openly as someone played and sang "I'll Get By." It was not so much the terrible Mr. Mayer or Mr. Warner or even the more sympathetic Mr. Zanuck or Mr. Selznick who effected their complete disenchantment with the employment they had chosen over their often more rewarding free-lance writing; it was the rivalry among themselves engineered by those bosses and their deputies that pitted Fitzgerald against Oppenheimer, John Howard Lawson against Donald Ogden Stewart, Ben Hecht against everybody.

Irving Thalberg, who has been lifted to that pantheon of film untouchables because of his reputation for "tasteful" films, was the architect at Metro of a "backup" policy that would impell Oppenheimer to confront deputy boss Bernard Hyman and say, "I'm working on *No More Ladies* and there's a writer following me." "Follow" to a Hollywood writer meant reworking the same material, scrapping all or part of what you had written. Your fame meant nothing under the circumstances; your credit slid off a film as easily as jelly. This happened to everyone: Sherwood, Huxley, Hecht, Faulkner, Parker; there were no exceptions.

It was accepted, this disregard of what you had spent hours and weeks conceiving, because Hollywood was a very different game from New York publishing and the theater. Here, your fame had taken you among other elite of the world to the moon and there were short men chewing on dead cigars who ruled the planet. You early learned to follow orders since this was, after all, an alien place, but it was also something that all the world saw and delighted in—just its very existence was a wonder. Moonshine, of course, but beguiling. And these major talents usually stayed on despite the semiliteracy of several of their bosses. It was not inconceivable that essayist and novelist Aldous Huxley might be assigned to do a farcical adaptation of *Mother Was a Marine.* He braced himself for it at any time. If he had been given the project, he would have sat down and seriously pondered all of the funny angles he could think of. He had not offered himself for hire to the studios just to make trouble. Like most, he went along, rarely protesting, only remarking (in this case, to Anita Loos) on how curious it all was. "The tag," he wrote her, "which you like will probably have to go, as the censors cannot permit anyone who has ever committed adultery to be shown as being happy!"

Only a few writers dared turn down a project—those who didn't give a damn or played a convincing role of not caring. Rebels such as these were, in many cases, in deep trouble with the producers when the Blacklist began, since, in Hollywood, rebelliousness and "radicalism" often went hand-in-hand.

There were a few writers, like John Howard Lawson, who had come into the industry on the strength of a well-received book or play. In Lawson's case, it was the expressionistic play *Processional* (1925), which depicted the average American as the victim of the Ku Klux Klan, capitalism, and other social "ills," all done in a "jazz symphony" style that created its own

buffer zone between itself and the audience so that entertainment did not become assault. George Abbott, who was soon
to become one of the most successful stage directors of all
time, played an angular and volatile "Dynamite Jones," gadfly
of the American way.

Processional provoked controversy, so it followed that its
author had some original ideas that might be profitably
utilized by films. Lawson's political views were not those you
would care to discuss with him over a leisurely dinner, but
that was all right. Let the Behrmans and the Sherwoods and
the Connellys be lionized. Lawson had other things on his
mind, not the least of which was helping to win substantial
recognition for his fellow screenwriters. Also, he was wary of
Hollywood moguls, although he had respect for Thalberg. He
knew that Hollywood treated eminent figures in the world of
arts and letters with casual scorn and that these people came
and went more rapidly in the first years of sound (the early
thirties) than at any other time.

Possibly feeling there was no way to penetrate the egoism of
nearly everyone in Hollywood, all those self-interested souls
whose chief concern with movements sent them to the
drugstore rather than to the barricades, Lawson tried to flee
the Hollywood trap in 1931, when he had another play ready
for Broadway production. But with its failure, by 1933 he was
back, forearmed, this time, and ready to do something specific
about the plight of the filmwriter. He was hired back by
Metro because they needed his talent. It is also possible that
Sam Marx, head of Metro's story department, and Irving
Thalberg had been alerted to Lawson's militancy and were
quick to rehire him in order to keep an eye on him.

When Lawson attempted to enlist all writers in their newly
formed union, the Screen Writers Guild, which he had helped
found, Thalberg and Marx were ready with a company union
of their own, the Screen Playwrights, with four rightist
scenarists on the prowl for members—Laurence Stallings,

James McGuinness, John Emmett Rogers, and John Lee Mahin.*

Young writers just in from the East were proselytized from two equally militant directions the moment they set foot on studio property. Even the rather liberal George Oppenheimer was induced to come into the Screen Playwrights for a brief time, but he soon realized his error and rejoined the Guild, where, as a measure of contrition, he served on the Board and in every capacity he had time for.

The Screen Writers Guild eventually overcame its phony rival and became the screenwriters' strongest protector. But it took years and a couple of strikes to win the minimal protection necessary to hoist up the writer to a level where acknowledgment was visible on the screen that he had contributed to the creation of the film about to unreel. The hardest-won recognition of all was that of credits, which were, as Lawson recalled, "a free-for-all. Anyone could get the credit who could get hold of the producer and convince him that he had done the crucial work on a picture. And the producers often gave the credit to their personal friends. I had this happen to me again and again and again. The Guild was by no means the perfect solution. There was still a lot of competition among writers and there was a very bad atmosphere about writing and about production generally. But writers now do have the right to demand credit and the Guild was finally recognized in 1940–41."

But whichever guild they landed in, whether they were recognized for their work or not, money and creature comfort undid many of them unless and until they fled the California

---

*Mahin had come into films from a Madison Avenue ad agency, where he created the advertising slogan, "Are you mouth happy?" His career in films was enhanced by his screenplay of Howard Hawks's production *Scarface.* The director was grateful to Mahin for writing into the script a "director's touch"—the moment when a gangster about to be slain by a rival gang torpedo in a bowling alley lets the ball go, the pins fall down except one that wobbles a bit, then falls, too, and we know the man is dead. This bit of business, in turn, was suggested to Mahin by his friend Charles Lederer.

hills. With the tension of waiting for a royalty check to pay the
rent or the mortgage installment, with the rigors of winter—
shoveling out a driveway in Connecticut in the middle of
February—a writer is kept on his mettle. In Hollywood, only
the most highly motivated writers—Lillian Hellman, with her
great show of not caring, Christopher Isherwood, Thornton
Wilder, and Nathanael West—seemed unaffected by the
temptations of the slower, sun-drenched atmosphere.

Isherwood lived a little apart from the mainstream of
Hollywood life. "If I have books," he said by way of
explaining his detachment, "it's almost as good as having the
people there, from a purely cultural point of view. But I have
lived a great deal in countries where English was not the
language and where all *that* has been going on in my head
[more] than any place else. . . . I don't think that I bring very
much to films. I think that films bring a great deal to me. By
working in this medium, which is a medium of visualization
primarily, I learned a great, great deal, which I could use in
my books. I never really saw things before."

Thornton Wilder, on his way to dinner one night with the
Charles MacArthurs (she was Helen Hayes) and actress Ruth
Gordon, put a curse upon the place, telling them: "You know,
one day someone is going to approach this area and it will be
entirely desert. There will be nothing left standing, stone
upon stone, but those large nails that the old men throw at the
horseshoes in MacArthur Park. That's all that's going to be
left standing above ground. The reason is that God never
meant man to live here. Man has come and invaded a
desert . . . and he has tortured this desert into giving up
sustenance and growth to him and he has defeated and
perverted the purposes of God. And this is going to be
destroyed." He said this in all seriousness. *The Skin of Our
Teeth* was yet to be written, but he was probably thinking
about it.

Some managed by being themselves with few or no concessions made to the traditional role of employee. Jack Warner, in his autobiography, recalls buying Raymond Chandler's thriller *The Big Sleep*, which

> had Humphrey Bogart's name on it, whether or not by design. . . . I don't recall who mentioned [*William*] Faulkner's name—he had not yet won the Nobel or Pulitzer prize [!!!]—but I thought it was an exciting idea. Jerry Wald brought him to Burbank, and I gave him a sumptuous office with two attractive secretaries, and I said: 'No one's going to bother you here, Mr. Faulkner. Your time will be your own.'
>
> "'Thank you, Mr. Warner,' he said, 'but if it's all the same to you, I'd rather work at home.'
>
> "'Now, we don't expect you to punch any clocks, Mr. Faulkner,' I said. 'You can come and go as you please.'
>
> "'I would prefer *not* to work in an office,' he said stubbornly.
>
> "Some weeks later, when something urgent arose in connection with the script, I asked Bill Schaefer to call Faulkner.
>
> "'You know he works at home,' Bill said.
>
> "'Of course. Call him at home.'
>
> "'This is long distance. We're ready on your call to Mr. Faulkner.'
>
> "'Long distance?' I almost yelled.
>
> "'Yes, sir,' the operator said. 'He's in Oxford, Mississippi.'
>
> "'Mr. Faulkner, how could you do this to me? How could you leave town without letting me know? You said you'd be working at home.'
>
> "'This is my home,' Faulkner said patiently. 'I live in Mississippi.'"

For many of the others who occupied cubicles or even plush offices in the writers' buildings, novels and short stories often went unwritten, plays got no farther than an outline and opening scene.

And there were at least two of their number, Dorothy

Parker and F. Scott Fitzgerald, alike in so many ways, whose surrender to Hollywood was made because of an inner conviction that what they were writing or intended to write would not measure up to the work that had been applauded in the past. Fitzgerald would be revived by the change and, as his peculiar "goofiness" when drunk began to isolate him from the writers' colony, he suddenly came face to face with himself. He got his first crystalline view of himself there in Hollywood and, though shaken, he was able to set down this image with a complexity and depth that were new in his work.

Fitzgerald and Mrs. Parker shared an enormous insecurity; they would come into rooms wondering if someone might challenge their presence at any moment. Dorothy Parker attempted to conceal this with a bright smile and a devastating quip. As Fitzgerald began to be avoided as "strange," Mrs. Parker was courted because of her wit, which in quotation began to rival Samuel Goldwyn's mangled English (and they were equally misquoted), and she was rarely omitted from any guest list out of fear of what she might say about such an errant hostess.

Both of these writers had been drinking their way to what they apparently hoped would be an early grave but only Fitzgerald would succeed. Meanwhile, there was the anonymity of the movie writer to cover any blast from the critics, although Scott entertained a notion for a long time of launching a major new career as a star writer of films, another Ben Hecht but with a more acute sensibility. Not least, he needed the money desperately, but it would be Mrs. Parker, who was much less anxious to succeed, who would make a successful transition to films (with the aid of her hardworking writer husband Alan Campbell) and enjoy the sudden affluence Fitzgerald had known only in the twenties.

Mrs. Parker, who knew him from back East, thought Fitzgerald more interesting as a human being and a writer than Hemingway. "Hemingway always bored me," she said late in life. "You can see how that would be. Fitzgerald was sweet. And he wanted to be nice. And Ernest didn't want to be nice. He just wanted to be worshipped. . . . Scott never found himself. He was still always at Princeton. He was awfully sad. He would dance Princeton, you know. . . . He was very touching, I thought. He irritated the life out of you. He was awfully slowed up, and I guess that happens to people. . . ."

And so was she, Mrs. Parker, "slowed up" by the time of her arrival in Hollywood. She was always planning to write far more than she ever produced. And in Hollywood, like Fitzgerald she would have to fight the chaos of her private life. But somehow, against overwhelming odds, both would succeed in sustaining their literary reputations.

6.

Scott Fitzgerald had come and gone very quickly in 1931. The advance word was that he needed the money, and yet his fame, which had been as vast as Sinclair Lewis's or Theodore Dreiser's, the other big literary guns of his day, had not diminished by much. One of his most enduring short stories, *Babylon Revisited*, had appeared in the February 21 issue of *The Saturday Evening Post*, one of eight of his stories the *Post* would publish that year.

During his weeks at Metro, the King Vidors looked after him with genuine affection and the Irving Thalbergs (she was Norma Shearer) invited him to their larger affairs.

And he was not unknown in the film colony. In 1927 John Considine of United Artists offered him an assignment to write "a fine modern college story for Constance Talmadge." He and his wife Zelda trained West and settled into the posh Ambassador Hotel in a four-apartment bungalow which they shared with John Barrymore, actress Carmel Myers, and another writer (also photographer) Carl Van Vechten.

In that peak year of the twenties, Scott and Zelda met the stars on an equal footing, many of the players fawning over this super-celebrity of the literary world, although few had read his books. One who had was actress Lois Moran,* a honey blonde whom the newspaper columnists called "one of the screen's perennial Vassar girls." In 1927 she was still riding the crest of a wave of popularity begun the year before when she appeared as "Rosemary," Lon Chaney's daughter in *The Road to Mandalay.* Scott was to remember both the film and the heroine's name. Miss Moran was to become his "Rosemary," the peripatetic film star who seldom made a trip without her mother in *Tender Is the Night,* Scott's most ambitious and mature completed novel (1934).

Scott's friendship with Lois Moran has been described as a flirtation, but it was more serious and less physical than that. In a letter apparently intended for Zelda but never mailed, Scott was to write: ". . . I woke up in Hollywood no longer my egotistic, certain self but a mixture of Ernest in fine clothes and Gerald [Murphy] with a career—and Charlie McArthur with a past. Anybody that could make me believe that, like Lois Moran did, was precious to me."

Zelda had an electric presence and a heightened sense of life that was an oddness to her neighbors in Alabama and a "zing" to her new friends in Scott's Bohemian circles. But she had Scott's obsessive need to be admired without the talent to sustain it.† She was more than simply jealous of Lois Moran. It is probable that her first breakdown was triggered by her

---

*It was Miss Moran's notion that Scott should play opposite her in a motion picture. Scott actually appeared before the cameras in a screen test, an episode unique in the annals of America's literary giants, although Hemingway loved to be photographed and would do the voice-over narration for *The Spanish Earth* in 1937. Zelda wrote in disappointment to daughter Scottie that "Daddy . . . wouldn't do it." After viewing the screen test, Scott decided against an acting career.

---

†She did have a gift for expressing herself in an original fashion. She painted for a time and, more successfully, wrote one novel, *Save Me the Waltz,* published by Scott's house, Scribner's.

intense irritation over his "affair" (Scott was to call it that in a letter to one of Zelda's psychiatrists, Dr. Mildred Squires) with the actress. Miss Moran had studied ballet in Paris, so it is not surprising that, once back in France in the winter of 1929-1930, Zelda was at the practice bar, a thirty-year-old woman studying classical ballet to the exclusion of all else.

By 1931, Zelda already was alienated from Scott much of the time and moving in and out of the shadows of incipient schizophrenia, her delicate Southern beauty ravaged by emotional strain. There was certainly a case to be made by her supporters who believed that Scott had been nearly as mad as she, and it was one of those terrible alliances in which both parties were emotionally disturbed at times, each blaming his failure and depressions on the other.

Scott had another close female companion during the weeks when he was laboring over a Jean Harlow vehicle, *The Redheaded Woman.* Carmel Myers was a silent screen star who had made a faltering transition to talkies and retired from films (as would Lois Moran); in 1931, she starred in *West of Broadway* opposite John Gilbert, winning favorable reviews that applauded her new "more sophisticated" film characterization, but the public responded apathetically and she soon left the movies to accept a starring role in a Broadway musical comedy, *Let 'Em Eat Cake,* with music by the Gershwins (1933). Miss Myers and several other loyal friends, including the Vidors, the Charlie MacArthurs, and George Oppenheimer, formed an alliance against the creeping social alienation that threatened him because of his heavy drinking.

The Redheaded Woman was not going well. It had been derived from an inferior copy of Scott's own style and province by Katharine Brush. He ignored the work's origins and even its superficiality, and attempted to impart some wisdom and perception to what was a synthetic carbon copy of an early Fitzgerald. It did not work, and the studio brought in Anita Loos to replace him. Anita had written the first major Harlow-Gable success, *Hold Your Man,* the previous year, and would write two more before the platinum blonde's tragically premature death in 1937. Earlier, while Scott was still working on his draft, Anita had given him some reassurance and emotional support. But neither could she forget that in the late twenties back on Long Island, Scott had threatened to kill her and Zelda during one of his drunken rages. Even Zelda was terrified, sensing that he was serious, and they had run across the street to Ring Lardner's for help.

Surely there was an echo of this earlier, murderous incident in his head as he cleaned out his desk, prior to his departure, but his feelings on the subject of the film were primarily those of rejection and even despair. "I ran afoul of a bastard named de Sano [*a collaborator Metro had brought in to try to salvage the Fitzgerald script*], since a suicide, and let myself be gypped out of command. I wrote the picture and he changed as I wrote. I tried to get at Thalberg but was erroneously warned against it as 'bad taste.' Result—a bad script. I left with the money, for this was a contract for weekly payments, but disillusioned and disgusted, vowing never to go back tho they said it wasn't my fault and asked me to stay." All of this in a letter to his daughter, whom he treated alternately as his confidante in such private moments and as the daughter of a stern father, quick to scold.

There are some film historians who believe that Hollywood was never itself a destructive agent in writing careers, that those authors whose muse dried up or whose works became smaller were on the skids anyway and in any climate. But Scott was a special case. He no longer felt the need to do colorful turns that would bring down the house. He has been depicted as a shambling wreck by literally dozens of witnesses, friends, and acquaintances who were privy to his bouts with alcoholism, his filmscript failures, or some social gaffe or evidence of his insecurity. Following his death, a number of them turned a quick dollar by sending in their reminiscences to a popular monthly. Scott had been doing the same thing, both for the cash and as a spiritual purgative, during his last decade, and his mistress, Sheilah Graham, who was also his salvation for more than three years, made a whole second career out of a series of memoirs, *Beloved Infidel, College of One, The Rest of the Story,* and *The Garden of Allah,* which has a chapter on Scott. But in actual fact he was maturing as a writer, going beyond the perfection of form of *The Great Gatsby* to something more profound. His work in the thirties had taken on a depth that coincided with and was fostered by the tragedies befalling him in life, including his failure in Hollywood. Budd Schulberg's novel *The Disenchanted* (inspired by his brief collaboration with Scott on a weak and shallow movie about Dartmouth's winter carnival,) was doubtless the high water mark in this flood of "Fitzgerald in dissolution."

Scott took Hollywood much too seriously. He fled East, where he pulled himself together both as a person and as a leading novelist. He was able to shed some of his sense of insecurity, even anonymity, at La Paix, an old mansion he rented near Baltimore.

But it was possible for Charlie Lederer, raised in Hollywood (or taken there by his aunt, the star Marion Davies, at no more than eleven or twelve years of age), to see it as a place for neither expiation nor forced labor. He would drive in through the studio gates at an early hour, wave to the guard at the gate, enter his ground-floor office and within minutes, climb out the window. Then he would spend the day at his favorite pub or tennis club, (he always wore his tennis whites to work), returning in the late afternoon the same way and impressing everyone with his industry. Lillian Hellman writes of spending days with another writer at the Goldwyn Studios attempting to inscribe several condoms with yet another colleague's name, since by some fluke his photo had appeared on little matchboxes made in Europe and they thought boxed condoms stamped "with the compliments of Henry C. Potter" a great joke.

A genius at procrastination, another Charlie, this one

surnamed MacArthur—moving in the same circle as Lederer,
they were known as the two Charlies—began to peeve
producer Hunt Stromberg by failing to deliver a filmscript by
a certain deadline. Stromberg finally demanded to see the
work on which MacArthur ostensibly had been toiling.
Charlie M. grabbed a pile of miscellaneous letters, carbon
copies, memos, and old bills, anything close to manuscript
size, and rushed it in to Stromberg's office, waving the pile
aloft and declaring, "Here it is. It's here, Hunt. But it's not
worthy of you and it isn't worthy of the studio, and I'm not
going to give this to the studio," at which point he began
shredding the papers into confetti, a form of sleight of hand to
distract Stromberg from the various shapes and colors of the
paper. "It's not worthy of you," Charlie insisted. "You're
better than this and I'm going to do better than this." But then
soon afterward, the script was delivered. MacArthur was
known to be conscientious, and Lederer was not hired and
rehired simply for his pranks and goofing off, but they both,
like many others, enjoyed teasing and tormenting their bosses.

There was "bad blood" between David O. Selznick and
MacArthur. Helen Hayes MacArthur recalled a fight on the
grounds of their Hollywood estate between her husband and
Selznick that blackened Charlie's eyes and put Selznick in the
hospital. "He couldn't see David," she said, "without getting
into a fight with him. I don't know what it was. . . . It was
one of the worst brawls that Hollywood had known and only
was broken up when Irene [Mayer] Selznick, realizing that her
husband was getting the worst of it, took off her slipper and
began to beat Charlie over the head with her heel." Charlie
Lederer believed that Selznick was jealous of Charlie M. in
some way as a writer. Selznick fancied himself a writer; also a
casting director, director, set and costume designer, and press
agent; but his interference in all of these areas sustained his
reputation as a perfectionist.

"Get the producer" might have been great fun, but those

who played it could receive a dismissal notice instead of a tolerant smile. Producers became "writer shy" around the less reclusive writers and no one was more so than Selznick. During a collaboration of Charlie Lederer and Ben Hecht on a movie to star John Barrymore, *Topaze,* being produced by Selznick for RKO (1933), Charlie was fired suddenly and for no apparent reason.

"My agent," Charlie L. recalled, "said it seemed to be my fault. 'What the hell are you talking about?' I asked. 'Well,' said the agent, 'it seems that Selznick says he can't stand your smirking at the story conferences. He can't sit in the room with you smirking all the time.' I didn't know that I smirked. 'If I did,' I said, 'it was involuntary and I don't like to take the rap for an involuntary tic.' Henri d'Arrast was the director on the film and I wanted Harry to make the picture." Selznick told him that if he came in and apologized for smirking, everything would be all right. Charlie L. went in and said, "Mr. Selznick, I'm awfully sorry about this. I have nothing to smirk about. I hope you'll forgive me." Selznick forgave him and he was reinstated, although upon its release Selznick withheld credit from him as collaborator on the screenplay. This did not sit well with Charlie; there would be further contretemps and the truce would not last.

There was no Hollywood writer without his version of the "dunderhead" producing one of his scripts. There were a number of incompetent producers but everyone knew Selznick was not. The writer and the producer were the classic antagonists of Hollywood and you were not "in the club" until you had an anecdote to recount, usually cautiously, in circles where it would not cost you your job. It helped keep the interior under control and artistic frustration to a minimum. But the exterior was treated to a gentle dew at sunrise (although few writers ever were awake to be aware of it), and sunshine nearly every day that would give them a poolside tan. Most of them urban-raised and -attuned, they

had to learn to live with birdsong at dawn, and sometimes
halfway through the night, windows that framed not a
bustling blur of humanity but palm fronds and lots of blue sky
and the glaring white of a neighbor's villa in the sun. Your
days were measured not by your several appointments but by
the miles that lay between them, hence there were fewer of
them than in the East. Your friendly gas station was even
more familiar than Lucey's Bar or Henry's, where the pre-
tense of Eastern-style barroom camaraderie was insisted upon
and was even fairly convincing.

Yet most of them knew in their hearts that while their
presence en masse was making American films more mature
and literate, the spiritual cost to themselves was high and their
huge salaries had reduced most of them to hirelings besotted
by California languour.

7.

Charles MacArthur had not proved difficult to get when
Irving Thalberg sent out the first feeler. Many of his cronies
were already in the West. The Algonquin Round Table in
New York—that lunchtime shooting gallery where often you
or your work were the target—was defunct.

The Algonquin had been for many years a spiritual harbor
to writers and actors. The Round Table had come into
existence not by design but by the fact of the hotel's restaurant
being such a congenial meeting place in the theater district,
courtesy of its owner Frank Case. (It still is, although Case is
no longer with us.) Dorothy Parker, Robert Benchley, and
Robert E. Sherwood were among the earliest "members,"
while Alexander Woollcott considered himself a founder.*
Cover artist and portraitist Neysa McMein was perhaps the
most striking of the ladies who were regulars. Casual parties at

---

*Woollcott was introduced to the pleasures of the Algonquin by Brock Pemberton.

her studio were planned at the Round Table and there were wall-to-wall crowds attending as invited guests or "with a friend."

George S. Kaufman was a frequent drop-in. His favorite lunch-table amusement was word games. Harpo Marx, an occasional guest, recalls in his memoirs some of the Round Table's offerings:

KAUFMAN: Want to hear me give a sentence using the word "punctilious"?

WOOLLCOTT: Give me a sentence using the word "punctilious."

KAUFMAN: I know a man who has two daughters Lizzie and Tillie. Lizzie is all right, but you have no idea how punctilious.

HERMAN MANKIEWICZ: You know, it's hard to hear what a bearded man is saying. He can't speak above a whisker.

BENCHLEY: Have you heard the one about the little boy on the train?

KAUFMAN: (Who's heard it twenty times; for some strange reason its Benchley's favorite joke.) No.

BENCHLEY: A man gets on the train with his little boy, and gives the conductor only one ticket. "How old's your kid?" the conductor says, and the father says he's four years old. "He looks at least twelve to me," says the conductor, and the father says, "Can I help it if he worries?"

The talk was witty in most cases and such items as the above were usually picked up by F.P.A. (Franklin P. Adams) and published in his *Conning Tower* column.

Edna Ferber called their influence "tonic." "The people they could not and would not stand," she continued, "were the bores, hypocrites, sentimentalists, and the socially pretentious. They were ruthless toward charlatans, toward the pompous and the mentally and artistically dishonest. Casually incisive, they had a terrible integrity about their work and a boundless ambition."

The enduring legend of never-to-be-surpassed wit and one-upmanship of the Algonquin Round Table has led to an uncritical view of its members. George S. Kaufman has not passed the test of time as a major comic playwright. His life; his headlined affair with Mary Astor; his indulgent, bright wife Beatrice, in one case, and classically beautiful wife Leueen, in the other, were more interesting than his work. . His true brilliance was more apparent in the drawing room than in the theatre. *You Can't Take It With You* (with Moss Hart) and *Stage Door* (with Edna Ferber) enjoy occasional revivals, but playwright George Kelly, whose career Kaufman's for a time eclipsed, now seems much surer of a place in America's permanent theater repertory with *The Show Off* and *The Big Butter and Egg Man.*

F.P.A. (Franklin P. Adams), Alec Woollcott, Heywood Broun all belong to the twenties and thirties but have not survived as major figures in the world of letters, although again Woollcott's flamboyance and ubiquitousness have given him stature as a writer beyond his real literary achievement. Edna Ferber's *Show Boat*, adapted from her novel, has passed into America's musical theater repertory due to the enduring popularity of her story and one of Jerome Kern's more enchanting scores. But her other books, excluding her luminous autobiography, *A Peculiar Treasure,* and a splendid book of short stories, *"Nobody's in Town,"* have become period pieces.

Marc Connelly and Sherwood were probably the most significant early regulars, with Mrs. Parker close on their heels. All were soon on their way West and the ironic fact was that Hollywood, which was a favorite target for their humor, was quietly attracting a far more important literary crowd during the heyday of the Algonquin group—Preston Sturges had arrived in town, Scott Fitzgerald, Ben Hecht, Donald Ogden Stewart, S. N. Behrman, Guy Bolton and P. G. Wodehouse; the list goes on and on.

But it is the New Yorker's habit to lend an aura of

uniqueness and splendor to its old institutions. The Round Table was the most literary and amusing of them in our century and thus its history looms larger than the reality of the group itself.

It terminated quietly, eliminated by events much bigger than it could deal with through its intramural humor. Three years into the Depression, it became a bit precious and reminiscent of Louis XVI to lunch on your friends' weaknesses or indulge in comic banter while the world was collapsing just outside.

Charlie MacArthur was between writing projects. In point of fact, he was *usually* between projects. It is the hardest thing in the world for any writer of value to sit down at his typewriter and write, and everyone has a variety of dodges— sorting through bills (writers' bills are often dog-eared from just this process), reading "background material," which may be that detective novel received in the mail yesterday, raking the leaves to clear the mind as well as the yard, or simply saying the hell with it and taking off for that cocktail party at five on East Sixty-third Street. Charlie often said "the hell with it." Some called him lazy, others a perfectionist; Scott Fitzgerald said that others do and Charlie simply *is*. But whatever he *was*, he was delighted to accept Thalberg's offer and hasten West with wife Helen, where they would join the Ben Hechts, the Marc Connellys, the Robert Sherwoods, and the Charlie Lederers, except that now his social life would have to be fitted in around his ten-to-four chore at the studio every day.

For the MacArthurs, it was a new beginning and all the old, festering sores of New York were behind them—the women to whom Charlie was gallant to the last, the reckless hosts and hostesses who knew Charlie could drink all of them into unconsciousness and still be on his feet, and, not least, the one-sidedness of Helen's fame and Charlie's charm.

Helen Hayes MacArthur already had become one of three

first ladies of the stage (the other two being Lynn Fontanne and Katharine Cornell—America rarely doing things by halves or even by ones), but Helen felt or at least declared she felt that she had hogged the spotlight for much too long. Charlie's big stage success in collaboration with Ben Hecht, *The Front Page,* had opened in 1928; he and Helen were married that same year, it having been agreed that they would wed when he had attained a success as large as her own.

Perhaps Thalberg knew that the moment had come when MacArthur would say "yes" to an offer. His wife was pregnant and temporarily off the stage and he would soon have a child to support. The contrast between collaborator Hecht, who often juggled as many as four or five film projects, could not have been sharper. If Charlie was a writer who seldom wrote, if his preoccupation with living the life of a playwright-charmer kept him from the typewriter, now at last he was going to be corralled by the one man in Hollywood who allegedly had the taste and wisdom to get the most and best out of him.

And so the MacArthurs trained West, where they were given a dizzying round of welcoming parties. Young expectant mother Helen was gayer than anyone had heard (she was relieved that their life had been pulled together for once and it was no longer an improvised day-by-day matter) and Charlie embraced old friends from New York, Bobby Benchley, Marc Connelly, Don Stewart, and, not least, Ben Hecht and his wife Rose.

Soon after their arrival, Charlie and director King Vidor became tennis partners—they were working for the same man, Thalberg, and had fallen into an easy rapport. Vidor invited the MacArthurs to come up to the ranch he shared with his wife Eleanor Boardman so that Helen could have her baby there. Helen recalls them as "just close and loving friends—laughing friends. All of Charlie's friends out there were laughing friends. . . . But then there was that nut, John

Gilbert, the quintessence of actor, if you will . . . a great attitudinizer, and Laurence Stallings. [Eleanor] was close to Marion Davies and we used to go to Marion's all the time. . . . Charlie adored her and he was a great admirer of Hearst. He had worked for him and he just thought he was the greatest newspaper man there was. Gilbert annoyed Charlie a lot. He was like a bad boy. I remember Gilbert was going through the tragedy of losing Garbo—they had broken up after he had done the house up on the hill for her with gold hot and cold plumbing fixtures with her initials on them . . . and he was always going to kill himself, always telling Charlie that he was going to do this. Once he came down and asked Charlie to please knock him out, hit him. And Charlie was so weary of him and just didn't want to take the trouble. . . ."

After baby Mary was born, the MacArthurs began looking for a place of their own. An estate consisting of a mansion and twenty acres behind the Metro studios in Culver City was available. It once had been owned by Grace Moore and seemed a little grand but just the place in which the Mac-Arthurs could reciprocate the numerous dinners and cocktail parties their social lives had accumulated while Helen was *enceinte* (and Charlie had had to go alone much of the time). It was known as "the Youngworth Ranch" and it was covered with acres of artichokes. Even level-headed Helen had done nothing to resist. She was not content to be considered a soggy blanket—her reputation back East. Here she was being given a social reprieve. The MacArthur Ranch would be a magnet for all that was gayest in the film town, all the best minds, the brightest pranksters, the Charlie Lederers (fun), the Walter Wangers and the Irving Thalbergs (the power elite), the Marc Connellys (Broadway), and, of course, the Vidors and the Ben Hechts (loyal to the last).

But disillusion set in early that summer of 1930. Artichokes when ripening attracted flies, and anyone wandering out onto the MacArthur patio did so at his peril. Or so Charlie began to complain that they did. He began complaining about a host of things and soon the studio and its limitations, often stifling, were among them.

He was becoming nearly as friendly with Irving Thalberg, who had creative control of the studio, as he was with Vidor. Irving found Charlie relaxing to be around, with his easy, quizzical smile and seeming sense of never being in a rush to finish anything. (Irving had not seen his private agony as Helen had—that need to leave his literary mark; the determination to experience every possible avenue of life; both desires aborted time and again.) He and Irving would mull over ideas together and Charlie's initial awe of this most powerful superproducer evaporated as he realized how unsure the man was about so many things. There was the matter of Irving's delicate health and, like Scott Fitzgerald, he would not hesitate to confide that all was not well with him. Friends told Charlie *everything*. They used him as more than a sympathetic ear; he was a dumping ground for pent-up emotions and, while he listened and clucked and nodded his head, it began to tell on him. He complained bitterly to Helen that nearly everyone he knew had a problem, usually unsolvable.

Thalberg reflected what was best and worst in Hollywood at the time. The glossy films turned out in the thirties under his aegis were vastly popular. He once told screenwriter Allen Rivkin that he was the only man in Hollywood who had his finger on the public's pulse. *Quo vadis* Zanuck, Selznick, Schulberg? If he was a delicate man, he yet had the perquisite ego to put his identifying stamp on nearly fifty films a year.

The comedies and dramas of Robert Montgomery were a finishing school for the have-nots (the exceptions *The Big House* and *Night Must Fall*), the romantic melodramas of Garbo were a predictable lot of boudoirs and salons and sleighs scooting through chateau country redeemed by Garbo herself (the exceptions, *Anna Christie* and *Ninotchka*, of course). And there were *Grand Hotel, Mutiny on the Bounty, The Good Earth,* the Harlow films, the Marx Brothers comedies, *Romeo and Juliet, The Barretts of Wimpole Street* and the Dressler-Beery series. Perhaps a couple of dozen distinguished films and several dozen gleaming entertainments, highly perishable.

Still, entertainment was the essence of a Metro film. No need to think. Lewis Stone provided the knotted brow and solemn thought; Marie Dressler the tinge of disrespect for the mighty; Jeanette MacDonald and Nelson Eddy the classical tone; Robert Montgomery and William Powell the zippy repartee.

So it is not surprising that Irving Thalberg was soon insisting upon adapting Helen Hayes MacArthur—the human being with dignity—from a stage star into a leading actress of the screen. As successful as she had been on the stage, she was still reaching a limited audience compared with the millions around the earth who would see her in the movies.

This passion for stars and the involved and often calculated business of creating them was something Thalberg shared with Louis B. Mayer, the head of the Culver City studio. Thalberg could not resist casting such a populous film as *Dinner at Eight* with five of his most important stars and eight of his lesser ones. About the only supporting actors in the movie were those playing maids and other hotel employees.

But making Helen Hayes a glamorous film queen was no small process, since she was not only diminutive but plain. A bit earlier, producer Walter Wanger had told her, "There ought to be a place for you in pictures. You're half comic and half human." They eventually found that she had "one good side" (one profile that could be made up and lighted to reflect screen glamour), and Charlie set about to rewrite her first film, *The Sin of Madelon Claudet.*

Madelon's sin was that she was made pregnant (pregnancy

was to play a considerable role in Miss Hayes's life in the early thirties) by an untalented artist and then rejected by a farm youth who could not live with "her shame." It was a reworking of *Madame X*, which had been one of the early talking picture successes with Ruth Chatterton. It even carried over one of the same actors, Lewis Stone.

The New York Times echoed the general feeling that it was "virtually suspenseless" because of its similarity to the earlier movie. "And added to this is the piling on of the agony in a fashion which will cause almost anybody to think that Madelon's nemesis is not fate, but the studio producer. . . . When she is down, she must fall lower. . . . When she applies for a domestic position, she is a second too late. . . . She must walk the streets to get money, most of which she sends to an old doctor for the education of her son."

Under the calm Charlie projected was almost constant tension. He was on another movie when *Madelon* was being previewed and the writing was not going to his satisfaction. He was drinking heavily. That preview night, his wife declined to see her own picture, and Charlie had come back really shaken by the experience. When one of the trade papers blasted the movie the following day (a foretaste of what lay ahead), Charlie sat across from Helen reading the review and crying—nothing melodramatic, just big tears coursing down his cheeks. She held him in her arms for a long time; Helen mothered him, among much else. Helen Hayes MacArthur would be criticized by a number of Charlie's cronies as being "too proper" and severe, a charge also leveled at Gertrude Benchley, who rarely left the Benchley home in Westchester County, New York, but Helen held Charlie together for many years, until his death in fact.

Charlie did not even get screen credit for his work on *Madelon*, which may have seemed a blessing in the face of those reviews, but later, as the public flocked to see one of America's great actresses in her movie debut and the Academy voted her an Oscar for her performance, that lack of recognition hurt more than a little. He had tailored his revision to his wife's talents and had reworked whole scenes a day before they were to be shot. Helen recalls one scene in particular he added: "When Madelon comes out of prison, and she'd been in there for . . . several years . . . and as she walked along, there was a tree, the branches were low and she reached up just without saying anything, without any reference to it and just touched the branches of the tree as she went under it. . . . People thought I was a genius because I had thought to touch the branches of the tree. Well, it was all written down there in the script."

One film followed another for Helen Hayes—*Arrowsmith* by Sinclair Lewis, Hemingway's affecting love story of World War I, *A Farewell to Arms,* and *The White Sister*—her dignity and stage fame combining to make Hollywood offer her their most impressive leading men, Colman, Cooper, and Gable as well as their most important literary properties. The MacArthurs' New York life pattern was repeating itself in the West with even sharper contrasts. Helen's film career quickly began to eclipse that of her writer husband. Thalberg's brilliant notion had reduced Charlie to being prince consort to a leading film star.

But he was gracious about it—grace being instinctual with him—only a little too ready perhaps to agree with her complaints about the increasing demands upon her time. And, of course, they began running on different schedules. She was up before dawn to be off to the studio while he was sleeping off the party of the night before. Sometimes she would protest the whole contrived waffle of stardom, but it did her little good. There were contracts and commitments, and their lives were fitted in around them. She determined to flee at the earliest possible moment and they both looked toward the East in the hope that there lay their eventual salvation.

8.

Prohibition had been repealed, but American morality still took a serious turn in 1933. No more high jinks. Sally Rand, performing with her fans and nothing else at the Chicago World's Fair, was arrested and convicted "for willfully performing an obscene and indecent dance in a public place." Later, explaining to reporters how she was able to continue with her act, the most popular attraction at the Fair, she held up three little pieces of sheer silk gauze. "This," she said smiling, "is the difference between decency and indecency."

Enforcement of the Code in American films was a few months away and Mae West was the eighth most popular performer on the screen. Miss West was given full credit for saving Paramount from bankruptcy during the Depression. She should have been given a citation for keeping the screen liberated for more than two years as the pressure groups mounted the ramparts and leveled their guns on Hollywood. If she initiated the eventual attack that would end in a rout of the free and inquiring spirit, someone had to be the target.

On March 10, 1933, at five-thirty in the afternoon, the four Marx Brothers and their mother Minnie were gathered around the bedside of their dying father and husband. Suddenly the floor began to tremble and the walls to shake. Harpo, who was not especially religious, became a believer on the spot. The old man's bed began to roll forward as Chico leaped out of the way. Minnie Marx mumbled Yiddish prayers to such a spectacular departure. Then the room was quiet, old Mr. Marx's bed rolled back to its place against the wall, and the vigil resumed. Long Beach was levelled during those three or four astonishing minutes in the most devastating California earthquake since 1906.

Director William K. Howard's *The Power and the Glory* (1933), with Spencer Tracy cast as Tom Garner, a rugged tycoon, anticipated *Citizen Kane* by eight years, flashing back through the man's life and cutting in an old friend's varying attitudes toward him as a voice-over narration. This Fox production was written by Preston Sturges and produced by Jesse Lasky, who had moved over from Paramount.

Sturges, like Ben Hecht a Chicagoan (but only by birth; his childhood was spent shuttling between America and France), was on the set throughout the filming of this innovative film.

Samuel Goldwyn, impressed by the visual power and strong story of *The Power and the Glory*, hired Sturges to adapt Tolstoy's *Resurrection* for his new star Anna Sten. But Sturges was not yet a big enough name to be an attraction for Goldwyn and his adaptation was not used. Even George Oppenheimer had suffered some ignominy at the Goldwyn Studios when he was there because his name was not Moss Hart or George S. Kaufman. Goldwyn hired "household words" and built a career for his excellent taste simply because he never bought an unknown quantity.

He was the only Hollywood studio head who remained fixed in his aims and in the public mind as someone of unchanging and undiluted quality throughout the great period of talking pictures.

Goldwyn's talent was not creative in any sense. It was acquisitive. He wanted to produce films so rich in every detail—performance, direction, script and atmosphere—audiences would be attracted by the combination, not by only one of its parts. During World War Two, when he became increasingly reliant upon one star, Danny Kaye, to carry the movie, his fortunes faltered a bit. The Kaye films were accepted at first but, as with any mannered personality, overexposure made inroads on his audience appeal. Much earlier, the same thing had happened to Goldwyn with Eddie Cantor.

Then he was saved by William Wyler's *The Best Years of Our Lives*, Hollywood's moment of real triumph in the immediate postwar years and a clarification of where American films stood in those years of the rise of neorealism. The difference between American realism as expressed in this Robert E. Sherwood script and the Italians' neorealism was one of focus. It was the difference between an oil by Thomas Eakins and one by Matisse, between a gifted documentarian with a concern for light and shadow and an impressionist very much involved in giving us his own view. And, of course, there was no turning back once American filmmakers had come in contact with real life again. The Code administrators had to expand their staff. Scripts were analyzed scene by scene. Bartering began—"We'll allow you one plunging neckline if you keep the drunken mother off-screen."

Goldwyn always had stood alone among the independent "one-man" studios. (Perhaps here we should define "independent" as meaning a studio without its own major theater chain. This meant that most of its product had to be sold on its merits rather than as part of a "block" of films.) But in the mid-thirties Goldwyn's supremacy was threatened by three rivals: David O. Selznick, whose standards of quality matched Goldwyn's but who had not yet severed his connection with Metro; Darryl F. Zanuck, who had just formed Twentieth Century Pictures with the assistance of Joseph Schenck; and veteran, allegedly unloved, Harry Cohn, whose Columbia Pictures had released *It Happened One Night* with two borrowed stars, Clark Gable (Metro) and Claudette Colbert (Paramount). Overnight, the tawdry programmer factory on Gower Street was elevated to the leading independent studio. Jack Holt, Cohn's rugged leading man of indisputable masculinity, no longer was the studio's *raison d'être*. Director Frank Capra was given carte blanche to make comedies with half-million-dollar budgets.

Still another surprising success, Richard Boleslavski's *Theodora Goes Wild*, with Irene Dunne, emerged, awards were won, Cohn's office enlarged, and Capra was told to proceed with a costly, escapist production, *Lost Horizon*.

When Capra told Cohn the film would cost two million dollars, Cohn dropped his fork in the diner of a train. "Two million? For Chrissake, that's half our whole year's budget!"

But Cohn had a hunch about the James Hilton romantic adventure. Possibly the setting, Tibet, suggested escape of such a high order audiences would respond on a tremendous scale. There was no taint of Hitler or the Depression; rather the opposite. Civilization was to be saved in a setting of airy splendor. The whole point of the book as told to Cohn was that Shangri-La, the Tibetan lamasery where much of the action was set, was to be a repository of all that was finest in the world. Let the rest of the world kill themselves—here was peace and tranquillity, knowledge and beauty. And *time,* man's greatest enemy after Hitler, stood relatively still there. *What possibilities!* thought Cohn.

Capra took screenwriter Robert Riskin to the desert and left him there to struggle with Robert Conway (the hero) and the High Lama while director Capra concentrated on getting the background of Tibet as accurate as possible.

Of all of the films of the 1930s and 1940s, two films appear more frequently than any others among both film critics' and ardent moviegoers' all-time favorites. One is *Lost Horizon* and the other is *Citizen Kane.* The first was an adventure tale on the grand scale not so terribly different in its plot ingredients from H. Rider Haggard's *She,* but there is an essential difference. The motivation of *She* (a thousand-year-old white woman who rules a hidden black kingdom in the wild mountainous bush country of Africa) is narcissism and lust; that of *Lost Horizon* is the altruistic hope of saving the finest and most useful knowledge of civilization in a world gone mad. The "ageless" heroine of *Lost Horizon* (Jane Wyatt) uses no coercion to keep the handsome outsider by her side. She is confident that he will come back, and he does. *She* bathes in the fire of eternal youth once too often in the vain hope of keeping the English youth who has blundered into her kingdom and become her captive as her prince consort. *She* is reduced to ashes rather like the Tibetan "girl" in *Lost Horizon* (played by Margo) who dares to venture out of the Valley of the Blue Moon and is turned into a two-hundred-year-old crone before the horrified eyes of her lover (hero Robert Conway's younger brother). Author James Hilton undoubtedly was influenced by the much earlier book, but he had the wisdom to play upon the terrible insecurity of the average reader, threatened as the latter was by war, totalitarianism, and personal insolvency. In The Valley of the Blue Moon, all wants were mystically satisfied—it was something in the buoyant air.

Since both author Hilton and scenarist Riskin carefully omitted any specific references to world leaders, particular wars, or any geography beyond the setting in the Himalayas and London, to which Robert Conway would return briefly, the film moved into that same realm of timelessness sustained by the book itself.

In Capra's autobiography, *The Name Above the Title*, he gives us some background on how this film classic was assembled.

> The first order of business was how to re-create and photograph Shangri-La, a magnificent lamasery that overlooked, from its perch on a cliff, the warm, verdant Valley of the Blue Moon; an earthly paradise so secluded, so isolated, so protected from the world and its cold winds by a ring of high peaks, that time—unruffled and unmeasured—offered life its richest savor. The inhabitants of this cloistered Eden observed a sunset as men in the outer world heard the striking of a clock, and with much less care.
>
> Shangri-La was hidden in the uncharted Himalayas—a thousand miles from nowhere. . . . We re-created the mountain-locked Valley of the Blue Moon—its peaceful village by a peaceful stream, under the tranquil primacy of the lamasery on a cliff—in miniature. We built the exterior of the lamasery full size

on the Columbia "ranch" in Burbank—its sunlit walls splayed with gnarled, centuries-old vines that dripped with fragrant blossoms; its broad, pink stairway that beckoned to the great portico; its acres of flat white roofs that shimmered in the sun at various levels. . . .

Stephen Goosson, the art director, did a superlative job in designing and building the settings for *Lost Horizon*. His colorful sketches and paintings of Shangri-La and its people still adorn the walls of art lovers. . . . Tibetans are Orientals, but taller, rangier than the Chinese or Japanese. Again we had recourse to our non-Chinese but Oriental stand-bys—Pala Indians from the San Diego Mountains. (Years later, I was a guest of Indian film director Chetan Anand, at his Juhn Beach home near Bombay. He asked where, in Tibet, had I shot his favorite picture, *Lost Horizon*. He was astonished to hear that I had never set foot in Tibet. But those were real Tibetans, he insisted. No, I said, they were American Indians. He upheld his unbelief by asserting vehemently that, while visiting a certain Tibetan lamasery, he had read all about the making of Lost Horizon in its "secret books.")

Films that have become classics over the years are made with many of the same risks as failures. Robert Riskin was Capra's favorite writer *(Lady for a Day, It Happened One Night, The Whole Town's Talking, Mr. Deeds Goes to Town)*. It seemed a magic combination and yet the first preview of *Lost Horizon* was a disaster. Riskin had written a long opening sequence showing the actual burning of Baskul. For reasons known only to the fates that govern hits and misses in the film business, this frame was faulty for the adventure to follow. Doubtless, the prolonged violence leading to flight and escape was wrong if rooted in a *real* situation. The movie needed wonder and slight bafflement from the beginning; the audience needed to be kept in the dark. They should ponder over why a girl of the streets (Isabel Jewell), probably tubercular, was flying away from danger into skies above the towering Himalayan peaks.

Capra lost three nights of sleep, then decided to destroy the opening two reels of the city's burning, actually throwing them in an incinerator. The second preview was an exciting event, with the audience thrilled, even exalted, by the scope of Conway's mission and concern over its success—the fate of civilization seemed to be riding on his decision of whether to stay and take over Shangri-La from the expiring High Lama or go back to the *real world* that could never understand his motives in "escaping" to Tibet.

The film altered Columbia's image for all time, paving the way for the glossy, high-budgeted star vehicles of Rita Hayworth throughout the forties. The studio's programmers continued to be filmed but on a reduced scale. Capra and Riskin had made Harry Cohn rise above "Poverty Row" and be mentioned in the same breath with Mayer, Goldwyn, Zanuck, and Jack Warner.

9.

Sometime in the fall of 1933, Charlie MacArthur, without a word to anyone, disappeared from his California home. His disappearance was not terribly out of character. It had happened before, and his wife was not greatly alarmed. In fact, she did not know he was gone until she got an urgent call from Irving Thalberg. It was Charlie's whim to take off unannounced. When Helen was about to give birth to Mary and Charles was finishing up a movie script, he decided to go back East by way of the Panama Canal and booked passage on a United Fruit Line ship. In Havana, he went barring long enough to miss the boat's departure. Anita Loos cabled him money for a few clothes and his fare back to New York.

At the time of this unscheduled exit, Helen was touring with Helen Menken in *Mary of Scotland*, and Irving's first notion was that she was pregnant again. "Why else," he asked when he finally located her in Pittsburgh, "would Charlie run out on me like this?"

The Thalbergs and the MacArthurs had returned from a joint trip to Cuba and Europe only the previous summer. Irving had had a bad heart attack earlier in the year, grave troubles with Nick Schenck and the studio, and the Mac-Arthurs were charming, intelligent and easy company. Norma thought their going with them was the best medicine in the world. Helen was rushed to the pier still in makeup and in a Catholic nurse's uniform (for *The White Sister*, completed late that afternoon).

Helen assured Irving from her Pittsburgh hotel suite that she was not pregnant and promised to let him know when Charlie turned up. It was one of the accommodations Helen had made to her husband that there never was any need for explanations about his movements or his actions. Such a loose leash enabled an intense, wandering Irishman to remain married to the same woman for twenty-eight years, until his death.

But the feeling he had of throwing away his talent on a script he hadn't the slightest interest in was more than he could contain. When he had attempted to reason with Irving, and persuade him to do something more original, since that was the only way MacArthur could be induced to remain in Hollywood, he encountered the stubborn will that had allowed this youthful production chief to survive in a world of Mayers, Schulbergs, and Goldwyns. He had been asked, ordered finally, to make something fresh out of Michael Arlen's *The Green Hat*.

Only the year before—or perhaps a year and a half—he had tangled with Metro production chief Bernard Hyman (a little lower than Thalberg) over rewrites on *Rasputin and the Empress*. Hyman had insisted that a rape scene be added to make the assassination of the "mad monk" (played by Lionel Barrymore) more acceptable to the audience. "We don't need it," Charlie had insisted. In fact, he saw the integrity of his entire script being compromised by Hyman's artistic myopia. But Hyman declared that audiences would not believe that

Rasputin's assassin, "Prince Chegodieff" (played by brother John Barrymore), would kill him simply out of his love for Mother Russia.

The rape had gone into the film and added fuel to a massive libel suit launched by the aging aristocrat, Prince Youssepov, on whom the character of the assassin was based. That lawsuit would drag on for years and finally be lost to the aristocratic plaintiff. At that early point, however, even Charlie Mac-Arthur was included among the defendants, alongside Loews, Inc., and Bernard Hyman, and it was with more of a shudder than a smile that Helen asked Charlie if he thought the Russians would like the furnishings they were putting into their eastern home in Nyack. They already had persuaded the Ben Hechts to settle there when Ben felt he had to make the complete transition to the role of serious writer. Perhaps the ire he aroused in moguls such as Mayer was part of it; in the East, he could snap at the hand that fed him with impunity. And he and Charlie could write their plays and he his books and short stories.

Helen was very close to Norma Shearer Thalberg in those days—with some wonder and awe. Norma was so perfect in her manners and apparently so dedicated to Irving's health, his status, and his privacy, it *was* awesome. The rupture between their husbands ended it. Miss Shearer's convictions were Irving's while he was alive, at least after their marriage. Before that, she was a coolly ambitious lady who had made capturing Irving a year-long project.

Irving could not have been more amazed or hurt by Charlie's defection. Indeed, he would not even accept the fact. But when he saw Charlie's resolution plain, the closeness dissolved.

Charlie's decision was made with no personal bias; with only professional integrity at stake. But for him that was more than enough. Thalberg's choice of *The Green Hat* upon his return from Europe was a fairly typical Thalbergian move.

His aim, Charlie finally saw, was to give a gloss to the hoariest of projects (*Anna Karenina* had been made twice by him, both versions starring Garbo), to make old ideas seem new through seamless craftsmanship. Charlie was appalled that Thalberg had so chosen, with all the world to choose from, with all the freedom ever given a Hollywood film man to make a really exciting *new* movie! *The Green Hat* had begun to date before the end of the twenties. It was, for Charlie, the epitome of all that was hokey and falsely sentimental and cheaply chic in that decade.

It would be unfair not to point out that that same mind could go through identical processes and come up with something very right. With *The Barretts of Wimpole Street*, released only a year after Charlie fled Metro, Thalberg's obsessional need to star his wife Norma Shearer in nearly every one of his own films met up with the perfect vehicle. She was intelligent-looking, despite a slight cast in one eye; she was delicate and could have been believably an invalid. She was also the perfect victim to the villainies of old Mr. Barrett as played by the superb Charles Laughton. What is more, Norma Shearer does not seem to date on revival. There is a timeless femininity about her.

Charlie's seeming perfidy was only one of several Thalberg suffered that year. One rumor, persistent in Hollywood after his departure on vacation, was that he had throat surgery performed in Europe. If true, it cannot be documented. Hollywood was always burying Irving or putting him prematurely in intensive care. Prior to that, he had been depressed by the shooting death of Paul Bern. Ben Hecht and others believed that a discarded mistress had killed Bern, enraged by his marriage to star Jean Harlow. Bern had been one of Thalberg's closest associates. The official word was that it was suicide.

Director Edmund Goulding (who had come to Hollywood initially as a writer, doing the original script of *Broadway*

Melody) took over the writing chore Charlie MacArthur had walked away from. The Norma Shearer vehicle was eventually released in 1934 as *Riptide* and faintly praised as having style, taste; nearly everything, in fact, except a decent story. Goulding had taken almost equal parts of Michael Arlen's *The Green Hat* and Somerset Maugham's *Our Betters* as sources for the plot and characters. The assumption is that the studio paid both authors for these borrowings, but it is equally possible that only Goulding was rewarded. Thalberg, according to Salka Viertel's memoirs, was not above literary piracy. She writes of an incident involving Garbo's *Queen Christina*, which she originally had written in collaboration with Peg Le Vino after many months of historical research. Garbo had taken the manuscript to Thalberg to read and his reaction was enthusiastic. He then attempted to put Mrs. Viertel on salary as a Metro writer and said nothing about buying *Queen Christina*. When Mrs. Viertel brought up the subject, suggesting that the studio make a deal with both ladies for the property, Thalberg said charmingly, "But there is nothing to buy. You have no copyright. Anybody can come and write a story on a historical subject." Eventually he was forced to pay $7,500 for the screen story.

But Charlie MacArthur and Thalberg were through as professional associates, although they would keep in touch (at a distance) until Thalberg's death three years later. It was not to be the end of the MacArthur film career, however. That had scarcely begun. Yet he knew that early how Hollywood used and abused the literary man. Even Thalberg, for all his vaunted reverence for the printed word and admiration of those who created it, was not above making an author feel anonymous and inept; his power sufficient to render him unaware of a writer's feelings, even Charlie's or Scott Fitzgerald's or Don Stewart's as they cooled their heels in his outer office, waiting for what seemed hours for a word with the production overlord.

In recollection, many of them would call Thalberg a genius and he was, his gift being to make the banal look fresh again, to give the ugly realities of life a lovely unreality. But to their wives and pals, he was often an abuser of the talents he had bought and he appeared to believe that a man's pride was purchased along with his time. He had become an industry icon and remains one nearly forty years after his death.

Back East, licking his wounds, Charlie realized that he had been seduced by one of Metro's most successful blandishments, *money.* The credo at the studio was, if anyone is unhappy and has proved himself, raise his salary. Stars who had been hired as juveniles or starlets at $750 a week and had risen to great prominence after the first couple of years were usually increased to $2,000 or $2,500 a week to keep them and their agents in line. Authors the same. It was unique and costly and it virtually guaranteed that Metro would never lose a star or a writer over money differences. But they had lost Charlie MacArthur over a matter of integrity.

10.

The controversy over creative control of film never was more intensely examined and reexamined by critics and filmmakers than during that period in 1933 when *Thunder Over Mexico* was being previewed and finally released on about the same shaky footing as was *Citizen Kane* eight years later. There was a vast difference in quality and critical reception, however. In the instance of *Kane,* a capitalistic titan had attempted, with considerable success, to stifle a masterpiece. In the case of *Thunder,* an anticapitalist had endeavored to provide the means for a great film artist to create a masterpiece, but, anticapitalists seldom being multimillionaires, the means had run out after something more than a year of shooting parts of the hoped-for masterwork.

Ostensibly, the Mexican film had been produced and directed by Sergei Eisenstein, the Russian director-writer and creator of *Potemkin,* from a screenplay by his close friend and collaborator, Gregory Alexandrov. In actual fact, it was about 9,000 feet of film extracted by uncreative Hollywood hands from something over 175,000 feet shot by Eisenstein and his party during a fourteen-month stay in Mexico sponsored by the Upton Sinclairs; or, more particularly, "The Mexican Picture Trust" set up and managed by Mary Craig (Mrs. Sinclair). She and a group of friends and art patrons, including Otto Kahn, had staked over $75,000 on Eisenstein's delivering up an epic film on Mexico, its land and its people and past, especially its revolution. Very soon after his arrival there, Eisenstein was calling the movie (entitled *Qué Viva Mexico!* as long as it remained in his hands) "a symphony" although it was for many weeks formless and the Sinclairs were alarmed by its "lack of a story." Eisenstein stated then that it was his plan to tell five or six stories in semidocumentary style with nonprofessional Mexicans as actors; then weave the stories together layer upon layer "like a serape."

Eisenstein had with him a brilliant photographer, Edward Tissé, and at least part of the time, a British couple, Ivor and Hell Montague, as translators. They were all to be supervised by Mary Craig Sinclair's brother, Hunter S. Kimbrough, a Southern bond salesman on leave of absence, who would be in charge of costs and doling out money as well as obtaining film supplies, processing what had been shot, getting it through tight Mexican censorship, and attempting to curb Eisenstein's extravagance. No one, including the official Russian film agency, Amkino, ever denied this aspect of the gifted Russian's character, although the Sinclairs naively accepted Eisenstein's initial agreement to do the whole thing for $25,000. That figure was to triple over the months and possibly the budget would have gone right through the ceiling had not Upton Sinclair blown the whistle on the entire project in February 1932.

The irony in this last despairing gesture was that the Sinclairs, the most famous Socialists in America at the time, were going to free Eisenstein from the Hollywood slave mills as well as the Soviet propaganda mills. On leave from Sovkino, Eisenstein had come to Hollywood in 1930 to work for Paramount. Eventually he would write one of the "great unfilmed screenplays," an adaptation of Theodore Dreiser's *An American Tragedy*. The assignment was not as odd as it sounds. For many years Dreiser had remained among the most popular American authors available to Russians in translation. Eisenstein's long script departed from the original work in strange ways, according to those few who have read the script, possibly intended to show the youthful murderer's inability to break free from the malign grip of capitalistic greed and its often dehumanizing economic aspects. Paramount's story department was baffled by much of it and the adaptation was immediately assigned to others and the novel filmed while Eisenstein was still on the American continent.

Earlier, the Russian filmmaker had been given two other stories to attempt: *Glass House* and *Sutter's Gold*. A shooting schedule was asked for and worked out on the latter by Eisenstein. But both were shelved as "uncommercial." With his failure on *Tragedy*, a screenplay Eisenstein considered among his most significant, he faced the prospect of returning to Europe a capitalist reject (very much as Maurice Maeterlinck and a host of others had been before him). It was probably what Stalin, watching his progress through deputies' eyes, wanted.

Although his visa was running out (the American government was not overjoyed at having a "Bolshevik" of such influence spending so much time in the country), Eisenstein had no intention of returning to the Soviet Union under such ignominious circumstances. He sought film work in Spain, in India. Stalin believed he was "a deserter" and told Sinclair as much in a telegram.*

*For a fascinating look at much of the Sinclair-Eisenstein-Stalin, etc., correspondence, read *Sergei Eisenstein and Upton Sinclair: The Making and Unmaking of* Qué Viva Mexico! by Harry Geduld and Ronald Gottesman.

For a few days, Eisenstein and his group explored Los Angeles and attended services at Aimee Semple McPherson's Angelus Temple, where they observed her enormous appeal to a packed congregation. "She assured her audience," wrote Salka Viertel, who accompanied them, "that the Lord is sweet, and made gourmet sounds, tasting Jesus on her tongue. . . . The congregation drooled and smacked their lips. The Russians were delighted."

One of Eisenstein's biographers, Marie Seton, noted that Mexico had interested Eisenstein at least as far back as his first theatrical work, a production of Jack London's story, "The Mexican" (1920). He was familiar with Mexican folk culture. He had read Anita Brenner's *Idols Behind Altars*, and authors Geduld and Gottesman believe her book to be a "spiritual scenario" upon which Eisenstein and his writing assistant, Alexandrov, built several of the stories of their film. Miss Brenner wrote:

> . . . In Mexico, [death] is no longer a dreaded and a flattered guest. . . . The city jabs slyly at him, makes a clown of him. . . . Sufficient mourning and much respectful talk is partly something of the same obsequiousness the Aztecs had for their gods, and for the same reasons.

In Eisenstein's outline of the film to come, he extended Miss Brenner's observation:

> Death. Skulls of people. And skulls of stone. The horrible Aztec gods and the terrifying Yucatan deities. Huge ruins. Pyramids. A world that was and is no more. Endless rows of stones and columns. And faces. Faces of stone. And faces of flesh. The man of Yucatan today. The same man who lived thousands of years ago. Unmovable. Unchanging. Eternal. And the great wisdom of Mexico about death. The unity of death and life. The passing of one and the birth of the next one. The

eternal circle. And the still greater wisdom of Mexico:
the *enjoying* of this eternal circle. Death-Day in Mexico.
Day of the greatest fun and merriment. The day when
Mexico provokes death and makes fun of it—death is but
a step to another cycle of life—why then fear it!

The Sinclairs were long-standing friends of the Soviet Union.
Sinclair had accepted an invitation to visit Moscow and his
books were best sellers there.

Sinclair planned a picnic lunch for Eisenstein and his
friends at the ranch home of razor-blade millionaire King C.
Gillette, who was conspicuously not at home and the mansion
locked. But the handsomely landscaped garden was open and
inviting. The only *gaffe* on that sunny day was committed
by silent star Mary Miles Minter, who jarred the good
vibrations by making a long, incoherent speech about Communism and then asked Eisenstein why the Russians had
permitted the execution of the Tsar and his family. Eisenstein, who understood English perfectly, and the Viertels
were much embarrassed.

Nevertheless, the day was a success. Mary Craig Sinclair,
with much help from her author husband, who wrote dozens
of imploring letters to friends and friends of friends, managed
to raise the $25,000 Eisenstein said the project would cost. But
the warmth of that initial encounter soon evaporated. After
months of shooting, following delays caused by the rainy
season, illness, and a search for locations, the money was
exhausted and Eisenstein had only part of a movie assembled.
Supervisor Kimbrough was forced to cable for more and more
thousand-dollar drafts to keep the project from foundering.

[Foreign filmmakers who were giants in their own countries literally sold their souls to get significant work accomplished in America. F. W. Murnau, who made the film *Tabu*
in collaboration with Robert Flaherty and who was to die in a
car wreck in late 1931, had made all sorts of compromises
following his connection with Fox; and von Stroheim by 1932

had resumed his acting career, vowing never to direct a film again, his creative spirit wholly destroyed. Max Reinhardt, the most esteemed director in the German theatre, shortly would begin an "all-star" American film production of *A Midsummer Night's Dream*, which was snatched from total disaster mainly by James Cagney's performance as Bottom and a promotional campaign that pandered to the element of snobbery in most of us *(Reinhardt! Shakespeare!)* but retains a peculiar fascination since it featured nearly all of Warner Brothers' top performers—veterans of rowdy comedies, topical crime melodramas, and adventure films.].

About fifteen months after that fateful picnic, the Mexican film project was near collapse from financial depletion and a storm of tension and internecine warfare. Sinclair, ten months into the film and with no end in sight, had ordered his wife's deputy and brother, Hunter Kimbrough, to insist upon a work schedule with completion dates listed and strictly adhered to. According to Sinclair, "this sent Eisenstein into a frenzy."

The movie company split neatly into two parts: the artists and the philistines, and the Sinclairs and brother-in-law Hunter Kimbrough were the anti-art villains. Sinclair's own creative output had shriveled to next to nothing and he was a year behind schedule on his current book. His health was affected and his wife pleaded for them to get out of the thing. Meanwhile, in Mexico, Eisenstein's nerves "were shattered" and there were even rumors that his prolonged absence from the Soviet Union had caused him to fall out of favor with the government.

A letter from Eisenstein to "Zalka" Viertel reveals his bitterness:

Mexico, January 27, 1932

Dear Zalka!

It seems to be my fate that I should be heaping my despair upon you! In my Paramount days and after—but this time is the most desperate of all! I don't know how much Sinclair keeps you *au courant* about our activities and difficulties. If he does I may be as doomed in your eyes as I am in his. However, this is the situation:

You know that instead of the four-months' schedule and $25,000, which would have merely resulted in a pitiful travelogue, we have worked thirteen months and have spent $53,000, but we have a great film and have expanded the original idea. This expansion was achieved under incredible difficulties inflicted upon us by the behavior and bad management of Upton Sinclair's brother-in-law, Hunter Kimbrough. I am blamed for all sins committed and I accept it, under the condition that from now on I myself should be responsible, but not Mr. Kimbrough. Or we three: I, Alexandrov, and Tissé, should manage the whole thing until its completion. But I am facing a situation which, so far, had been completely unknown to me: blood relationship and family ties. Mr. Kimbrough was recalled, but then sent back with "increased powers" *as my supervisor,* which means that now he has the right to interfere in everything I do and make all the cuts! He presented me to Sinclair as a liar, blackmailer, and God-knows-what-else. My direct correspondence with Sinclair stopped, our only contact was through Kimbrough, who, an ambitious man, poisons our existence and creates an atmosphere in which it is impossible to work. I wrote this to Sinclair, whereupon he abruptly halted our work of thirteen months. The last part of my film, containing all the elements of a fifth act, is ruthlessly ripped out, and *you* know what this means. It's as if Ophelia were ripped out from *Hamlet,* or King Philip from *Don Carlos.*

We saved this episode . . . as a climax and the last to be filmed. It tells the story of the *Soldadera,* the women who, in hundreds, followed the Revolutionary army, taking care of their men, bearing their children, fighting at their side, burying them and taking care of the survivors. The incomparable drama and pathos of this sequence shows the birth of the new country. Exploited and suppressed by the Spaniards, it emerges as a free Mexico. Without this sequence the film loses meaning, unity, and its final dramatic impact. . . .

. . . We have 500 soldiers, which the Mexican Army

has given us for 30 days, 10,000 guns and 50 cannons, *all
for nothing.* We have discovered an incredible location
and have brilliantly solved the whole event in our
scenario. We need only $7,000 or $8,000 to finish it,
which we could do in a month, and then we would have a
truly marvelous film—and when I say it I *mean* it!—a
film with such mass scenes as no studio could attempt to
produce now! . . . 500 women in an endless cactus
desert, dragging through clouds of dust, household
goods, beds, their children, their wounded, their dead,
and the white-clad peasant soldiers following them. We
show the march into Mexico City—the Spanish Cathedral—the palaces. For the meeting of Villa and Zapata
we will have thousands of sports organizations—again
without pay—with the cathedral bells ringing the
Victory. . . . And all that has to be sacrificed because of
$8,000. . . . Sinclair stopped the production and intends
to throw before the people a truncated stump with the
heart ripped out! . . .

Seeing that the impasse with the Sinclairs was irremediable,
Mrs. Viertel had a screenwriter friend, Oliver H. P. Garrett,
intercede in Eisenstein's behalf and persuade David O. Selznick to take over responsibility for the production. Selznick
asked to see the footage but Mrs. Sinclair told him that
Eisenstein had been notified already that production had been
halted. "The film belongs to the Pasadena group and can
neither be sold nor financed by anybody."

When the abortion, *Thunder Over Mexico,* opened in New
York, critic Richard Watts, Jr., writing in the *Herald-Tribune,*
said:

> The quality of the film depends chiefly not upon its
> photographic effects, but upon its editing, as we say
> when discussing the esthetics of the cinema, the "mount-
> ing." The fame of the distinguished Russian director is
> based mainly on his great gift for so arranging the
> sequence, the length and the rhythm of his scenes that
> their interrelationship provides drama and significance

and dynamic forcefulness to episodes in themselves not
inherently overwhelming. . . . The Sinclair version is,
whatever its virtues, a makeshift edition of the idea that
Eisenstein had in mind for the work. . . . The concep-
tions of Eisenstein, while untried, suggest signs of
greatness, the work of the Messrs. Sinclair and Lesser
gives every indication of being strictly hack. . . . What
could have been a masterpiece emerges as a beautiful but
essentially unimpressive striving for melodrama.

Mary Craig Sinclair became, by degrees, anxiety-ridden,
distrustful, and, finally, convinced that Eisenstein was
steeped in perversity and moral rot. In a letter to a friend she
writes of Eisenstein's determination to desert the Soviet and
then refers to a man who was Seymour Stern's "partner in all
this devilish plotting" (to undermine the Sol Lesser version of
the film through critical rejection) as one of "the Master's"
Mexican "boyfriends." She became totally disenchanted with
the Soviet in the process of producing the movie. "I used to
tend toward Communism, and so did Upton! *Seeing* it in
practice—then hearing from other Socialists what the Communists do to Socialists everywhere—I have come to realize
that I can never be a Communist."

The fact seemed to be that Mary Sinclair was at heart a
capitalist, despite her long devotion to the Socialist cause.
When the break with Eisenstein came, it was she who turned
down every offer Amkino or Soyuskino (Soviet film agencies
in America and Russia) made to obtain a working print of the
tremendous footage so that Eisenstein might make his own
cuts of the incomplete film and salvage much of his original
concept. Apparently, she persuaded her husband that the
Russians were thoroughly deceitful and that every offer was
some sort of chicanery designed to dupe them out of either
money or control of the film. Her first loyalty was not to art,
as she perhaps believed that it was in the first instance, but to
her investors. The Sinclairs even tried to sell bullfighting
footage to Paramount for a melodrama they were planning

that would utilize that background. They allowed four separate films to be made from Eisenstein's footage, all eons away
from Eisenstein's "serape" scenario: *Thunder Over Mexico,* the
first, and *Death Day,* the second feature supervised by the Sol
Lesser firm; *Time in the Sun,* made from 16,000 feet purchased
by an Eisenstein partisan and biographer, Marie Seton; and
the remaining footage was sold to Bell and Howell, who cut it
into a number of "educational shorts" under the series title,
Mexican Symphony.

Around 1955, Jay Leyda, another Eisenstein disciple,
began to pull together a number of four-hour-long "Study
Films." At the same time, the Museum of Modern Art was
quietly assembling footage from all possible sources and, in
1966, Gregory Alexandrov announced his intention of cutting
a new, longer version of what he recalled that he and
Eisenstein had in mind back in 1931-32. In early 1969, film
footage was released by the Museum of Modern Art to
Gosfilmofond for Alexandrov's purpose. Eisenstein himself
had died in 1948.

If any of the foregoing seems outrageous to the purist, it is
only an extreme example of what the Hollywood screenwriter
and nearly all directors under hire to a studio had to endure.
Even as late as 1964, Lewis Milestone *(All Quiet on the Western
Front)* was pulled off the remake of *Mutiny on the Bounty*
because of friction with star Marlon Brando, and Sir Carol
Reed was flown in to complete the picture. There are snippets
of more than two dozen gifted hands in the making of *Gone
with the Wind,* including two directors and seven writers, but
David O. Selznick, like Mary Craig Sinclair, saw nothing
wrong in allowing these contributions, which had been
rendered anonymous by him, to remain in the released film.

Richard Watts, Jr., called Sinclair a "despoiler" of what
should have been a masterpiece and said, ". . . The synthetic
version of the picture is destined, I predict, to have the ill-fate
of annoying those who would have delighted in the original

conception, without keeping awake the people who are expected to delight in its conventional melodramatics." This judgment prevails today, and the strange alliance of ultraliberal author and Communist filmmaker took much away from Sinclair's reputation among Hollywood people. Some of them paid him grudging respect later during his campaign for governor on his "EPIC" program *(End Poverty in California)* when Louis B. Mayer arbitrarily took a percentage out of all Metro salaries as a contribution toward his defeat.

Whether the Mayer studio money helped or not, Sinclair was resoundingly beaten. But, ironically, even Louis B. Mayer, crass businessman that he was, never went as far as the Sinclairs did in ruining what could have been, like Fitzgerald's *The Last Tycoon*, a partial masterpiece.

11.

As the ranks of the unemployed swelled and President Roosevelt was attempting radical measures (that often worked) to keep the country from collapse, Hollywood began looking for material from another, pleasanter century to offer the Depression casualties some escape *(Little Women, Berkeley Square, Voltaire,* and *The Bowery)*. Then *It Happened One Night* and the screen version of Hecht and MacArthur's *Twentieth Century* brought adult comedy into sudden popularity. Great screen comedy right up to Laurel and Hardy, who seemed to have moved into a void created by the semiretirement of Chaplin, always had been innocent enough to be seen by all the family. It had a universality that touched the toddlers as well as grandma.

"Screwball" comedy of the thirties was something more special. The screenplay would be realistic on the surface, usually set in a placid backwater very much like any village or suburb. But then the bizarre would occur—that quiet, reticent lady writer down the block has written a sizzling sex novel, or that nice blonde next door, Hazel Flagg, is told she is suffering from a terminal disease (another Hecht work) and decides to throw caution to the winds and have herself a last fling in the big town. The trend continued for half a decade with Carole Lombard and Jean Arthur (Frank Capra's favorite leading lady in his light, sardonic period) kept before the cameras in one semifarce or another almost constantly.

While the gang wars that had preceded the repeal of the Volstead Act (Prohibition) had given Warner Brothers a reputation for dealing with reality, the crime film, too, was a form of escape. It was succeeded for a time by a cycle of films glorifying the G-man. The Warner *mise en scène* was always a slum, a working-class neighborhood, the bottom rung of show business, or a lower-middle-class section, and it had the stars to match. Glamour was not the stamp on their films, but the common man was. "As the thirties proceeded, Bette Davis' standing at the box-office dictated a shift in emphasis and Southhampton could be seen (at least corners of it) on the soundstages of Burbank as well as of Metro."

The idle rich were still to be seen on the screen impersonated by Constance Bennett, Kay Francis, Diana Wynyard, Leslie Howard, and Robert Montgomery. But 1933 was the year of Hitler and it was becoming the decade of the Third Reich. The world, as we all know, would be slow in reacting to its existence and its threat. "The little man,"—"the forgotten man" (which was even the title of a major song number in a Warner musical), the luckless dispirited man—was being recognized and turned either into a shock-troop robot abroad or a human being to be fed and housed. By the late thirties, as the Gestapo and Storm Troopers fanned out over the globe, there was also the man on the run, the hunted, the quarry. Hollywood utilized all of these men as story material and, interestingly, as war became a reality, Hollywood sensed that its unrealistic handling, its romanticization of war, had become passé.

The American's search for creature comfort served to deflect the harsh realities of fascism and Jew-baiting that were then beginning in Europe. It is ingrained in us and will always be with us, an inheritance of the early emigrants who came here "for a better life," the gold rush brigade, the Indian killers. So even though a greater emphasis on contemporary historical fact was underway on the American screen, at least, we were usually watching the rich reacting to it. Metro had its exceptions; its long-lived series films—The Hardy Family and Dr. Kildare; and you could count on the middle class being a standard background at Fox, and usually Paramount (unless Marlene Dietrich was involved). But the big stars at Metro reacted to financial disaster and distant wars in penthouses and Southhampton estates in nearly all of their high-budgeted films.

There was a gamble in this. Audiences were no longer enchanted by the frivolous. Families were breaking up and there were thousands of children moving around the country in empty boxcars. The apple sellers on the street corners were usually men in frayed suits with white shirts and carefully knotted ties. Films *were* an escape for the millions of jobless and those whose salaries had been slashed (even the film industry had cut everyone's salary in half). But what kind of escape?

As a last gasp of the old tradition, Fox had Billy Wilder's German film, *Ihre Hoheit Befiehlt,* adapted as a vehicle for Janet Gaynor *(Adorable)*. A fairy-tale princess, disguised as a commoner, falls in love with a guards officer, who, as it turns out, is really a prince. Back at the castle, she sees that he is promoted every week or so, as their clandestine romance ripens. Shortly, he is in command of the unit. Their disguises are stripped away by some of the most frantic plot turns since Sheridan and, at fade-out, they are allowed to come together as the natural royalty they really are. *Merde!* If Miss Gaynor had not become a national icon (as Will Rogers was and

Shirley Temple soon would be) over the past half-dozen years, screens might have been stormed and torn to shreds, although the movie was not much of a success. And if one had not been sent out humming the theme song ("You're so completely a-dorable") into the grim streets with their apple sellers. Ah, well, even those men polishing their nickel apples did not look in such terrible shape as you left the moviehouse. That is what is known as a postcinema glow. It made empty bellies tolerable, gave a glitter to eyes that needed new prescriptions, and, if you had been exposed to your betters for a couple of hours, put a ramrod in your spine. Someday a veteran box-office cashier will write her memoirs and tell us about those audiences leaving the theater after seeing *Conquest* or *The Great Ziegfeld*. That lady has seen revolutions aborted.

The three most popular actors in roles of high station were George Arliss in the early thirties, Warner Brothers house interpreter of the mighty; Paul Muni in the late thirties, again for Warners, Muni taking over upon Arliss's retirement; and, surprising nearly everyone, Charles Laughton, who had done a number of films in this country for Paramount, all of them moderately successful, but who astonished filmgoers and critics alike with *The Private Life of Henry VIII*, produced by Alexander Korda in 1933. Emil Jannings had done the role in Lubitsch's *Anna Boleyn* (released in America as *Deception* in 1920) and Lyn Harding had done something with his Henry in *When Knighthood Was in Flower*, the Marion Davies production of 1922, a humanized king with a sense of humor and not such a far cry from Laughton's blustering, sardonic monarch. The Laughton film played the Radio City Music Hall, one of the first British movies to do so, and that was a portent. It was the first great overseas success of a British film and Hollywood was not unmindful of the fact. Within less than a decade and a half there would be a steady procession of American film-writers, directors, and producers across the Atlantic into exile in England, where Korda or J. Arthur Rank would give a few of them sanctuary at a reduced salary, and, eventually, do even better than that.

12.

Scott Fitzgerald and Dorothy Parker were covering different aspects of the same territory in their literary work. Both were equally fascinated by the rich, but Mrs. Parker had an obsession about those who either admired or worked for them—all of those mousy ladies who live in drab two-room apartments and visit their "betters" for a charitable cocktail, all of those black or Irish servants who suffer in silence and *endure.* Both were gifted analysts of the woman in love or women suffering rejection or some other torment, while their men are nearly always less complicated and often vaguely defined or mysterious. The complexities of Dick Diver are created primarily by the superimposing of Fitzgerald's own brooding character on the beautifully civilized Gerald Murphy.*

They were unconscious puritans yet, in their world, they were constantly bumping into the deviant, recoiling, and then trying to put a face on their "unsophisticated" reactions. Fitzgerald's heroines and even minor female characters are described with a credibility and a sense of their interior beings that is much less frequent among his male cast. He saw the

---

*Joseph L. Mankiewicz has put this matter more eloquently than anyone I know. In his memoir on the making of *All About Eve,* he said: "It would be fascinating to do a film about a man in rebellion against 'manliness.' (Not necessarily a homosexual. [There's another of our society's rigidities; you're either 'manly' or queer . . .] Homosexuals—male and female—are constituents of a thoroughly viable third sex. Within it, the chances of success or failure in personal interrelationships need be neither more nor less than within any other. *If,* that is, our 'virtuous' and 'manly' society drops its vendetta against them.) . . . the films about the man in revolt against 'manliness.' I'd like to tell it by suggestion, by nuance and mood, by utilizing all of the subjective techniques and material you're supposed to eschew on portraying the male on stage or screen. Why the hell, for instance, shouldn't a man burst into tears? Or lose badly? Or be indecisive—or be irrationally afraid of the unknown or unseen—or smell good—or want peace?"

masculine/feminine components in all of us, but he seemed inhibited in ascribing feminine traits to a man unless he was "clinically ill." Fitzgerald describes an active homosexual, Francisco, whom he calls "the Chilean Queen," in *Tender Is the Night.* It was fairly advanced comment in his day, but this section, if published now, would bring loud protests from the Gay Liberationists, and legitimately, because Scott cannot disguise his contempt for what he considers to be a poisoned, lost soul so beyond salvation that psychiatrist Dick Diver rejects him as a patient.

Dorothy Parker had been born the daughter of a rich New York garment manufacturer ("a cloak-and-suiter," as she describes him). She had cut herself off from her family before she was twenty and had plunged into the life of a working journalist.

Money impressed her, especially *old* money (made by the Carnegies, Vanderbilts, and Rockefellers in another, quieter century), but meant nothing to her personally. She never would accept a loan from anyone who had not earned his money. She was nearly always broke or needing a financial lift to see her through some crisis despite the large royalty checks coming in during the thirties and the huge sums she earned from writing films.

The perfidious male impressed her even more. Despite her numerous affairs with attractive men, such as John McClain, Ross Evans, etc. or perhaps because of them, and two marriages, her verse and prose throb with feminine passion unfulfilled, romantic plans derailed by heedless males, who take showers instead of love's nectar during one-hour wartime leaves, who fail to return despairing telephone calls, and some who simply fail to return ("Oh, of course I'm coming back!" he said)—liars, cheats, preening vain creatures, enemies ("Scratch a lover, and find a foe").

As nearly everyone knows, she once wrote that Katharine Hepburn ran the gamut of human emotions from "A to B."

Mrs. Parker, forewarned and yet eyes bright with prospect, was to run the gamut of the trials and abuses of the writer in Hollywood, from A to Z, many of them self-inflicted. She even was set on fire by her producer, Hunt Stromberg, who finally came to terms with incipient pyromania by having a fifty-foot firehose installed in his home. She claimed poverty was her motive. She liked to tell of her Algonquin Roundtable days when she didn't have the wherewithal to buy her own lunch ("I was penniless much of the time, and so was Bob [Benchley].") But she was eager to get away from New York, where she was required to shine. She dismissed the Roundtable group as "just awful. You were always expected to be on, and nobody listened to anyone else. They waited for their chance to drop a *bon mot.*" If she was made uncomfortable by their relentless knifing of each other, she rarely showed it, and her own knife was not left idle on the tablecloth.

So it was that she and her new husband, Alan Campbell, as perfectly featured and built as any Broadway juvenile, came to Hollywood. They arrived in 1933 in a state of semidestitution to go on a combined salary beginning the following Monday at $5,000 a week for the two of them. Advances were given hurriedly. She had no clothes to speak of in her baggage. It was literally "rags to riches" and everyone was quick to set them up comfortably. George Oppenheimer loaned them his home; Metro took care of the rest.

Alan bore a superficial resemblance to Scott Fitzgerald, but his eyes were larger and sexier. In manner, they were kin. There was something of a chip on Alan's shoulder. His wife attributed this to his half-Jewishness (an ethnic background she shared, in reverse, her maiden name being Rothschild and no relation to the "House of . . ."), and they were both relieved that he had Scottish lineage where it counted. There was a streak of anti-Semitism in Dorothy which she did little to disguise and which her friends defensively attributed to her hatred of her father. Alan's mother's maiden name was

Eichel and Dorothy and Alan Campbell, deep in their cups, would shudder over the terrible fate they would have shared had *his* name been "Eichel." Since they worked in a largely Jewish-dominated industry, their worry is hard to justify, but both were hagridden throughout their years together by picayune doubts and "what if's?" so that no matter how comfortable they became physically, they projected a continuing feeling of insecurity, as though it would all end tomorrow.

Although Alan Campbell is included in this chronicle because he was married to Dorothy Parker, it was he who sat at the typewriter and did the real work of putting down on paper the technical and special language of the scriptwriter. Dorothy would sit nearby, often knitting, as Alan might ask, "Shall we make the mother a washerwoman," and Dorothy might say, "Oh yes, by all means, a washerwoman." Then she would read over what Alan had written and edit it and write in some witty dialogue, elevating the competent to the penetrating and, sometimes, the splendid.

But she resented nearly everything that Alan did for her. In their leaner days, he would also make the beds, cook, and do the dishes. He even would see that she went shopping and looked her best. Friends attest to his excellent taste, but apparently this had not always been the case. "He told me that he used to affect a cane and spats," Dorothy later confided to Wyatt Cooper. "Yes, he did. It was very touching. . . . He'd seen the wrong pictures. . . . And then he suddenly got very good taste indeed. He was wonderful at doing houses."

But Dorothy Parker could not bear being in anyone's debt, including her husband's. Gratitude for her was the vilest of human emotions. George Oppenheimer was to advance them the money for their first mansion and even loan them his silver service for their housewarming, but he was pointedly not invited to attend.

A few years later when they, too, were infected with the

Hollywood-escape virus, and bought a large farm in Bucks County, Pennsylvania, they purchased a home nearby for Alan's mother, hoping to keep her out of their hair since she would come up from Richmond and stay for weeks at a time. The arrangement did not work, according to Dorothy, since Mother was forever dropping in and there was no longer "Mother's room upstairs" where she could be shunted. She was in their living room or kitchen on her casual visits. Dorothy despised her mother-in-law and her "little ways" and declared she abhorred being called "daughter" by her.

Her loathing of kin was not confined to Alan's mother. She said her older sister, who was very beautiful and nine years her senior, attended Horace Mann High School in Manhattan where boy students predominated, but she was "very much interested in that" and later married "the most horrible, disgusting, outrageous German, the worst kind of German, you know." Her epithets, and they flew from her mouth with no apology, had a way of building into a kind of crescendo of revulsion. By the time of her death, she apparently had alienated or terrified nearly all of her own relatives so that only friends would call on her at her Manhattan hotel, never any family. In her early seventies, she would say that she had outlived them all (not quite true) and rather enjoyed, at seventy-three, thinking of herself as an orphan.

Her Hollywood years were marked by a similar kind of contempt for fraudulent or hypocritical chitchat. But, and this is terribly important, she somehow remained very conscious of manners to the end. And she felt strongly about the misfortunes of others, especially those who were unknown to her so that she could think of their problems with a neat abstraction. She arrived in California a far-left liberal and by the time of the Spanish Civil War she would be completely radicalized.

Her politics did not come, as is generally believed, by way of her guilt feelings over the money pouring into her joint bank account (and right out again). The execution of Sacco

and Vanzetti in 1927 had made her realize for the first time
that not only was there injustice in America, but corruption
of the basest sort was at the highest levels. Her good friend
Bob Benchley had encountered an associate of Judge Thayer's
(it was Thayer who condemned Sacco and Vanzetti) before
the sentencing and Benchley quoted the man as saying that
Thayer was going to "give those Bolsheviks what they
deserve."

Interestingly, only once did she write anything political and
then it was her much-anthologized, rather personal study of a
group in a war-front restaurant in Spain ("Soldiers of the
Republic"). Most of her remarkable short stories, especially
"The Lovely Leave," "A Telephone Call," "Dusk before
Fireworks," "Big Blonde" and "The Waltz," dealt with women
forlorn or forsaken or both. Her written prose was just the
opposite of her often splenetic speech. She even might be
called the last of the genteel Americans—in print.

Faithful and even deceitful servants people her stories like
wistful young girls in a Chaplin feature. There was something
of the social climber in Mrs. Parker, but, as with all her traits,
it was disguised as its opposite. Yet her interest in the
underdog and in unpopular causes kept this facet of her
character confined mostly to her published works. Oddly, she
was more open on the printed page than she was to many of
her friends.

From about 1934 on she became militantly active in all the
underdog causes that came to her attention. It was in that year
when she and Alan threw a huge buffet dinner in their new
mansion for the Scottsboro Boys. A *cause célèbre*, almost but
not quite on a level of significance as the Sacco-Vanzetti case,
the boys were nine young blacks who had been arrested in
Alabama in 1931 on the complaint of two white *demi-
mondaines*, Victoria Price and Ruby Bates, who had been
riding in a boxcar with three white men. During a fight
between the nine blacks and the white youths, the latter
jumped off the car and ran away, leaving the women behind.

They claimed that the blacks raped them, although medical evidence in court did not uphold this contention. Later, Ruby Bates repudiated her accusation in court. Eight of the blacks (one thirteen-year-old was released) were tried and sentenced to death. At this point, the ILD (International Labor Defense) entered the case, hiring the most successful criminal lawyer in New York, Sam Leibowitz, to lead the defense in seeking an appeal.

Dorothy received a call in her studio office that the boys were on their way to Hollywood, and she immediately began ringing up everyone she knew who was not a rabid reactionary. The Fredric Marches came that evening and the Donald Ogden Stewarts and actor Lionel Stander. There were other writers, as well as some producers and directors. Bill "Bojangles" Robinson danced for them and several thousand dollars was raised. It was her first step toward becoming a political activist; Alan simply stood by her side and smiled attractively. He was more typical of his breed; he was far more interested in the grosses of the movie they had just written than in politics. And, later, even the Un-American Activities Committee knew better than to call upon Alan Campbell to testify.

It would be hard to say just why Dorothy Parker enjoyed writing of and being with the extremely rich so very much. It should not be forgotten that she was born rich but had run away from it. Probably she thought money was all right if you weren't selfish about it and so long as it was not tainted by an acquisitiveness which she associated with her Jewish father. Wild stallions could not keep her from attending any soiree Mrs. Cole Porter or Sara Murphy might throw at Cap d'Antibes on the Riviera, when she was abroad. Her last public appearance was at a fashionable dinner party in her honor given by Gloria Vanderbilt Cooper and her husband and Dorothy's good friend Wyatt. She was buried in a golden sheath bought for her by Gloria for that evening three months before her death.

She had met Alan Campbell at the Howard Dietzes. Despite his stock company attractiveness, Dorothy was enchanted at once ("How could you not be?"). He was sweet-tempered when sober, with an endearing sort of wanting to be helpful. He was Dorothy Parker's *helpmate* in nearly every sense of the word. He was also "fun," for which he got high marks.

But, as we have seen, she resented anyone who helped her function. She gave Alan the back of her hand as often as not, tossing the words "faggot" and "homosexual" around indiscrimately but often in the context of a casual remark about her husband. This would set Alan's gleaming, perfect teeth on edge, and perhaps it made it easier for him to backslide into bisexual liaisons since the label already had been pinned on him.

She was herself not without beauty, being delicate-featured with large, sensitive eyes that belied their watchfulness. She favored large picture hats and satins and silks. Claiming to have been unloved as a child (her mother died during Dorothy's infancy and her stepmother would usually ask, "And what did you do for Jesus today?"), the adulation she received from her fiction and verse could not be lightly dismissed. It had to be handled in some fashion and Dorothy Parker managed it by accepting her fame as something not quite deserved but nevertheless a fact of her life. She had precise ways of dealing with it. There was a look of meek humility about her when she moved with the equally popular; she retained a look of perfect femininity, and she quickly deflated it when it threatened to get out of hand.

13.

The gap between Hollywood films and American audiences was narrowing. But not enough; a set designer's notion of how middle-class suburbia looked was still faintly ludicrous. In

Gregory LaCava's *My Man Godfrey* (1936), the worst days of
the Depression are recalled in the opening moments as we
move slowly over a hobo jungle on a smoldering dump
beneath the Brooklyn Bridge. William Powell wears a frayed
suit and a three days' growth of beard. When Carole Lombard
wanders into this unlikely setting, she is more than a vision—
we know that somehow she has come to save Powell. We even
forgive her crassness in putting this "forgotten man" on
display at a huge party of the rich as the prize specimen in a
scavenger hunt.

Audiences could relate to Miss Lombard. She probably said
"damn!" or "shit!" or worse when she banged her finger and
she had a frank way of looking into a camera as though it were
a nuisance that had to be tolerated as the only way you and I
could see how utterly candid and deep-down sincere she was.
Jean Arthur had much the same quality and at the same point
in time. They could easily be interchangeable in the parts they
played with the exception that when called for, Miss Lombard
could be a clothes horse as elegant as any Balenciaga could
wish for.

It took some time for the thought to sink in, but the
discovery was beginning to get through to the film community
that the public, which had accepted talking pictures with
something akin to rapture, quickly got used to spoken dialogue and in no time at all became bored if a movie was "all
talk." Ruth Chatterton, whose careful enunciation of the
English language put us all to shame, was already being put in
the shade by great faces and even more remarkable bodies.
Miss Chatterton was, beyond that careful voice, not the
sexiest woman of the thirties. Even her exquisitely right
portrayal of the desperate Fran Dodsworth could not save her
career.

Sensing this rejection of "talky" films ahead of nearly
everyone else, the Warner Brothers retooled their production
schedule literally overnight. On the tightest budgets known to

the major studios before or since, a string of snappy, topical
films emerged, many with the same stars: Joan Blondell,
Glenda Farrell, Joe E. Brown, Alice White, Ginger Rogers,
Edward G. Robinson, Dorothy Mackaill, Richard
Barthelmess, Kay Francis, Dick Powell, and Ruby Keeler,
and a stock company of supporting players, including the
inexpressibly disgruntled Ned Sparks. The "new" Warner-
First National stories were about petty gangsters, newspapermen, sailors, housewives, and kids starting out in show
business. These comedies and melodramas even had some
social content in them.

Jack Warner, sensitive to the political climate that followed
the imposition of the Blacklist in the late 1940s, does not
mention the fact in his autobiography, but he was a heavy
contributor to any decent cause that came to his attention.
Following a meeting of the Anti-Nazi League in the middle
1930s, he handed one of its members a check for $3,000. And
while he was known throughout the industry as a man who
worked his employees hard (all of his movies were filmed
quickly on a six-days-a-week schedule), the resultant reviews
gave him enormous satisfaction. He wrote: "There came a
period in the early thirties when the critics and trade paper
editors hopefully noted, as though a bad boy had been
reformed, that Warner Brothers had developed a social consciousness manifested in some of our films."

It was one of the more degrading spectacles of the days of
the Un-American Activities inquisition to see Jack Warner take
the witness stand to recant nearly in toto his pride in his
"social consciousness' as he cited individuals, most of them
writers, for injecting "un-American ideas" into screenplays.

But it was doubtless a joy to many of his present and former
employees with whom he was about as popular as Harry
Cohn. Sometimes, as was the case with the poignant Ann
Dvorak, it was a matter or pure recrimination that made him
so disliked. In his memoirs, he conceded that he had brought
Miss Dvorak to Warner Brothers because she had a "dainty,

unworldly quality that was rare in the actresses in Hollywood at the time." He continued:

> . . . in a five-year period she made nineteen pictures, including *G-Men, Three on a Match, Midnight Alibi,* and *The Crowd Roars.* Almost inevitably, she came down with the temperament disease. . . . I put her under suspension, and she never came back to the Burbank lot, which was too bad because she had a dazzling future until her quarreling agents snuffed it out.

But he often worked his performers into exhaustion or into oblivion. An instance of the latter was that of Alice White, who had a pixieish quality and was discovered on a movie set (Josef von Sternberg's) as a script girl. She was rushed into nearly a dozen films over a period of a little more than three years—the reason: The public found her delightful. She was "Lorelei Lee" in the first film version of Anita Loos' *Gentlemen Prefer Blondes* (1928). She was Dixie Dugan in *Show Girl,* The same in *Show Girl in Hollywood,* she was *The Girl from Woolworth's* (the public was beginning to wonder when they saw this movie before; maybe they changed the title), but something a bit different as the most innocent of the wide-eyed *Broadway Babies* (Miss White's career swings upward again), but then *Naughty Baby, Sweet Mama,* and *The Naughty Flirt.* She was being rushed from one film to the next, making a movie every three months. Her bright star burned to a cinder before 1932 and she was playing supporting roles for the rest of her movie career.

A more puzzling case and one having nothing to do with Jack Warner was that of Anna Sten. She had been trained as a film actress since she was fifteen when she was admitted to the Russian Film Academy. She had toured with one of the lesser Stanislavski companies, playing Pirandello, Ibsen, and Maeterlinck; then the Moscow Art Theater and nearly a dozen important Russian films. She had a cinematically perfect face

reminiscent of America's Nancy Carroll, but she was voluptuous, not frail. She had the sultry seductiveness of Dietrich
and Garbo and a more feminine voice than either. Samuel
Goldwyn signed her on the strength of her appearance in a
Dostoevski adaptation, slimmed her down, had her accent
refined by speech experts, and had Emile Zola's *Nana* adapted
for her Hollywood debut.

Miss Sten, with a decade of film experience behind her as
well as Russian stardom, was grateful but not overwhelmed
by Mr. Goldwyn's interest. She, and everyone around her,
assumed that *Nana* was simply the first step, and she settled in
California, had contemporary architect Richard J. Neutra
design her a hilltop home (which still stands, one of his finest,
as modern in spirit today as when it was built).

The Code dictated a change in the ending of *Nana* and
much else. It is more than possible that it was the administrators of the Code who killed off this most promising
newcomer and not "audiences' rejection of her," the most
common explanation of her sudden eclipse. As nearly every
reader knows, *Nana* is the story of a girl of the streets who is
made into a music-hall star by the possessive impresario
Greiner, who likes her saucy impudence and soon is profoundly in love with her. But Nana is a young woman;
Greiner is aging, probably impotent. She falls in love with a
dashing young officer, played by Phillips Holmes, and soon
they are spending a great deal of time in a villa, which in the
screen version appears to be her country home where she is
amused betweentimes by her former street companions. The
officer's brother is head of the neighboring household and
surprises the youth climbing in through his bedroom window
at dawn. The young man is sent off to Africa and the older
brother himself falls hopelessly in love with Nana.

Then Nana falls victim to a host of plot turns, all designed
to take her along the road to hell. Her letters to the young man
are never mailed by the jealous ex-street girl Rose and the

worldly housekeeper, and all of George's ardent letters to her are likewise destroyed. Believing herself abandoned by her one true love, she gives in to the importunate brother and allows herself to be set up in Paris in a sumptuous apartment, after Greiner has kicked her out of his theater and his life. But the older brother has connections and she is back on the boards, as popular as ever. Her young lover returns, finds Nana agitated about his being in *that* apartment (as well she should!) and hurries to get dressed so that they can go out "for a talk." Meanwhile the older brother returns as Nana is in the bedroom and the two brothers get into a terrible argument over her. Nana, overhearing the worst of it and knowing the encounter has killed any chance of her ever returning to George, shoots herself.

As *Nana*, Anna Sten could not have been better. They say that Goldwyn wanted another Garbo or Dietrich. Neither star could have got the insouciance and winning seductiveness out of the part that Miss Sten did. Even the film itself was not as foolish as more than half of Dietrich's early American films and it was as well-upholstered in design as any Garbo film. Dorothy Arzner, the only major woman director in Hollywood at the time, could only be faulted for keeping the movie in a passive frame throughout—perhaps the instinct of a woman of that day (1934). Nana's rebellions were piques, not the screen-shaking revolutions they should have been.

Further, the ending of the movie, dictated by the Code authorities, is banal. It should be understood that no faithful rendering of *Nana* could have passed the Code people. The list of "unacceptable" screen material from the classics was mountainous: *Death in Venice, Remembrance of Things Past, Sister Carrie, Maggie: A Girl of the Streets,* any biography of George Sand, unless revised to the point of absurdity. In Zola's book, Nana catches smallpox from a child and dies in a hotel with only Rose to hold her hand. Then, in death, the smallpox pustules break out on her face and her beauty disintegrates before Rose's horror-struck eyes (probably a medical impossibility). Obviously, Anna Sten's movie debut was not going to be willfully harmed by Zola's pre-Wildean fantasy as we fade out over Nana's hideously scarred face. Still, the disease was more original and even acceptable in screen terms than the claptrap pistol.

Anna Sten made an enchanting Nana with all of these things against her—the predictable meaningless ending and Phillips Holmes's beauty rivaling her own (it was the curse put upon Holmes's screen career; he also played Clyde Griffiths in the first sound version of *An American Tragedy*, the one that replaced the Eisenstein adaptation, but he never became a major star). It seems almost incredible in viewing the film today that the critics of that time were so unanimous in dismissing it as an unsuccessful attempt to saddle us with yet another exotic northern European. Her personal notices were, on the whole, favorable.

Sam Goldwyn's showman instincts told him that he was right (and he was) and he persisted, starring her in two more major films, a reasonably faithful and interesting version of Tolstoy's *Resurrection (We Live Again)* with Fredric March, and *The Wedding Night*, the least successful of the three, co-starring Gary Cooper, who started out as beautiful as Phillips Holmes but time was on his side and soon began etching a few lines of character and strength into his face. Cooper had no greater luck with Sam Goldwyn, however, than Anna Sten had. He was to have the most expensive failure of his career in *The Travels of Marco Polo*. Let it be said in the sure knowledge that *his* cloud had a silver lining, it was a bad year for Sam.

Dorothy Mackaill was the gift of Hull, England, to the movies. She preferred directors and writers to actors as beaux and especially disliked her principal leading man, Milton Sills. *(Courtesy Diana Fitzmaurice Cousins)*

ABOVE: *Fast and Loose.* Miriam Hopkins registers an undefinable emotion in her 1930 film debut, as Charles Starrett levels with her at the beach. *(Author's collection)* CENTER: The legend that John Gilbert was forced off the talking picture screen by a "high, fluty" voice is inaccurate. His voice simply had no distinction, and he disappeared along with dozens of others. *(Author's collection)* BELOW: Dolores Del Rio, whose film career spans half a century, was the only actress with one expression who would be welcomed by any filmmaker if the part was right. Today, she still looks much the same as she did in *Wonder Bar,* a 1933 movie with Al Jolson and Ricardo Cortez. In this film, she stabs Cortez during a public dance performance without flicking an eyelid. *(Author's collection)*

ABOVE: Gary Cooper, one of a breed of star personalities who endured. Beautifully laconic, he was a "reactor," inarticulate and yet eventually known for his Western nasality and "yeahups." Circa 1931. (*Author's collection*) CENTER: Production czar Will H. Hays with Jack Warner, 1928. Hays had The Code drafted, which became the bible of motion picture production in America. His imprint is lasting. (*Author's collection*) BELOW: Saucy Alice White, star of seven "Naughty But Nice" films in the early talkies. Unfortunately, they came out at three-month intervals and were mostly written from the same blueprint. The result: box-office death due to overexposure. 1930. (*Author's collection*)

ABOVE: Lily Vautier (Miriam Hopkins), a sneak thief herself whose pose as an aristocrat lasts about five minutes, looks impressed by Gaston Monescu's (Herbert Marshall) sleight-of-hand with her garter. Ernst Lubitsch's *Trouble in Paradise* (1932). *(Author's collection)* CENTER: Director Ernst Lubitsch in his Paramount office, 1932. His influence would be acknowledged by Billy Wilder and his style imitated by a score of others. *(Culver Pictures)* BELOW: Lubitsch urges Gary Cooper to put more vigor in his spanking of Claudette Colbert in *Bluebeard's Eighth Wife* (1937). *(Culver Pictures)*

ABOVE Mae West, actress and dramatist, was the main target of the Legion of Decency in 1934, but she survived for another five years. Here she cools off a steaming lover, Victor McLaglen, in *Klondike Annie* (1936), one of her original screenplays. *(Photo by Carola Rust)* BELOW: A rare photo of studio head Louis B. Mayer and his production chief Irving Thalberg, circa 1929. *(Culver Pictures)*

ABOVE: Dorothy Parker on the eve of her departure for Hollywood. *(Courtesy Charles Lederer)* CENTER: Frances Marion, a sultry Scheherazade, who earned more money from writing movies than any other of her sex. She wrote the screen version of *Dinner at Eight* (1933) and nearly all of the Dressler-Beery films. *(Culver Pictures)* BELOW: Anita Loos was the most social of all the Hollywood writers. Scott Fitzgerald once tried to kill her in a drunken rage; in half a dozen years she would replace him as screenwriter on a movie. Circa 1970, although she looked exactly the same forty years earlier. *(Courtesy Anita Loos)*

ABOVE: Robert Benchley in a rare pose of total composure and tranquillity before Hollywood success made him rich, more famous, and a man whose on-screen instructions to audiences would be followed at one's peril. *(Author's collection)* BELOW: Marc Connelly reaching for an elusive bit of dialogue in his Hollywood office during his collaboration on *Captains Courageous* (1937). *(Culver Pictures)*

ABOVE: One of the first writer-producers was Nunnally Johnson. Zanuck liked him because he had the guts to tell him and other studio bosses not to bother him while he was writing a script. His screenplay *The Grapes of Wrath* pleased its author, John Steinbeck, and they became fast friends. Circa 1935. *(Culver Pictures)* BELOW: The King of Hollywood, Clark Gable, circa 1934. *(Author's collection)*

ABOVE: Irving Thalberg yodeling over a beer at Marion Davies's Tyrolean party. Charles Lederer (Marion's nephew) at left is surprisingly sober while Louella Parsons at right is typically euphoric. 1934. *(Courtesy Charles Lederer)* CENTER: Joseph L. Mankiewicz was "an elemental force" in Hollywood. He believed that any first-rate writer could take control of his work by becoming its director or producer or both. Shown here at work with Ava Gardner during the shooting of *The Barefoot Contessa* (1954). Joan Crawford once wrote that he "took the suds out of soap opera." *(The Bettmann Archive)* BELOW: Slightly tarnished and world-weary ladies were a specialty of Joan Crawford, who has survived longer than any film star on this planet. F. Scott Fitzgerald wrote *Infidelity* for her, but she never got to film it. *(Author's collection)*

Fred Astaire and Ginger Rogers were the chief reasons Gershwin stayed on in Hollywood. His last alliance, with Samuel Goldwyn, was much less rewarding. *(Author's collection)*

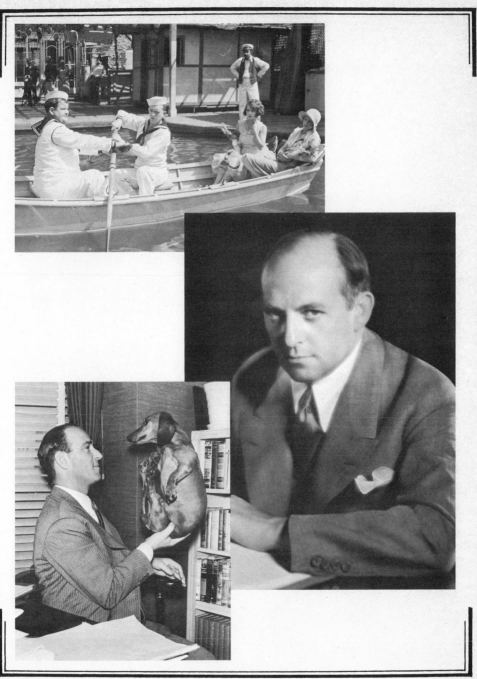

ABOVE: Stan Laurel wrote nearly all of the routines for himself and his partner Oliver Hardy in such vastly popular comedies as *Men O'War* (1929). The simplest invention of man could best Laurel in any encounter. The girls wonder if they have put their safety in the right hands. Laurel and Chaplin emerged from the same music-hall troupe in England. *(Author's collection)* CENTER: The "terrible" Harry Cohn, head of Columbia Pictures, a man of towering rages and predictable vulgarity, but with an instinct for making movies that are still being revived. Circa 1930. *(Culver Pictures)* BELOW: Screenwriter Robert Riskin, who did the script of *Lost Horizon.* Here he is in his studio office with his talented dachshund. *(Culver Pictures)*

ABOVE: Earlier, Colman had shown a flair for adventure in *Bulldog Drummond Strikes Back* (1934). *(Author's collection)* BELOW: *Lost Horizon* (1937) began with revolutionaries attacking a mysterious rescue aircraft. Here, Ronald Colman as Robert Conway and John Howard as his brother fend off bayonets before takeoff. *(Author's collection)*

William Faulkner at home in Oxford, Mississippi, where he wrote many of his film scripts.
(*Photo by Cartier-Bresson*)

Charles MacArthur and Ben Hecht in Astoria, Long Island, where they wrote the scripts and ran the show. 1934. *(Courtesy The Academy of Motion Picture Arts and Sciences Library)*

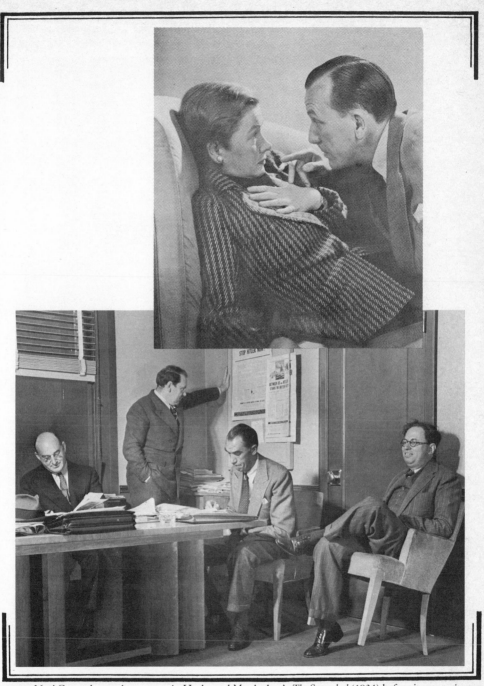

ABOVE: Noel Coward agreed to appear in Hecht and MacArthur's *The Scoundrel* (1934) before it was written. Here, in a scene from the movie, he intimidates Southampton's stage darling Hope Williams. *(Courtesy Universal Pictures)*   BELOW: The Playwrights Company at work in 1940. From left: S. N. Behrman, Maxwell Anderson, Robert E. Sherwood, and Elmer Rice. They all worked for the studios during part of this period. *(Culver Pictures)*

Studio czar Darryl F. Zanuck retooled production at Warner Brothers before starting his own company, Twentieth Century Pictures. That's the Twentieth Century Limited, appropriately enough. Circa 193-
(Culver Pictures)

ABOVE: Shakespeare authority Professor William Strunk of Cornell University was hired by Irving Thalberg to act as "literary adviser" on the *Romeo and Juliet* set. Here Professor Strunk studies the Talbott Jennings script with Irving Thalberg and David O. Selznick. 1935 *(Culver Pictures)* CENTER: There were few screenwriters as much admired in the film colony as Gene Fowler. He liked biographical subjects and wrote *Good Night, Sweet Prince* and *The Great Mouthpiece*, biographies of John Barrymore and lawyer William Fallon. *(Culver Pictures)* BELOW: Nathanael West saw more clearly than most that Hollywood could not survive as it was, but this black-humored prophet died before the Apocalypse in the West came to pass. *(Courtesy Farrar, Straus & Giroux)*

ABOVE: The exotic Margo made her screen debut as the mistress whom Claude Rains kills in *Crime Without Passion* (1934). *(Culver Pictures)* CENTER: Walter Wanger supervised the Eastern studios for Paramount when Hecht and MacArthur were producing their own films. Wanger was articulate (although given to hyperbole) and at home with the "400." Here, with wife Joan Bennett. *(Culver Pictures)* BELOW: B. P. Schulberg, studio head at Paramount until 1932. Under Schulberg, lurid melodramas and Limehouse hanky-panky were shelved for breezy revues with lots of hummable tunes and girls with good legs. By 1949, he was broke. Placing an ad in *Daily Variety* he wrote: "…Must we always wait until a productive pioneer is found dead in some obscure Hollywood hotel room before reflecting upon an indifferent and forgetful industry?" *(Culver Pictures)*

ABOVE: Sam Goldwyn and his wife Frances take a rare vacation, circa 1929. *(Culver Pictures)* BELOW: By 1947, Samuel Goldwyn Productions had won scores of Oscars, the Goldwyn pavilion-type mansion had drapes *outside* as well as in, and he was able to finance his films on his own. *(Culver Pictures)*

PART TWO
REBELLION
AND
RETREAT

The First Defector (1919)

During the trip to New York to open *Broken Blossoms*, Griffith had decided to take the next step in his quest for independence. He resented deeply having to pay such a large sum over cost to keep the rights to what he felt was his picture. He was more determined than ever that the only kind of front office he wanted to work for was his own. He wanted no more Marvins, Kennedys, Aitkens, or Zukors controlling him. While in New York he made arrangements to purchase a large estate on Orienta Point, a peninsula jutting out into Long Island Sound near Mamaroneck, New York. It was Griffith's intention to convert this estate into his own studio. Griffith's reasons for establishing his own studio in New York rather than California were probably at least twofold. He wanted to get away from the burgeoning business atmosphere of California, and New York was a return to his beginnings. Why not start over for himself near where it had all begun?

Robert M. Henderson,
D. W. Griffith: His Life and Work

1.

From this distance in time, it does seem odd that the initial efforts of the screenwriter to achieve some proper recognition, if not control, of his work should coincide with the first successful enforcement of the Code. Much of what he wished to be recognized for was pabulum and the wicked point of nearly every sophisticated comedy was blunted to such a degree that "movie versions" of the most mature books and plays were looked upon now as not adult but adulterated. Screenplays had been ironed out, bleached out of all "impurities" by the Hays Office.

What he really wanted was that illusive credit. Credits meant that his option would be renewed, that he would be able to hang on for another three months or six months when his future would be passed upon once again. He began to care less about the artistic content of what he was turning out and more about that $2,500 a week.

Certainly, there were some worthwhile films being made from material that was naive enough or "morally uplifting" enough to avoid the censors' blue pencils: Adventure films (*Lost Horizon* and *King Kong*, although the latter has been called a love story by some); certain comedies (*The Awful Truth*, based on a 1922 play, in which Ralph Bellamy played his convincing stock role of the innocent; he was, probably unwillingly, the Hays Office's guardian angel in any slightly naughty tale); suspense and horror films (*Frankenstein* represented the outer limits of what could pass the Code enforcers—there *was* that scene with the little girl, and here was the tale of a man presuming to grant life, but, like "Dr. Faustus," it is a morality play and the monster perishes. God dare not be mocked); love stories of the proper sort (*Goodbye, Mr. Chips* represents moviemaking ideally right by the censors' lights—a man, almost a misfit, redeemed by the love of a good woman).

If the story was as successful as any of these, the screen-writer involved understandably wanted recognition. *Control* over the script was something quite different. It was tough-minded, self-confident Joseph L. Mankiewicz who contended that any superior screenwriter would rise like cream in a bottle and control his own work—by taking over its direction or by becoming its producer. *He* had, and so had his brother Herman for a time. If they could (and perhaps he did not realize how exceptional they were), he seemed to feel that any writer who learned his craft *and* wrote exceptional scripts could. Joe, was to produce Scott Fitzgerald's *Three Comrades,* * which concerned itself with several ordinary men and one woman caught in the maelstrom created by Hitler, who also believed that the superior would rise and that mediocrities were expendable. The trouble in the latter's case was that his own notion of superiority was mediocre. But Joe Mankie-wicz's standards always have been resolutely high—in some instances, to his detriment.

What Joe Mankiewicz failed to take into account was the usual reticence of the writer personality in pushing himself forward. Joe himself was a natural force, a fundamental element almost as natural to Hollywood as the sound revolu-tion, Grauman's Chinese, or the mystique of Garbo. Joe was and is a forceful man whose unconsciously dictatorial bearing creates an impression, wrongly, that he believes himself infallible. Although "democratized" by casual clothes and an inevitable pipe, his bearing was more imperial than Louis B. Mayer's. (Joe wrote and directed both the film version of *Julius Caesar* with Marlon Brando as Antony and the monumental, disastrous *Cleopatra*, a movie so butchered by other hands he has disowned it.) Had he wanted it, he doubtless could have formed his own studio at any time. When Irving Thalberg's health began to wane around 1934, Louis B. Mayer seriously

---

*An adaptation of the novel by Erich Maria Remarque.

discussed the possibility of Joe taking over. Mayer had been impressed with his ceaseless flow of energy. "We need your *manpower*," Mayer told him.

But Joe insisted upon directing. "No!" Mayer shouted. "You will produce. You've got to crawl before you walk." And Joe told Mayer that was the best description of a producer that he ever had heard.

Joe did become a producer for Metro, and an important one sometime in the middle thirties, but writing was his real passion—and writing with a precision rare in films. Joan Crawford said that Joe took the suds out of soap opera and he wrote at least two of her vehicles, *Forsaking all Others* (1934) and *I Live My Life* (1935).* And about this same time, he did the script for *Manhattan Melodrama*, John Dillinger's last-attended movie.

While Mankiewicz never did become a film mogul and his neomilitary attitude toward underlings put a little distance between him and most of his co-workers, he is far more valuable as a touchstone in chronicling the great studio period than ever Irving Thalberg or David O. Selznick could be. He rose from a lowly title writer at the Berlin UFA studios (although he was born in Central Pennsylvania), through his Paramount days (where he managed by osmosis to write the archetypal Paramount film, *Million Dollar Legs*, (1932), then moved along to Metro, where he mastered the elegant unreality that allegedly elevated the taste of the masses for a couple of

---

*Mankiewicz is explicit in his memoirs about male characters on the screen: ". . . the 'man's role,' as presently in vogue, doesn't interest me very much as writer and/or director. He is invariably expected to pit himself physically against his adversary: to me, the least imaginative and interesting form of confrontation. His goals are usually restricted to, variously, conquering or amassing things. A fortune of money, an enemy country, a chain of factories, a series of broads—one or more loathsome children who, quite understandably, find him equally loathsome . . ."

". . . Women are, by comparison, as if assembled by the wind. They're made up of—and react to—tiny impulses. Inflections. Colors. Sounds. They hear things men cannot. And, further, react to stimuli men either can't feel or must reject as 'unmanly'."

decades, and on to Twentieth Century-Fox, where he wrote and directed the brilliant *A Letter to Three Wives* (1948), and performed the same chores on what is considered his finest work, *All About Eve* (1950).

That distance he kept between himself and nearly everyone else gave Mankiewicz special advantages. Unlike most directors and producers, he was nearly immune to pressures and corruption.

David O. Selznick was the complete film maker. He chose his properties carefully and, once chosen, went on twenty-four-hour schedules seeing them through to completion. The son of silent filmmaker Lewis J. Selznick, who had been done out of his fortune and much of his reputation by unscrupulous partners, Selznick had films in his genes. His first important assignment had been at Paramount, where he was a production aide to B. P. Schulberg.

There, he helped get productions under way and assigned titles to them. His titles—*Three Sinners, Dirigible, The Man I Love, The Wolf of Wall Street, Show Girl*—were considered so valuable he was paid $100 each for them, and one, *Dirigible*, was later sold to Columbia Pictures for filming, the title being sent along without any story accompanying it.

Garbo's contract in the early thirties at Metro called for her films being produced either by Irving Thalberg or by Selznick. Selznick did her *Anna Karenina* (1935). Always vigilant about having the best talents surrounding her work, Garbo pleaded for Selznick to stay with Metro when he was making his plans for forming his own company.

Oddly, most writers rarely turned down an offer to work with him despite his penchant for taking their work, fiddling with it, and then taking credit for its creation. Further, on some of his films, there would be six to ten writers, all working on the script at various times or in teams.

Joe Mankiewicz insisted that this was routine; that very often what a screenwriter (or a novelist brought in to write screenplays) set down on paper was unplayable. Mankiewicz had to learn to live with getting "frozen out" socially by an author whose work he had revised, even though it may have won an award. So did Selznick.

Yet Selznick was a man with far more literacy than Thalberg, far more meticulous than Zanuck (who had no subtlety at all when it came to the final cutting of a film and often reduced to pure action what had been tremulous and deeply felt emotion), more acquisitive than Goldwyn and with as much professional acumen. If he had any weakness beyond the ordinary mortal one of pursuing attractive young actresses around his study table, it was in being such a perfectionist. He would set his mind on one particular star or director or writer and word would get around town—usually to the ear of his brother agent Myron, who promptly would "stick him" for an exorbitant fee for their services. (Selznick claimed that Myron had forced him to pay thousands of dollars in excess of what Carole Lombard and Fredric March were worth to team them in *Nothing Sacred,* and the trouble was that once their fee was jacked up, there was small chance of getting it lowered again.)

2.

The suggestion has been made and circulated, chiefly by writers, since they are far more iconoclastic than any other group, that producers survive, for the most part, through connections, and the connection is often as primitive as the proboscis to the kiester. Following an elevator incident in which the seat of Louis B. Mayer's pants was caught in some elevator doors, a number of Metro writers expressed their immediate concern—"Was Arthur Freed badly hurt?"

When a writer becomes a producer, his contempt shrivels and his vision clears. And when a former writer and producer becomes a studio head, he no longer cares what is said about him. He has become a force that will shape careers, possibly

change the course of the Hollywood film; his fancies are those
of a Genghis Khan. If he is someone with a past as varied as
Darryl F. Zanuck, it is a prickly matter indeed attempting to
set the record straight.

After Zanuck had walked out on Warner Brothers in 1933,
he was courted by every studio in town. But he had left for a
high moral purpose—to make movies of his own. Twentieth
Century Pictures began functioning as a major independent
studio with just four stars: George Arliss at the very end of his
career, Constance Bennett badly in need of a hit, Loretta
Young just then beginning to mature as an actress, and
Raymond Griffith, who wanted to get out of acting and into
the production end. But it had financing brought in by Joe
Schenck, whose brother Nicholas was Board Chairman at
Metro; the services of William Goetz, Louis B. Mayer's
son-in-law; and the canny insight into audience appeal of
Zanuck, whose only rivals in this extrasensory field of vision
were Joe Mankiewicz and David O. Selznick. Thalberg was
only then beginning to slip and Hunt Stromberg was becoming far more reliable; Harry Cohn's developing gift would
confound Hollywood a good year later.

As a former writer himself, Zanuck knew that a movie
could be no better than its script and he brought two brilliant
screenwriters with him—Gene Fowler to adapt the life of
P. T. Barnum to the screen and Nunnally Johnson. Johnson's
byline at the time was chiefly known on the covers of *The
Saturday Evening Post* and at Paramount for some modest
successes written to order for Maurice Chevalier teamed with
Baby LeRoy *(A Bedtime Story)* and a likelier pair, Mary Boland
and Charlie Ruggles. Frankly, he was surprised that Zanuck
even had taken note of his presence in Hollywood. Johnson
was to spend most of the next thirty years working for
Zanuck.

Johnson's relationship with Zanuck was a simple one. He
would be given a story or a book and Zanuck didn't hear any

more from him until he brought him in a screenplay. "At first," Johnson said, "he wanted a treatment. After that, I liked to get straight into a screenplay on the assumption that this was the *final* screenplay. Now I'm not foolish enough to think that it would be, but at least it gave me a feeling—if I wrote it thinking that this was something they were going to shoot—this was not something that I could go over later. This attitude was good for a man like Zanuck, who had to turn out forty or fifty pictures a year because he didn't have to bother about me at all."

Zanuck's confidence in Johnson led him quickly to the notion of making him a producer, but Johnson was loudly vocal in making it clear that he could not help anyone produce a script. "I just didn't have any talent for that. Maybe I found too much fault with them." Later, he would be asked to produce his own scripts and that worked out much better.

Gene Fowler, a former newspaperman, biographer (John Barrymore, Bill Fallon), and playwright (*The Great Magoo*, in collaboration with Ben Hecht) was as acerbic as Hecht in describing the hokum of Hollywood. Metro had loaned Wallace Beery to Twentieth Century (remember William Goetz, the Mayer son-in-law, was Zanuck's aide). Director Walter Lang, another man of competence who did not know that Zanuck had his eye on him, was brought in to direct. As part of the promotion of *Barnum*, Fowler's screenplay was going to be published by Covici, Friede, the first American screenplay ever to appear in book form.

In Fowler's Foreword to that volume, he gives us a thorough background of the film in production:

> Mr. Darryl Zanuck, the producer of this picture, is hopscotching up and down the concrete pavement. He even invades Brother Goldwyn's sacred sward. He scents a commercial success in this picture. Mr. Zanuck wears a yellow polo shirt and carries a long cigar as though it were a mallet. This sprightly gentlemen is

recently returned from Africa, where he riddled an
elephant, cut down a rhino, shot a water buffalo in
the eye, and extinguished a family of melancholy
gnus. . . . This scenario . . . violates most of the canons
of literature and kicks history squarely in the groin. It
seeks to create and sustain a mood in consonance with an
era of pioneer showmanship.

Whenever one thinks highly of his own ability as a
writer or an actor, let him visit any of the sets which are
built for Hollywood productions. He will come away
with a somewhat sad conviction that here, among the
designers, the set dressers, and the builders, is exempli-
fied the only honesty Hollywood knows. . . . Their
names are not emblazoned on great screens. . . . Yet in
the tiddleywinks world of celluloid people and amid the
cries of drooling censors who sleep on dunghills and
consort with French postcards, these forthright artisans
stand as something tangible, real, and constructive.
Their work is reasonably free from politics, untouched
by bigotry, independent of the nigger-rich snobbery of
the cinematic potentates and of the monkey business of
smokehouse Othellos and constipated Ophelias of Beverly Hills. . . . The creator of a motion-picture set, and
the one who "dresses" it, must do his or her work so well
that *no one will notice it.* This fact alone conspires to keep
the labors of these people anonymous. There must be a
fine balance, a superb restraint in the physical creation of
a background.

Fowler's screen biography of *The Mighty Barnum* (1934) was
typical of the early Zanuck films for his newly formed
company. It was rich in background, and America's past was
re-created with a naive gusto. It was a big, sprawling production with Barnum's American "Museum" as its principal set,
with street scenes of antebellum New York, interiors of
Barnum's Bridgeport villa, *Iranistan*, Battery Park's Castle
Garden, saloons and hotels of the period.

There are considerable resemblances between the screen

work of Gene Fowler and Ben Hecht. They were most congenially assigned to American legends. Fowler's *Billy the Kid* (1941) with Robert Taylor as the Kid, was his last major assignment and it was a considerable success. But Fowler wrote less than twenty screenplays and remained a book author despite the lasting impression he made upon the town. And his books, especially *The Great Mouthpiece* (the life of Fallon) and *Good Night, Sweet Prince* (John Barrymore) were extraordinarily successful. His life of Mack Sennett *(Father Goose)* and his own memoirs *(A Solo in Tom-Toms)* are out-of-print but worth seeking out.

Zanuck's impact upon Hollywood in 1934, '35 and '36 was profound. He was producing films with the broad, detailed canvas of Selznick. He was choosy about his properties and careful in his casting and every other detail. But then, with the merger with Fox in 1935, the tone began to change, subtly at first, and even as late as 1941 he was personally supervising a film even more carefully assembled than his early Twentieth films: *How Green Was My Valley.* But the pressures of turning out forty to fifty films a year, many of them delegated to Sol Wurtzel, began to show. Twentieth Century-Fox was beginning to resemble the product of Warners, which Zanuck had set upon a permanent, profitable course. A stock company of Fox stars was formed consisting of Shirley Temple, Warner Baxter, Don Ameche, Tyrone Power, Alice Faye, Betty Grable, Linda Darnell, Sonja Henie, Dan Dailey, Gene Tierney, and Clifton Webb. In the 1950s, Marilyn Monroe was added.

Americana was exploited, not re-created. Backstage stories predominated with the same predictability as Warners' old crime films. Subtle nuances of such a work as *A Tree Grows in Brooklyn* (1945) were edited out, either in the script itself or in the final cut. And the sad fact is that world film audiences did not seem to notice the difference.

3.

So the excitement of a new brand of movie soon faded as its image began to resemble the others in town. Success bred sameness.

The day of the independents had not arrived. Orson Welles was slated to become, essentially, a two-year wonder, permanently handicapped by grave offense to one of the most powerful men in the film industry and in America, William Randolph Hearst. There seemed to be no one at all in the middle thirties who cared enough about the American screen to alter its formula-bound course.

The only group to discuss attempting something different was the writers. They were the ones who were asked to make the compromises; Lillian Hellman, specifically, was the one who was asked to change the sex of the tardily-declared lover in her adaptation of *The Children's Hour,* removing the lesbian tinge. A decade later, there was some effort to take the central romantic figure from Charles Jackson's novel, "The Fall of Valor," an early and rather antiseptic study of a homosexual, and change him from a man into Joan Crawford. Aldous Huxley was the one asked to remove the happy ending for the adulterous lovers in his own *The Gioconda Smile* (known in America as *A Woman's Vengeance* [1947]). There was grumbling and disdain, but the writers as a body or as individuals were powerless to alter the content of any film unless they had become its producer.

Ben Hecht and Charlie MacArthur decided to take a stand "and liberate the screen." The movie version of their hit play, *Twentieth Century,* had done a couple of things beyond making them temporarily rich. It had established the remarkable Carole Lombard as the loveliest comedienne since Marion Davies, who was retiring at about that time, and it had shown the movie public a side of John Barrymore which his Hollywood intimates had known about for years—his ability to make his own huge ego the the target of biting satire, a form of self-abuse he eventually would run into the ground, rather as Tallulah Bankhead was to do a few years later.*

Then the money was gone—furnishings for their Nyack places, nurses for the children (the MacArthurs had adopted a boy whom they called James). Hecht's money was funneled into his several establishments and personal charities. Whoever can account for where thousands go? We can remember the quarters we spend on magazines, the dimes for coffee, but what author unless he has written a text on bookkeeping ever knows where his royalties go?

So things were thinning out for both Charlie MacArthur and Ben Hecht. For Hecht, such emergencies usually were met by asking his agent to drum up some rewrite job. He often had four or five such projects going at one and the same time. But not for Charlie. Few Hollywood employers believed that he could deliver more than one script every six months. People get reputations, unfortunately.

If they could do it twice (*The Front Page* had preceded *Twentieth Century* by five years), the boys reasoned they could do it again. The illusory feeling of a vast fortune pouring into their hands just after the play opened to rave reviews followed at once by the movie sale gave them the confidence to plunge immediately into a new work. Their muse was not fed so much by a fresh inspiration as by a distinct euphoria that was

---

*The production of *Rasputin and the Empress* required more than three months of shooting and the use of a number of huge sound stages. On one of them, the Kremlin cathedral was reproduced full-scale. There were four very young ladies in the cast, the most innocent-looking being actress Anne Shirley. At the time, Miss Shirley was not even featured; she played the least important of the young princesses. They were all in awe of the Barrymores, but there was one day when John failed to show up. The rumor was, as Miss Shirley remembered, "that Mr. Barrymore didn't feel well. I thought that was what was meant but as you get older, you know that perhaps Mr. Barrymore had been to a party. . . . We waited and waited for hours and he arrived—I couldn't be accurate but perhaps at two-thirty in the afternoon. Ethel had been waiting, tapping her fingers. . . . And Barrymore made his entrance, fully dressed, ready to go to work and looking fabulous, and he walked onto the set and came straight to me, who was the smallest young lady, and said, shaking his finger, 'Don't you ever do that again!' ")

shared by the two collaborators and they were borne aloft by it for a few weeks. They sat in one Nyack study or another and turned out at least half a dozen first acts. It was the second that always did them in.

Confirmed Easterners now, with Ben and wife Rose having bought a house on the Hudson ("It was Charlie who lured me to Nyack. He had been raised on a hill outside the town where his father had tended a sort of tabernacle"), they wanted far more than the money the movies could give them for their work; they wanted lasting fame as Broadway playwrights. In his memoirs, Ben writes: "We finished only a few of the plays we started. . . . I sigh, remembering . . . the merry plots we lost and forgot. We were lavish fellows and we gave no damn for anything except our youth, and how to keep it going in the teeth of bald spots and graying sideburns, and, God forgive us, even paunches."

Ben never alludes to the fact, but undoubtedly much of what they collaborated on was "make work" that might lead to something profitable but more than likely would not. It was a discipline that kept Charlie away from the bottle and too many parties, and Ben admits that the only thing that kept him from a major encounter with "those two vaudevillians, Haig and Haig" was his romantic nature. For Ben, a passionate love affair could keep him high for weeks.

Few surviving friends of Ben's fail to mention his need for young ladies (and some not so young), usually actresses and not always in need of money, who could respond to his Edwardian ardor. His wife, Rose Caylor Hecht, as attractive as any of Ben's amours and more perceptive than most (she was a novelist twice published), rarely was heard to complain of Ben's "midinettes." And it is certain that she rarely nagged, for that was something Ben could not abide. She had the good sense to see that these side-affairs kept her man's life in some kind of balance.

Ben, the nostalgia-purveyor of old Chicago and the acrid

nay-sayer of Hollywood, had become messianic about Manhattan and its environs. When he told Charlie that they would stay in the East and make their own movies away from the bosses, Charlie believed. Ben Hecht was a power. They both wanted their freedom and somehow they would find a way to win it. D. W. Griffith had done it. So in the end he went broke. So does nearly everyone in the end.

Ben Hecht became notorious for characterizing Hollywood, where he made his million (a conservative figure) as a place of corruption. (It is totally impossible to determine the gross income from filmwriting earned by Hecht, the most successful screenwriter ever. There were at least a dozen instances, some of them witnessed by otherwise reliable men, where he was paid "under the table" at cut-rate fees for all or parts of scripts so that his wife Rose, who handled his income tax, would never learn of the transaction. Some say he did it to support friends whom Rose considered undesirables; others insist that he was keeping "a love nest" and that the lady in question had expensive tastes.) But under or over the pay table, Hecht snarled at the bosses and sometimes, they swear, sank his incisors into their beneficent hands.

In castigating the bosses, he was careful to explain,

> I do not mean . . . writers or directors. These harassed toilers are no more than the lowest of *Unteroffizieren* in movieland. The orders come from the tents of a dozen invisible generals. The "vision" is theirs. They keep a visionary eye glued to the fact that the lower in class in entertainment product is, the more people will buy it.
> . . . These dozen Tops of the industry have nothing to do with the making of movies. They have to do only with the sort of movies that are to be made—commercial ones. There is no murmur of revolt.

Ben Hecht by this time was well on his way to becoming a legend. He was a phenomenon and a prodigy of production.

While his closest friends, including MacArthur, Lederer, Dr. Sam Hirshfeld, and Harpo Marx, as well as wife Rose, saw his warmth and his zest for life, they could not fail to see his absorption in his own past. If the average American misses a great deal by living in the future much of the time, Ben seemed to enjoy the present most by framing it in his own past.

His face held a mystery. There was something of the sensualist in him (in repose, there was a slight resemblance to W. Somerset Maugham). This leathery, lived-in face was at odds with his familial concerns. Besides his brilliant wife, his girlfriends (always one at a time), he harbored homeless and penniless friends (Max Bodenheim, the poet, lived with the Hechts for years), various members of his family beyond his wife and daughters, a home at Oceanside two hours from Los Angeles, a house on the Hudson, and a flat in New York.

Ben may or may not have been a compulsive writer, even though he habitually arose at five and was at his typewriter by six. His homes, family, bedmates, friends, and charities (often synonymous) kept him screwed to his typing chair.

Ben's character and preoccupations were something David O. Selznick much appreciated. Aside from Ben's later political involvements, they were very much alike. Besides their romantic natures, so similar in focus and sentiment, they both had large contingents of family and friends camping at their various domiciles. And they shared an enthusiasm for exciting and mature films. Selznick was protective toward Ben and was disinclined to listen to Louis B. Mayer's angry denunciations. Mayer was his father-in-law for a time (until Selznick married Jennifer Jones) but he never did have much influence on him.

Ben began to age quickly in his forties. His face was like a film negative; it recorded his every peccadillo and gave him the look of a sybarite when caught off-guard, but this was deceptive. His nature was really avuncular.

On the clean page of a sheet of paper as he began page one, his outlook changed abruptly. The tinge of cynicism running through much of his writing reflected a prolonged encounter with a community of ruinously self-indulgent human beings.

This would not be especially deplorable; we find them everywhere—even Aunt Agatha in Cedar Falls. But in Hollywood, the necessity for a good press bred hypocrisy. It was not so terrible that one of the more glamorous leading ladies was, in reality, a lesbian and it was unremarkable (out there) when she was cast opposite a beautiful male who was one of the most-pursued homosexuals in town. Perhaps a third of all leading men were either similarly inclined or ready to move in either direction. But their press agents threw a protective cloak over all of their real-life affairs and the public fed such tabloid fantasy as a daily chronicle of an unrequited love affair between the aggressive leading lady and a male star, whom she was always standing up or letting down. The actress, in the best vamp tradition, embraced her leading men on screen and kissed *them*, and made the gesture sophisticated and "continental" rather than laughable, as was the case with the old Theda Bara films. The real Hollywood and its fan magazine interpretation were two quite separate things, and no one living there ever confused the two.

So they began in an empty office on the old Paramount lot in Astoria—three thousand miles away from all that hypocrisy, where they could write about anything that popped into their heads. Hecht and MacArthur, the team of rebels who were going to take on the Mayers, the Laemmles, the DeMilles, the Warners, and the Cohns and make them see that crap was not concomitant with entertainment.

Ben was careful in setting down later the names of a handful of producers who actually "were equal or superior to the writers with whom they worked. These producers were a new kind of nonwriting writer hatched by the movies—as Australia produced wingless birds. They wrote without pencils or even words. Using a sort of mimelike talent, they could make up things like writers . . . there weren't many. David O. Selznick, Sam Goldwyn, Darryl Zanuck, Walter Wanger, Irving Thalberg seem to exhaust the list. . . . Lest it look as if I'm inclined to curtsey only to the highest, I recall other studio pharaohs who were as helpful on a job as so many Will-o'-the-Mills. . . ."

Yet in his autobiography, *A Child of the Century,* Ben would suggest that no subtleties of difference existed among the filmmakers:

> Two generations of Americans have been informed nightly that a woman who betrayed her husband (or a husband his wife) could never find happiness; that sex was no fun without a mother-in-law and a rubber plant around; that women who fornicated just for pleasure ended up as harlots or washerwomen; that any man who was sexually active in his youth later lost the one girl he truly loved; that a man who indulged in sharp practices to get ahead in the world ended in poverty and with even his own children turning on him; that any man who broke the laws, man's or God's, must always die, or go to jail, or become a monk, or restore the money he stole before wandering off into the desert; that anyone who didn't believe in God (and said so out loud) was set right by seeing an angel or witnessing some feat of levitation by one of the characters; that an honest heart must always recover from a train wreck or a score of bullets and win the girl it loved; that the most potent and brilliant of villains are powerless before little children, parish priests, or young virgins with large boobies. . . .

In Astoria, Long Island, Ben Hecht and Charles Mac-Arthur would attempt to turn this formula upside down. They said as much in their several manifestos. But, whatever they did, they knew they would have to get around the Production Authority, the Will Hays office. Below the thin ice they were skating over was the slough of the Code and its "don'ts."

After Walter Wanger, who ran the east coast Paramount Studios, the man most interested in what Hecht and Mac-Arthur were doing was Will H. Hays. Hays had come to the Producers Association in 1922, following his years as Postmaster General in the Harding administration. He was an inoffensive man who reserved his hard-hitting remarks for a defense of God and Christian ideals. He was on close terms with Louis B. Mayer, William Randolph Hearst, and Irving Thalberg. He was something of a name-dropper, as are most Rotarians lifted to high office, but then his own name was as famous as any during the twenty-three years he reigned as "Film Czar."

Writing in his memoirs of local censorship boards, Hays said:

> Out of these grass-roots experiences came a group of generalizations that seemed to indicate fairly accurately the prevailing moral sense of the United States and Canada. These were composite judgments founded on scores of opinions. Though censor boards differed widely in some of the specific rulings—in one state it was held immoral for a young wife to indicate, even by knitting booties, that she expected a baby. . . .

"Don'ts" as adopted in the original draft of the Code follow:

> Pointed profanity—by either title or lip: this includes the words *God, Lord, Jesus, Christ* (unless they be used reverently in connection with proper religious ceremonies), *hell, damn, gawd,* and every other profane and vulgar expression however it may be spelled.
>
> Any licentious or suggestive nudity—in fact or in silhouette; and any lecherous or licentious notice thereof by other characters in the picture.
>
> The illegal traffic in drugs.
>
> Any inference of Sex perversion.
>
> White slavery.
>
> Miscegenation (sex relationships between the white and black races).

Sex hygiene and venereal diseases.
Scenes of actual childbirth—in fact or in silhouette.
Children's sex organs.
Ridicule of the clergy.
Willful offense to any nation, race, or creed.

By 1930, after many violations of the Code, which had not yet been strictly enforced, Hays got together a group of "experts" in the field of morality, including appropriately enough, a Father Lord (Daniel A., of the faculty of St. Louis University) and Martin Quigley, a Chicago publisher and friend of Hays of "exceptional moral and intellectual quality" and a man who had become known to the industry for his editorial "spankings." Their job was to draft a *new* Code. Hays writes that

> A matter that came in for a lot of discussion was the definition of "realism" and the distinction between realism and romance. We all agreed that as far as possible life should not be presented in such a way as to place in the minds of youth false values of life. . . . What had hitherto passed for realism had actually been "literalism," an entirely different thing. Realism, meaning fidelity to life, is desirable, but the term had been corrupted by the literalists.

Will Hays and Father Lord were going to reshape the content of American films through this curious interpretation of "realism." Not "were going to," but "*did*." What is "desirable realism" but an idealization of life, a sugar-coating of reality—resulting in romanticization of war, glorified hovels, the failure to ever show a harridan on the screen as a mother, or an unrepentant harlot? For the eleven years of complete enforcement of the movie Code by the Hays Office (from 1934 through 1945) and then its subsequent enforcement by Joseph Breen and Geoffrey Shurlock, Hollywood acquired a reputation throughout the world for *an unrealistic view of life*, for a fantasizing of life that gradually one took for granted as being "typically Hollywood."

The possibility that realism when refracted by an original view such as O'Neill's or Hemingway's might be art and not "literalism" never seemed to occur to these formulators of the Code.

So the Codemakers went for *Romance.*

> . . . We agreed that it is the lesser of two evils. There is a sense in which the movies, as a product of our century and civilization, are certain to be saddled with one or the other and must make a choice. We analyzed all these things. But we were concerned, after all, in getting out a code. We were not missionaries whose job was to found a new civilization, but movie men bent on making our art conform to the best of this civilization. I believe we succeeded.

Thus, the Code was drafted by a former Postmaster General, a Jesuit whose only previous contact with films was as technical adviser on *The King of Kings* (Father Lord, of course), and a publisher.

A committee of producers chaired by Irving Thalberg studied the Lord-Quigley draft. These men redefined vulgarity (proscribed) as "the treatment of low, disgusting, unpleasant, though not necessarily evil, subjects." Forbidden also were all scenes of carnal passion, immodest costumes, and improper dances.

Then the Legion of Decency, a Catholic censoring body, was formed in April 1934, demanding pledges from all Catholics to remain away from offensive movies *and even theaters where such pictures were shown as a matter of policy.* The Code simply had to be enforced and Hays writes, like a Biblical prophet,

> The movement was like an avenging fire, seeking to clean as it burned. . . . It took the form of a popular move-

ment, in some cases the clergy being obliged to restrain their people from boycotting even decent shows and condemning all movies!

Billy Wilder was to say that the trick was to get around the restrictions of the Code and there is small doubt that he and his collaborators succeeded as well as any in doing just that. But still, this sort of evasion meant that the triumph of amorality that epitomized the films of Lubitsch—Wilder's mentor and greatest influence—could never be fully exploited by Wilder.

As though in answer to the Legion of Decency, filming began on *Crime without Passion* that same spring, 1934, script by MacArthur and Hecht, produced by Hecht and MacArthur, and directed by the same team with considerable help from Lee Garmes, the cinematographer who believed in what they were doing. Garmes may have entertained some doubts along the way, and toward the end of this four-picture operation his own talent appears to have been going down with the leaking craft. But Garmes proved indispensable and possibly was the most disciplined of all the men behind the camera working there.

The next eighteen months have been called many things, from "a brave experiment" to "A Miracle in Astoria." But it started off with such high ebullience, such explosive relief! Here were two of the most maverick writers ever corralled by Hollywood suddenly on their own and a continent away from the bosses they despised. They were like boys released from a reformatory.

One of their first evenings, the Hechts and MacArthurs with friends—Charlie Lederer, who had been flown East to take a "supervisory" post, Fannie Brice, and Billy Rose—did Coney Island from one end to the other. Helen Hayes MacArthur remembered that there was a freak show on the midway, . . . "and they had the Missing Link there. . . . I don't know where he came from. He was kind of chocolate brown. I don't think he was African . . . probably from the Caribbean or something, and he had a tall, pointed, pear-shaped head. He was a weird creature. And they hired him. At the freak show they had him dressed up in a grass skirt or something . . . but he wasn't fully clothed. He was exotic in his attire. Well, they put him in a gray flannel suit and tie and everything and they took him and put him in the office and called a press conference and had him announced as their executive producer. How they ever got the pictures on with all those little things they were doing, I'll never know. It was not disciplined. It was controlled chaos. . . . But the movies (in Hollywood) weren't disciplined. They were slow, tedious, and, I think, very spendthrift."

It was their major premise that serious, well-crafted movies could be made on low budgets, and with the writers as their own producers, much of the profits would redound to them. More fools they! There is more evil legerdemain going on in a major studio bookkeeping department than Merlin ever dreamed of. Whatever the profits, unless you spend a small fortune having the studio accounts audited, you can get a warranty as foolproof as any from General Motors (but not from the studio itself) that you will rarely see a penny of it. There will be several dozen secretaries you never knew existed and who never came within two thousand miles of your production headquarters, press agents whose clippings never were received, travel expenses for personnel who never reached you: the list is endless and insidious. It is the way movies are still made unless you get the film financed yourself.

Walter Wanger could not be blamed when no profits ever came into Hecht and MacArthur's hands. He was on a payroll as head of Paramount's Astoria division. An earlier confrontation with B. P. Schulberg had led to his departure from Hollywood, and, like Hecht and MacArthur, he told his friends that it was good to be back in civilization. He was a man who spent a great deal of time at Twenty-One and was one of the few film men who knew most of Society's "400" on first-name terms. Of all the producers, including Thalberg and Selznick, none was more truly respected as a man of intelligence and impeccable taste than Wanger.

Wanger, who died in 1968, left behind no notes to inform us of his own reaction to the circus he was asked to supervise known as Hecht-MacArthur Productions. But he was at least a nominal liberal awake to the persuasive powers of the screen. He had been friendly to writers from the first and saw them rightly as the true creators of films.

Wanger was a model of his kind; in women (he first had married Follies showgirl Justine Johnstone and, later, Joan Bennett), in clothes, restaurants; and he believed in the early thirties that films were meant to entertain.

Everything seemed to be clicking perfectly as Lee Garmes's camera rolled on the first setup on *Crime without Passion*. To keep Will Hays hanging by his thumbs, the story began with every indication of showing an unscrupulous lawyer, Lee Gentry (played with dissolute eloquence by Claude Rains in his second film role), killing his mistress because he is tired of her, and apparently getting away with it.

The mistress was played by Margo in her film debut. The venture at Astoria looked more promising every day to the Paramount spies reporting back to the West Coast. While there were traces of plot developments similar to Charles Laughton's great success *Payment Deferred*, Hecht and MacArthur managed with considerable success to keep Mr. Hays and the audience guessing until the denouement, when Rains must pay for his crime. In a masterful deployment of the split screen, we see a coolly logical Rains dictating to his frightened self just how to clear himself.

Crime without Passion was a great success in New York, although much of the rest of the country seemed to overlook it. It is doubtful that it earned back its cost (something over

$100,000) until after repeated revivals. In our day, it has gone into the repertory of classic American films along with the next Hecht-MacArthur collaboration, *The Scoundrel.*

4.

The boys from Chicago had made a bold attempt to be accepted among the talent elite during their stay at Astoria. It was a group that numbered Nunnally Johnson, Ernst Lubitsch, Preston Sturges, Joseph L. Mankiewicz, Sidney Howard, and Billy Wilder. For reasons that will become clear later, all of these men would make it and be able to control their own work during the next decade except for three— Hecht and MacArthur and Herman Mankiewicz.

Ben Hecht, who was the chief power behind Hecht and MacArthur, failed because he had not created commercial successes. It was a shattering, a disillusioning experience; enough to make him seriously believe that America was peopled by yahoos or something more sinister; they had been lobotomized by the defenders of their purity, those Legions, American and of Decency.

Walter Wanger, who would be looking in on the Hecht-MacArthur experiment from time to time, but altogether giving them their head, was not considered terribly serious as a filmmaker until after his exposure to Hecht and MacArthur at work.

A year after the last of the Astoria experiments was released, Wanger left Paramount to begin a series of independent films (for United Artists) that were on a much higher level than anything done by the rebels from Chicago: *You Only Live Once* (directed by Fritz Lang), *History Is Made at Night* (from Vincent Sheean's *Personal History*), Alfred Hitchcock's *Foreign Correspondent*, and John Ford's *The Long Voyage Home.* Just prior to leaving Paramount, he had produced *The*

President Vanishes, Private Worlds (a study of a mental institution several years ahead of *The Snake Pit*) and *Every Night at Eight*. By 1936 he would have a dozen major stars under personal contract and he thought at least two of them, Charles Boyer and Madeleine Carroll, suitable for almost any role, even for a time after he had optioned Hecht and MacArthur's adaptation of *Wuthering Heights*, believing Boyer to be the perfect Heathcliffe, French accent and all. It was not an unintelligent choice.

Wanger had two conflicting qualities. He had a small but droll sense of humor and once announced with a perfectly straight face that he was planning to film Alva Johnston's biography of Sam Goldwyn and was looking for a young man to play the youthful Sam as an enterprising glove salesman.

Wanger was also, despite his literacy, hopelessly naive about politics. He returned from a vacation in Italy in July 1936 praising the Fascist state, extolling Mussolini, and insisting that the African War (the invasion of Ethiopia) had not halted Il Duce's rebuilding of Italy. "There is no poverty and no beggars. No kids in the street—all in uniform. New buildings. New roads. Terrific!" This was his manner of speech. Clipped phrases; enthusiasm.

He hadn't been in Italy for eighteen years and the contrast shocked him into a euphoria which he would live to regret. About Mussolini himself, he said that he was "Plain! Simple! Sympathetic! Marvelous man!" He spoke of collaborating with the Italian dictator on a Cinema City (actually built by Il Duce as Cinecittà and still used today)—Mussolini would provide the physical plant and Wanger would produce at least two movies there a year. When Wanger sensed the hostility of the public and even of Hollywood to this proposal, it was quietly shelved and he would become more militant than any other producer in defending democratic ideals when threatened by the Fascists.

Neither MacArthur nor Hecht yet knew that they had not moved up among the astral bodies. The fog machines at the Paramount Studios would work overtime on their next big film with Noel Coward, but enormous publicity had clouded their actual status. They were getting major interviews in every trade and movie magazine weekly, and radio interviews by the dozen.

Hecht enjoyed the spotlight even more than MacArthur. It was not immediately revealed that that fraction of their scripts left to the director was really being handled by Lee Garmes. Garmes would not be fully credited for his contribution until Hecht wrote his memoirs in the early 1950s. Then he would say,

> Standing on a set, Lee saw a hundred more things than I did. He saw shadows around mouths and eyes invisible to me, highlights on desktops, ink stands, and trouser legs. He spotted wrong reflections and mysterious obstructions—shoulders that blocked faces in the background, hands that masked distant and vital objects. These were all hazards that no look of mine could detect. He corrected them with a constant murmur of instructions.

Indeed, Garmes was heard constantly shouting "Cut!" at the end of every scene, an expression usually reserved to the director.

5.

Noel Coward had loathed the Ben Hecht version of *Design for Living*. He made a claim of never having seen it. But Coward had seen *Crime without Passion* and he had admired *Twentieth Century*. He was not the sort to let a little thing like a mauled and unrecognizable adaptation of one of his finest plays stand in the way of what would be his acting debut in films.

The Scoundrel, as outlined to him by MacArthur and Hecht
before a line of it had been written, appealed to him. It was,
on the face of it, a vehicle for Coward, and that made the
whole thing irresistible especially since Helen Hayes had been
promised him in the role of the poetess (a promise unfulfilled).
The filmwriters and Wanger got him to sign a contract and
then Hecht and MacArthur were off to Charleston, South
Carolina, to fill in such gaps as the necessary script.

Everyone in the New York theater and its environs was
eager to get in on the act now that the experiment was proving
such a notable success: even Alexander Woollcott was brought
on camera in the gossipy role of Vanderveer Veyden. Young
actress Julie Haydon, George Jean Nathan's protégée, was
given the feminine lead, and the elegant Hope Williams
begged for a chance to play a lesser role and got it.

"The Scoundrel" is Anthony Mallare, killed in an air crash,
whose restless spirit roves among those he knew to find
someone, *anyone*, who will mourn him. The film loses a little
of its impact when the audience discovers that there is no one
among the shallow creatures who were this egocentric publisher's friends who ever will shed a tear. Yet Coward
redeemed it all with a performance of total conviction. Julie
Haydon as a poetess tossed aside by Coward was equally
splendid. Only the ending failed to satisfy, and although no
one else seemed to get it, perhaps the screenwriters were
saying that even God didn't care enough about him and
atomized what was left of his frazzled spirit.

MacArthur and Hecht thought that the battle had been won
for the screenwriter with *The Scoundrel* (1935). It played the
Radio City Music Hall and nearly all of the reviews in this
country were favorable. But once again they had erred
commercially. Noel Coward was not a household word in
Rapid City or even in Dubuque. There seemed to be something a bit effete about him in the prairie theaters and
everyone in the film with the exception of poor Julie Haydon

was absolutely morally "rotten." The team had produced an oddity; a fascinating portrait of a man with whom not more than 5 percent of the audience could make contact.

A third film, *Once in a Blue Moon*, starring Jimmy Savo, was probably intended as a political parable, but it was so inept it was not even announced on the Paramount schedule and crept out two years later in a remote Boston theater, where it sold a few tickets as "the worst movie ever made." There was something wistful about the wide-eyed Savo caught in the Russian Revolution, where his role as clown merely makes him seem an all-too-obvious target for the bullying Bolsheviks. Actually, this film was shot second at Astoria, but it remained as an "unfinished project" in the cans for months.

Then came the last, *Soak the Rich*, which fared better than *Once in a Blue Moon*, but much less well than *The Scoundrel* or *Crime without Passion*. It was about college radicals in an era when that was really *avant-garde*. The credo of the film was spoken by one of the rebels' supporters:

> Theirs is not radicalism, sir. They will grow up to be quite conventional gentlemen. While they are young they sing, struggle, and dream of something else. A few years ago it was the fashion to be Don Juans. Today ideas have taken the place of drink and revolt is the latest form of necking.

This reads like Hecht and probably is. The chief college radical is John Howard, who is involved in protesting the dismissal of a Professor Popper (who has composed a pamphlet advocating a "Soak the Rich" plan). A tycoon (Walter Connolly) does not take his student daughter's flirtation with radicalism lightly. The young lady is played by an ingenue named Mary Taylor, actually herself the daughter of a tycoon, who had a substantial role in this, due in no small part to her close association with Ben Hecht, but who never appeared in films again. No one seemed to regret this.

Soak the Rich had opened in February and, at least, they had made the Astor on Broadway with that one. Mary Taylor received no critical comment at all on her acting in *The New York Times*, rather, Frank S. Nugent wrote that in the role of the daughter of the tycoon, she "needs a spanking, insists upon enrolling in his private university, promptly becomes enamored of the chief college radical—Mr. John Howard will do—and is involved in one of those typical undergraduate protests against the dismissal of Professor Popper, who has written a pamphlet endorsing the soak-the-rich program." And this was one of their better notices, since Nugent conceded that Hecht and MacArthur's "spoofing of youth in revolt is frequently amusing and the quality of the dialogue proves that the premier filmmakers of Astoria have lost none of their wit. The same, alas, cannot be said of their sense of direction."

The wolves were snarling at the doors of their neighboring houses on the Hudson. Then word came to them that Sam Goldwyn was flying to New York to look into some properties. Ben tossed the daily *Variety* aside and was on the phone with Goldwyn within five minutes. He told the veteran producer that he and Charlie had a truly brilliant story idea.

Goldwyn wanted to know the theme, but Ben declined to give him any details over the phone.

Charlie groaned when Ben rushed over to tell him "the good news."

It was not unusual for Ben to try to peddle one of his lesser stories for a quick dollar, but Charlie declined in every case to participate. "Ben," he told his friend and collaborator, "Now look. I'll go if you promise me that if I dislike the story you're telling him, you stop it and say that you've changed your mind or some such alibi, but don't . . . *I won't* sit still and be put in a spot like that." So Ben said that was O.K., and they went off to their meeting. Before they went in, Ben asked,

"How am I going to know if you don't like what I'm telling him?"

"I'll get up from wherever I am and walk over to the window."

Ben thought that was all right, but Charlie, desperate as he was for cash, was still apprehensive. "For Christ's sake, remember! Don't tell those lurid opium-den plots of yours."

Ben nodded and they sat down with Goldwyn.

"Now, what do you boys have for me?" Goldwyn asked, rubbing his hands together in anticipation. And Ben began a tale that opened in a smoke-filled room in London's Limehouse. He had not got to "Limehouse" before Charlie began edging toward the window. "A man known to have criminal contacts on the highest level was——" And there Charlie stood next to the window as Goldwyn looked on, rather bewildered by the performance.

Ben neatly switched tales and now they were in a Brazilian jungle with some crooked rustlers and Charlie walked back to join them, a grim warning look in Ben's direction. But as the plot began to thicken, with the pitiful bellows of stolen steer rising high above waters carrying the improvised raft used by the rustlers to transport their stolen goods-on-the-hoof and the raft capsizing into the Amazon and deadly piranhas swimming in for the kill, once again. Charlie did his slow ramble to the window, but Ben pretended that he didn't see him and kept elaborating on the plot. The piranhas were now working over the rustlers—the Code, you know. They were on the 27th floor, but Charlie opened the window and, as Goldwyn looked on more than a little aghast—he no longer could hear Ben's jungle fable (even though Ben had a way of making the outrageously bad sound good in the telling)—Charlie climbed out onto the windowledge. Then Goldwyn screamed, Ben stopped talking, and the two men pulled Charlie MacArthur back to safety.

So the Astoria revolution began sputtering and within a few weeks both Hecht and MacArthur were pinning their hopes on their adaptation of Emily Bronte's *Wuthering Heights,* which Walter Wanger had read while at Astoria and on which he had taken an option.

Rose Hecht was in Europe around this time, a little disheartened, it is said, by Ben's romantic involvements while playing the role of producer. There was talk of divorce, but nothing came of it and he entreated her to come back. She came and they left at once for the Coast where Sam Goldwyn had a job for the team of Hecht and MacArthur—as writers.

The dream of control over the script would have to be put out of mind for a while or turn on in someone else's mind. Hecht and MacArthur were back in the tunnel with the miner's light and a pick. But the pay at the end of the day was very good. And if anyone knew the low life that populated San Francisco's *Barbary Coast* in the early 1900s, it was these ex-newspapermen who at one time or another had witnessed just about every iniquity indulged in by man.

6.

When I am doing something commercial
I am working secretly to make it flop. . . .
   —*Pollikoff* in Ben Hecht's
   Spectre of the Rose

Hecht and MacArthur had spent well over a year attempting to do just the opposite; create what they believed was both artistic and so revolutionary audiences would rush to see their productions out of curiosity, if nothing else. Unhappily, no one, including D. W. Griffith, Orson Welles, von Stroheim, or Chaplin in his experimental phase, ever has proved their assumption true.

One of Hecht's own former employers (and his rescuer in

1936 with *Hurricane*), Samuel Goldwyn, was carefully putting together a movie all through the latter half of 1935 and early '36 that was both more mature and more "revolutionary" than anything attempted at Astoria. Oddly enough, the script concerned one of the Code's foremost interdictions—it presented adultery as more satisfactory than a rotten marriage. Sidney Howard, in adapting Sinclair Lewis's *Dodsworth* to the screen (from his earlier play version) was to fashion a drama that has not dated very much in the nearly forty years since its release. Audiences still come close to jeering Ruth Chatterton as Fran Dodsworth when she cries out in disbelief, "He's gone ashore! He's gone ashore!" and applauding as "the other woman" Edith Cortwright (glowingly played by Mary Astor) suddenly sees Sam Dodsworth (Walter Huston) in the skiff bringing him back to her and her home on the Bay of Naples.

Even more curiously in these annals, the film *Dodsworth* antedated F. Scott Fitzgerald's unfilmed project *Infidelity* by more than two years. *Dodsworth* was called *Infidelity* in its Italian release. Scott's fear was that the subject itself would send the Code Authority wardens into a panic, but this could hardly be true when *Dodsworth* already had covered the territory on a much more profound level than Scott's story would attempt. There are vague similarities in character motivation in the two scripts but there is one major distinction that makes Howard's *Dodsworth* a compelling film and Fitzgerald's *Infidelity* a snobbish disaster—audiences care about Sam Dodsworth and Edith Cortwright (his inamorata). All of Fitzgerald's characters are on the level of Fran Dodsworth, egocentrists who deserve one another, which leaves us with no true hero or heroine.

It is interesting that the American literary giants with the greatest stylistic faults—Dreiser, Lewis, and O'Neill—have contributed far more powerful and viable screen material (adapted by others) than those whose than those whose styles have been more admired—Hemingway, Fitzgerald, and

Faulkner. The answer in O'Neill's case lies in his handling of the raw material of his drama; his plays are borne along through sheer emotive force. In the instances of Dreiser and Lewis, their screen adaptability must lie in their pure Americanism in Lewis's case and in their universality in Dreiser's; their novels are true-to-life; they are not subtly plotted; and they are etched onto a broad canvas, leaving the adaptor free to put in as much or as little detail as he likes.

Samuel Goldwyn's production of *The Hurricane* was shooting from a script by veteran Dudley Nichols as adapted by Salka Viertel's old friend Oliver H. P. Garrett. Director John Ford was plainly unhappy over the wordiness and the plot changes (some of them demanded by the Code Authority— uncomplicated Polynesian natives living as Nordhoff and Hall saw them already had transgressed the Code before a camera turned).

Goldwyn, like a dozen other producers in trouble before him, phoned Ben Hecht and explained his problem. "You've got seventy-two hours, Ben, to get me out of trouble."

And then Ben began a ritual he had performed a dozen times before. He barricaded himself behind his oceanside study door with Rose supplying him with coffee and sandwiches. He tossed dozens of pages of dialogue into the wastebasket, threw out all of the meandering added plot, allowed the film to rise or fall on the strength of the biggest display of nature on a rampage ever to be filmed, so that whatever violation of the Code's notion of Polynesian morality might be would be frozen and stillborn in those wardens' minds as they sat spellbound before the biggest blow to ever blast an audience from its seats. For less than three days' work Ben was awarded $25,000.

When the film was released in November 1937, *The Times* called special-effects man James Basevi's hurricane by all odds his masterwork, and he had created the earthquake in *San*

Francisco and the locust plague in *The Good Earth*. "It is a hurricane to film your eyes with spindrift," wrote critic Frank S. Nugent, "to beat at your ears with its thunder, to clutch at your heart and send your diaphragm vaulting over your floating rib into the region just south of your tonsils. . . . Palms are torn up by their roots and go swinging clumsily through howling space; coral reefs are torn apart and fling their jagged fragments against a defenseless beach; great combers surge over the land and engulf men and women whose screams of terror are in pantomime, mocked to silence by the howling rage of the wind. If this is make-believe, nature must make the best of it; she has been played to perfection."

The Hecht-MacArthur experiment was deemed a failure at the time. The films had lost money; *unforgivable*. One could not even be released; it had to be sneaked out in the dead of night like oversized garbage. The boys' attempt had polarized attitudes toward the screenwriter. They had made it much more difficult for any writer to gain control over his film.

But the passing years would treat the Astoria revolution as kindly as any painful first love. *The Scoundrel* and *Crime without Passion* would become cult classics, which meant that thousands would see them because it was *de rigueur* in some particular set without the faintest notion of why anyone as callous as Anthony Mallare should care whether anyone had loved him or not. No studio is magnanimous enough to finance such films. They simply happen, like accidents. They are taken up by film students and patrons of New York's Elgin, Thalia, St. Marks, and the Museum of Modern Art, and these enthusiasts can't seem to see them enough. *Harold and Maude* (1970), the story of a necrophiliac youth in love with an eighty-year-old woman who appears to be living in a converted caboose, was ignored on its first release, but cultists have come close to making it a financial miracle for Paramount. There are rumors that Marilyn's last film, *The Misfits*, recently moved into the black fourteen years after its release.

But in the middle and late thirties a quieter revolution was under way in Hollywood that was far more significant than the Long Island adventure. John Ford's *The Informer* (1935), a film made at RKO that seemed shot on location, was a drama of the IRA in Dublin and the first serious examination by a major Hollywood director and studio of a current political problem. In the years ahead there would be scores of them, enough to make serious rents in the straitjacket of the Code. And, oddly, it would be through them that more recognizably human characters would move onto the screen. I say "oddly" because purely political films are usually not very human; they are dealing in broad ideas, abstractions (even *The Great Dictator* errs in this direction). But the classic films of the Depression era *(Dead End, The Grapes of Wrath, Wild Boys of the Road)* led almost directly into the antifascist (and sometimes anticolonial) films of the late thirties and early forties.

Freedom of a sort was at hand for the Hollywood film, but it was to lead to an even harsher and more repressive effort by outside forces to dictate not only content but *who* would be allowed to make the film—from the director and writer to the supporting players.

PART THREE

FITZGERALD RETURNS, DOROTHY PARKER GOES TO THE FRONT

1.

In May of 1936, European newspapers, mostly to the right, began publishing stories of riots and disorders in Spain.

The stories were distortions, exaggerations, and lies, but they were printed whenever the left (or "Bolsheviks") loomed as a threat at election time in any Western nation. In reality, the Civil Guard was shooting down strikers; a liberal who was more centrist than rightist, President Manuel Azaña, was running the country in a constitutional manner, supported by all of the workers and even a few Communists. But wages were below a subsistence level; it was very much like France on the eve of the Revolution. The military elite was plotting against the government of Manuel Azaña together with the high clergy and the industrialists and financiers, not to restore the monarchy, which they had already got rid of, but to rule in its place.

These were the extreme rightists, the *Falange,* who were out to take over the country with Generalisimo Franco as his country's "Saviour" and Christian civilization's "by blotting out the menace of Marxism."

The Nazis were already well into the Civil War as Franco's allies, feeding propaganda through Goebbels' machinery into the German press; they were supplying Franco with arms and ammunition; and there were German spies in every city and village throughout Spain. The Spanish workers in control knew their neighbors well and were continually hauling out village and town agents in the pay of the Nazis and usually executing them without ceremony. The democratic system was being put aside "temporarily" in order to save its supporters from a worse tyranny. Snipers were everywhere and men, women, and children being picked off from rooftops; low-flying planes machine-gunned indiscriminately.

If 1936 was a bad year for the world, it was almost equally bad for Hollywood, although sudden death from the sky cannot be seriously equated with plummeting box-office grosses.

Eighty-five percent of all movie theaters were showing double features. The Academy Award really was given that season because Luise Rainer wept in close-up over the telephone as Anna Held in *The Great Ziegfeld*. Kate Hepburn tried regally to dispel a label of box-office poison with a dark-hued biography of *Mary of Scotland* and failed. Dietrich attempted to do the same in a shade of Technicolor that might be described as "Night on the Desert" in *The Garden of Allah* and failed even more dismally. But there were some compensations.

Chaplin released his last film with only sound effects and music—*Modern Times,* and the theme song, *Smile ("Though Your Heart Is Breaking"),* set the mood for an iffy year for everyone. Ginger Rogers and Fred Astaire's *Swing Time, My Man Godfrey, San Francisco* (with the visual tricks stealing the movie from Clark Gable and Jeanette MacDonald), and *Mr. Deeds Goes to Town* were the major successes and usually managed to play the first-run circuits without a second feature detracting from their impact. There were two prestige productions from Metro, Garbo's *Camille* and Thalberg's *Romeo and Juliet,* with Norma Shearer defying time (she was thirty-five) as Shakespeare's dewy heroine in a shimmering version of the classic. Donald Ogden Stewart, who had become exceedingly valuable as a rewrite man to Thalberg, was on the set of the Shakespeare work through most of its production, although Talbot Jennings, another Thalberg favorite, had written the screenplay and got the credit.

Benchley, Stewart, and Dorothy Parker, off-screen and away from crowds, were probably of themselves their own greatest amusement. Screams of mirth and steady squeals of someone being tickled with a feather would roll out the doors and windows of any suite or living room where they had cornered themselves. No joke could be remembered. Just a scrap of a phrase would be uttered recalling something else, of course, and the mirth was not merely in danger of being uncontained; it threatened the peace of the neighborhood. Mrs. Parker called Benchley "Fred," usually upon greeting him, as though this was the most Babbitty name she could think of. To keep things even more familial, Benchley had been best man at Don's wedding to Beatrice Ames in 1926. Benchley, in a word or two, had enormous kindness and humor in nearly equal amounts. He had generosity. Women found him wildly attractive, although he was no John Gilbert. Perhaps it was his gallantry and his slight but clear awareness of any feminine charm. He came down from Larchmont a righteous and moral paragon and he was steam-rollered by the most deliriously unrighteous folk east of the Mississippi.

But it was in 1936 that Don Stewart swung to the left.

With Fredric March and his wife Florence Eldridge as performers, Stewart got the Anti-Nazi League to sponsor a reading of Irwin Shaw's antiwar play *Bury the Dead*. Shaw was then relatively unknown; this was his first play and was still unproduced. Stewart was chairman and helped with the collections, which were "big." Apparently, the money was to help stop the fascists in Spain.

The morning of the day of the reading, Sam Marx, Metro's story editor, came around to Stewart's office and asked how his screenplay was progressing and then said, "*Irving* won't like it if you take part in this." But Stewart chaired that meeting and countless others like it.

Beatrice Ames, divorced over thirty-five years from Don Stewart, remembered his "left turn" in an even more detailed fashion. Don, she recalled, was working on *Romeo and Juliet*.

"The children were having their naps," Mrs. Ames recalled. "It was a Thursday—the staff's afternoon off. Later, I would take the children to the Bel Air Beach Club and they'd paddle around and have a good time. The doorbell rang. That was unusual at three o'clock in the afternoon. So I went downstairs and answered it. And there stood an awfully nice-looking young man with shining red hair. And he had a little bag in his hand—overnight kind of thing. And he said, 'Are you Mrs. Stewart?' And I said, 'Yes.' 'Well,' he said, 'Is Mr. Stewart here?'

" 'No,' I told him, 'he's at the studio. He's very busy. I don't know whether you could talk to him' I never called him at the studio because he might be on the set. But I asked, 'Is it important?' 'Yes,' the young man said, 'It *is* important.'

"So I took him into the bar and made him a drink and gave him the telephone after I got the studio. And I just heard him say as I went through the bar into the living room on my way toward the staircase, 'Mr. Stewart, Kyle Crichton sent me. It's rather urgent that I see you.'

"On the steps, I asked the young man, 'What did he say?' 'He's coming right over.' "

Beatrice Stewart continued her Thursday routine, taking the children outside, where they played around a patio and the tennis court. Finally, Don showed up. He seemed very nervous; the young man was with him. "I forgot this was Thursday," he said. "It's the day everybody goes out. My wife's alone with the children."

The youth said, "That's quite all right with me, but we must have a conference at once."

None of this is especially ominous, although Bea Ames believed the young man to be a Communist field worker. (Kyle Crichton was called a Communist by John O'Hara in a letter to his brother written in the mid-thirties. He has been mentioned by others as having had leftist beliefs, but so had the majority of intellectuals of the time. Crichton was not a screenwriter but a magazine editor and writer, whose byline was well-known to readers of *Collier's* and other weeklies. Under the pseudonym of Robert Forsythe he wrote a column, "Redder Than the Rose," for the far-left *New Masses* Magazine.)

Metro and Hollywood needed Stewart—he was valuable to Thalberg and to Metro—and if there is one lesson to be learned from the years of the Blacklist that would come within a decade, it was *to make yourself valuable; irreplaceable*. Gale Sondergaard would stand up in crowded places and make speeches in a vain effort to keep her husband, Herbert Biberman, from prison, and she would not only fail; she, too, would be blacklisted. Biberman was one of the Hollywood Ten and a director of considerable daring, who early in his career had staged the Soviet play *Roar China*, in which a large battleship surrounded by a real moat appeared on stage with sampans floating in front of it; on the screen, he had had a substantial success in *Meet Nero Wolfe*. His wife, Miss Sondergaard, was a respected stage and screen actress who had won an Academy Award as best supporting actress in *Anthony Adverse* (1936), but that was not enough to keep her from becoming a pariah in the film community and the Bibermans were unemployables for nearly twenty years.

Lauren Bacall, although she did not have Miss Sondergaard's eloquence, flew to Washington with her husband, Humphrey Bogart, to denounce that same committee that was sending Gale Sondergaard's husband to jail and returned to her Holmby Hills mansion where the couple's bills would be met by their astronomical salaries, their films would continue to be made, and only gentle rebuke would come their way from Jack Warner and others.

In mid-August, *Romeo and Juliet* premiered in half a dozen cities, including New York, where Frank Nugent praised it in *The New York Times*. Public response, however, seemed more inclined toward George Jean Nathan's opinion as set down in his book, *The Morning After the First Night*:

> The story that the film throws before your eyes, begauded and over-elaborately produced as it is, impresses the spectator as being less one of ancient strife between

the houses of Montague and Capulet than between those
of D. W. Griffith and Cecil B. De Mille. . . . Leslie
Howard's Romeo suggests that he has swallowed an
air-cooling plant. . . . Norma Shearer is pictorially satis-
fying as Juliet but, save in one or two short scenes that
call upon her harsher moods, purveys the feeling that she
is simply reciting, like a schoolgirl, a well-learned lesson.

Well, no one in Hollywood aside from Dorothy Parker,
Oscar Levant, and Ben Hecht ever paid the slightest heed to
George Jean Nathan. He was nearly as much of a curmudgeon
as H. L. Mencken, but at least Mencken came out for a frolic
once in a while.

On Labor Day weekend, the Thalbergs were relaxing
at the Del Monte Club near Pebble Beach. This is nearly 300
miles north of Hollywood but it is a verdant and elegant
wooded retreat almost on the Pacific. Harpo Marx had come
along and several Metro directors and their wives.

Pebble Beach is a foggy resort on the cool side and that may
have precipitated Irving's cold. But however it began, his
condition worsened in early September so that Norma sent for
Dr. Franz (Fritz) Groedel, Irving's physician from Bad Nauheim (who, incidentally was William Randolph Hearst's
doctor on the Continent), who was now a refugee from
Nazism practicing in Manhattan.

Thalberg now was suffering from pneumonia, his heart was
weakening, and he felt hopeless about his prospects. Louis B.
Mayer spent the morning of September 14th at his desk, his
hands locked together, praying for a miracle. None was really
expected and none came. The phone rang shortly before noon
to inform him that Thalberg was dead. He closed the studio
for the day and drove down to the beach to pay his respects.

Back East, Charlie MacArthur was alone on his Nyack
tennis court with a basket of balls, banging them against a
wall. Helen went down from the house after hearing the news

on the radio and Charlie sensed her standing there but he kept on banging the balls, finally saying, "I know."

For all of Thalberg's reliance upon the familiar and the proven, he had a belief in movies that was contagious. If he had been physically stronger, he might have left his mark on American films, one as lasting as that of Griffith or Chaplin. But dying when he did, he became a martyr to the "tasteful" film; his striving for perfection had destroyed him. It is unfortunate that there is such little excitement in perfection since the Thalbergians had a hand in the running of Metro at least for a number of years after his death. *Marie Antoinette* was completed; and I wouldn't be surprised to learn that *Mrs. Miniver* and a whole host of other faultless ladies and gentlemen were spiritual progeny of Irving Thalberg. Perhaps, if Thalberg's place in American films is ever properly evaluated and the myth shaken out of his fascinating saga, we will discover that he became a power at a time when American films needed a direction and he believed the camera's sight should be vertical and not horizontal.

2.

Part of the Thalberg legacy was that the American (or the Chinese or the Viennese) had to be nice. It did not begin with him, but he refined it and even made it a necessity. There was an American theatrical tradition, certainly as old as *Our American Cousin,* and carried over into the movies, that it was not enough to be good. This goodness had to shine like a beacon from within.

This niceness colors all of the work of Mary Pickford, continued to shine out at us in the persons of Ronald Reagan, George Murphy, early Dick Powell, Ruby Keeler, Judy Garland, Jeanette MacDonald, and is the essence of the current British Julie Andrews, who, I have a strong feeling, was not nearly so "nice" back home. It has fostered a "niceness" in the American image that persists and, since many of us aren't very "nice," has caused us to be hypocritical in our social selves. Its counterfeit has destroyed many a marriage and friendship. The alleged mass murderer of numerous young boys in Texas was known by everyone as a "nice man." The neighborhood of a "nice" New York City youth was shocked when he raped a woman old enough to be his grandmother.

In the 1930s, as America was becoming a bastion of much that was "good" in the world, President Roosevelt began sending "goodwill" ambassadors to Latin America and elsewhere. Alcoholics, Don Juans, and other unnice diplomats were carefully kept away from these missions. And it was at this same time that Shirley Temple became the most popular American film star anywhere.

Shirley was sweet, with a round, cherubic countenance and just enough baby fat to keep her story writers away from "little slavey" fare. Typical of the genre was *Poor Little Rich Girl* (1936) written by Gladys Lehman and Harry Tugend. In this film, Shirley plays the daughter of a handsome widower (Michael Whalen), a soap tycoon who has turned to radio advertising to compete with a rival. Shirley is mostly in the care of a grim, unsmiling governess (Sara Hayden) and sees her father all too seldom. But when they do meet of an evening, they cuddle in front of a radio listening to his company's show and singing love songs to each other ("When I'm with You"), a fairly typical liberty taken in Shirley's films, with no incestuous allusions intended.

Shirley ruefully tells her dad that she is lonely, that she has no playmates, so he decides to pack her off to a girl's boarding school. In a fairly incredible plot turn, she eludes the keepers who are taking her upstate to the school and runs free in the big city for several days. Dad doesn't discover that she is not enrolled and happily established in the school until he hears her singing on his rival's radio show. At the railway station on her way to freedom, she stops a tall black porter and asks him his name. "Rufus Washington Jefferson," he says. "All by yourself?" she wonders and there is a little determined way she has of speaking that allows her to get away with it. In the street, she follows an organ-grinder (Henry Armetta) and his monkey home and then tells him her name is "Betsy Ware" (a fiction). "I'm on a vacation. I used to live in an orphanage, but they were awfully mean to me." A bit later, since the scenarists quickly exhaust the ethnic possibilities of the Armetta household, she falls in with a couple of singing vaudevillians (Alice Faye and Jack Haley) who are given the same line (the orphanage bit) and work her into their act. When they discover their error, Miss Faye tells her partner, "I told you she didn't jump out of a hat." Miss Faye is agreeably persuasive as a slightly faded blonde. In order to give the story added suspense, there is a dirty middle-aged man who attempts to entice Shirley away from the singing and dancing Dolans with the old candy routine, but even sweet little Shirley is onto that one and never mind the unnice connotations. Her presence keeps us from pondering over the man's existence in a story so lightweight it threatens to float off the screen at any moment.

The following year, British author Graham Greene, in one of his infrequent essays on film, wrote that he found Shirley's "oddly precocious body . . . as voluptuous in gray flannel trousers as Miss Dietrich's," suggesting that the child star's aging male fans were drawn to her films by more than her acting talents. Twentieth Century-Fox sued for libel and won a settlement of $9,800, a modest sum, it would seem, to give guarantee of the little darling's innocence.

At regular four- and five-month intervals, Temple films emerged from Zanuck's incredibly successful studio, where entertainment of the most wholesome sort was becoming a staple. He was about to make a film star out of skater Sonja

Henie. His leading men—Ameche, Power, Fonda—were "noble" types, so noble, in fact, that certain of their leading ladies looked slightly whorish by contrast.

In Miss Temple's next film, *Captain January,* the grim Sara Hayden attempts to get her away from a semiliterate old lighthouse keeper, played by Guy Kibbee—to put her in an institution, naturally. Miss Hayden again fails, but not before we have been treated to a few bars of "At the Cod Fish Ball" sung by Miss Temple and Kibbee.

By 1937, Zanuck had induced veteran director John Ford to guide Shirley through her most ambitious part yet, a loose adaptation by Ernest Pascal and Julien Josephson of Rudyard Kipling's *Wee Willie Winkie.* In this, she had Victor McLaglen, June Lang, and C. Aubrey Smith as co-stars, along with the inevitable Mr. Whalen. The film was something of a comedown for McLaglen after his sterling successes in *The Informer* and *The Lost Patrol* and his role was a pale carbon of his old Captain Flagg character of *What Price Glory?* In the movie, Shirley succeeds in routing thousands of bewildered Indian tribesmen in a victory for the Queen. *New York Times* critic Frank Nugent warned his readers that "Miss Temple will get us all if we don't watch out."

The point made so effectively by Shirley Temple was that Americans are dear, sweet-natured, and willing to share our bounty with all now that the Indians are dead. (Jane Withers had a meteoric rise to a point high on the box-office ten at about this time proving just the opposite—a clever promotion by studio czar Zanuck, although Miss Withers disappeared from sight in three years or less.*) These were qualities at odds with the intentions of the bombardiers eliminating Dresden and other European cities as well as Hiroshima and Nagasaki within about seven years. They were at odds, too, with those

---

*Jane Withers surfaced as a performer in the 1960s as "Josephine, The Plumber" in a series of cleanser commercials. Her income from this employment has probably exceeded her earnings as a star in the 1930s.

who shut doors in the faces of the Okies seeking a handout on the road West.

3.

Janet Gaynor had made a substantial reputation for herself (unwillingly, I'm sure, at least part of the time) as the nicest Nellie on the block. She seemed to have inherited the most commercial features of Pearl White and Mary Pickford. If some heinous individual was not attempting to do his worst with her, then the elements (floods, war, or, if she was lucky, a simple cloudburst) took over. Through it all, she had a beatific smile, a kind of insipid Gioconda smile to put a literary frame around it. And, needless to say, she had a huge following.

And apparently she hated it. She wanted to play at least one role of substance before she died. When her contract with Fox expired, she saw that it was not renewed. She informed her agent that she had played her last "Daddy's Girl" (see Fitzgerald: *Tender Is the Night*).

There were others in Hollywood who were breaking out of the old molds as well. Walter Wanger seemed to have become involved with the greater theater of a world in chaos and had abandoned for all time his earlier persuasion that entertainment was the prerequisite of any good movie.

In 1935, David O. Selznick "went International" to do just the opposite. Selznick, International, his new producing organization, would make some remarkable pictures during the four years of its most intensive activity, but there would be no effort to capture on camera what was happening on the world's stage. He first would film a children's classic of the nineteenth century, *Little Lord Fauntleroy*, starring his "David Copperfield" Freddie Bartholomew, a considerable success released earlier that year while Selznick was still at Metro; then he turned to a trite romance that was foredoomed, *The*

Garden of Allah, inspired as much by Charles Boyer's success in the Casbah in Walter Wanger's *Algiers* as by the hoary romance by Robert K. Hitchens, and it was a resounding failure despite the presence of Marlene Dietrich. Its cost and its total loss were disheartening to Selznick and to those who had gone into partnership with him (principal stockholders brother Myron Selznick and Irving Thalberg, John Hay— "Jock" Whitney, C. V. Whitney, and Mrs. Joan Payson Whitney's sister).

When Fox first realized that Janet Gaynor was becoming restive and that her "Pickford" days were over, producer Sol Wurtzel, who supervised nearly all of Fox's films except those personally produced by Zanuck, told playwright S. N. Behrman, "Why not *Anna Karenina* with a note of hope at the end for Gaynor?" But now, in late 1935, Miss Gaynor already had a major film in release made at Metro. It was about a not-very-old spinster who finally lands the catch of the season *(Small Town Girl).* Seeing that film, something clicked in the mind of David O. Selznick.

Years ago, Selznick had made a seriocomedy about Hollywood with Lowell Sherman and Constance Bennett called *What Price Hollywood?* The film ended with the death of Sherman and fell between two stools, but Selznick always had believed in the idea and kept discussing it with writers.

Now Selznick asked novelist and screenwriter Robert Carson to prepare a shooting script of a movie about a has-been star who falls in love with an actress on the rise. One of the first titles Selznick appended to it was *The Stars Below.* In 1937, in a memo to his long-time aide Daniel O'Shea, Selznick wrote:

> *Star Is Born* [he finally had hit upon something close to being right] is much more my story than Wellman's [William A., the director signed to shoot the picture] or Carson's. I refused to take credit on it simply as a matter of policy, and if the picture is as good as we hope, they

are the beneficiaries. Certainly Wellman contributed a
great deal, but then any director does that on any story.
The actual original idea, the story line, and the vast
majority of the story ideas of the scenes themselves, are
my own.

With the germ of the movie coming out of Selznick's head
and many of the scenes as well, the writing of this film should
have been comparatively easy. But, as he did on nearly every
film he ever made, Selznick wanted to "ensure its being as
perfect as possible" by having two teams of writers working
on it: Robert Carson and William Wellman making up the first
team and Dorothy Parker and Alan Campbell the second.
Selznick eventually credited Mrs. Parker and Campbell with
the final dialogue and some "amendments in the scenes," even
though "ninety-five percent of the dialogue in that picture was
actually straight out of life and was straight 'reportage.'" Mrs.
Parker's ear for local dialogue being what it was, it was
possible for her now to pour all of her venom—and it had been
accumulating for over three years—into what some reviewers
would call "savage satire." The sharks around Vicki Lester
ready to rip her failing husband to shreds were sharks Mrs.
Parker had observed at first hand.

But the irony was to come later. *A Star Is Born* won
Academy nominations for all of its principals: actor Fredric
March, actress Janet Gaynor, and best picture. It *won* Oscars
for writers Robert Carson and William Wellman, but because
Selznick had decided that rewriting most of the dialogue and
changing scenes was a "refinement" and not a substantial
contribution to the actual writing, the Campbells were neither
announced as collaborators at the time of the film's release nor
did they share the only Oscar won by the film.

A Star Is Born was, until *Sunset Boulevard* was released
thirteen years later, the most successful film on Hollywood
ever made. It recouped the losses from *The Garden of Allah*
and allowed the spendthrift Selznick to keep from foundering

during the next three years prior to production of *Rebecca* and *Gone with the Wind.*

Those four years of Selznick International were golden ones, with only one or two failures to mar the record. They would never come again for the gifted producer, perhaps at that period the most creative filmmaker in Hollywood. But no one knew that then, or even guessed, especially David O. Selznick.

4.

> The third Hollywood venture. Two failures behind me though one no fault of mine. . . . I want to profit by these two experiences—I must be very tactful, but keep my hand on the wheel from the start—find out the key man among the bosses and the most malleable among the collaborators—then fight the rest tooth and nail until, in fact or in effect, I'm alone on the picture. That's the only way I can do my best work. Given a break I can make them double this contract in two years.
>
> —F. Scott Fitzgerald in a letter to his daughter

In July 1937, Scott Fitzgerald was back in Hollywood, settled into one of the bungalows at the Garden of Allah Hotel. He was over $40,000 in debt* but agent Harold Ober had got him a contract at Metro for six months with options at $1,000 a week. "There are clauses in the contract," Scott wrote Max Perkins, "which allow certain off-periods but it postpones a book for quite a while. . . . Ernest [Hemingway] came like a whirlwind . . . raised $1,000 bills won by Miriam

---

*An inheritance from his mother soon would reduce some of this indebtedness.

Hopkins fresh from the gaming table, the rumor is $14,000 in one night (for Spanish War Relief).

"Everyone is very nice to me, surprised and rather relieved that I don't drink. I am happier than I've been for several years."

Helen Hayes MacArthur brought Scottie (Frances Scott Key Fitzgerald), Scott's daughter, out on the train with her and their young Mary. Scottie was then around sixteen and about to enter Vassar.

Scottie stayed with the MacArthurs most of that summer in a bungalow at the Beverly Hills Hotel. No one today can quite remember why Scott didn't take her into his own apartment but perhaps the responsibility was more than he could handle along with his abstinence and his studio work.

Late in July, Marc Connelly invited Sheilah Graham to a Writers' Guild dinner dance at the Coconut Grove. They were seated at a table for ten and nearby was Dorothy Parker's table, also a small crowd. Then suddenly Sheilah found herself alone and saw Fitzgerald was likewise alone.

"The thought flashed through my mind," she wrote later, "he should get out into the sun, he needs light and air and warmth. Then he leaned forward and said, smiling across the two tables, 'I like you.'

5.

At Helen Hayes's suggestion, Scottie had wired ahead while they were crossing the desert that their train would be arriving that afternoon and that she would be looking forward to having dinner with her father.

It just happened that Scott had made a dinner date with Sheilah Graham for that evening, Scottie's arrival having slipped his mind entirely. According to Sheilah Graham, Sheilah held him to the date: "I stared at the telegram, astonished at the intensity of my disappointment."

She was engaged to marry a titled Englishman in six months. "Yet suddenly I knew I must see Scott again. Nothing else mattered. I telephoned him. 'Scott,' I said, 'it makes no difference, your daughter being here. I'd like to meet her. Can't we all go to dinner?"

Scott agreed to pick her up at seven. It was a tense evening with Scott fussing over Scottie endlessly. He was ill-at-ease in the role of father, but it was evident he wanted to make up for all those months of absence, that void Scottie must feel.

"But Scott would come (after that first evening)," Helen Hayes was to recall, "and we'd all go out to dinner every night. Oh he was always a spellbinder to me—wonderful, articulate, charming, tender, a beautiful human being."

To the literary set, particularly Dorothy Parker, Sheilah Graham could not have been more inappropriate for someone like Scott. Always on the teetering edge of saying or doing the wrong thing, Scott needed an educated, sensitive helpmate. He never had allowed himself to have one, unless Lois Moran could be put on that level, but she had been more the product of a finishing school and a bright supportive friend.

Sheilah noticed that the more literate Hollywoodites deferred to Scott. His was a mind they respected. And yet for months early in their relationship she had never read any of his books and thought that he was the author of *Flaming Youth.*

When she discovered what a strong bond remained between Scott and Zelda, this was very hard for Sheilah to accept. She may have imagined Zelda as a slatternly lost soul who drifted about in sacklike dresses with no waistline. Sheilah could not know what it was like when the world waited breathlessly, a little foolishly, for Scott and Zelda's next move. They had been a golden pair. Sheilah seemed to lose her bearings for a while. She flirted openly with other men in front of Scott. What had she to lose? Certainly, there was no future with him.

In her book *Beloved Infidel* (written with Gerold Frank), Sheilah Graham emerges as a martyr to a literary icon who embarrassed her in public with his drunkenness. But there were some of Scott's friends who could not believe that any man would take for long the abuse she is supposed to have heaped upon him. There are clues in *The Last Tycoon* that Sheilah ("Kathleen" in the book) would "not have accepted a bad lover," so there is reason to believe that he pressed himself to perform in bed with some virility.

Dorothy Parker and too many of Scott's other friends from back East attempted "to disassociate him" from Sheilah, a subtle form of blackballing the one person who was holding the pieces together. Snobbery was behind some of this ostracism. Sometimes at dinner, Sheilah could not avoid following the butler with her eyes as he served a tray of food. That obsessional regard for appetizing fare doubtless could be traced to her years in a London orphanage, but it was there.

Scott, the terrible puritan, was hopelessly involved with a woman he would call his "paramour" to friends. And as if to demonstrate her flightiness, it is said that following a quarrel, she took up briefly with war correspondent Quentin Reynolds, a portly and slightly swaggering writer with an internationally-known magazine byline.*

She may have thought at the time that she could have done better than Scott Fitzgerald materially. She still had her fresh British complexion, her lithe figure. But she was ridding herself rapidly of her cockney expressions and had enrolled in Scott's "College of One," which gave them both huge satisfaction. He was a frustrated schoolmaster and she was anxious to be up to the mark with his friends. Whole hours of every day were dedicated to Keats and Spinoza, Kafka and Thomas Hardy. They eventually moved on to the Elizabethan poets

---

*In Sheilah Graham's "confessions," *A State of Heat* (1972), she would seem to deny any intimacy with Reynolds, writing: "I liked Quentin and his close friend John McClain but neither appealed to me physically."

and Marx. If she didn't assimilate all of their works, at least she knew who they were and what most of them were about.

They met in mid-1937 and he was to live another three and a half years—the years of *Three Comrades, The Last Tycoon*, the most important work of the last half decade of his life. Sheilah Graham was there holding him intact when the crockery threatened to fly to pieces altogether. His sense of guilt over Zelda's breakdown was undermining his own fragile stability. Fitzgerald would not have accepted the long-term friendship of a male friend to see him through this dark, final period (that old andryogynous bugaboo of his again) but Sheilah, his dear "Sheilo," he would and it would be in her apartment that he would die.

Let it be said at once that Scott had not "gone to ruin," as so many have depicted him. He had a quiet grace about him and he still wore clothes with a flair. Sheilah has described them as a rather "twenties" tatterdemalion. Actually he was nearly always well-tailored except when lounging about his apartment. In novelist Anthony Powell's words" . . . snapshots tend to give him an air of swagger, a kind of cockiness, he did not at all possess. . . . There was no hint at all of the cantankerousness that undoubtedly lay beneath the surface. . . . In a railway carriage or bar, one would have wondered who this man could be."

At a luncheon with Powell, Scott divulged a favorite theme of his—the difference between the American and British way of life. It was his way of getting "under the skin" of a project. He regretted sadly the contemporary lack of culture in America, using as an example how surprised a friend was that he would use the word "cinquecento."

Before Irving Thalberg's death at thirty-seven in September 1936, Fitzgerald had been invited to an informal Sunday afternoon party at the Thalbergs' beach home in Santa Monica. Mrs. Thalberg (Norma Shearer) had been around the film community long enough to spot a drunk when she saw one, but Fitzgerald *seemed* sober when he proposed that a pianist be found so that he might sing an old ballad about "man's best friend." Film star Ramon Novarro accompanied him as he sang about a dog, then a second stanza as simpleminded as the first and then a third. There was considerable restlessness and even annoyance among the other guests as the song meandred along. Later Fitzgerald made it the basis of one of his finest short stories, "Crazy Sunday," but said that it had actually occurred on a Sunday at the home of director King Vidor. (There are also elements in this long story, for example, the plane crash that claims the life of the producer, that later would be utilized in *The Last Tycoon*.) After this gaucherie, Fitzgerald received a note from either Norma Shearer or Mrs. King Vidor (Eleanor Boardman), telling him that he was "one of the most agreeable persons at our tea."

He had become a man who needed his friends and Sheilah Graham and Dorothy Parker, antipathetic to each other, remained among the closest—but in quite different compartments of his life.

A Yank at Oxford was to be the first film made by Metro at its new studios in Denham, England. Its story was not particularly distinguished; about an American football player who attends Oxford but assumes a role of disdain for both school and the British.

An attractive girl student (at "St. Cynthia's"), played by Maureen O'Sullivan, decides to whittle him down to size but instead they fall in love.

Although he was later taken off the script, an example of Scott's dialogue survives and remains in the completed film:

221. CLOSE SHOT   LEE & MOLLY *in Punt*
MOLLY *(breathlessly):* Good morning.
LEE: *Such* a . . . good morning.
The boat swirls into the way of another and is bumped.

VOICE *(O.S. mildly caustic)*: Will you rub the sleep out of
  your eyes?
They look off laughing, then Molly pretends to rub
the sleep out of her eyes.
LEE *(stopping her)* Don't do that. If that's sleep . . . leave
  it. It's the best sleep I ever saw.
The punt starts drifting.
MOLLY: Idiot!
LEE: I'm not really—just happy!
MOLLY *(sees they are drifting)*: Look! The pole!

The CAMERA PANS with LEE as he leaps to the stern,
makes a desperate grab for the pole, which sticks up in
the mud as the punt drifts away from it. But it's too late.
LEE cannot reach the pole.

222. ANOTHER ANGLE
LEE, laughing, lets the pole go, rolls over in the stern to
  face MOLLY, and picks up a paddle,
LEE: I'm glad we're rid of that bally thing. Made me feel
  like a gondolier.
MOLLY: (sits down near LEE with lifted eyebrows) Did I
  hear you say "bally"?
LEE *(grins as he paddles along)*: Sure.
MOLLY *(shaking her head—mock warning)*: Umm! Wait til
  you take that accent back to Lakedale!

Some of this scene was cut, of course, when the film was
edited. Yet the essence remained. Scott's dialogue revisions
made Molly much less austere. He suggested changing her
opening remark to Lee from

I thought I'd have some coffee with you.

to:

Room for one more?

George Oppenheimer, who was one of the writers called in
to take over the script, hated his studio with as much passion

as Fitzgerald feared it and was known as one of "the Katzen-
jammer Kids" because of the pranks he liked to play on the
studio bosses (Charles Lederer and Harry Kurnitz were the
other "Kids"). He loved Fitzgerald as a literary man and was
devoted to him. As a publisher and cofounder of the Viking
Press before his Hollywood days, Oppenheimer had seen a
great deal of Fitzgerald back in New York. When Fitzgerald
arrived in Hollywood, he was glad to see a familiar face and
would go down to the Oppenheimer house, sometimes with
his daughter, Scottie, on one of her visits to Hollywood
because he knew Oppenheimer was "decent" and not apt to
scandalize his daughter. Whenever Oppenheimer gave a
party, he would ask Scott to come.

Even though it was to his disadvantage, since the more
dialogue a new writer could get included in a shooting script,
the more certain that he would get a screen credit, Oppenheimer pleaded with director Jack Conway to keep a number
of Fitzgerald scenes, including the dialogue between "Yank"
Robert Taylor and his slightly snobbish British girlfriend
Maureen O'Sullivan. Oppenheimer's plea was acceded to
and it remains one of the most affecting scenes in the film.

Scott was trying his damndest to succeed in making the
transition from a novelist to a screenwriter.

Daughter Scottie was "having the time of her young life,
dining with Crawford, Shearer, etc., talking to Fred Astaire
and her other heroes. I am very proud of her."

It was believed that being in this most social inn—The
Garden of Allah—he would be drawn out of himself. Only
the year before, he had written *The Crack-Up*, a candid
examination of a personality in the process of fracturing. "Of
course," he wrote, "all life is a process of breaking down. . . .
One should . . . be able to see that things are hopeless and yet
be determined to make them otherwise. This philosophy
fitted on to my early adult life, when I saw the improbable,
the implausible, often the 'impossible,' come true. Life was
something you dominated if you were any good." He further

elaborated this theme by saying that he had "cracked" not physically, nor mentally, but spiritually, that the savor of life was gone, that he pretended to enjoy the company of others, that even the ritual of brushing his teeth had become an ordeal for him.

The essay, so chillingly accurate, had appeared in *Esquire* Magazine and everyone in Hollywood had taken the trouble to read it. Friends urged him not to have it published, but he had insisted upon it and when he returned to Hollywood, there was one more blight on his reputation—the time not being an era of public confession. But good-natured Bob Benchley attempted to ignore the article's existence and invited him to parties in his apartment and elsewhere, as did Eddie Mayer and Dorothy Parker. There is some substance to a belief that Mrs. Parker now found Scott easier to take than before. She always had felt uneasy in Scott's presence—a certain unnerving sensibility that kept her on edge. But now he had proved himself as vulnerable as she was and able to write at first hand about it, which she was not.

And, Scott and Sheilah were not such an odd match as some believed. Sheilah had alienated as many powerful Hollywood folk as Fitzgerald had, with his heavy drinking and his sad confessions. If Fitzgerald's candor and brashness in the twenties had been excessive, wholly exploited as he was as the darling of the Roaring Decade, Sheilah's had been more so as she strove upward to some influence and power in the gossip field.

But she made it evident that her affair with Fitzgerald was not platonic. Fitzgerald's paleness, his pensiveness, had moved her to change her marriage plans and made her forget her dream of becoming a marchioness. She and Fitzgerald kept their separate establishments, but within a matter of weeks, they had become lovers.

With Sheilah, he could relax and not dwell on his present failures. She was, as she herself admitted, ideally equipped to deal with Hollywood types. She was full of pretensions, her background sheer invention. She would say nothing publicly of her Dickensian childhood until nearly twenty years after Fitzgerald's death. Still, she could lessen his insecurity when he moved among the moguls, lesser producers, stars, and famed writers and directors by telling him what she knew of their pasts. She was a notorious rattler of skeletons—that being a great part of her movie column's popularity—and Fitzgerald had doted on gossip and innuendo since his years at Princeton.

Sheilah collected her stories and brought them back to his Garden of Allah apartment or his cottage at Malibu Beach, which he leased next, where she would distract him with her gossip for long hours. And she also had her tender side. When he went on his first alcoholic binge in her presence, they were on a plane to Chicago and Fitzgerald was asking the stewardess and fellow passengers if they had ever heard of him, "of F. Scott Fitzgerald, the very well-known writer." Liquor made him both egotistical and, eventually, hostile. He was a nasty drunk. But Sheilah did not fight back as Zelda had done. She took his taunts and when he was outrageous in public, she flushed with all the embarrassment that would have been his had he been sober. In the four years or so of their relationship, she would see him turn to the bottle after every real or fancied slight or difficulty. But she saw him as more than a lover. She was discovering books she had never heard of; she helped him survive a time in his life when suicide might have been much the simpler solution.

He left town in a mood of the keenest despair, spending some time with Zelda and Scottie and, far from Hollywood, began to set down the first notes of his novel based on his close professional affiliation with Thalberg, *The Last Tycoon*.

With the novel taking shape, Fitzgerald felt it imperative to get back to the Coast where his characters were living, among them "Kathleen" (Sheilah Graham). And he had been assigned his most important property yet—*Three Comrades*, the Remarque novel about the coming of Nazism to Germany, its effects upon friendships and family. Joe Mankiewicz, a man who considered himself a fine screenwriter (and had awards to prove it later), was the producer and Frank Borzage (of *Seventh Heaven* fame) the director. Originally Spencer Tracy was to have starred but that role went instead to Robert Young, who would join the stars already signed to the production— Margaret Sullavan, perhaps the most sensitive heroine in American films, Robert Taylor, and Franchot Tone.

Fitzgerald's screenplay was brilliant, but there were moments when, forgetting that he was *adapting* a novel rather than *writing one*, he gave his characters far too much to say. Mankiewicz called in a collaborator, Ted Paramore, who finally got co-screen credit with the film. Beyond this, Mankiewicz himself rewrote large sections of the film. Later he would do the same thing on *Woman of the Year* (1942), and when screenwriters Ring Lardner, Jr., and Michael Kanin won their Oscars for best screenplay they declined to accept Mankiewicz's congratulations.

Today Mankiewicz is slightly bitter about his few months of work with Fitzgerald. "I pissed on the American flag. I dared to rewrite Scott Fitzgerald's dialogue when Maggie Sullavan pulled me off into a corner of the soundstage and said 'You've got to do something about this dialogue for Christ's sake! I can't speak it!'"

Scott wrote Mankiewicz a letter he never mailed (January 29, 1938), "to say I'm disillusioned is putting it mildly. For nineteen years, with two years out for sickness, I've written best-selling entertainment, and my dialogue is supposedly right up at the top. But I learn from the script that you've suddenly decided that it isn't good dialogue and you can take a few hours off and do much better." Scott went on to say that he was convinced that Mankiewicz had a flop on his hands.

But Scott was wrong. Mankiewicz's moviemaking instincts

were completely right. Mankiewicz got his start doing title-writing at the old UFA studios in Berlin. Although a native American, he had, like Isherwood, lived part of the twenties in Germany. So he had two advantages over Scott. He had spent several years in the locale of the film and he had the most acutely sensitive feel for what plays on a movie screen of any man in Hollywood. And he would get furious when any "upstart," even one named Scott Fitzgerald, began lecturing him on a business he had matured in a good decade ago. "Why should a writer demand *any* control over his screen work unless he has written a first-rate script?"

"The last third of *Woman of the Year* absolutely died. It was a disaster. Mike and Ring were not available. John Lee Mahin and I got down and we rewrote the last act. The sequence when—trying to make breakfast for him. And this is what the audience loved. They loved to see—the image of Kate (Hepburn), the superior woman, shattered. So that the woman in the audience could nudge her husband and say, "You see, I can make your breakfast. She can't make his breakfast." And they loved that. . . . And naturally I didn't take any credit.

Another thing people don't stop to think about is that dialogue written for a novel and dialogue written for a stage play or a screenplay are two entirely different—one is ingested through the eye and is a cerebral thing, and the other comes in through the ear and has to have an emotional response."

The result of all this "heartache" for Scott was that he got an extended contract from Metro when the film was previewed. Louis B. Mayer shook his hand and offered his congratulations. He had arrived as a screenwriter with help, just as ninety percent of the other successful writers had done. And the taste was bitter.

Prior to the film's release, Mayer screened the film for a Nazi consulate officer, who voiced objections to the hooliganism of the Nazis and asked if they couldn't be changed to Communists. Mayer thought this a fine idea and told Mankiewicz to take care of it, but the latter objected violently, threatening to leave the studio. It remained an anti-Nazi film, perhaps the most poignant ever made.

Mayer's casual attitude—that the political background of such a film could be changed as simply as changing hats— should be remembered. He would get into serious trouble later with a film glorifying the Russian Communists as staunch fighters for freedom in *Song of Russia*, perhaps the most incredible of anomalies since Mayer was a far-right Republican.

6.

On August 18, 1937, Dorothy Parker and Alan Campbell sailed on the *Normandie* for France in the company of Lillian Hellman. Dorothy had bought herself an entire new outfit for the occasion—a dress in a dark pumpkin shade and a hat with a broad brim and high peaked crown that was a bit outrageous. She seemed to be anticipating Halloween by more than two months.

She and Alan met the few reporters who knew they were aboard but she almost impishly declined to drop any *bon mots* for publication. Most of the ship reporters were thronged about Miss Constance Bennett, as well as several dozen autograph seekers. Also aboard was Grover Whalen, who was helping to pull together a World's Fair in 1939, the last anyone would see for a very long time.

Lillian Hellman was not disposed to join the Campbells for a festive farewell to New York Harbor. Alan made her nervous with "his pretend-good-natured feminine gibes." I suspect that Alan's sexual ambiguity bothered her more than a little. There were few others close to Mrs. Parker who found Alan effeminate or his wit on the feminine-bitchy side. But Lillian Hellman liked her men as rugged as she was (and she was a rigorously self-contained little woman who could hold her own with the toughest of company and in the most primitive of circumstances). When this masculine quality was combined with a profound dignity as well (as in the person of Dashiell Hammett), that was sheer good fortune.

The Campbells introduced Lillian to the Gerald Murphys. Hemingway came up from Spain and, while it did not especially thrill Dorothy to see this "unnice person" who courted flattery, especially about his *machismo,* which Lillian found so lacking in Alan, everyone was impressed with his no-nonsense advocacy of a strong stand by the free world against Franco.

Lillian had gone into partnership with Hemingway early in the year together with John Dos Passos, the Dutch Communist film director Joris Ivens, and others, calling themselves Contemporary Historians, Inc. A documentary on the Spanish Civil War had been produced by Ivens, with Hemingway often helping to seek out provocative and impressive ruins or actions. This film, called *The Spanish Earth,* was frankly partisan, but gave audiences a horrifying preview of the devastation modern weapons would bring to the world as the war widened in scope. It was impossible to be neutral about the film and one can but wonder if some who saw it in the United States were not driven farther into isolationism by it rather than angered by the butchers who were spilling the blood.

Hemingway received credit as author of the "screenplay," which he richly deserved. It was Ivens's film, but Hemingway particularly had helped block it out and find locations, and had roamed the world seeking money for its production. It is the most complete and accurate account we have of that conflict or possibly of *any* war. It is four months of hell compressed into a film of less than two hours.

Lillian got bored with the Campbells' "fancy friends," got in touch with a childhood friend named Julia, and was soon deeply involved in smuggling money by way of the Moscow-Berlin Express to "buy out" Jews, political persons, and others being hunted down in Germany at the time. Like Hemingway, she needed to do something more than contribute money to anti-Nazi causes and, being the solid dramatist that she was, was excited by the danger in her role in such an enterprise.

Dorothy and Alan returned to Hollywood, but Lillian stayed on in Europe and after a series of dramatic movements around the Continent was "On the Road to Madrid, October 22, 1937."

> Luis and I had known each other since seven o'clock in the morning. At three in the afternoon, coming down the long hot stretch of the road to Aranjuez, we were tired of each other. We were tired, too, of the sun and the road and the warm, squashed grapes lying between us on the seat. I guess we had talked too much: of the war, of automobiles, of my passport, of the long purplish plus-fours that he had bought from a hotel clerk in Valencia. I had admired them, had not admired his driving.

After several narrow escapes through his bad driving, she is able to take the wheel, eventually coming across a mountain village with a high steeple. . . . "Where there is a church that high, there are people that poor," Luis tells her. "They will give us something."

They are given wine and some food in a room with a fireplace and a table. There is a blond lady, with bleached hair, who prepares the food and understands from Luis, although he has no faith in her understanding, that Lillian is a writer for the stage, so he "erases" that and tells them she is Charlie Chaplin's sister.

> "[The blond lady] touched my hair. 'You do something to it?'
> "'Yes, I said, sometimes I have it bleached. At the roots.'
> "'I know,' she said, 'that was my work in Madrid. What color is it that you were born with?'

"I laughed. 'I don't know. I've forgotten. . . .'" Then the blonde gives Lillian directions to a beauty parlor on the Calle de la Cruz. "'Tell her I did not have the baby. . . . Tell her she must put soap in bleach and do good job.'"

"Four or five days later I tried to find Maria's. Maybe I had misunderstood the blond lady or maybe the Calle de la Cruz had been bombed away."

In this journal, as in her future memoirs, Lillian Hellman was to display a distinctive humanity leavened by humor that must have been the side she showed Dorothy Parker. It allowed Lillian to remain herself wherever she happened to land, but the sight of real war did something to Mrs. Parker. Prior to her departure for California, she wrote several dispatches for *The New Masses,* in one of which she wrote: "The only group I have ever been affiliated with is that not particularly brave little band that hid its nakedness of heart and mind under the out-of-date garment of a sense of humor." Perhaps the least wise remark of her life since many of the volunteers streaming into Spain from all parts of the Free World, especially the Americans, retained their sanity by hanging onto their sense of humor. If there was anything in her makeup that could be called unique, just as humanness and take-me-as-I-am was Lillian Hellman's, it was her wit. But now she abjured its use as a frivolity.

It is interesting that both Dorothy Parker and Lillian Hellman would write of war from cafes. In her story on the Spanish Civil War, "Soldiers of the Republic," Mrs. Parker gives us a clear view of the clientele in one in Valencia:

> They were all farmers and farmers' sons from a district so poor that you try not to remember that there is that kind of poverty. Their village was next that one where the old men and the sick men and the women and children had gone, on a holiday, to the bullring, and the planes had come over and dropped bombs on the bullring, and the old men and the sick men and the women and the children were more than two hundred. . . .

These Spanish peasants were not too different from those shown at the opening of John Howard Lawson's script for Walter Wanger, *Blockade*,*

This film shows Fonda meeting with a foreign double agent (Madeleine Carroll, then under personal contract to Wanger and given first consideration on every Wanger property the way Norma Shearer had been a bit earlier at Metro). The girl's father turns out to be an agent for the opposite side (not positively identified as "Falangist" or "fascist," nor is Fonda's side ever called "loyalist" or "Republican)." There is a massive shelling of the city; the girl is trapped in the wreckage and Fonda saves her. The girl's father is killed in the scuffle and her own execution is stayed by Fonda's intervention.

Despite the caution Lawson had taken in the writing, Generalísimo Franco bristled when informed of the film's story. The Civil War was not yet over; American volunteers with the Popular Front of the Republican Army were still being killed in action. Walter Wanger, who as late as 1936 had been praising Mussolini for "cleaning up Italy," was now perturbed by possible sanctions or boycotting of his new film in those parts of Europe, and that included about half of it, now controlled or occupied by the Axis. He was getting bolder as world events educated him. In March 1937 he denounced the Hays Office Production Code as antiquated and outmoded. On May 15, 1938, he sent a wire to Secretary of State Cordell Hull giving him details of his censorship dispute as received from his London office. The London cable to Wanger reads:

---

*Although they were mostly Indian-looking Spanish from Central Casting—Chicanos, except for one soft-voiced, nasal, and idealistic peasant (Henry Fonda), who matures quickly into a loyalist leader. One accepted native Americans in roles such as this because the American film star had become universal both in appeal and in appearance. He could play anything and only the most snide moviephobe would object.

Understand here from authentic source Franco will bitterly resent any adverse criticism in your Spanish picture "Blockade." Fear retaliation in Spain and Italy on future films after war is over [*Franco's victory was apparently a foregone expectation.*] Suggest you contact Italian film envoy in New York and reassure him. Gossip here is that Hollywood is hotbed of political adventurers reporting on current film production. What is actual status of "Blockade"?

The effect of this upon the film was slight, although it may have been at that point that identification of all armies was removed through editing. Secretary Hull stood ready to make the proper moves if the film should be banned abroad.

Wanger told reporters that during production of the movie several strangers managed to get through the studio gates and headed for the sets (at General Service Studio), many of which showed the devastation of Spain's Civil War. It was a tough day for studio police since no sooner would one of the strangers be thrown out than another would appear. Wanger saw the serious significance of this.

This is simply another incident in a series, which proves that either Hollywood must assert itself or disappear as a producing center. Not only do we meekly take intimidation from abroad, but we jump obediently when almost anybody in this country says "Frog."

It's ridiculous and I for one don't intend to continue. I'm going to release this Spanish picture, as is, and if it's banned in Europe, I'll have to take my loss. It cost me $900,000 to make. To get my money back, I must have a general world release.

Fact is, this foreign censorship problem is getting so serious that all productions may be forced to make pictures cheaply and for home consumption alone. That might solve a lot of problems and it certainly would make for better pictures. At least we could do films for the

American market, which we never would dare release in the world exchanges.*

For example, we could do *The 40 Days of Musa Dagh* by Franz Werfel. It's one of the finest, most dramatic novels I ever read, but it concerns the siege by the Turkish army of a group of starving Armenians atop a mountain, so Europe wouldn't let us make it. One of the biggest studios here owns the rights to this book, but it dares not produce it.

Another case in point is Vincent Sheehan's *Personal History.*† This is one of the best of the war correspondents' books. . . . I bought it because I thought it would make a good picture, but wouldn't you know, I've had protests from every nation mentioned in Sheehan's book.

Equally as serious is the unofficial censorship in America, which Hollywood takes like a little lamb. Only last week, the candy bar people jumped on one company because Shirley Temple was urged in a picture to eat a decent meal, rather than a nutty-squashy bar, or whatever it was.

7.

In one of his letters, Fitzgerald indicates to a friend that when the Great War got America involved, as it surely would do, then he would like to be a war correspondent. It is a romantic fantasy, of course. His poor health would never have allowed it, even if death had not intervened.

During the final months of the Spanish Civil War, from February 1938, to April 1939, when the Republican govern-

---

*By 1940, Wanger's prediction was coming true as the Axis banned American-made movies, but by 1942, the armed services had become Hollywood's biggest customer and Hollywood movies were being shown from the South China Sea to Casablanca and all Free World points in between.

---

†Made later by Wanger himself as *History Is Made at Night*—but not much resembling Sheehan's book since after all Wanger was well-grounded in Hollywood story protocol—and released in September 1939, with nearly all controversy deleted from the script. It starred Jean Arthur and Charles Boyer.

ment finally capitulated to the crushing force of the Axis coalition and Generalísimo Franco entered Madrid, Scott remained in Hollywood working on seven films, three of them having capricious self-centered women as their heroines (*Infidelity*—never produced; *The Women*, from Clare Booth Luce's play; and *Marie Antoinette*). A fourth film was meant to be a distinguished project, *Madame Curie*, based upon her daughter's biography, but Scott's version was not filmed. Only one film, *Air Raid*, had anything to do with the war and that was a month's work after Scott had been dropped by Metro.

It was beginning to be Hemingway's time in the world and yet, in a curious way, his end, too. We went into the war with memories of *A Farewell to Arms* and *For Whom the Bell Tolls* vivid in our minds and we came out as disillusioned *with Hemingway* as with war itself. The enormity of Hitler's evil had cast a pall over heroes and heroics.

And so it didn't really matter that while Chamberlain was flying to Munich, Scott was attempting to pull together an original screenplay for producer Hunt Stromberg entitled *Infidelity*.

In a letter to Max Perkins dated March 4th, 1938, Scott tells him that he is "writing a new Crawford picture. . . . Though based on a magazine story, it is practically an original. I like the work and have a better producer than before—Hunt Stromberg, a sort of one-finger Thalberg, without Thalberg's scope, but with his intense power of work and his absorption in his job." (He was undervaluing Stromberg's contribution to Metro here.)

While Scott's obsession with good breeding and background becomes overriding in this script, allowing the scenarist to treat the only sympathetic character in the work *(Iris)* with what amounts to contempt, there are obvious advances over his earlier screen work here.

The opening of *Infidelity* is clean, no extraneous movement of the camera. Two gentlemen, in tails and in their cups, are

looking over the crowd at the Waldorf Roof with binoculars to
see if there is anything interesting happening. They focus on a
handsome couple near ringside. Within the frame of the
binoculars

> . . . Their lips move appropriately but we hear nothing.
> They have just been served a light supper by a waiter
> who now retires. Nicolas (the man) makes a polite
> reference to the floor show which she (Althea, the wife)
> answers with a courteous smile, such as one gives to a
> stranger. The smile fades rather quickly, however, and
> their eyes meet for a moment, gravely—but not as if they
> were strangers' eyes, for with a stranger, some conversa-
> tion would have to go with such a look.

The curious drunks are thoroughly mystified and give up their
game and we pick up Nicolas's and Althea's lukewarm love
story.

Althea was meant to be played by Joan Crawford, who had
graduated from playing shopgirls with tired feet to imper-
sonating women of the world with some breeding in their
bones. Fitzgerald carefully has put in Althea's mouth little
"human" phrases that had become familiar in Crawford films.
Despite her breeding, in the early, happier episode, she calls
Nicolas "my man" and when he is leaving her on board the
Conte di Savoia for a trip to Italy to visit her invalid mother,
she tells him, "This is the awfullest thing that ever happened.
I can't stand it." But then he adds a Scott-Zelda touch that
certainly would have raised Crawford's eyebrows when she
read it:

> She grabs his hand and begins to jump up and down. He
> jumps with her and, unsmiling, like two children, they
> jump in a circle, shouting:
>
> ALTHEA and NICOLAS: We—can't—stand—it.
> We—can't—stand—it.

Door opens and stewardess puts her head in.
STEWARDESS: Is anything wrong?
They stop jumping and look at her.
NICOLAS and ALTHEA *(together)*: Ye-e-s-s-s.
Everything.

An old girlfriend, apparently a former secretary from upstate who says she has appropriated her name "Iris" from Michael Arlen's *The Green Hat*, shows up at Nicolas's smart Wall Street office on the second weekend of Althea's absence. Nicolas takes her to their townhouse, dismisses the old couple for the weekend ("Go to Atlantic City or something"), hires an agency butler who mispronounces his name in front of Iris, and eventually, although it is typical of the period (and preferable at that) that we don't see the act or any part of it, they go to bed.

Althea comes home a week early, sees the girl still *déshabillée*. The girl runs off (no one seems to care where) and then Althea's mother, who is soon onto the difficulty, throws her daughter together with an old flame to shake her out of her lethargy. Nicolas, lost and yet always very cool and in control of his emotions, gives a party at their Long Island estate for his brother and a bevy of chorines.

The old beau summoned by Mama gets nowhere, but Althea does bump into a young doctor just canned from a hospital she supports because of his fooling around with one of the "probationary nurses." One can but wonder why she was put on probation, but the doctor is dark, and, as Fitzgerald notes, "We love him because he hasn't let his being fired get him down." Within minutes, Althea and the wickedly smiling despoiler of nurses are in a believable embrace in a little grove of trees that takes one back to the preserve in Lady Chatterley. On that note, Fitzgerald was told to abandon his script.

His hour or so of high-toned philandering had offended Joseph Breen, who was now running the office vacated by

Will Hays (who moved to an honorary position). All major scripts that might be considered indelicate were being screened in advance by the Breen Office.

But Scott believed in his script (with considerable encouragement from Stromberg, who could see that he had mastered the sort of crisp prose Crawford spoke so well). On May 10, 1938, he sent Stromberg a several-page "New Treatment and End of *Infidelity.*"

> I ask you to look at this situation for the end. . . .
>
> First, let me state it in terms of parallel, highly justified in this case because adultery is a form of thievery. It is regarded as such in the standard book on situations (Polti's 36 situations).
>
> A certain man, in cooperation with an unknown accomplice, has stolen from his partner. The partnership is dissolved.
>
> After ten years the partners meet. The thieving partner has been forgiven in a certain way but has not been reinstated in partnership nor does he expect it. He finds, though, that his unknown accomplice has returned and is engaged in once again trying to steal from his former partner.
>
> What shall we do? In many ways he understands and likes his former accomplice. On the other hand, he does not like to see his former partner cheated again. He is in a serious dilemma.
>
> He steps in to right the wrong. In the process of so doing, it is necessary that the old accomplice be ruined—and also that he shall be received back into partnership.
>
> A Catholic like Breen would, I think, accept the morale of this situation completely. The thieving partner is redeemed. The unreformed accomplice is punished.

Then Scott transfers this situation to *Infidelity* and we have Nicholas (he is using a new spelling for his hero's name) and Iris guilty before the law. It is Iris who was unpunished at the time, who is ruined by the slip. It is Iris who goes downhill and through weakness, when the same situation comes up again, acts in the weak way. She has met Althea (who dosn't know who she is) and is letting the restless Alex (Althea's old beau) pay court to her. This is understandable on Alex's part because he is a playboy and because Althea has never been able to love him completely.

For nearly five months, Scott worked on revisions. Sometimes, the story itself would stray. Throughout February and into the spring of 1938 he is sending off notes to producer Stromberg. In one of them, he writes, "The problem still remains to dig up some attractive man, perferably an unknown, for the young doctor who comes out of the darkness to play his significant part for a moment in Althea's life—a real problem in casting because it presents a novel twist."

In his new treatment, prepared in May, he speaks of Iris "going rotten." Poor Iris, without any breeding at all, must be the pivot upon which swings the approval or disapproval of the Breen Office. Since she has no background, except her lower middle-class situation upstate, she is expendable. Or so Scott sees it.

But the project was shelved. Perhaps Miss Crawford didn't care for the changes. (Scott feverishly got off a note substituting Myrna Loy in the lead.) Today, of course, it is a period piece, but points rather clearly to Scott's bias toward the rich and well-bred.

He was not jobless for long, but he rested for a few days at the sublet estate of Edward Everett Horton he and Sheilah had rented. It was known as "Belly Acres" and that upset him but it was less damp than the beachhouse and Sheilah had done what she could to make it comfortable for both of them. It was located in the San Fernando Valley, which is generally warmer than Hollywood. Scott had his own bedroom balcony, where he could pace, getting rid of some of the tension that had been building up at Metro.

In January 1939, David O. Selznick asked Fitzgerald to

have a look at the screenplay of *Gone with the Wind,* which had been in preparation many months. He was instructed not to add any dialogue that did not come from novelist Margaret Mitchell's typewriter, but he was asked to "touch it up." For the two or three weeks he was on the picture, he did what he could to make it more cinematic, removing phony dialogue and bringing in silences where they were more effective than speech. Much of his work remained in the shooting script but he was not given a credit line.

The role of hired hand in Hollywood galled him and the gin intake increased. After a drinking binge in town, he picked up two hobos on the road back to Encino, brought them to Belly Acres, gave them drinks, and then attempted to give them his wardrobe, which they were quite willing to take. Sheilah came home to find them with his Brooks Brothers suits draped on their arms and his shirts piled up. "Will you please put down those clothes and go?" she asked them.

"These are my friends," Fitzgerald protested, and there was a threatening note in his voice. "Old friends." Sheilah would have none of it and said she was going to call the police. The men left, but Scott clearly felt humiliated. Presently he was hurling the bowl of soup she gave him across the room and when she attempted to clean up the mess, he slapped her hard enough to make her ears ring. His secretary, a Miss Steffen, heard the commotion and attempted to intervene, but he put on an extended performance for Miss Steffen to demonstrate what "a fake" Sheilah was. "She's right out of the slums of London. She was raised in an orphanage. Her name's not Sheilah Graham, it's Lily Sheil. Lily Sheil!" And then he hopped around like a crazed Rumpelstilskin, chanting, "*Lily Sheil, Lily Sheil, Lily Sheil . . .*" When the secretary tried to stop this outrage, he kicked her hard in the shins.

The psychopathic strangeness continued. The next day he threatened to kill Sheilah. It was not the first time he had made such a threat to a woman, but *how serious is an alcoholic?*

Sheilah had to ponder. He already had slapped her. Would a knife or a gun be next? He kept a gun for security reasons in one of the bedroom drawers.

On that occasion, he could not find it, and while he searched Sheilah called the police and said she was being held against her will and gave the address. This desperate action broke the spell and he allowed her to leave the house. When she got back to her Hollywood pied-à-terre, he was on the phone asking if she got home safely. "That's a joke!" Sheilah cried and hung up in tears. It was not the end of her ordeal, however, for the threats continued, by phone and wire, until she had to consult a lawyer to determine how she might find some peace of mind.

Fitzgerald, abashed, flew East to take Zelda from the sanitarium on a trip to Cuba, something she had been wanting to do for a long time.

Calamity struck again. In Cuba, Fitzgerald attempted to break up a cockfight, feeling it was needlessly cruel. In the process, he was badly beaten up, so badly that upon his arrival back in New York, Frank Case, manager of the Algonquin Hotel where he went from the boat, promptly had him placed in Doctors' Hospital. Zelda went back to Asheville alone. His biographer Mizener writes that Fitzgerald was anxious that his agent, Harold Ober, not know that he had been injured in a fight with Cubans since Ober might think (and rightly!) that alcohol had again got him into difficulties. So he created a "bad recurrence of tuberculosis" with temperature charts and chest X-rays. Ober probably did not believe it, but he was forced to go along with the story since Fitzgerald circulated it among all of his friends on both coasts and even told it to his daughter.

His money was running out and, for once, Ober had failed to come through with a loan hoping that his author would get back to the writing desk and at least turn out a new story for *Esquire*. Scott dismissed Ober and began marketing his work directly, selling most of it to Arnold Gingrich, *Esquire's* publisher.

By the end of September 1939, he was able to get to his desk long enough to sort through his hundreds of notes for *The Last Tycoon* and begin putting them into rough form as a book. He wrote his daughter that the novel was "his first labor of love . . . since . . . *Infidelity* . . . I am alive again."

Six thousand words into the work, he attempted to get *Collier's* Magazine, which was interested in the idea, to come up with an advance on what they said they would pay for an acceptable final draft, suggested as being worth $30,000. This material was not enough for them to come to a judgment and he asked his editor, Max Perkins, at Scribner's, to rush it to the *Saturday Evening Post.* The *Post* declined, wanting more of the manuscript for a decision and he was back where he started—badly needing money.

Help again came from Hollywood, this time from producer Lester Cowan, who bought the screen rights to Fitzgerald's story "Babylon Revisited" for $800 and was willing to pay him an additional $5000 for writing a screen version of it. While he worked at this, Columbia Pictures, Cowan's home studio, doled out small sums to Fitzgerald for living expenses. There is little doubt, too, that Sheilah helped him out. They were taking up life together again at the Valley home in Encino and certainly his income could not have supported such an establishment alone. He worked very hard on his script, up to six hours a day, and then they would dine quietly together and sit on the balcony, listening to crickets or sometimes the hoofbeats of horses as westerns were being filmed nearby.

In April 1940, he gave up the house and Sheilah found him a small apartment in Hollywood and they shared her maid. By June, when the fall of France made him melancholy for a while, recalling the times there with Zelda and the Gerald Murphys, he heard from Cowan that his script of "Babylon," now entitled *Cosmopolitan,* was to be shelved for a while.

Surprisingly, he was not thrown back into an alcoholic retreat. Instead, he worked on his novel and sought other screen work.

In the fall of 1940, Scott wrote that he was "coming out of hibernation" to attend a cocktail party at Dorothy Parker's for the Countess Tolstoy.

Doubtless, the guest of honor's illustrious name inspired Scott's social excursion after his weeks of withdrawal. The Countess was married to the great Leo's grandson, Ilya Andreyevich Tolstoy, but she was better known to Mrs. Parker and to scores of others, including Scott, as Bea Ames, the former Mrs. Donald Ogden Stewart. Scott *had* to be a little curious about the elevation of the lively and flirtatious Bea Stewart to the heights of White Russian aristocracy.

Dorothy and Alan had found a small estate on North Camden Drive, but it was not yet ready for them and they were living meanwhile at the Chateau Marmont. In a spend-thrift moment, Dorothy had persuaded Alan to lease a house for six months on North Palm Drive so they would have a proper place in which to entertain. To the best of anyone's knowledge, that party for Bea Ames Tolstoy was the house's only use by the Campbells.

With the fall of France completing the Nazis' domination of continental Europe, the Russian invasion months away, and the aerial bombardment of England well under way, the Tolstoys were war refugees. Since Bea's former husband, Don Stewart, had been active in ultraliberal causes for at least five years, it made one wonder if her marriage to a White Russian was not a reaction against all those years of Don's militancy. But perhaps not; his causes were nearly all Dorothy Parker's and Bea considered Dorothy her dearest friend.

If Ilya Andreyevich failed to get his American citizenship, the Tolstoys would be going back to a war-racked Europe. So the party was on that footing, a kind of all-star replay of *Idiot's*

Delight, with Ruth Chatterton and her then husband George
Brent, Richard and Jessica Barthelmess, Fredric March and
his wife Florence Eldridge, and Kay Francis. Dorothy had
pushed her personal biases aside and even invited Laurence
Stallings, who was a Southerner of the most reactionary sort
and who looked upon the oncoming war as simply another
romantic interlude in American life. Indeed, he was Hollywood's expert on the camaraderie of "doughboys," a word
he appropriated and later wrote an entire book around.
Stallings had been sent with the American Expeditionary
Force to France in 1917 and had come home with a wooden
leg, which, after a couple of martinis, he was inclined to
display—the sacrifice of a "redblooded American." Bea was
amused by his pretensions and told everyone that he had
suffered multiple fractures of his leg through a fall from an
upper berth in a troop train.

Scott found this company a distraction from the battle to
complete *The Last Tycoon.* He and Bea Tolstoy spent a few
minutes alone in a corner where he regretted that her ex-
husband Don was not present so that he could discuss some of
his problems on the book. Scott respected Don Stewart's
critical judgment. Bea did not mind the allusion to her "ex."
She was too much in love with the Count to be sensitive about
the recent past. Scott probably noticed her joy, but said
nothing about it. He was sweet and gentle, and his pale
handsomeness gave him a kind of opalescence, a fevered
translucency. In Andrew Turnbull's phrase, it was "as if he
had been erased."

The only hint in any of Scott's writings that he was truly
apolitical and, had his death not intervened, would have
blossomed finally as a screenwriting professional in the wake
of the Blacklist, is contained in a letter to Max Perkins in June
of that year. He wonders how Ernest (Hemingway) feels
about things. "Is he angry or has he a philosophic attitude?
The Allies are thoroughly licked, that much is certain, and I

am sorry for a lot of people. As I write Scottie, many of her friends will probably die in the swamps of Bolivia." He followed the war on the radio and in the press and seemed to feel, like so many others, that the German *Blitzkrieg* was akin to a force of nature.

Except for a dinner at Nathanael West's house, that was the last time anyone in Hollywood saw Scott in public. His night sweats had begun again and he was on a round of sedatives, heart medication, and injections for an old tubercular lesion that had reopened. Writing in longhand, as he always did, his block on the *The Last Tycoon* dissolved suddenly and he wrote obsessively every day as long as his strength held out. He was propped up in bed and the pages encircled him; some of it was first draft, and he got a good deal of the entire story down on paper, but when it looked as though *Collier's* might take it for serialization, he began going over the early chapters carefully, editing himself as he went, writing final copy. By December he had completed six chapters of *The Last Tycoon;* remarkably vivid likenesses of Thalberg in Monroe Stahr and Sheilah in Kathleen; prose nearly as spare and perfect as that in *The Great Gatsby.* He got as far as Cecilia Brady finally being invited by Monroe Stahr to spend the night with him at Doug Fairbanks's ranch; it has taken her 128 pages to accomplish this but, in transit, we have seen the insularity, insensitivity (except for Stahr and Cecilia) and gross ambition of Hollywood magnified only slightly. Fitzgerald had set it "safely in a period of five years ago to obtain detachment, but now that Europe is tumbling about our ears this also seems to be for the best. It is an escape into a lavish, romantic past that perhaps will not come again into our time."

Christmas week, Scott felt well enough to accompany Sheilah to a preview, but as they got up to leave, he stumbled and nearly fell. He seemed improved the next day and even cheerful. He spoke with Sheilah about the possibility of his going abroad as a correspondent when "we're in it." "Ernest won't have that field to himself then." The old rivalry stirred and seemed to be an evidence of returning vitality. Then he sat in the living room with Sheilah and looked over a *Princeton Alumni Weekly*, writing in the margins of an article on football. He ate two chocolate bars (he was on sweets as a substitute for gin).

Sheilah saw "out of the corner of my eye—as you see something when you are not looking directly at it—I saw him suddenly start up out of his chair, clutch the mantelpiece and, without a sound, fall to the floor. . . . My mind whirled with thoughts. He's fainted. What do you do when someone faints? You pour brandy down his throat." But Sheilah Graham hesitated, fearful that it would start that terrible battle with the bottle all over again. Instead, she loosened his collar and thought that his faint had lasted an awfully long time. Frantic, she tried the brandy anyway, but she realized that was folly when it ran down his chin.

Scott was dead that 21st of December, 1940, at forty-four. Sheilah Graham, like Marion Davies eleven years later upon the death of her lover William Randolph Hearst, was pushed back in the wings and the family took over.

Fitzgerald was laid out in an undertaking establishment on Washington Avenue in one of Pierce Brothers' parlors (they were the best undertakers in Los Angeles, the western equivalent of Campbell's in New York), his casket resting in the "William Wordsworth Room," with a copy of Wordsworth's book of poems open at "Crossing the Bar" on a table near the entry. As one viewer, Frank Scully, noted "laid out to look like a cross between a floorwalker and a wax dummy in the window of a two-pants tailor. But in technicolor. Not a line showed in his face *(which was unremarkable since Scott only wrinkled about the hands).* His hair was parted slightly to one side. None of it was gray." Those wrinkled hands, according to Scully, gave him away and he wrote that "he actually had suffered and died an old man."

Dorothy Parker came to the funeral parlor, something she

was loath to do always, but she stood looking at his body for several minutes and then, repeating what "Owl-eyes" says of Gatsby, said in a low voice, "The poor son-of-a-bitch." She had remarked half a dozen times to Beatrice Ames Tolstoy, George Oppenheimer, and others what "a horse's ass" Fitzgerald had become, but at the end she was one of the few to come and mourn. She loved him for what he had been and for what he had become. She was devoted to original, creative minds and she was just as fanatic about the fallen and the lame. Fitzgerald had been both and doubtless she suspected that the same fate lay just ahead for herself.

The day after Scott Fitzgerald died, Nathanael West, on a hunting trip through the Imperial Valley with his wife Eileen, ran through a stop sign. He and his wife were killed. "Pep" West was thirty-seven and, like Fitzgerald, had expended a great deal of creative energy in setting down his impressions of Hollywood. But there were essential differences. West had written from the bottom, the substratum of the place, looking up from such a distance it was difficult to imagine the existence of those legendary creatures running the studio Scott was writing about. Where Scott was admiring, West was acid. And West had got *The Day of the Locust* published a year earlier so that it was read and admired by Scott and, very possibly, influenced him.

The most remarkable thing about Scott Fitzgerald's and Nathanael West's Hollywood years was the manner in which it fed their creative impulses. Neither was very successful as a screenwriter, although Scott's *Three Comrades* has become a film classic, yet both saw that the blandness imposed by "self-censorship" had rendered the movies unadult and puerile, or, in Scott's words, "nothing more nor less than an industry to manufacture children's wet goods," and the place itself "a dump . . . a hideous town, pointed up by the insulting gardens of its rich, full of the human spirit at a new low of debasement."

8.

Back in the spring of 1937, Aldous Huxley and his wife Maria had been among the first wave of eminent refugees from a Europe that was now literally plunged into darkness. They had crossed the continent leisurely, finding Charlottesville "moldy,"· Duke University exciting, where experiments in supranormal experiences, including extrasensory perception, had been launched under the supervision of Professor J. B. Rhine, and Dillard College, an all-black school in New Orleans, "rather depressing."

Huxley despite the critical and even popular success of such novels as *Antic Hay, Chrome Yellow,* and *Brave New World,* was nearly as concerned as any other professional writer about *Ends and Means.* That was the title of a new book which he was finishing during his first American summer spent on Frieda Lawrence's San Cristobal ranch in the mountains of New Mexico, a "very extraordinary place—more than 8,000 feet up in a clearing in the woods, which are composed of pine, aspen, and oak-scrub. Below in the plain . . . is the sage-brush desert . . . with the canyon of the Rio Grande running through the midst and blue mountains beyond." It was a dramatic landscape and it seemed clear that the West was much the most interesting part of America he'd discovered.

While at San Cristobal he received an inquiry from a Los Angeles bookseller, Jacob Zeitlin, about representing him with the studios. He sat down and wrote Zeitlin a careful reply, listing his "properties" that might be filmable. Among them was "The Gioconda Smile," which was filmed years afterward by Universal, and *Point Counter Point,* which, much later, became a fascinating television series, done in five parts. *Brave New World* had been sold to a studio earlier but there were no plans afoot for filming it.

In the fall, Huxley wrote a first-draft treatment of a film to be called *Success* but there were no takers. He also authorized

Zeitlin to make discreet inquiries at the studios to determine whether there might be screenwriting available to him.

That winter, still undecided about where they should settle, they went back East to the old John Jacob Astor estate near Rhinebeck, in the Hudson Valley in New York, and near his old friend, William Seabrook. They stayed at a "cottage" built in the French style, among old river families, whom he described as being bankrupt, dotty, or both.

His acute intelligence did not make him a literary specialist. He had a curiosity about everything around him, especially man. In a letter to Priestley from his snow-bound cottage on a book called *Sex and Culture* recently published, he observed that as man becomes more promiscuous his attention to other matters declines accordingly and "along with it the intensity of the emotions connected with other matters."

But *man* could be observed in more salubrious climes and America's frigid northeast began to get to the Huxleys. In early February they bought a car and set off for California. In the Arizona desert he fell ill with respiratory inflammation and spent nearly four weeks in a Tucson hospital. By mid-March, however, he and Maria were settled into a rented house on North Laurel Avenue in Hollywood, exactly one block south of where Scott Fitzgerald had been living at the time of his death.

In July, Huxley was put under contract by Metro after they had asked him to do a film on the life of Mme. Curie. Producer Sidney Franklin, who had the discussion with Huxley about it, said nothing about the possibility that his script might not be used. (Scott Fitzgerald was to take over Huxley's "too literary" adaptation in November and work three months on it. Neither Huxley's nor Fitzgerald's version was eventually filmed but an entirely different screenplay written by playwright Paul Osborn with Paul H. Rameau.)

"I shall enjoy doing the job," he wrote his brother Julian, ". . . and it also has the merit of being so enormously overpaid that I hope to be able to save enough in a few weeks to keep me a year without having to bother about anything else. Garbo will do Mme. Curie and there is to be an intelligent director, George Kukor (*Cukor*, who was to become one of Aldous's dearest friends)." But, of course, Garbo was not persuaded out of her retirement to play the role and it went to Greer Garson. Very early in the game, however, he was on to the changeableness that pervaded moviemaking. He expected that his treatment would go through twenty pairs of hands before reaching the cameras.

Garbo had become friendly with the Huxleys through Salka Viertel, who was the doyenne of the Santa Monica Canyon community where many refugees from Europe, including Thomas and Heinrich Mann, were finding comfortable accommodations. Through one or the other, they also met Anita Loos, and fell in love with her on sight.

9.

By Christmas, 1938, director William Wyler had Sam Goldwyn's production of Hecht and MacArthur's *Wuthering Heights* well into the shooting stage.

Goldwyn had sent a background unit to the wild moors of England late in the fall, but it was to be entirely shot in the studios despite its eventual feeling of great lonely spaces, dunes and desolation.

The earlier squabbles over who should play Cathy having been resolved with the firm announcement of Merle Oberon's casting, there was only some mild speculation about their giving the role of Heathcliffe to Olivier. Wyler was insistent but Goldwyn was unhappy about his "unusual face."

When finally the film opened at the Rivoli Theatre in New York, the most astounding thing about it was its freshness; its sense of being an original despite Emily Bronte's book.

No one since has approached the spareness or the harshness

of the dialogue the two collaborators drew out of Miss Bronte's northern England dialect. It so far surpassed anything either of them had done for the screen before, even their friends were stunned.

As Heathcliffe, Olivier was diabolical, possessed, everything Miss Bronte had imagined and more—he was somehow appealing, the way Karloff's monster was or *King Kong*, but with a face and body that women would find more exciting than Boyer or Cooper and, during those years of his triumphs in *Wuthering Heights* and *Rebecca*, Gable himself. When Heathcliffe returns to Cathy and Edgar's home to pay a social call (unwelcomed by Edgar) and says, "I'm neither a thief nor a stranger. I'm merely your neighbor," there was just enough menace in his tone to set the drama on its collision course irrevocably.

No novel within memory ever has had the excitement or cinematic improvements added to it that *Wuthering Heights* received from Ben Hecht and Charles MacArthur.

The New York Film Critics voted it the best film of the year—over *Gone with the Wind*. It won an Oscar for Gregg Toland for his brooding, misty cinematography and a nomination but not the Oscar as best picture.

Olivier, tight-lipped and as tightly coiled as a perfectly designed explosive, would virtually duplicate the malevolence of his Heathcliffe performance as Max de Winter—with certain refinements. It was to become the Olivier "type" until he broke the mold with *Pride and Prejudice* and *That Hamilton Woman*. Then, of course, with his successful film *Hamlet*, he was back again as "the old Olivier."

10.

In 1939, after a world tour with his friend and companion W. H. Auden lasting several years, Christopher Isherwood arrived in town.

The Berlin Stories (or *Goodbye to Berlin*), a book that was to
have a very long life and numerous incarnations, was about to
come out, but his royalty advance was long spent and he was
living in modest circumstances.

The hero of *The Berlin Stories* was Isherwood himself, only
slightly disguised, and Sally Bowles, his irrepressible neighbor, was a girl he knew in his Berlin *pension*. He is unable to
respond to her sexuality, which first upsets her since she is
attractive and is getting by largely on her appeal to men. Then
a very deep understanding and bond develops between them.
(The film version of *Cabaret*, based upon Sally and the young
man, is the most financially successful adaptation.)

Isherwood had lived in half a dozen or more places with
poet W. H. Auden for at least five years. But Auden had
wanted to try New York and Isherwood chose California.

In the early thirties, Berlin had become impossible for any
politically aware intellectual and, in Isherwood's words,
"Hitler's coming to power made me what one of my German
friends has described as an 'honorary refugee.'"

In Santa Monica he visited his friends the Viertels. Back in
London, he had worked on a screenplay for Bertolt Viertel to
direct. It was called *Little Friend*; it starred Nova Pilbeam and
it was a success even in New York (in 1934).

Isherwood also saw much of writer Gerald Heard and met
the Huxleys. He began to meet established Hollywood
legends—Anita Loos, Garbo, and Selznick. So his life was
pulled together once more as it had been for several years in
Berlin.

The Viertels made him one of the family (as they had done
with Garbo and others). Salka fascinated him. She formerly
had been a distinguished actress on the Berlin stage, although
she was actually Polish. (Salka always spoke with Garbo in
German.)

Isherwood originally had met Bertolt Viertel through the
original of Sally Bowles (Isherwood hadn't lost touch with

"Sally" as his narrator did in the story). She had been Bertolt's secretary for a time and, like Salka, she always believed in recommending her friends whenever she could push them ahead a bit.

Nobody at the British studio had heard of Isherwood at that time but Bertolt liked him and he liked his writing, which was very flattering and profitable at that moment.

In California, Salka got in touch with Gottfried Reinhardt, Max's son, who had become a producer at Metro and was putting into production Charlie Lederer's "spoof" of the Russians *Comrade X*, an ill-fated movie that would come out just after the Russian takeover of Finland, rile audiences to the point of booing and, in Long Beach, actually ripping up theater seats and hurling them at the screen.

Reinhardt got Isherwood employment as a contract writer for Metro. He was to do a number of what he called "patch jobs" on others' scripts, until he got a major screenplay of his own to do—*Rage in Heaven*, which was to be an Ingrid Bergman film and a considerable success, written in collaboration with Robert Thoeren.

Thoeren himself deserves a mention. He was a German-speaking actor who had been making a movie in France when he learned the Gestapo was hunting him. He fled the studio and bummed around the south of France until he encountered a famed operatic diva, who found his handsomeness compelling enough to prompt her to offer him a job—as her chauffeur (and bedmate). Thoeren rejected her offer unless she would sing an aria of his choice during the sex act. He and his songbird shuttled around that part of Europe that was free until the Nazis got too close again and he fled to America. The diva's soprano could be heard almost every night trilling over the transom of some of Europe's better-class hotels.

There are certain super celebrities of the twentieth century who hold such fascination for the average reader, books based

upon their lives would fill several good-sized libraries. The list
is not very long, but the number of biographies, profiles,
memoirs and "new looks" is prodigious:

Isadora Duncan, T. E. Lawrence, F. Scott Fitzgerald,
Gertrude Stein, Charles Chaplin, Garbo, Ernest Hemingway, Woodrow Wilson, Franklin and Eleanor Roosevelt,
Winston Churchill, Lenin, Hitler, Stalin, John Kennedy as a
martyred president, and William Randolph Hearst.

For a decade or more earlier in this century, there was a
vogue for chronicles based on the hyperactive Teddy Roosevelt and the blond and slumbrous Prince of Wales (later
Edward VIII and interest in him magnified a thousand fold
with a deluge of books on "the romance of the century," his
alliance with Wallis Warfield Simpson), just as there has been
a run of books about the Kennedy family in our own day.
Vogues such as these are, I fear, no more durable than was the
public's obsessional interest in Rudolph Valentino and Mayor
Jimmy Walker in the twenties. The difference between these
two groups of the famed is basically one of substance. How
real is their fame? Is it the result of a flamboyant life style or a
unique and valuable persona or the inflatus of press agentry?
Is it based on a fierce individualism that leaves the world a
little changed for their having lived or is it built, like the
proverbial house of cards, on a sheaf of press releases in one or
two of which may be tucked an evocative slogan ("The woman
in black appeared again yesterday at Valentino's tomb on the
anniversary of his death")?

William Randolph Hearst lived nearly ninety years, mostly
in America, and only his childhood was fairly unremarkable.
He was something of a sissy, preferring the company of his
mother to anyone else, and antique Greek vases and gold
ornaments turned out by Cellini to baseball mitts and sleds.
He especially liked elegantly furnished rooms filled with
flowers from his mother's flourishing rear garden at their San
Francisco town house.

If little Willie Hearst had not inherited his father's lust for power, he likely would have turned out queer. His upbringing provided the classic prerequisites for irremediable gayness—a mostly absent father (Senator George Hearst, who had made his fortune as a miner and was never much at home in his wife's period rooms); an indulgent, loving mother; no interest in sports or roughhouse play with his peers. But Willie very early developed a taste for off-caste young women. At first, they were waitresses, but he quickly graduated to showgirls.

At very nearly the same time, he discovered that he liked the out-of-doors—on his own very special terms. He profoundly loved his mother Phoebe's ranch down the coast in the mountainous, coastal region above San Luis Obispo. A secret dream of his was gathering his favorite showgirls and entertaining them with hot dogs and baked beans at a "cookout" on the ranch.

But young Hearst knew that he needed something more than an old California spread (even if it was over 300,000 acres) to attract showgirls or any other worldling to such a remote place.

At least a dozen Americans of great wealth have carried out the nesting instinct in a most peculiar way—by building home-museums: industrialist James Deering's *Vizcaya* in Florida, George W. Vanderbilt's *Biltmore* in North Carolina, Jay Gould's Gothic revival restoration of *Lyndhurst* in New York state, Cornelius Vanderbilt's *The Breakers* in Newport, and, not least, William Randolph Hearst's *La Casa Grande* in San Simeon, California, among others.

A man who wanted to be listened to, who wanted to alter the course of his country, if possible, had to find a voice. When Hearst's father gave him the San Francisco *Chronicle*, young Hearst had a powerful instrument at hand, and when his chain of newspapers was expanded across the nation, there was no denying it. Hearst was a feared and often strident voice in the land. He had much to do with creating the climate of agitation and jingoism that led us into the Spanish-

American war. He began to be noticed beyond our borders. He became, in fact, for good or ill, the most influential American leader outside the government for a minimum of two generations.

Physically, he was a huge bear of a man, well over six feet, with sloping shoulders, a long oval face with surprisingly small eyes that nevertheless could look "right through you" with their piercing blueness. And a voice that contradicted everything else; its near falsetto quality was politely over-looked by those newly met and occasionally imitated quite easily by his friends.

Add to all this a fascination with the movies and the money to make his own and you have a man of the sort Hollywood rarely attracts and seldom holds, a Howard Hughes in reverse. Hearst had begun shooting films long before he met Marion Davies, the Ziegfeld showgirl. His initial big star was the brunette Alma Rubens, who later died of drugs. But he and Marion soon were inseparable (except on those familial occasions when wife Millicent, another former showgirl, needed his presence at an important function), and the legend was begun. There would be few authors going up Hearst's mountain to *La Casa Grande* and seeing the "daddy bear" in residence with his piquant and droll blond pal who failed to write something about it. Aldous Huxley even used something close to Marion's real name in his first draft of "After Many a Summer Dies the Swan"—Dowlys, which is very close to Douras, but later changed the blond's name to Miss Maunciple. And certainly Huxley's old tycoon in his castle with his ageless carp and his struggle to prolong his life was based upon Hearst.

Herman Mankiewicz was bolder. He considered Hearst and his mistress in residence at the feudal mountain castle the perfect components for a screenplay that would have a great deal to say about the tyranny of unlimited power, its chief victim being the man who flaunted it.

But *Citizen Kane* very nearly was the ruin of Mankiewicz. After its release in 1941, his credits thinned down to just a trickle. From three or more scripts a year (he wrote six in 1930), he was down to half a dozen throughout the entire span of a decade (1941–1952). Failing health and too much booze do not explain it; they followed in its wake. He died in 1953.

The furies unleashed by the Hearst Corporation* against Herman Mankiewicz and Orson Welles's movie of *Citizen Kane* have no parallel in this history (except possibly the British boycott of Ben Hecht because of his outspoken condemnation of their mishandling of Israeli immigrants).

Mankiewicz had to scrounge around for work, despite his having won the Oscar (which Welles shared as "co-author").

And there were subtler forms of abuse. In 1946, five years after the film's release, Mankiewicz was driving home from a drink or two (according to his widow) at Romanoff's and he sideswiped a car driven by Mrs. Lee Gershwin. Mrs. Gershwin was taking her maid to the bus and the maid had minor injuries, but one of Hearst's lawyers strolling the grounds of Marion Davies's Lexington Road estate said he had witnessed the accident.

The morning Hearst daily had headlines about Herman Mankiewicz being involved in a traffic crash. There were bold and as yet unproved allegations about drunk driving. This precipitated a court action and weeks of appearances by the Mankiewiczes in court (Sara, his wife, went for moral support). There began to loom very large in their lives the spectre of living a life on probation with some unseen judge ready to pounce whenever Herman tripped, as everyone does occasionally.

The widow keeps Herman's Oscar at the center of her

---

*Clearly, Hearst knew what the Corporation was doing to keep *Kane* from a general release, but it was his executives who carried out the embargo, chief among them, son Bill, Jr.

mantelpiece, but for many years until his death at 56 it must have resembled Poe's raven. The film was fated to remain in limbo for more than a decade or until a new generation of film-goers discovered it. Its initial play-dates were all in special showings, some at theatres converted hastily from legitimate theatre houses (the Hearst Corporation had seen to it that no major distributor would release it through normal channels). Then, in the 1950s, colleges discovered the film and it would be shown in local art houses. It slowly acquired the reputation of being the most exciting American sound film ever made and remains so to this day. Largely overlooked in this belated praise is its creator, Herman Mankiewicz, a gifted writer whose career was eclipsed in his lifetime by his more powerful and effectual brother, Joe, and whose memory has been all but obscured by the fulsome praise lavished on Orson Welles, the man who made Mankiewicz's script a reality. (Ironically, Welles suffered from the same character flaws as Hearst but, not being subsidized by a fortune, could not indulge them.)

ABOVE: Anna Sten arrived in Hollywood in 1933 and had architect Richard Neutra build her this contemporary hilltop house, where she romped with her dog and had her thick Russian accent modified. *(Author's collection)* BELOW: She then appeared in Samuel Goldwyn's *Nana* with too-handsome Phillips Holmes, and, for reasons unknown to this day, the critics and public rejected her. In none of the reviews, however, was either her beauty or her acting talent dismissed. *(Culver Pictures)*

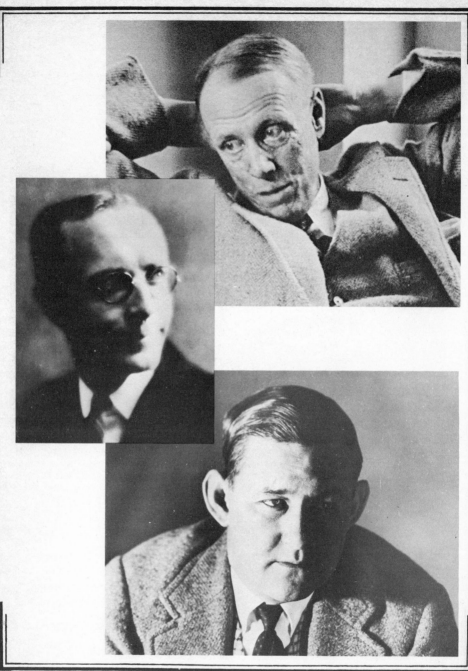

ABOVE: Sinclair Lewis, whose *Dodsworth* and *Arrowsmith* made memorable films. *It Can't Happen Here* allowed us a glimpse of the seamy underside of democracy—the flag-waving superpatriots who denounced him and his book. Because of pressure within and outside the film industry, the movie was never made. *(Photo by Alfred Eisenstadt)* CENTER: Donald Ogden Stewart, rich man's companion and jester in the twenties, radical in the thirties. *(Courtesy Academy of Motion Picture Arts and Sciences)* BELOW: John O'Hara was brought to Hollywood prematurely (on the strength of his first novel) and was allowed to sit out much of his first contract without an assignment. Paramount unwittingly subsidized his career as a major novelist before dropping him. The studios made this "mistake" numerous times. *(Culver Pictures)*

ABOVE: George Oppenheimer was called in so often to doctor ailing screenplays, someone, not very seriously, thought his first name was "And." Here (about 1935) he lolls with a friend's dog. *(Courtesy George Oppenheimer)* CENTER: Gay Beatrice Stewart sails into a friend's home in Beverly Hills. By 1938, she already was divorced from Donald Ogden Stewart and had become the Countess Tolstoy. *(Courtesy Beatrice Ames)* BELOW: The Alan Campbells at home with dog Jack. Dorothy Parker Campbell never was known to be without dog. The script Alan holds is *A Star Is Born;* the year, 1936. *(Courtesy Beatrice Ames)*

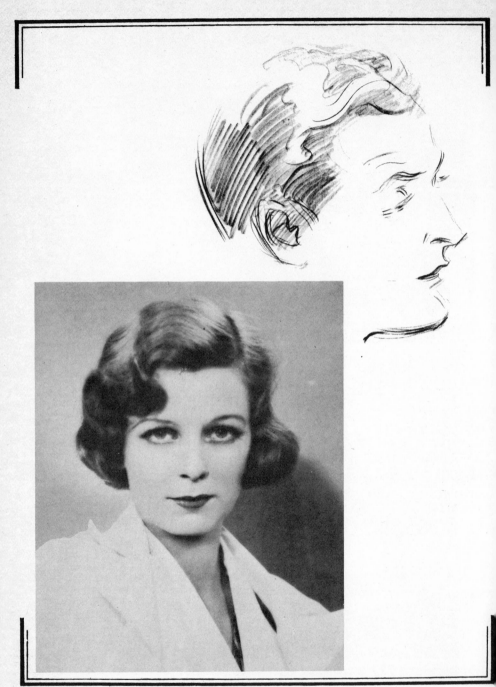

ABOVE: Scott Fitzgerald was one of the few literati who wanted to be remembered for his movies as well as his fiction. In this James Montgomery Flagg drawing we see him at the crest, as popular as almost any film star of the day, before he had experienced frustration and disappointment in the studios. *(Courtesy Princeton University)* BELOW: Star of Scott Fitzgerald's adaptation of *Three Comrades*, Margaret Sullavan lacked the driving ambition of Joan Crawford, but her vulnerability and talent made her life-abused, sick, or dying heroines more to be treasured than pitied. *(Author's collection)*

ABOVE: H. G. Wells visits a movie studio to watch *Anthony Adverse* being produced by Warner Brothers. Left to right: Mervyn Le Roy, the director, Fredric March as "Anthony," Wells, and studio head Jack L. Warner. March later became politically militant, putting his career on the line, but he was too important to be blacklisted. *(Author's collection)* BELOW: Janet Gaynor arrives at the premiere of *A Star Is Born* (1937) with her husband, the designer, Adrian. *(Author's collection)*

ABOVE: A scene from Hecht and MacArthur's *Wuthering Heights*, perhaps the finest adaptation of a classic ever made in America. From left, Geraldine Fitzgerald, Merle Oberon, and David Niven (1939). *(Author's collection)*   CENTER: The last photo taken of Sidney Howard before his tragic accidental death four months before the Atlanta premiere of *Gone with the Wind*, for which he was given sole screenplay credit. Although Howard did only a portion of the script, Selznick didn't want the credits on the film cluttered with the more than half-dozen writers hired to do scenes or rewrites. *(Culver Pictures)*   BELOW: A still from Daphne du Maurier's *Rebecca*, adapted by Robert E. Sherwood. Joan Fontaine is the ill-at-ease second Mrs. de Winter while Laurence Olivier is the haunted husband. 1940. *(Culver Pictures)*

ABOVE: Zanuck's biggest star Shirley Temple already knows at six how to handle a Broadway Runyon type such as Sorrowful Jones *(Adolphe Menjou)* in *Little Miss Marker* (1934). This one was made on loan-out at Paramount. *(Author's collection)* CENTER: World War I "Doughboy" specialist Laurence Stallings confers with director King Vidor on a Civil War romance, *So Red the Rose* (1930). *(Culver Pictures)* BELOW: Charlie Lederer comes to "work" in Astoria. MacArthur and Hecht at middle and right. Margo is obscured by a hand. 1935. *(Courtesy Charles Lederer)*

ABOVE: Norma Shearer in *A Free Soul* with Leslie Howard (1931). *(Author's collection)*   BELOW: In *Riptide*, her husband's remake of Michael Arlen's *The Green Hat*, Miss Shearer engages in some chic banter with Robert Montgomery (1934). *(Author's collection)*

ABOVE: Metro player Aileen Pringle, semiofficial greeter to the literati arriving from the East. *(Author's collection)* CENTER: "Her cheeks lit to a lovely flame, like the thrilling flush of children after their cold baths. ...Her fine forehead sloped gently up to where her hair...burst into love-locks and waves and curlicues of an ash blonde and gold...eyes...bright, clear, wet, and shining...." Thus Scott Fitzgerald described Rosemary Hoyt, film star, in *Tender Is the Night*. Lois Moran was his model. Circa 1928. *(Author's collection)* BELOW: Zelda Fitzgerald at sixteen. She slimmed down soon after this was taken and became the belle of Montgomery. *(Courtesy Harper & Row)*

Garbo's presence was perhaps the most magnetic of the lures attracting the world's writers to Hollywood, excepting money, of course. She "created" one screenwriter, bringing her friend Salka Viertel to her studio to help keep her scripts literate, although she preferred movie gossip magazines to Tolstoy or Proust. Circa 1928. *(Culver Pictures)*

ABOVE: Dietrich in focus, taken by Anton Bruehl, circa 1937. *(Courtesy* Cinema Arts) CENTER: No one entertained more troops during World War II than Marlene Dietrich. Here, Dietrich shows her famous legs at the request of the author during a visit to a military hospital in southern Italy, 1944. *(Author's collection)* BELOW: Fannie Brice was a pal to Ben Hecht, Charlie MacArthur, and myriad other creative members of the film colony. *(Photo by Dudley P. Lee)*

ABOVE: George Bernard Shaw, seen here, was one of a dozen world celebrities enchanted by Marion Davies. Another, Charlie Chaplin, follows discreetly behind them. William Randolph Hearst, the most significant of her champions, had the "bungalow" (visible in the background) built for her use at Metro-Goldwyn-Mayer. 1933. *(Author's collection)* BELOW: Kay Francis, who married story editor Kenneth MacKenna, and performed for Lubitsch, was the ideal lady of easy virtue who never showed it except in her mocking eyes. Here she gently works over Ronald Colman in *Cynara* (1933). *(Author's collection)*

ABOVE: Paulette Goddard married Chaplin, eventually became Erich Maria Remarque's wife and then widow, and always has known what she wanted and got it. *(Photo by Paramount; author's collection)* CENTER & BELOW: In modeling and movies since she was a toddler, Anne Shirley married writer-producer Adrian Scott and retired from films to become a homemaker. They divorced after political pressures destroyed Scott's livelihood; he became one of the "Hollywood Ten" and his chief occupation was defendant in a long series of court battles. She then wed screenwriter Charles Lederer, also in and around movies all his life. That marriage proved enduring. Circa 1938. *(Photo by Coburn for Columbia Pictures; courtesy Anne Lederer)*

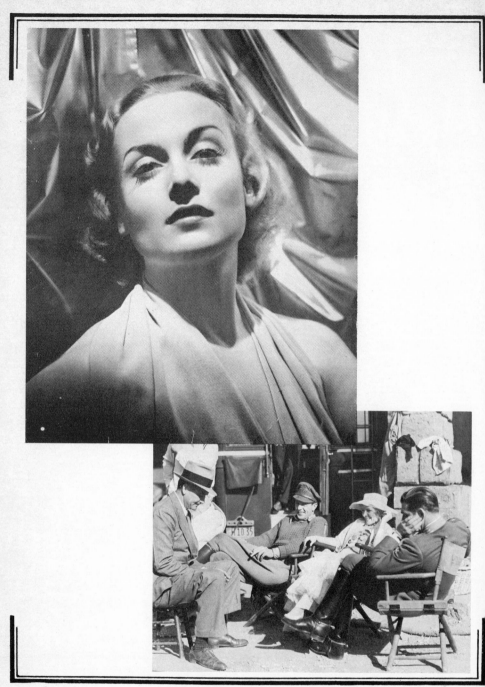

ABOVE: Carole Lombard was the first great beauty to become a "screwball comedienne." Irene Dunne and Katharine Hepburn followed. *(Photo by Hurrell; author's collection)* BELOW: Helen Hayes (Mrs. Charles MacArthur) relaxes on the set of *The White Sister* (1933) with director Victor Fleming, her former leading man *(A Farewell to Arms)*, Gary Cooper and a dozing co-star Clark Gable. That's Donald Ogden Stewart in the all-white outfit. *(Author's collection)*

PART FOUR

OF IDIOT'S
DELIGHT
AND
RELATED
MATTERS

1.

Robert E. Sherwood looked upon Hollywood as a playground. He seemed to believe it was morally corruptive. Charlie Lederer, a relatively free soul for whom the town was simply *home* and who argued that it was no more Bohemian than Omaha, described Sherwood as being about nine feet tall with a face even longer than he was. But in the West there was a determined sort of gaiety in him.

Howard Hughes, Goldwyn, and Thalberg all had hired Sherwood at one time or another. Probably the least of his labors was *Cock of the Air*, a 1932 collaboration with Charlie Lederer. Its flyweight plot defies analysis, but it was not even a trifling success.* The following year he wrote another flop musical comedy in *Roman Scandals* for Goldwyn and grasped the first opportunity to get back to "civilization" with the London production of his Periclean drama, *Acropolis*. This, too, was not a success and with his marriage to Mary Brandon foundering, it was Sherwood's bleakest period.

Sherwood had been an anglophile since his college days and had volunteered to serve with the Canadian Black Watch in World War One. Gassed in France, he was never to enjoy perfect health again. By the mid-thirties, he had a serious case of *tic douloureux*, a painful facial malady that kept him lying quiet on a sofa for hours at a time with cloths over his eyes. With the earnings of *Reunion in Vienna* (1931), he had bought a country estate in Surrey, England. It was there, at Great Enton, his affair with Madeline Connelly, wife of his closest friend Marc, began, which was to lead to a nasty divorce action, an agonizing custody battle for Sherwood's daughter Mary, and the loss of Connelly's friendship. The two men had

---

*His collaborator Charles Lederer called the film's scenario "an unlickable, absolutely frightful story, about a man whose girl was encased in a suit of armor and the man who was after her (the villain, I suppose) came up to her with a can opener, at which point she became hysterical with fear."

been extremely close. Their triangular situation resembled
that recounted in Truffaut's film *Jules et Jim*, with Connelly in
the role of the anxious-to-please Jules, but this parallel cannot
be pushed too far. Connelly saw Sherwood as the man with
the difficult wife, and he was right, but then someone made an
overture and his own marriage was on the rocks. And
Sherwood himself was no extroverted "Jim." He was often a
brooding man who more than most carried the burden of the
world on his shoulders. He agonized over the Free World's
disastrous waltz toward the holocaust as much as any world
leader and it was no surprise to his friends when he was called
in by Roosevelt soon after hostilities began in Europe as one of
his three principal speech writers. Sherwood held that semiofficial post until Roosevelt's death in 1945 and once told a
friend that there was no thrill in the theater comparable to
hearing one's lines delivered by the President. But that was all
much later.

Sherwood took his second wife, Madeline, to Great Enton
in a bid to pull their lives together. His return to England
coincided neatly with Alexander Korda's first major effort to
make British films that would be worthy of world attention.
Under Korda's aegis, Sherwood wrote *The Scarlet Pimpernel*
(1935), an adventure film set during the French Revolution;
The Ghost Goes West (1936), a delightful piece of whimsey
about a handsome ghost (Robert Donat) haunting a castle
bought by a Hearst-like American tycoon (Eugene Pallette) to
be reassembled in America; and new scenes and dialogue for
Rembrandt (1936). If Sherwood had not been a keen analyst of
film and its development (going back to his years as a critic for
the old *Life* Magazine), he might have believed for a time that
England was cornering the market in good movies and that he
had a hand in a number of them.

Sherwood's English idyl was not to last. He had gone back
to New York in 1936 for the productions of his *Idiot's Delight*
and his version of Jacques Deval's *Tovarish*. In 1938, he was

again in America for the production of *Abe Lincoln in Illinois,* which was to win him the Pulitzer Prize. That same year, he had been summoned once more to Hollywood for the movie of *Idiot's Delight.* The round of parties began again, this time a welcome respite from his deep concern over the war in Europe. In Hollywood, unless you had a political commitment (generally radical), it was not considered good form to wax serious over the coffee and cigars. An interesting sidelight was that the men always dispersed to the library or billiard room after dinner and the women to the parlor. It was a strange custom to find in the movie colony, but it had antecedents in the days of the pioneer West when an identical separation of the sexes occurred on such occasions. In the words of Sherwood's biographer John Mason Brown:

> . . . he dined with such friends as Polly and Sidney Howard, the Irving Berlins, the Goldwyns, Clarence Brown, and George Oppenheimer. One very pleasant evening stood out for him because it outlasted its pleasures. It was the night he spent playing "the Game" at Dorothy Parker's *(Mrs. Parker adored word games of every sort as she excelled at them)* and Alan Campbell's with Dashiell Hammett, King Vidor, Sam Hoffenstein, James Hilton, and F. Scott Fitzgerald. He was delighted to see Fitzgerald again, a "ghost" unencountered since he was writing *The Beautiful and the Damned.* Saddened, too. "A marvelous writer, a first-rate mind, and a tortured spirit. If he could only get back into his stride."

Like so many evenings that preceded and followed it, there was far too much liquor available and consumed. There appear to be only two roads to follow in Hollywood—the one that leads to cirrhosis and an early grave or the way to the cross. Sherwood was never religiously inclined, and the following morning he was a nursing "a gruesome hangover," despite a commitment to go out to the beach to read his script of *Idiot's Delight* to the stars of the upcoming film—Norma

Shearer as "Irene" and Clark Gable as "Harry Van." Despite his temporary physical incapacity, Sherwood was relieved to note upon reading the last page that the movie script had gained something by the omission of the stronger antiwar sentiments of the play. It was less of a tract and more of a moving drama with universal appeal.

Sherwood admired Gable's easy masculinity as well as Miss Shearer's unequivocal femininity. It was not always so easy to know where you stood. Sherwood's own nearly unconscious *machismo* was fairly well established in the film colony, but there were times when the cutting edge of his prejudices seemed a bit too carefully honed. At one of Sam Goldwyn's weighty English dinners, a group of men were sitting in the study talking about a play of Sherwood's which was concerned with Hannibal's turning away from the gates of Rome (*The Road to Rome*). Sherwood suddenly asked, "Whatever became of that lousy little fairy that acted as a sort of pimp for Jane Cowl?" There was a dead silence. Then a short man unknown to most of the men in the room stood up and said with a tinge of belligerency, "I was the lousy little pervert who went around with Miss Cowl at that time." Without a second's delay, Sherwood asked, "Well, whatever became of you?"

Sexual identity always has been a problem for men involved in show business, since bisexuality is so common. And there is something androgynous about any serious writer. He has to see the world through the eyes of both sexes. This can lead an author into a kind of post-Neanderthal stance, coloring his public and private behavior (Norman Mailer) or into open admission of sexual divergence that is the basis and strength of most of his published work (Christopher Isherwood). Or a writer's sexual identity can be an open secret and yet carefully screened out of his writing for the most part (E. M. Forster, W. Somerset Maugham, and one American comic dramatist of immense stature—now deceased—who had two ambitions beyond sustaining his successful theatrical career: One was to write a serious play that would be well-received, which he completed and saw fail, and the other was to cure himself of his penchant for attractive young men with nice smiles, the last being the most expensive to subsidize since it entailed paying enormous bills from an ever-changing eminent psychiatrist).

In New York, all variations of sexuality have been assimilated and tolerated in theatrical circles. Hollywood appeared to have been traumatized early by the clear-cut he-man and feminine roles played out upon the screen of a day gone by. There was the additional complication of the sexually demanding film queen, whose desires were not satisfied by a small stable of studs. She had to be teased and toadied to by an entire platoon of employees, from the lowest drugstore "go-for" to her producer. Unless she had the sympathetic insight of a Marilyn Monroe (who had half a dozen gay friends of both sexes), she was apt to be virulently antihomosexual, spouting innumerable "fag" jokes and, through the bias of her gutter speech, keeping away the sexual weaklings, or as she viewed them, the misfits. She would make rare exceptions in order to get a first-rate hairdresser or designer, but she usually couldn't avoid being patronizing to them. And then when she reached her sixties, declined to take character roles, and retired to the East (they usually made themselves inaccessible as "landmarks"), they surrounded themselves with sycophantic and often beautiful young men who act as a sort of living mirror, reflecting back to the ex-goddess only what she wants to believe of herself. It would be unkind to call her a hypocrite; she has become a lost soul. Since gayness is rapidly becoming little more than a personal oddity, no more remarkable than left-handedness, where this will leave the film queens of the future one can but sadly wonder.

Meanwhile, Hollywood itself is several years behind the times, and even today gay writers, directors, actors, and producers are very much where they were forty years ago—

forced to form a subgroup within the film colony itself with individuals emerging from time to time for one-shot social occasions among the man-woman social groups that dominate.

Sherwood had adapted his own successful "twilight comedy" for Hunt Stromberg at Metro. Since America was nominally neutral, all references to Axis leaders had been removed from his original text, but its theme—the idiocy of war as a solution to anything—remained. It was a stylish film and its "universality" was a part of its chic appeal. The distant bombers came from nowhere and retreated to nowhere. There is a great difference between a slit trench and a cocktail lounge.

But Clark Gable hoofed badly, as he was supposed to do with "les Blondes" in his second-rate nightclub routine, and he was engagingly "Harry Van" with all his foolish bravado. Norma Shearer, in a blond wig and a slinky gown, made an impressive comeback from her monumental failure in *Marie Antoinette* (on which Sherwood had collaborated for no credit). Her phony Russian accent seemed almost right and there was some evidence that she should have attempted comedy years earlier (she had done Sherwood's *Reunion in Vienna* in 1931 for the screen without any notable success). She probably saw in the role of Irene something she could identify with—a pieced-together dignity, a rather charming pretension to good breeding.

As in the play, we see these two second-raters reveal themselves totally as fear of doomsday approaches. Their pasts are not very attractive, which is much of the point, but they are observed with an honesty that was rare in films.

Sherwood, probably because the Code people insisted that the original defiant chorus of "Onward Christian Soldiers" was irreverent, ended his movie with Gable banging out a jazz tune on the piano as Norma "trucks" (a form of jitterbugging) while the bombs fall and the walls collapse.

Sherwood would be involved with war and political matters for more than four years, but first David O. Selznick had asked him to step in and rewrite the screen version of Daphne du Maurier's incredibly successful *Rebecca*.

Selznick's acquisition of the second-most-popular "film" book in the world in the late thirties (after his coup with *Gone with the Wind*), had a minor guessing game going on among writers when it was rumored in Hollywood that Selznick had turned down director Alfred Hitchcock's personally super-vised version written by the Hitchcock specialist Joan Har-rison with Philip MacDonald. Sidney Howard and Sam Behrman "were not available." Hitchcock's insistence upon its being adapted by an English author came to naught: both Clemence Dane and Hugh Walpole were unwilling to come to America; even Miss du Maurier was asked, but declined.

Sherwood's fee for the film was high but he was quite satisfactory to Hitchcock. Sherwood's single concern for several days was that Selznick might cast his Scarlett O'Hara (Vivien Leigh) as the second wife, apparently to satisfy Laurence Olivier, who already had been cast as Max de Winter.

Sherwood got into a three-way "casting direction" position. Selznick first ruled out Olivia de Havilland, who wanted the part, because she had contractual commitments with both Goldwyn and Warner Brothers. This left them with three candidates: Margaret Sullavan, Joan Fontaine (Miss de Havil-land's sister), and Anne Baxter.

Selznick's personal choice was Miss Fontaine. He was to say:

> I had pretty well decided to forget her for the role since I couldn't get anybody on the studio staff, excepting only Hal Kern [*Selznick's head film editor*], or anybody in the New York office, to agree with me that she was physical-ly an ideal choice for the role and that from a perform-ance standpoint she obviously (or, at least, so *I* thought)

was the only one who seemed to know completely what
the part was all about.

Then Hitchcock swung around to her after listening to
Sherwood on what the role required. Sherwood's and Selz-
nick's view prevailed and she went on to win every conceiv-
able award for her performance, including an Academy
Award nomination. *Rebecca* won the Oscar as best picture.
Selznick's second in a row. And Olivier won an Academy
Award nomination for his role.

Oddly, although Sherwood *had written* the best movie of the
year, his screenplay lost the Oscar to Donald Ogden Stewart's
adaptation of *The Philadelphia Story*, a much easier task. (And
that was the year, too, when Preston Sturges proved himself a
sound gambler in persuading Paramount to hire him to direct
his own screenplay of *The Great McGinty* and winning the
Oscar for the best screen original.) Sherwood would win at
the war's end, however, for *The Best Years of Our Lives.*

The Sherwoods never would return to Hollywood on
anything but a transient basis. He was, he assured everyone,
happy to be gone from it.

2.

The movie business had never been better. With the swastika
flapping like a huge carrion bird over three-quarters of Europe
and huge parts of Africa, the Free World needed more
distraction than *Amos 'n' Andy* could give them. Radio was on
the wane; it was mainly the bearer of bad news or the
delightful riffs of Jimmy Dorsey or Benny Goodman.

Those over thirty, who preferred Guy Lombardo, went to
the movies for their Saturday night diversion and the choices
were becoming more varied.

Charlie Lederer was sharing in this bonanza with three
major films in release in 1940. The first, *His Girl Friday*, was

written in eleven weeks of semi-lounging around director Howard Hawks's desert home at Palm Springs, and came near the end of almost a decade of zany humor. The genre began in 1930 with King Vidor's *Not So Dumb*, the film version of Marc Connelly's *Dulcy* starring Marion Davies, and would taper off as Hollywood felt compelled by world events to be less "madcap." Within two years, the species would be gone altogether, although comedy—mainly in the satirical vein of Preston Sturges—would attain its highest point of audience acceptance during the war years. The essential ingredients were a comedienne of more than passing attractiveness, frantic action and plotting, such convulsive laughter that the audience often missed a line of equally hilarious repartee.

The shooting script (the final version of the screenplay that is used for the actual production) evolved through a process that had become a ritual in Hollywood. First there was the story conference, attended by the producer, director, and the screenwriter. Artistic requirements usually gave way before budgetary ones, although many emendations and outright cuts made in the name of costs have resulted in better movies.

Such was the case in Charlie Lederer's retooling of Hecht and MacArthur's *The Front Page*. Not that the original work was improved upon, although there are numerous film buffs who insist that it was. But so extensive was Lederer's reworking, the screenplay must be considered an original with major credit for its success and durability being shared by Lederer with director Howard Hawks, whose notion it was to make reporter Hildy Johnson a girl instead of a man. Hawks was an excellent critic but no collaborator in the sense Lubitsch was. Hawks would say, "Not bad," or he would tell the writer why he didn't like a particular scene and it would be rewritten. This process might be repeated half a dozen times—a trial and error sort of construction.

In an early draft of the opening scene of the screenplay,

Lederer had "Hildegarde" Johnson (Rosalind Russell) in a courtroom in the process of getting a divorce from her newspaper boss, Walter Burns. In the smooth, razor-sharp opening scene as produced, Hildy breezes into the city room of her former employer, fresh from the Reno divorce courts and Bermuda. She can't wait to tell Burns that she already has bagged a second trophy in the battle of the sexes and that he is cooling his heels in the newspaper's outer office.

Hildy and Burns immediately go at each other almost as of old, but divorce has sheathed the knives. Part of the "cruelty" she complained of in an earlier draft of the screenplay was Burns's sending her down many fathoms into the ocean to get a story on a sunken submarine (and on her honeymoon). In the film itself, she trots out an old complaint about being sent down several hundred feet into a coal mine, to which Burns immediately replies, "But we scooped the country on that one!"

Hildy has her future hopes pinned on a quiet future in Albany with an insurance salesman (Ralph Bellamy) and his widowed mother. She properly has doubts about Mama, but she is willing to take the risk. She tries to persuade herself that she is relieved, that she can't wait to get on that train to Albany with Bruce and his mother. But she protests too much: "I know all about reporters—a lot of damned buttin-skies with only nickels in their pockets."

Tossed out of draft two or three was a vignette with Bruce on the phone and Burns overhearing him recite: "Hildy, Hildy, I love Hildy. If that's a crime, then I am guildy." Put in at the last moment was a marvelous touch as Burns goes out to meet "this paragon" waiting in the outer office and immediately goes up to an eighty-year-old man and takes his hand, congratulating him to the venerable gentleman's perplexity. Then Burns insists on taking Hildy and Bruce to a nearby reporter's hangout for a disastrous lunch. It is Burns's intention to see that Hildy is trapped into returning to the paper to do a story on a murderer about to be hanged for shooting a policeman. But Hildy strikes a bargain with him. She will delay her departure for Albany two hours and do an interview with the condemned man, Earl Williams (John Qualen), if Burns will buy a $25,000 life insurance policy from Bruce. She is so familiar with Burns's deviousness she will not proceed until a doctor has examined her ex-husband and boss and Burns has given Bruce a certified check for $2,500 as a down payment on the policy.

In Hildy's interview with Williams she is all compassion and Williams, nearly inured to hard-boiled interviews from an endless parade of newspapermen, responds. Hildy is the first sensitive human being he has met since he was taken in for the night by a prostitute, Molly, on her usual beat.

Hildy learns very quickly that Williams is a maverick Socialist who once heard a soapbox orator harangue a crowd about the need of "production for use." Its banality is lost on Williams; to him, it is a revelation. Then, asks Hildy, "When you were using that gun to shoot a cop, guns are made for shooting and that was your philosophy at work—*production for use.*" "Yes!" he agrees at once. Finally, someone understands his muddled mind and he is ecstatic.

Burns and Hildy also discover that one last psychiatrist, a Dr. Egelhoffer, is to examine Williams that very afternoon to determine whether the man is sane or not. They also believe that the mayor, who is running for reelection, wants Williams hanged on schedule to give the public a compelling example of his campaign propaganda on the need for law and order.

Lederer first wrote the actual examination scene in which Egelhoffer decides that Williams should reenact the crime and borrows Sheriff Hartman's gun. It is interestingly written and might have been used, if a more spectacular effect had not been decided upon by Hawks. The early version follows:

EGELHOFFER: We shall now reenact the crime . . .
You are Earl . . .
WILLIAMS. And I am the policeman.

He hands the gun to Williams and then backs up
a few paces.

EGELHOFFER: So—I say to you, "Earl Williams, you
are under arrest!"—and you point your gun at me.

. . . Williams does so.

EGELHOFFER: Then what did you do?

Williams hesitates for a moment and then pulls
the trigger.[Sheriff] Hartman promptly dives under
the desk.

(CLOSE SHOT   EGELHOFFER)

*(His hands clasped over his abdomen, he stares at
Williams searchingly.)*

EGELHOFFER: Yes, Yes—dementia praecox.

He topples to the floor.

As the earlier version continues, Williams escapes and the
hysterical pitch of the film picks up at this midway point and
rushes without letup to its frantic conclusion. In the finally
produced film, Hildy and the other reporters are gathered
waiting in the press room of the Criminal Courts Building.
Somewhere below them, Williams is having his psychiatric
examination. Then a single shot is heard, shouts, and, as the
reporters rush to the windows to look out, we see, from their
angle, dozens of policemen with shotguns and machine guns
scurrying about shooting wildly—Williams has broken out.

Bruce has been kept out of the way by Burns, who has
managed to have him arrested on a variety of trumped-up
charges, including "mashing," a thirties' type of sexual pass a
man gives a woman not his acquaintance, usually on the street
or in a moviehouse (and in Bruce's case brought by a blond
demi-mondaine fainting in front of him—in the hire of Walter
Burns), and finally passing counterfeit money (given him by
Burns, of course).

Bruce's white-haired old mother, impatient over missing
one train after another, blunders into the wild press room of
the Criminal Courts Building as the search is on for Williams.

There she discovers that Hildy has the fugitive concealed in a roll-top desk belonging to a rival newspaper. Burns has the old lady carried out bodily and taken to a safe place, from which she eventually escapes to press kidnapping charges on him.

Hildy and Burns nearly succeed in turning over their prize fugitive to the governor (instead of to the corrupt local mayor) when the mayor and Sheriff Hartman arrest them for aiding an escaped criminal and kidnapping. As they stand in handcuffs, a bumbling messenger (Billy Gilbert) bearing a reprieve for Williams manages to get into the room and declares that he has talked the matter over with his wife and that he cannot accept the mayor's bribe of money and a job in order to delay the delivery of the reprieve until after the hanging.

Justice, for a refreshing change, triumphs, and the mayor attempts to blame the "whole misunderstanding" on Sheriff Hartman.

Bruce and his disheveled mother meanwhile have managed to get to the train station, where he phones Hildy to say that he is taking the nine o'clock train whether she comes or not. Burns pretends indifference and urges her to get on her way, but she drags her feet, hurt by his attitude and emotionally unable to walk out the door and into a new life. (In an early draft, Hildy and Bruce go off to their train after Burns insists on giving her his inscribed watch. "Thanks, Walter," she tells him, "I'm going to be awfully proud of this." They depart for Albany and Burns instructs his aide Duffy to "send a wire to the Chief of Police at Albany and tell him to meet that train and arrest Hildy Johnson and bring her back here. . . . The little crook stole my watch.")

But motion picture protocol (Bellamy *never* won the girl in his comedies) and logic won the day in reworking the final scene and Hildy chooses to let the Albany train go without her. Burns even suggests that they get remarried "in Niagara Falls," since there's a story along the way he would like to pick up.

Charlie Lederer got into screenwriting because he played

tennis. In those days, there was not the rash of tennis courts and players we have today. A fourth at tennis was always welcome. Charlie was rather good at it, playing mostly with actor Matt Moore's crowd, which generally included Charlie Chaplin, Cedric Gibbons (the art director), and sometimes movie director Lewis Milestone, known as "Milly." Milestone was trying to lose some weight.

"Milly" thought Charlie was very bright. The young Davies "scion" would make an occasional jape that would get a laugh. He *was* a bright and superior conversationalist. Milly asked him if he would care to write some pictures. "You'll start at $75 a week," he said. Charlie was to do the screen version of *The Front Page,* not so surprisingly. It had been bought for the movies by Howard Hughes and Milestone was to direct.

Milestone's faith in Charlie was not misplaced. The film had a considerable success (although it failed to become a "classic" in the manner of Lederer's much later transsexual version) and it led to another assignment.

We have observed already Selznick's acute sensitivity to the expression on an employee's face. The incident over Charlie's smirking had been forgiven but all that humility on Charlie's part was most unnatural. He suffered in comparative silence until one particular Mayfair night (*Mayfairs* were social gatherings at the Ambassador Hotel or some equally elegant spot where writers, producers, and directors and their wives mingled on a very democratic level. They were infrequent but they brought everyone together at least once or twice during the year). David came in wearing his white tie and tails and looking precisely like Teddy Roosevelt laid out in state.

Charlie Lederer was in Irving Thalberg's party that night and Thalberg and Selznick didn't see eye to eye. Charlie got drunk and shortly was moving up to the Selznick table. He said, "Hey, David how are you? Oh! Those are the wrong buttons, David." Selznick looked at his shirt studs in perplexity and glowered. MacArthur overheard it and it set him to chuckling. Then he came up and said, "Oh, how are things, David? Oh, wrong buttons, David!" It was like Penrod's experiences at the party. They got everyone to go by Selznick's table and say, "Wrong buttons, David." Selznick turned green with rage finally and electricity came out of his hair. The angrier he got, the more the two Charlies laughed.

Falling back on the old humility, Lederer and MacArthur sent Selznick a wire saying, "Please forgive us for what we said about your clothes at the Mayfair Night. We were drunk, and, besides, who are we to tell David Selznick anything about buttons or for that matter, buttonholes? (Signed) MacArthur and Lederer." Monday morning when Charlie Lederer walked onto the RKO lot he was greeted by two gentlemen bouncers who assisted him out. His belongings were piled up for him to take away. It was a very funny feud and while Selznick may have believed that he had bounced a problem out of his life, Charlie did not agree. That night he sat down and in about five minutes turned out the lyrics to a song, which were destined to survive as one of the crustier laments of Hollywood:

> Someone had to marry Irene Mayer,
> Someone had to have the guts to lay her.
> Someone had to win her
> Without throwing up his dinner,
> That's why David was born.

The song got to New York within twenty-four hours, probably by telephone. Charlie heaped additional scorn upon his ex-boss by giving him a nickname, which stuck until his death. He called him "Chinchilla Head" because of that unruly, curly hair of his.

By 1933, Charlie Lederer was settled in on the Metro lot without the help of his aunt, Marion Davies, who was the social queen bee of the studio and could tell Louis B. Mayer to

do practically anything and he would do it. Whether what
Mayer feared was losing her as a star (and she *was* a
comedienne of extraordinary gifts) or incurring the wrath of
her patron, William Randolph Hearst, no one seemed to know
with any certainty.

Being more reckless by nature than most of his peers,
Charlie joined Laurence Stallings and others in cracking wise
about Selznick's cast for his upcoming *Dinner at Eight.* "I
understand," he said, "that if he marries the other Mayer
sister, they're going to give him Garbo, too." He didn't realize
that a door had opened behind him during this rather jejune
sally. Selznick stood there and bellowed, "Another crack out
of you and you can go get your check." Irrepressible jokester
that he was, Charlie said, "What good would that do? The
banks are closed." Of course, he was out again. But that's
when he got a job with Hecht and MacArthur, who had that
deal with Walter Wanger back in Astoria, Long Island.

Sometimes Charlie's need for personal revenge wrought
extensive physical damage. When he was young he was
working with director Leo McCarey doing a picture called
Polly of the Circus with his aunt Marion. He had become very
fond of Leo. After three weeks' work on the film, McCarey
was called in and fired by Paul Bern, the producer, and was
given no reason. Leo had hoped to do more significant pictures
than the Laurel and Hardy comedies which he had been
directing up to that time. After Leo's firing, Bern and Charlie
had a very brief and unpleasant exchange and Charlie wound
up holding a burning copy of the *Hollywood Reporter* under the
faucets of the sprinkling system in the ceiling of the executive
building at Metro. The water responded to the heat as in the
days of Noah and the entire bookkeeping department on the
first floor was awash and on the second floor they started
putting oarlocks on the windows. Leo and he had a rather
scary time of it when the fire chief discovered the burned
Reporter, which Charlie stupidly had let fall to the floor. Leo

squeaked by this crisis only when a secretary vouched for him to a fire chief who asked threateningly, "Does anyone here know this guy?"

For Hecht and MacArthur, Charlie worked on a picture called *Soak the Rich* which he is convinced was only released on boats (liners crossing the Atlantic) and then a really terrible musical starring Ben Hecht's daughter Edwina and Jimmy Savo *(Once in a Blue Moon)*. It was not a success. The company folded and he went back to Hollywood and got a job as assistant to Irving Thalberg.

He was co-producer of *A Night at the Opera*. He loved Irving. The fact that Thalberg had a feud with Selznick did not make him uncharming to Charlie. He was in this post about six months, leaving in 1936 when his sister Pepi died. He was asked to find some amusing material for Elizabeth Barrett Browning to jazz up the screen version of the play on the Barretts. And he did pictures like *I Love You Again* and *Love Crazy* and films for Bill Powell and Myrna Loy.

Around this time, when he was on a trip to Germany with the Hearst party, he wound up (as always) at Bad Nauheim for the cure. A telegram came from Anita Loos, who was then at Baden-Baden. "Never mind G. Get H." and it was bravely signed "Anita." The hotel manager accompanied the messenger who delivered it and Charlie remembered his look was wide-eyed and extremely alert to any false move. He expected the Storm Troopers at any moment, but they never came. Possibly he was saved by the fact that he had just had his head shaved and rather resembled one of them, at least a pocket version.

Lederer was about as casual in his approach to working as any of the veteran professionals handling writing assignments. When the pressure was on him, he would deliver and that kept him solvent. His rich aunt Marion was always impressed by the large sums he could earn when the spirit (and a contract) took hold of him.

Equally playful but more energetic was Preston Sturges. He was not the first writer to direct his own script, but he had persuaded Paramount to let him direct (for a $10 fee) his own original screenplay, *Down Went McGinty* in late 1939. Brian Donlevy was McGinty, an amoral politician far too oblivious and careless of public opinion to rank in the Watergate class, a party hack who rises to great power. The film was made for less than $300,000 and won an Oscar for Sturges and unlimited status at his studio.

Scott Fitzgerald had written his wife: "They've let a certain writer here direct his own picture and he has made such a go of it that there may be a different feeling about that soon. If I had that chance, I would attain my real goal in coming here in the first place." His illusions about his true status in Hollywood remained intact to the end.

But Sturges had Charlie Lederer's playfulness. He loved gags and he enjoyed fooling around with contraptions, some of his own invention. As a youth, he had invented kissproof lipstick for his mother, Mary Desti, who loaned Isadora Duncan that fateful scarf (that killed her). She was an eccentric Bohemian who was also an entrepreneur, the owner of a cosmetic line; Preston managed the New York branch for a time.

It was this amalgam of filmmaker and ex-merchandiser that kept him more truly outside the Hollywood hierarchy and more feared than any other individual at that level of power. In a very real sense, he was one of them. A lipstick salesman rather than a glove wholesaler, he also had genius and talent, something none of the studio bosses possessed. The success of his films at the box office sustained him, but nearly all of the old studio chiefs were waiting for him to slip. Knowing this, he had his own table at the Paramount commissary where he would preside; he bought more fancy cars than he needed; and he established two restaurants, one of them, the Players, a success for a while and Sturges's principal hangout. He created his own circle of friends but had few confidants. He was much admired but at a comfortable distance.

They could not have been more unlike—director and star. Preston Sturges (Edmund P. Biden) had come to Hollywood by dint of a considerable comedy success in New York (*Strictly Dishonorable*, 1929) and by way of Paris and Chicago with long, Bohemian *vacances* during his formative years with his mother in the Isadora Duncan set abroad. Veronica Lake (Constance Ockleman Keane) had entered Hollywood, as had thousands of other young ladies, brought there by an ambitious mother.

Veronica's (or *Connie's*) advance reputation was not such as to encourage Sturges to take her on for the role of *The Girl with No Name* in *Sullivan's Travels* (1941). "The Girl" had to know how to act and Connie's only previous appearance had been as the diminuitive blonde with the unmanageable hairdo in Mitchell Leisen's *I Wanted Wings*. The reviewers had not been especially welcoming. Everyone agreed that an actress with only one eye visible had something unique but her emotional range was less than Kate Hepburn's during the mercifully brief *The Lake*. Uncertain about how a star should behave (how could she not be?), she adopted a tough, unladylike stance.

But this appealed to Sturges when he finally felt ready to do his "Hollywood" film, his own *What Price Hollywood?* He was a bit on the defensive himself. Despite a string of successes, he fitted no known mold as a moviemaker.

His insistence upon total control over his films was not purely an ego thing as with Orson Welles, who would put his name on everything connected with his films whether he did the work or not. Their mutual emergence as double-threat talents during the same period (1940–41) was simple coincidence. Welles never could learn to write sparely, as the best movies require. (Proper writing credit on Welles's best films already has been given to those who performed the creative act of setting the words down in script form, after which he took over.) When he is on his own in the writing of a script, he is frankly tiresome (*Immortal Story* is the latest example). So in actual fact, they were different talents and yet, in a sense, total filmmakers with an extraordinary talent for translating their vision to the screen.

By the time of *Sullivan's Travels,* which relates the spiritual torment of a successful film director who wants his next film to be "a true canvas of the suffering of humanity," Sturges had been almost reluctantly advanced by his studio bosses to "A" features with stars of the caliber of Barbara Stanwyck and Henry Fonda and now he had Joel McCrea, as John L. Sullivan, and Veronica Lake, the studio's overnight bitch-goddess, in the leads. His modestly budgeted films made money; they were attracting foreign audiences, and he was becoming a "writer's writer" (Lederer on Sturges: "God! What a marvelous talent!"). He had everything going for him except the blessing of the head of his studio, William LeBaron, and eventually he had that, too. Sturges was a satirist who knew what he was doing, probably one of the rarest birds known to the arts. Over the years, Hollywood has encountered some near-misses: Ernie Kovacs, Mel Brooks, and, earlier, the Chaplin of *The Great Dictator.* But here, on their payroll, was a man who had total command of the film idiom; who had at his disposal a brilliant cutter, Stuart Gilmore; a colorful stock company of character actors (William Demarest, Georgia Caine, Porter Hall), and who was so fiendishly clever they never knew whether he was idealizing Mom or Santa Claus or putting them down. At times it seemed that he had decided to cut out the horseplay and be "American" as everyone hoped he would be. Let us say that Preston Sturges was an enigma.

An Aside — Veronica Lake

We met in London in the summer of 1969. "Veronica Lake, or Connie Ockleman, or Connie Keane, take your choice," the greeting came from a very tiny bleached-blond lady indicating a certain vagueness at her center that was disconcerting.

She was promoting her autobiography, ghostwritten, but "every goddamned word from my guts," which again made everything shadowy with no clean lines to determine where you stood. We exchanged books and in mine, she wrote:

St. Swithens Day

Fred--

The best of all to your "Norma Jean" and all others.

Love,

"Veronica"
alias Connie

Chiswick Mall on the Thames, London 7/15/69

I was with a male companion and she seized upon this alliance before she could possibly have known its significance by declaring her absolute tolerance for all of life's misfits, of which she counted herself one.

It seemed that life had dealt her a dirty deal and that was film stardom. It had come when she was eighteen or nineteen and she couldn't handle it, so she used bitchery as a weapon and when that didn't work, booze.

We were approximately the same age, but years of what must have been unending binges had given her eyes a slight puffiness. The famous tresses had thinned out and been bobbed short; there was the merest trace of a wattle under her chin. But, oddly, the total effect was not unattractive, only a peculiar hardness in her eyes that flickered on and off like some beacon of warning.

The pub-restaurant was in her neighborhood, a middle-class London area on the Thames with a waterfront air about it, especially at night when fog drifted up from the river. The food was Portuguese and the owner Greek. He looked after "Connie" with a paternal manner and exacted promises from my friend and me that we would see her to her front door. Over a leisurely, slightly greasy dinner, the three of us consumed approximately fifteen Scotches and two large bottles of white wine. By ten-thirty, I was in need of some fresh air for my dull headache.

Taking Veronica Lake to her front door was not enough. The old "understanding and tolerance bit" preceded it and she assured us with a slightly rum laugh that she had no designs upon either of us, but we must take her upstairs. So up we went into her boardinghouse, three flights of rickety stairs to an unattractive blue-enameled room with a bare bulb. "Now how about some tea or a nightcap?"

I waggled my hand in protest. "No nightcap for me. A little tea would be fine." And off went one of the world's most famous women of the Second World War in search of a tea kettle in the community kitchen shared by all the boarders on her floor.

She was back in seconds, almost before I could take in any of the few details of the room; a tattered movie poster from *The Blue Dahlia* with its stoical leading man and lady—Alan Ladd and Veronica Lake; the perfectly cool sex combination, or, to put it another way, the least *sizzling* movie combination since Tom Mix and Tonto.

"Sarah, she's my best friend here, already has the tea kettle in use." And instead of sitting on the edge of the narrow daybed covered by a worn chintz coverlet, which is where she told us she slept, she stood in the center of the room. "Sorry," she told my friend, who had indicated a nightcap would suit him fine. "I drank the last of the Scotch this morning."

This seemed to be a peculiarly abrupt ending to an overlong drinking bout, but I was on my feet at once while my friend sat in his red-painted mission chair, quite at a loss. He was South American and used to dinner evenings trailing off into the wee hours after heads-together song sessions, a few merengues done to tunes in the head if absolutely necessary.

"Call me tomorrow. We'll get together again in my new place. I'm taking a little maisonette with my own kitchen and everything."

"Come on, Charlie," I said. "The lady needs her beauty rest . . ." And this sentence was interrupted by a killing glance from Connie that implied "Don't shit me! I *know* I'm over the hill."

Charlie soon got the point with a little prodding and we went down the stairs in darkness. "Sorry," Connie said from the gloom at the top of the stairs. "The bulb's burned out. Don't forget. Tomorrow." A door closed above us and we stumbled somehow to the bottom.*

3.

René Clair, who, as James Agee pointed out, was probably Sturges's mentor and whose view of life most closely approximates Sturges's once said, "Preston is like a man from the Italian Renaissance; he wants to do everything at once. If he could slow down, he would be great; he has an enormous gift and he should be one of our leading creators. I wish he would be a little more selfish and worry about his reputation."

Sturges's French background in his formative years (he was selling cosmetics for his mother in Deauville at sixteen), doubtless gave him the objectivity about Americans to see the

---

*Veronica Lake died of acute hepatitis in a New England clinic in 1973.

absurdities clearly. His use of Eddie Bracken as an inept, hopelessly befuddled misfit in two successive films was a precursor of, and perhaps even inspired François Truffaut to build, an entire series of feature-length films around a Gallicized version of the same man: "Antoine Doniel" as played by Jean-Pierre Léaud.

Truffaut in *Bed and Board* and *Stolen Kisses*, etc., seems to be working more rapidly than Sturges. The films seem more improvised and under less complete control of their creator than the Eddie Bracken "poor soul" films of Sturges.

Films today are looser, so the Antoine Doniel films can trail off inconclusively. But in Sturges's day comedy scripts had to be tight *and* conclusive.

For example in *The Miracle at Morgan's Creek* the inept hero Norval wonders if the infant (for whom he will be a father substitute) is a boy or a girl and is escorted by the new mother's slyly wicked sister to the nursery window where he is shown six babies. He wonders which is his and "Trudy's." "All of them" is sister Emmy's gesture, whereupon Norval collapses.

When he recovers, "he becomes increasingly happy, for, as Shakespeare said: 'Some are *born* great, some achieve greatness, and some have greatness thrust upon them.'"

Sturges had served in the Air Corps in the First World War (he was born in 1898) so he was not obligated to enter any of the services when war was declared in 1941. The content of his films and even his pricking of the pomposity of superpatriotism and the gung-ho spirit in his masterpiece *Hail the Conquering Hero,** which will come up a little later, suggest

---

**Hail the Conquering Hero* is a nearly pure example of "the Hottentot formula," a phrase much used by Hollywood writers to describe a screenplay built around a fluke triumph over ineptitude. It had its antecedents in much of early- and mid-career Chaplin, nearly all of the work of Harold Lloyd, and was taken into Hollywood argot when a screenwriter at Warner Brothers was assigned to build a script around a hero, who knew nothing about riding a horse, being compelled to ride a horse named "Hottentot" and win the race.

that he considered war about as feckless an enterprise as reading the last chapter first of a detective novel.

War created a new situation for Hollywood. The demand for its product (the Armed Forces being the biggest distributor) never had been greater, but the talent pool had been drained so that only the old, the halt, and the alien were available. Even the careful Mr. Hitchcock was forced to make eight films during the war years, beginning with *Foreign Correspondent* (1940) and ending with *Notorious* (1946), nearly all having some connection with the war or the Nazis.

Director William Dieterle made ten, including *Dr. Erlich's Magic Bullet* (1940) and *All That Money Can Buy* (1941). Ernst Lubitsch averaged a film a year throughout this period, although with decreasing power and effectiveness; George Cukor managed eight.

Among the writers sent off to war, the two Charlies, MacArthur and Lederer, both wound up in Burma at one point, as did George Oppenheimer. Oppenheimer had been surprised earlier by a visit from Charlie and Virginia Lederer at Fort Roach, the studio become propaganda and training-film center. Charlie arrived in his (then) first lieutenant's uniform bringing George a carton of presents: a white feather (for cowardice), two rubber ducks for the bathtub, a Japanese compass, a Tyrolean hat with feather, a yo-yo, and a file of *House Beautiful* magazines. Sherwood and Alan Campbell were in London, moving in quite different military circles. Dorothy Parker felt that Alan's volunteering for duty abroad was a subtle evasion of his marital responsibilities and perhaps she was proved right. When the war ended, Alan remained overseas in London. Dorothy announced to her friends that the reason for this turn of events was a love affair with another man. She told Alan she was getting a divorce and she did.

Ben Hecht was quietly working with a group in New York to make the State of Israel a reality; but he was able to continue doing rewrite jobs and managed to do much of the writing on three highly regarded films of those years: *Tales of*

Manhattan (1942), *Spellbound* (1945), and *Notorious* (1946). Another film, *The Spectre of the Rose* (1946), an original also produced and directed by Hecht, will be examined presently, as it represented both a distinct break with the past for him as well as a possible breakthrough for the small-budgeted art-house film in America.

4.

After the phony heroics of Hollywood's version of *The Moon Is Down* in 1943, there was an uneasy feeling, especially among soldier audiences, that Hollywood was going to turn the war into hokum, a war that might at that very moment be a Spitfire or a German fighter doing a deadly aerial ballet above the amphitheater where you were seated.

Then Howard Hawks, who was not only very good at such antics as *Bringing Up Baby* and *His Girl Friday* but at dramas in which men feel a very strong emotional bond between them, made *Air Force,* in which a nine-man crew struggle through an aerial attack to keep their plane air-borne and functioning as a weapon.

Inspired by a suggestion of General "Hap" Arnold, it had its original screenplay mapped out by Hawks with his writer Dudley Nichols, a veteran of early talkies. Its aerial sequences were as exciting as those in *Hell's Angels* but there were additional spectacles, such as the Battle of the Coral Sea, re-created for the film, and the bombing of Hickam Field, which brought us into the war.

Gunner "Winocki" (John Garfield) is the outsider, the man eager to get his years of enlistment and the army behind him (before he learns that the Japanese have attacked Hawaii and all such contracts are "invalidated").

It was a fairly typical Garfield performance, which had become so polished in its unheroics, its stresses, and its anal pains beyond number, his roles wrote themselves in most cases.

His first screen role after his stage success in *Golden Boy*—the itinerant composer in *Four Daughters*—established the pattern for a long string of losers, East Side misfits and iconoclasts who were automatically against the majority (except in this case where we were all in it together, misfits and patriots).

His New York accent never left him, nor did his growing legions of fans, mainly female. When the script was brilliant, he was superbly himself, as in *The Postman Always Rings Twice*. So cleverly did he play the drifter, the man whose chance of licking adversity is minimal, he was never to win an Oscar although he would win a nomination (for *Body and Soul*, 1947).

Eventually, his personality began to dictate the shape of the movies that were his vehicles, as in *Dust Be My Destiny*. Then he would rebel and head for the New York stage, where he made a number of appearances during his all-too-brief screen career. His politics were as individualistic as his screen image and, while it riled Jack Warner, he was too valuable to throw to the witch-hunters—for a time.

5.

Sometimes a producer (or, more often today, a director) will back into a movie project during an abortive effort at something else. Such was the approach of Darryl F. Zanuck into the most interesting film of his long career, *Wilson*. In Zanuck's own words:

> For some time, I had been mulling over another idea altogether—a picture dealing with the life of the late Samuel Gompers, the great labor leader. It seemed to me at the time that a constructive, carefully documented film about Gompers would not only be a worthwhile undertaking from a dramatic standpoint but that it might also contribute something to lessening the tensions developing in our economic system.
>
> But as I continued to delve into the subject, with the

aid of Lamar Trotti, one of the screen's most capable
writers, I found myself more and more often confronted
with the name of Woodrow Wilson, the record of his
accomplishments and the part he played in Gompers'
career.*

Zanuck dropped the Gompers project and began a major
film production based on Wilson's life, especially his political
and war years. Lamar Trotti, his choice of screenwriter, was a
former newspaperman who had begun his movie career as a
New York assistant to the Production Code administrator,
Will H. Hays, oddly enough, the year of Wilson's death. He
was a staff writer at the old Fox studios when Zanuck merged
his Twentieth Century Pictures in 1935. Trotti turned out to
be one of the most dependable and talented assets brought into
the new combine from Fox (the others, and they were few,
being Shirley Temple, Will Rogers, whose death by air-crash
loomed just ahead, Janet Gaynor, Warner Baxter, and Warner
Oland). Trotti, then, was invaluable to Zanuck as Twentieth
Century-Fox films began to take on an identity. Alone or in
association with someone else, usually Sonya Levien, he
wrote *In Old Chicago, A Bell for Adano, Alexander's Ragtime
Band, Drums Along the Mohawk* and *Tales of Manhattan.* Quite
naturally, he was an authority on the "do's" and "don'ts" of
screenwriting, but he had the faculty of keeping his scripts
free of even the faintest attack on America's puritan ideals
while retaining a high level of entertainment. He wrote
numerous pseudo-biographical films to star Tyrone Power
and Don Ameche or both. Zanuck's films, as the thirties
proceeded in their historically inhumane way, were mostly
musicals or flimsily based on some historic event or individu-

---

*Samuel Gompers, a cigarmaker born in England, helped develop the American
Federation of Labor, of which he was President for over thirty years. He was close to
Wilson at the Paris Peace Conference, 1918–19, in his capacity as President of the
International Committee on Labor Legislation. They remained close, both personally
and officially, until Wilson's death in 1924, just ten months before Gompers's.

al. They were written and produced quickly, nearly always with casts drawn from the studio's roster of leading players. Sol Wurtzel was in overall charge of the less important movies.

So there was little to prepare filmgoers, many of whom were in uniform in 1944 when *Wilson* was released, for its careful and historically accurate plea for peace. Only twice before in his career had Zanuck produced such a delicately wrought production, and both had been best-selling novels, *The Grapes of Wrath* (1940) and *How Green Was My Valley* (1941). In the case of the John Steinbeck novel, for which he had paid $100,000, Zanuck was doubly cautious, to avoid offending either the novelist or his screenwriter, Nunnally Johnson. Johnson had been known to tell his bosses that he didn't want any producer "pecking around" his work. "It could delay me a month and if you don't like what I've written, it could upset me."

But Zanuck knew that Trotti was a man who had no serious objections to sitting down with the producer and taking the script apart. Zanuck frequently asserted that he "thought like a writer" and it is true that he did have the writer's point-of-view on most of his productions. With *Wilson*, Zanuck wanted to go against the grain of all his earlier films. He was going all out for a message. "I saw how destructive of humanity war was, and how innocent of its causes were those who had to do the fighting. Again and again as I saw our boys dying and suffering the thought occurred: why had not something been done to prevent this futile sacrifice?" Let's not forget that word *futile*, for it suggests a pacifist to whom all wars are abhorrent. If the war to prevent Hitler from imposing his paranoia on half the world was futile, then no war ever has any justification. And certainly with the postwar rise to prosperity of West Germany, the affluence of the Japanese, and the strange lack of concern for human needs demonstrated by the "civilized" British during the disgraceful Crete Internment episode, as well as a similar lack of critical concern about the Palestinians by the former internees, there is a serious question as to whether the Second World War achieved much of anything beyond eliminating some 50,000,000 persons from the earth, many of them unfortunately with the finest minds and most acute sensibilities. If this is an age of mediocrity, it should not surprise those of us who kept score: a great many of our most brilliant minds—political leaders, painters, writers, scientists, philosophers, and even film-makers perished. Perhaps more significantly, cadres of the young were gassed, bombed, or otherwise annihilated whose gifts were lost to the world before they were even partially realized. Chasms of mediocrity may well span two generations.

With Zanuck placed on an inactive list by the Army, he plunged into the production like a man possessed. His aim was to contribute "toward bringing a better world into being." His task was not going to be an easy one and he knew it. "We had learned," he said, "through bitter experience that any attempt to deal realistically with the problems of the day was bound to bring down on us a flood of vituperation and criticism from special groups. . . . The risk each time was so great and the complications so vexing that such pictures [as *The Grapes of Wrath*—a success—and *The Ox-Bow Incident*—a failure] seemed hardly worth the effort and pain." And beyond this, he was concerned about the box-office receipts from such pictures. He would ensure that *Wilson* had redeeming entertainment values. "This is not a cynical decision made in the hope of profit. . . . A picture must have an audience.

"To be truly successful," Zanuck continued, "to make its point, a picture must be a financial success at the box office. It must be seen by the maximum number of people. If it fails at the box office it merely means, particularly in a serious film, that the point has failed to get across. Artistically and technically, it may be perfect. But unless people wish to see it and do, it is still a failure. It has failed because it was made to be seen." By this definition, *Citizen Kane,* released in 1940, was a failure and is so considered within the industry.

And, deplorably, because in many ways it is Zanuck's monument, his finest achievement, so did *Wilson* fail. For reasons best known to himself, there was only one performer in the entire cast who had any wide popular appeal. Ever since *Dark Victory* and *Wuthering Heights.* Geraldine Fitzgerald had been climbing steadily upward. Her name was now above the title in all of her films, and she had that rare self-assurance in performing that can only come from years of theatrical experience. But for the part of Wilson, Zanuck cast a comparative unknown, Alexander Knox.

It was a brilliant casting. Knox *was* the dry pedagogue, the self-righteous moralizer, the human and vulnerable pacifist, who could be swayed. What's more, Knox had a dry style of acting that made his hundreds of lines bearable, a bit akin to sitting on a sand dune and allowing the sea breeze to gently waft about your ears. But in the clinch, during an impassioned speech, there was real indignation audible to jerk you to attention and these jerks came often. The script is filled with homely touches illumined by Wilsonian oratory. A prime example is the scene in the railway canteen, where wife Edith (Geraldine Fitzgerald) is serving coffee at the counter and the President is washing dishes in the back. A number of soldiers are guessing about the identity of the attractive lady, obviously someone of distinction. One of the doughboys tells her, "They been trying to tell me you're the President's wife." "Really?" she says with some amusement. "They can't string me!" "You don't think I look the part?" "I say you don't!" Then Edith smiles and says, "I agree with you. But when you come back from France, if you'll come to the White House, I'll do my best to look as I should. *(And she hands him the cup of coffee.)* Or, better still, why don't you speak to the President himself about it."

The boy turns and sees the President, drops the cup in astonishment, and Wilson smiles and says, "Slippery, aren't they?" The boys gather round their Commander in Chief, taking it all in to tell their grandchildren one day, and telling him where they come from and what ethnic group they belong to. "This is all very interesting, boys," Wilson says with some attempt at camaraderie, "and I want you to remember it. . . . Here we are—men of all races—with different backgrounds and ancestries—working together for a common purpose. That's what's made America what it is—and that's what the whole world must learn to do some day. . . . I know there are some people who say that this is just another war to protect the great fortunes, or for some other economic reason. But don't believe them! If anybody tries to tell you that universal peace is just an idle dream, tell him he's a liar! Say your President said that you're fighting this war so there won't have to be any more wars. And that when we get through with it, we're going to sit down with the people of other countries who feel as we do and work out some plan which will make it unnecessary for boys like you—and your sons—to have to go out and shoot one another. Maybe we'll call it a League—or maybe we'll call it something else. But whatever it is, that's what you boys are going to France for. And with the help of God, that's what you're going to get! Now good-bye boys, and—God bless you all."

It would be windy rhetoric except that we have been given over an hour's build-up toward this point. We have seen Wilson as the President of Princeton in such an ambience of campus life, every member of the audience is saturated with it—strolling glee clubs sending up their songs at dusk, a lost football game, a handsome young student who is like a son to Wilson. So imbued is the *mise en scène* with old Nassau, surely to the fascinated audience it is good for half a credit toward some degree or other. We have followed Wilson as the reluctant politician and we have watched him give the shaft to a forerunner of Boss Hague in the Jersey City area.

It is a sprawling, purely American film. It re-creates the
1912 Democratic convention with an accuracy for detail that
does not overlook a host of flapping paper fans and sweat-
soaked shirts. And this attention to detail is only the un-
derpinning to a narrative that rivets the attention, quite unlike
Zanuck's later attempts, *The Longest Day,* about the Allied
invasion of France, and *Tora! Tora! Tora!,* about the Japanese
aerial attack on Pearl Harbor, both 1962, and both having no
more of an impact than a footnote to a story we anticipate but
never see.

Wilson was on all of the ten best films of the year lists in
1944; it was nominated for an Academy Award but lost out to
Going My Way. Alexander Knox was nominated for an Award
as best actor but Bing Crosby won as the priest in the winning
film. It lost much of its $4,000,000 cost and yet, like *Citizen
Kane,* doubtless will survive its maker and this century, since
somehow Zanuck's soul flicked onto the celluloid. And it is
interesting to realize that this was the most message-oriented
film ever made by a major studio to survive the reviewers.
Had such a film been written by John Howard Lawson or
Ring Lardner, Jr., rather than Lamar Trotti, or been directed
by Edward Dmytryk, Robert Rossen, or Joseph Losey rather
than Henry King, *Wilson* would have been analyzed and taken
apart for attempting to propagandize the troops and home-
front with pacifist dogma in the midst of a war we were only
then beginning to win. But it was very much like President
Nixon's amazing trip to Peking. Zanuck had the background
of a savvy showman and could gamble on a theme of such
political dimensions precisely because he always had been out
to win audiences and not converts.

An Aside—Geraldine Fitzgerald

When the Warner Brothers brought Geraldine Fitzgerald
from New York, where she had done a play with Orson
Welles for his Mercury Theatre *(Heartbreak House),* Jack

Warner had no notion that he was taking on an eloquent-voiced Irish termagant, who would be on suspension nearly half the time. He would not succeed, in a temper flare-up, in snuffing out her career as he had with Ann Dvorak, nor would he try. Perhaps the difference between the fates of these stars lay in the fact that Jack Warner had created Ann Dvorak, given her the star buildup, while Geraldine Fitzgerald had come to him under the usual seven-year contract by way of the Gate Theatre, Dublin, the British screen (*Turn of the Tide* and *The Mill on the Floss*), and Orson Welles. In other words, her credentials went beyond the Warner Brothers stock company.

Her first role just happened to be a stunner—that of Bette Davis's closest friend Anne in *Dark Victory*. The Gods seemed to be going out of its way for Miss Fitzgerald. Nearly everyone recalls the story in which Judith Traherne (Bette Davis) learns that she is dying of a brain tumor and the drama is in her courageous acceptance of the oncoming darkness. One of the most memorable scenes in film history is that in which, as Judith is planting bulbs in her garden with Anne at her side, she suddenly remarks that the sun has gone under a cloud.

Miss Fitzgerald had a clause in her contract allowing her to spend half the year on her own. She thought with this freedom that she could do movies and plays independently of Warners, but this never worked out. The good things never came along at the right moment. This ill fortune was to handicap her seriously throughout her film career. With two or three exceptions, all of her contract films would be fairly run-of-the-mine efforts, her performances being their principal virtue in most cases. *Dark Victory* and *Wuthering Heights*,* her first American films, and the latter on loan-out, would remain her best during her Warner Brothers days and she

---

*The Samuel Goldwyn production, released through United Artists.

would not have a real opportunity as a star until *Wilson*, which came near the end of her seven-year contract, also on loan-out.

But she settled into the life with some ease, moving in a civilized crowd, which included Charlie Lederer. He recently had completed writing his version of Hecht and MacArthur's *The Front Page*. *His Girl Friday* was about to go before the cameras. Charlie liked Geraldine on sight and nicknamed her "Jelly".

When it was clear after the preview that she was well-launched by her American role, Charlie and another friend, Allan "Pinky" Miller, a lawyer-agent and Zeppo Marx's brother-in-law (which gave him a certain eclat), escorted her to Lamaze for a celebration dinner.

Charlie had a compulsive urge to make the pleasurable memorable and that could only be done by *doing something beyond* the routine of just sitting in an elegant restaurant and having a few drinks. Down the block from Lamaze was one of the chapels in the Utter-McKinley burial chain. The only odd thing about that particular branch was that it had a steeple with a clock on it, but no hands on the clock. While Geraldine, who was patient and understanding, even admiring of this side of Charlie, waited alone at Lamaze with her celebration drink, Charlie and Pinky entered the mortuary chapel, found no one animate moving about, climbed into the steeple, and, with Pinky holding him by the feet, Charlie painted five to twelve on the clock face. There was only one slight repercussion from this slightly scandalous act (it might have been construed as a desecration except for the fact that there were several dozen Utter-McKinley chapels in California, all as identical as so many White Towers). Universal Pictures chief Carl Laemmle, Jr., was nearly arrested the next day and charged with the "crime." He had paused in his car to laugh at the prank long enough for a sheriff staked out nearby to nab him.

But there was precious little to celebrate again. The parts that came Geraldine's way were nearly all bland, in that

flattening-out process that Hollywood studios utilized in order
to satisfy the Code as well as their collective audience "with a
fourteen-year-old's mind." She routinely turned down nearly
everything and went on suspension. She didn't understand
Mr. Warner. She had come to Hollywood believing that the
men who employed the artists were artists themselves—an
Irish fantasy perhaps. The fact that they were businessmen
and little more was unknown to her. "The depths of my
nonunderstanding were abysmal," she recalls. "They should
have had someone on the lot who understood the artist and his
needs. They would have saved themselves a lot of time and
worry."

Jack Warner's threats brought Geraldine into line when she
wanted to play "Cathy" in *Wuthering Heights* (he had
made a loan-out deal with Goldwyn) and she settled for
Isabella, drabber, less fiery, but a role of extraordinary humanness. Her scenes were among the best in the
picture. I suspect that Ben Hecht and Charles MacArthur
focused on Isabella to bring Emily Bronte's novel out of
the nineteenth century and into a tightly coiled reality
for twentieth-century audiences.

But Geraldine disliked being on the set whenever she wasn't
needed for a scene. She couldn't bear seeing Merle Oberon do a
role she believed herself more suited to—"with my background, I knew I could play the role. I thought these things
counted."

She did enjoy working with Olivier, however. Even then,
she says, "we knew he was an artist of the first rank. And
remember he was not 'Olivier' then, just 'Laurence Olivier.'
Goldwyn didn't even like his face, far too unusual, with those
lowering brows and smoldering eyes. Well, for that day there
was something far out about his face, something elemental.
But today, what man wouldn't give to be born with such a
face! Olivier was a great human being, terribly compassionate."

"It was very rare for a part to be cast exactly the way the director or the author wanted it. There were other factors that mattered more—*commitments.*" And then she pauses for a moment, her face reflecting that keen sensibility and intelligence that were her trade-mark actually. "The only exception that I can think of is Clark Gable as Rhett Butler. The public wanted him. Margaret Mitchell. Everyone." Parenthetically, someone recommended Geraldine to David O. Selznick for the part of Melanie, but he told them, "Never having seen Geraldine Fitzgerald, I can't make any comment about her." This was before the release of her first American film.

Geraldine is not quite sure *Wuthering Heights* is a better film than *Gone With the Wind,* although some critics believe that it is. "They are of different genres really. *Gone with the Wind* is that wonderful thing, a perfect popular movie, a people's art, and a movie like that has a very long life. *Wuthering Heights* is a work of art esthetically, the best possible creation of the performing arts."

Wilson falls somewhere between these two genres and was made, Geraldine believes, "for prestige purposes. It was a bold thing for Zanuck to do (coming, as it did, during the war). He wanted to make his contribution toward telling Americans something about the way Wilson was treated in his fight for the League."

While Geraldine Fitzgerald in no way minimizes the value of *Wilson* to her own career and American films, she realizes that the rather banal dialogue given her by Lamar Trotti in her role as Edith Gault Wilson is about the weakest in the picture. "But there's a reason for that. There was a much stronger series of characterizations tabled for that film and a much stronger blast against the people who blocked the League of Nations. When they started to make the film, they found that most of the people were still alive and they wouldn't give their permission. Mrs. Gault was still alive, so there was no chance of getting through to the more negative aspects of her personality. As the kids say today, *no way.* She would only accept this bland—we're back to that word again—characterization which had no color in it at all, which could not offend (her) but which could not please (the audience) either. So I tried to do what I could to capture what I had heard were her 'agreeable ways.' I don't know whether she really was agreeable, but I went after that. We were forced to iron that film out and it's a terrific shame."

She remembers that Zanuck was around all the time. "There was nothing he wouldn't attend to. That's the mark of a great producer, that attention to every little detail. That's why Sam Goldwyn was a very good producer. I recall Goldwyn commenting one day, 'You call that makeup? I call it breakup.' Now what I have against Jack Warner is that he didn't supervise every detail. Hal Wallis did. I don't think Jack Warner ever made a film that was *his* film."

One of the most remarkable aspects of both the Bronte film and *Wilson* is their sense of place, their belonging to a certain moment in time and particular setting. This was no accident but the result of many hours of research and re-creating the moors and, for *Wilson,* the Princeton campus, the convention building and the White House. The White House was so accurately reproduced that when Geraldine finally visited the actual residence in Washington she knew where everything was, what was in all the rooms.

Henry King has a considerable competence in his direction of *Wilson's* small scenes but when you get to the convention, then, as Geraldine puts it, "you see an absolute master at work."

Geraldine Fitzgerald's unfavorable impressions of the American film industry as experienced by her at Warner Brothers kept her from renewing her contract in 1945. "It had been like working in an institution. For example, if you wanted to talk to one of the writers, you had to get a pass that would get you through to the front office where they had the writers' section. There was no moment when you were treated as a responsible person who might have the same goals as a producer (who had the run of the place). You were treated like a recalcitrant person who had been bought and now must be overseen to carry out what they were supposed to, like on a plantation. They were dreadful people. And it's amazing the number of distinguished people who were treated this way. But by the time I got there, Warner didn't treat Bette [Davis] badly any more because they had a number of knock-down-and-drag-out fights and she had come out on top and was number one at the box office."

Geraldine left Hollywood with her young son Michael in 1946 to marry a New Yorker, Stuart Scheftel. She had a daughter, Susan, and never went back except on short assignments for individual pictures. Her most memorable later film role was in 1965: that of Marilyn Birchfield, friend to *The Pawnbroker*, the Jew in Harlem who, as a survivor of the holocaust, is one of the walking dead.

Somewhere along the way she came upon a social consciousness, an awakening to the needs of others, something she didn't have much of except for friends and family back in Hollywood. She didn't get caught in "the meat grinder" of the Blacklist, like so many of her close friends, because she had never been "clubbable." When the Blacklist extended into the television industry and she was up for a role and they asked her to sign a loyalty statement, she threatened to sign "yes" to all their questions and have it published in the *New York Post*. She was hired for the part without the oath.

6.

Quite different from *Wilson* but far more successful with both soldier and civilian audiences was Preston Sturges's *Hail the Conquering Hero*, released the same year (1944).

Unhappily for both Paramount and Sturges, by the time of

this broadside attack against political chicanery and false and sentimentalized chauvinism, Sturges had skipped the lot and gone into partnership with Howard Hughes. (Who has ever come out ahead in such an alliance?)

The plot is Runyonesque (another strong Sturges influence). An asthmatic 4-F (unfit for service) played by Eddie Bracken, a Marine reject named Woodrow Truesmith whose father was a bemedaled Marine hero of World War I, has been hiding out—staying away from his home in a tiny Midwestern town because of his sense of shame over being rejected. Meanwhile, his best girl (Ella Raines) has become engaged to the incumbent mayor's son, Forrest Noble (Sturges's names are Dickensian).

A group of Marines on furlough on the same train as Woodrow listen to his story and decide to do him "the favor" of backing up his story that he is heroically serving his country somewhere. One named "Bugsy" is especially upset to learn that Woodrow has not been in touch with his mother and tells him, "You ought to be ashamed of yourself." The others explain that Bugsy is from a Home. "He never had any mother."

Woodrow's mother is informed of his homecoming and, unknown to him, a great celebration is planned, one in which the candidates for mayor will take active parts and perhaps share in some of the glory radiating around Woodrow.

Woodrow's old girlfriend is encouraged to forget her present relationship long enough to kiss him in greeting over Forrest Noble's feeble protest.

A maverick political group headed by the local doctor decides to urge Woodrow to step in as a shoo-in mayoralty substitute for their candidate, the doctor. Woodrow panics and nearly runs off.

Noble and his backers smell a rat and phone the San Diego Marine Base. They have all the particulars on Woodrow's medical rejection and are about to expose him. But, confounding them, Woodrow confesses his "crime" and his friends' complicity. In a complete reversal, the townspeople hail his honesty and nominate him anyway.

The Marines continue on their way as Woodrow whispers "Semper Fidelis."

Sturges only made one film for Hughes, *The Sin of Harold Diddlebock* (or *Mad Wednesday*) for which Harold Lloyd came out of retirement. It was released twice, under two different titles with indifferent box-office action both times out.

The crux of the action concerns a rare event in Harold Diddlebock's life—he has misplaced a day. During this twenty-four-hour loss, he has bought a circus, which he eventually unloads at a profit. Meanwhile, we are treated to a continuous flow of sight-gags, many of them straight out of Lloyd's *Safety Last,* with Lloyd, a character named "Wormy," and a lion dangling from a skyscraper.

Sturges's career then went into a decline having much to do with his ego clashing with Hughes's, film projects that didn't work out, and assignments in which he had little interest.

By the late fifties, he was in France, unwanted by Hollywood—the closest parallel in talking pictures to the decline and fall of D. W. Griffith. He made one film there, *The French They Are a Funny Race* (1957) or *Les Carnets du Major Thompson.* It was not a success. He died in 1959.

PART FIVE

FEAR
AND
DISSOLUTION

How do you protect people like me? That is what I want to know. That is why I feel we should outlaw the Party.

John Garfield to the House Un-American
Activities Committee, 1951

1.

In late 1946, Ben Hecht was recovering from a serious illness. He had been involved with three films that year, one of which, *The Spectre of the Rose,* he had both written and directed (again with the considerable help of cinematographer Lee Garmes).

Hecht was taking himself seriously as a screenwriter now and trying hard to rack up some arty works that might bear comparison with such foreign films as *Open City, Children of Paradise* (which, incidentally, has a feeling similar to *The Spectre of the Rose)* and *Dead of Night.*

The Spectre of the Rose (1946) was Ben Hecht's attempt to duplicate, using Hollywood technicians and actors, the verisimilitude and stark dramatic lines of the typical foreign import then taking over the screens of the art houses of our major cities and college towns. The original manuscript on which this film is based gives credit for the original play to "John Martin and Lenny Adelson" and adds "from a story by Ben Hecht." When the production reached its premiere engagement at the Republic Theatre in New York (it was financed and released by Republic Pictures), the credits read simply "written, directed, and produced by Ben Hecht."

There were really two writing Ben Hechts. One was a brilliant scenarist with an eye for the odd little piece of action or character. It is the Hecht of *Nothing Sacred, Wuthering Heights, Gone with the Wind, Spellbound,* and *Notorious.* Then there was the Hecht who wished to be remembered, who looked back to Anatole France for inspiration rather than to Hitchcock or Selznick or Bill Wyler. He wrote a number of sardonic novels that dated faster than "Jurgen." He looked for the ironies of life with a desperation bred of a conviction that no decent story could exist without them. He had Oscar Wilde's turn of mind without Wilde's turn of phrase. Hecht's strength was in the vernacular, not in the epigrammatic.

In *The Spectre of the Rose,* Hecht gives us a fairly convincing and irritating portrait of a second-rate impresario, Max Pollikoff (brilliantly played by Marilyn's drama coach Michael Chekhov), attempting to pull together a profitable ballet program to star a once greatly gifted male dancer, André Sanine, who has had a mental breakdown and possibly murdered his own wife during his last public appearance in the classic ballet version of "The Spectre of the Rose." "Madame La Sylph," in whose spacious top-floor studio ballet classes are trained, is approached by Pollikoff in an effort to help get this questionable production on the boards. In one of her classes is Sanine's present girlfriend and the one who has been nursing him back to health. As "La Sylph," Judith Anderson is as flinty as she was in *Rebecca,* but her footing in this "neorealism" of Hecht's is slippery. She remains safely strident and forbidding.

If some of this reminds you of the tragedy of Nijinsky, there seems little doubt that this is where Hecht derived the notion for his work. But the madness of a great dancer ends the resemblance. Nijinsky was more than slightly androgynous; he was sustained for a long time by an impresario who was in love with him. His mind was dulled by mental illness and even retarded by present standards. Hecht's Sanine tells the balky Madame La Sylph (whom he calls "Mama," perhaps to suggest at least a trace of infantilism): "Why fight Polly? I'm going to dance. If not for Polly, for someone else. But I'm going to dance."

The contrast between the crass agent or producer (who is another kind of impresario) and the artist is sharply drawn. Given total freedom by Republic studio head Herbert Yates, Hecht could indulge himself and make the producer the real villain of the piece.

Jones, the set designer's agent, knows nothing about the ballet for which his client is drawing the stage designs (and very little about grammar): "What's this here ballet about?" he asks.

Lionel, the designer, explains: "It's the story of a girl who comes home from a ball and falls asleep. She dreams of a beautiful man dressed like a Rose who comes through the window. She rises in her dream, dances with him, and the beautiful man, to a final burst of music, leaps out of the window and her dream. . . . The last time Sanine danced *Spectre of the Rose*, they closed on a sudden, violent death and a mental crack-up."

Jones replied: "Yeah, I heard. For three nights they were a smash—then Sanine's wife dropped dead on the stage. No wonder the show closed. What do ya do for an encore?"

The humor, such as it is, goes on in this grim way, and when the ballet finally flits across the screen, it is not breathtaking, as in *The Red Shoes* two years later; it is second-rate. The only fascination is the morbid one of wondering when the mad Sanine will plunge the knife into his present sweetheart, Haidi, who is dancing with him.

But the attempt—to make a low-budget "artistic" film in Hollywood that could fairly compete with the films of Rossellini and Carl Dreyer, Cocteau and Max Ophuls—was ambitious and worthy of the filmgoers' attention. It was a flawed, overmelodramatic and stagy film reminiscent of a much more harrowing and sure-footed exercise along the same lines written as a ballet by Gian-Carlo Menotti a few months later, *The Medium*. The difference between the two was that *The Medium* was shorn of epigrams, of overarticulate characters who talk out every little bit of action and exposition. Even in its later movie version, *The Medium* was less stagy than Hecht's film. But *The Spectre of the Rose* was a mistake that was attended by nearly all serious moviegoers and there were a number of them who spoke of it kindly for it had the smell of culture about it.

Hecht was also deeply into political activities, mainly a sub-rosa but very committed role in the American branch of the *Irgun*. Israel already had become an independent state and it did not wish to give the world the impression that it was coming into the community of nations as an armed camp. But it was secretly arming itself to the teeth against possible Arab attacks and the *Irgun* was supplying both guns and trained military leaders.

Hecht was giving the *Irgun* a substantial part of every fee he received and had been for some time. He had written pamphlets, newspaper advertisements, press releases. During his convalescence, he was visited by another prominent Jew, Bernard Baruch, who had come to inform Hecht that he appreciated all that he was doing. Baruch added that he was reserving his energies for later. "I am like the buffalo hunter," he told Hecht. "I lie in the tall buffalo grass and wait until just the right moment and then I spring up out of the grass with my gun and make the kill." Hecht said that he was glad to know that Baruch was going to spring up some time, the men shook hands and Baruch left.

The next day, Hecht was resting at his poolside with Charlie Lederer. The two men were playing cribbage when a shadow fell across the board. A huge man wearing a black suit asked, "Mind if I come in?" His question was singular since they were outside, but Hecht seemed to find it amusing.

The man explained that he was a gun supplier and that he could get as many guns for the *Irgun* as they needed. Hecht was annoyed at that point and told the man that he was neither a depot nor the representative of one.

"I come to you," the man said, "because your name means something. I will need a receipt for the guns I supply."

Hecht finally said that he would discuss the matter with his friends in the *Irgun* but that his answer would probably be no.

Lederer, less sophisticated than Hecht in political matters, was appalled. He wondered why Hecht would work for years to help get arms to the *Irgun* and then, when a major deal for them was offered, turn it down. Hecht quickly replied that there was something not quite on the level. "Someone," he said, "wants to make my life more miserable than it already is." (A clue to his growing disillusionment with wealth and success.) "There is such a thing as the Alien and Sedition Act." Of course, that act specifically prohibits any American citizen from dealing in or supplying weapons to a foreign power. Hecht would give the *Irgun* and other causes more than half his income, but he was not about to go to jail for any of them.

2.

Writers as a breed are often unpleasant. Some are as sweet as asphodels but many are cads and bounders, forever cadging from their friends and even from their enemies, when that shining opportunity presents itself. For every generous, humane and compassionate Aldous Huxley, there are two or three Clifford Odetses, but usually with a fifth of that playwright's talent. Fascinated and moved by humanity *in extremis,* they will fight the good fight *abstractly,* send dollars to Republican Spain, but they will often plunder a personal relationship until it is bare. They make gestures of belonging to the human race and some pride themselves on their normality—nearly all find fatherhood an unbelievable, mixed blessing. Since the omniscient eye of a writer can't take sexual sides, proof of virility calls for hosannahs.

They are usually ill-at-ease among their social inferiors, although they like to pretend a great democracy within themselves. Messenger boys think of them as snobs or "tough." Many are tight with a quarter. They are as vain as leading men and those who make a thing of their *machismo* can get themselves jobs when a leading lady wants them to do her script.

In Hollywood, strangely, much of their confidence, hard-won through best-sellerdom or a hit play, is drained away after a few weeks of sitting in a cubicle in the writer's building of a studio. A literary lion in New York will fidget at a

battered desk and wonder just how he offended Zanuck or
Jack Warner. He will rarely know whether he offended
Goldwyn or not, not until option time. Fitzgerald, in describing Stahr-Thalberg, projected his fear of the studio chief and
there are a number of scenes in his novel in which Stahr
wields the whip over his hirelings, but Thalberg's displeasure
in actuality was always covert, passed along to others to
activate or articulate, hoarded against some future day of
reckoning.

So in the years just ahead, we must consider the fact of most
writers having large egos and few friends. There were to be
some cold winters ahead and some psychological footing is
needed.

The end of the war brought a flood of writers back into the
mainstream of Hollywood production. Audiences never had
been greater in numbers.

Some of the writers were new. The old system still
prevailed. Published novelists and produced playwrights were
summoned and nearly all came.

The administrators of the Code had to bow to new pressures brought about by more mature audiences. Many young
men had "grown up" in the war; they had seen the world. Pap
or bland entertainment no longer held their interest.

And there were vague predictions and very real experiments in network television going on.

A certain freedom—far short of permissiveness—prevailed.
In John Garfield's *Body and Soul,* we understood that he and
his girlfriend were "living together" for a time.

Body and Soul was written by Abraham Polonsky and
directed by Robert Rossen. Both men would be of interest to
the House Un-American Activities Committee, which that
year—1947—was turning its attention to what they termed
the "communicative arts."

Their studio was new and fairly audacious. Enterprise
Productions had been founded after the war with Charles

Einfeld, head of Twentieth Century-Fox publicity, and Loew's, Inc., having principal control. They had $11 million from the Bank of America and commitments from Garfield, Ginger Rogers, and Ingrid Bergman. Bergman's career had not yet got into difficulties over her affair with Rossellini, but Miss Rogers and Garfield wanted to turn theirs around.

An Aside — John Garfield

We met as Garfield was completing a tour of the half-dozen mental wards our medical corps had set up in a former insane asylum. In another section, on an upper floor, political prisoners from the recently deposed and defeated fascist regime were jammed together. That fact interested Garfield. "What's being done for them?" he wanted to know. I shrugged. In point of fact, I tried not to think about it, since there was absolutely nothing that I, as a lowly enlisted man, could do about their misery.

"Figures," Garfield said, and his mind seemed to flick away from the subject just as mine did—uneasily.

He sat in the front seat of the jeep next to the driver as we drove back the two blocks or so from the mental ward of the army hospital where I was assigned to the sprawling military quadrangle where the medical wards, headquarters, and officers' mess were located in Aversa, Italy. It was the winter of 1944-45; the agonizing Anzio campaign, which had swamped our facility with several hundred more patients than we could properly take care of, was months behind us, and Rome had been liberated early that summer.

Garfield seemed to show no interest in the soldier driver but turned around to smile at me, then gave me a conspiratorial wink as though I were another Lower East Sider who had copped a free ride on the subway. "How do you manage a setup like this?" he asked.

His question puzzled me for a moment. I'd never thought of

myself, a T-4 (equivalent to a sergeant) working in the psychiatric wards as having any sort of "setup." Then I realized he was referring to my temporary job as "movie star escort."

"This isn't my regular job. Only when some celebrity comes to the hospital. The last was over two months ago— Humphrey Bogart and his wife, the day before they were asked to leave Italy. They were mixed up in some hotel brawl down in Naples."

Garfield showed no surprise but asked, "What do you do regular then?"

"A little bit of everything. Help hold down a violent patient about to wreck the joint. Last time, I had a grip of a left ankle. Take dictation on mental cases."

"I noticed you seemed to be at home there," Garfield said, and now he grinned as we were pulling up in front of headquarters. The Colonel was standing on the steps waiting for us. I, of course, was meant to be invisible at such times, but Garfield reached back and gripped my shoulder as he got out of the jeep. "You're a nice kid. When you get back home, drop around some time. Where you from?"

"New Jersey."

"Hell, that's just across the river. Good luck, Sergeant."

Then the driver turned around, a slightly hostile look on his face. I slipped out of the jeep without thanking him for the ride and walked back to the mental ward where I belonged.

Essentially, *Body and Soul* is about an almost first-rate fighter named "Charlie" who would sell his own mother to a promoter to get a crack at the title. It is about corruption, the corrosive effect of racketeers moving into decent lives and changing them forever.

Charlie meets a fairly successful designer, Peg (Lili Palmer), and they decide to try living together. She has reservations about a permanent relationship or marriage because, even from a distance, she smells the greed in the men surrounding Charlie.

Charlie sells out most of the interest in himself (percentages of his winnings) early in his rise. He is literally owned "body and soul" by an odious Mafia type named Roberts, whose front man is an equally noxious person named Quinn (doubtless the Irish have taken a beating here to keep the Italians from picketing the film).

Charlie accidentally kills a Negro boxer named Ben with a head punch at a training camp. Ben is an ex-champ on the way down whom Charlie has injured in an earlier public match.

Enraged by the trap he has allowed himself to be drawn into through his driving ambition, Charlie agrees to throw a big fight but does not. He double-crosses the mobsters who think they have him all wrapped up.

Despite their mutual fears, he and Peg go out into the foggy night relieved. "Everybody dies," he says. Charlie has become philosophical during what may be the last day or week of his life.

The film achieved what Garfield was seeking—he was playing strong roles and he was working with friends who shared his political convictions. If some of them were Communists, that was their business.

He was through with Warner Brothers and felt independent—he was his own man for a sweet four years or until the financing dried up.

Then suddenly, after weeks of inquisitory sessions in government hearing rooms where he repeatedly declined to name associates, Polonsky or Rossen or Lawson or anyone else, he believed might be a Communist; there were no job offers.

His final movie, *He Ran All the Way*, also produced by Bob Roberts, was not a success. Garfield himself was fine, believable in his alternating cunning and fear. But the movie flopped, no regular studio would hire him, and within less than a year and a half of sitting in various homes and apartments and brooding about his future, he was dead—in a lady-friend's home—of a heart attack.

3.

Much has been written about the 1947 investigation of possible Communist infiltration in the American film industry, or, more particularly, in Hollywood. A great deal of this literature or commentary is impassioned, on one side or the other. Those books that came out while some filmwriters were awaiting trial or final court appeal for contempt of Congress (*The Hollywood Ten* by Gordon Kahn, *The Red Plot Against America* by Robert E. Stripling, and *The Time of the Toad* by Dalton Trumbo) are all fascinating pamphleteering, the Trumbo work rising at moments through its pure contempt and revulsion to heights of rhetoric seldom equaled.

That was nearly thirty years ago and time has given us perspective. It seems clear now that there was no real "plot," no conspiracy in Hollywood, and equally clear that the radical politics of a number of Hollywood writers, chiefly John Howard Lawson, Dalton Trumbo, and Donald Ogden Stewart, among the "name" scenarists, had come to the attention of House Un-American Activities Committee Chairman J. Parnell Thomas (New Jersey) and his fellow members, including Richard Nixon. It now turns out that both these former Congressmen were opportunistic and small-minded, bent upon advancing their personal fortunes at almost any cost. One wonders anew about other "big cases"—Hiss-Chambers and the Rosenbergs.

Politicians except in the rarest of cases are in the business of politics, not in the service of the public. That goes for the Russians as well as the Americans. Abraham Polonsky, who talks freely of his Communist involvement years ago "when it was exciting, adventurous, interesting!" says this with a glint of some not-quite dead radicalism in his eye.

The movies were completely apolitical. They counted houses, not votes. If a star or a director or a writer helped bring in the crowds, no one cared if he was a Townsendite or a Socialist. You could be sure that his politics never got on the screen unless by government edict (which was to happen to that old reactionary, Louis B. Mayer).

Harry Cohn, allegedly the most unpopular, Simon Legree-ish, venal studio head in Hollywood, regarded the invasion of the Congressional investigators as not simple madness but a crude attempt to do him out of a great deal of money. He knew Robert Rossen was a gifted writer and director. To hound a man so sensitive, so important to the *Industry!* It angered Cohn almost to the point of apoplexy.

Chapters back in this account, we went over very carefully the pressures of Generalísimo Franco to stop production on Walter Wanger's *Blockade* written by John Howard Lawson.

Now Lawson was one of the investigators' chief targets. His name seemed to be the first on every informer's lips. But Cohn lost sleep wondering who found these informers, where these "schmucks" came from? Who was paying unemployed agitators to undermine a profitable industry that did no one anything but good?

There was clearly no one in the government afraid that Communist propaganda was being "slipped into" *Blockade.* Nationalities were dropped almost always at the request of this government or that but the confrontation between Wanger and Franco was over making the film in the first place. No foreign government ever told a Hollywood producer whether he could make a movie or not. Was this now a first step of the U.S. Government toward telling Hollywood what they could make? If they eventually eliminated or scared off most of the directors and writers, they certainly were telling the studios what they could make. *Crap!* said Cohn, and he brazenly overlooked the Blacklist then beginning to circulate ever so discreetly.

Chairman Thomas's theory—or perhaps it was propounded to him by his counsel Robert Stripling or even advanced as a possibility by one of the parade of "friendly witnesses"—was that the films being produced in Hollywood written by these men and others whom they had proselytized (another facet of the theory: they were a kind of spreading blight) were subtly tinged with Soviet propaganda.

One of the things marking the principal "friendly witness" (the novelist Ayn Rand) and the leading "unfriendly" one, Lawson, was their determined lack of humor. Lawson's explanation of this peculiar state of affairs was set down by him in a book on the movies (*Film: the Creative Process*, 1963):

> "Today, when the American screen seems to have lost its ability to laugh, it is well to realize that there can be no comedy when fear or stupidity prevent recognition of the evils and absurdities that surround us."

It reminds us of Dorothy Parker's "Soldiers of the Republic" in which she feared that a sense of humor at such moments was a frivolity. But Mrs. Parker soon regained hers and it was her only such lapse.

Miss Rand was a Russian ex-patriate or emigrée, who had left Russia in 1926. During the more than twenty years since, she had developed a certain facility for writing in English, marred perhaps by her grim determination to advance her own brand of philosophy, which she eventually called "objectivism," but which was in fact an unregenerate form of individualism that ignored the needs of other people altogether. It was diametrically opposed to Soviet collectivism. One of her novels, *The Fountainhead*, became a best seller in 1943 and went into numerous printings. It told of a young architect who had designed a housing project, only to find that, during the actual construction, the builders had changed his plans. He not only disowned it as his creation, he blew it up. In October 1947, she came to contribute what she could to the cause of advancing self-interest in America by reciting her critique of *Song of Russia,* a film made by Metro in 1944 during our alliance with the Soviet Union against the Axis war machine that by the end of the European war had crushed out the lives of some seventeen million of her former countrymen. She called it a completely naive propaganda film that had not helped Soviet-American relations. "I don't believe," she said, "that the morale of anybody can be built up by a lie. If there was nothing good that we could truthfully say about Russia, then it would have been better to say nothing at all."

Committee member John MacDowell of Pennsylvania revealed a slight levity in questioning Miss Rand. "You paint a very dismal picture of Russia. You made a great point about the number of children who were unhappy. Doesn't anybody smile in Russia any more?"

"Well, if you ask me literally, pretty much no."

"They don't smile?" he wondered a bit wistfully and even smiled for her.

"Not quite that way; no. If they do, it is privately and accidentally. Certainly, it is not social. They don't smile in approval of their system."

And so it went as the only relaxed man in the room gently probed the motives and beliefs of this grim-jawed, mannish-looking woman. "Don't they walk across town to visit their mother-in-law or somebody?"

Miss Rand was losing her poise. "Look," she said as though Representative MacDowell was slightly obtuse, "it is very hard to explain. It is almost impossible to convey to a free people what it is like to live in a totalitarian dictatorship. . . . It is in a way good that you can't even conceive of what it is like. Certainly they have friends and mothers-in-law. They try to live a human life, but you understand it is totally inhuman. Try to imagine what it is like if you are in constant terror from morning till night and at night you are waiting for the doorbell to ring, where you are afraid of anything and everybody, living in a country where human life is nothing, less than nothing. . . ."

It was especially difficult for the genial Mr. MacDowell to imagine over 200,000,000 Russians lying every night in their unhappy beds waiting for doorbells to ring, but Miss Rand got headlines the next day and her dark-haired boyish bob and dark, objectivist eyes were seen in nearly every photo section.

Louis B. Mayer, whose studio had produced the film being given a bad review by Miss Rand, had been born in Minsk, Russia, which is not so terribly far from Miss Rand's home town of Leningrad, but some twenty years earlier. Secretly, he quaked at the thought that Metro was being called to account for something he had thought a patriotic gesture at the time. According to "friendly" Robert Taylor, the Office of War Information had urged the film on Mayer.

Taylor's voluntary stand, his superpatriotism, called for a kind of vacuous courage. It did him small good and it is likely it cost him some fans. No one cheers actors on soapboxes. But then he had the bad luck to have been chosen (as Louis B. Mayer's favorite) to play the conductor in *Song of Russia*. Taylor was now exercising the right of vocal hindsight, correcting his faulty judgment in the past so that everyone would know, in case they cared a hoot, just where Robert Taylor stood.

Taylor had been the hero of the wretched movie, playing the role of a young American conductor who is sent to Russia to do a series of concerts, meets a lovely Russian village lass, and invites her to see Moscow with him. (Miss Rand asserted that the "Moscow" of the film showed beautiful restaurants and lakes with swans. "The streets are clean and prosperous-looking. . . . There is a park where you see happy little children in white blouses running around. . . . They are not homeless children in rags. . . . Then they attend a luxurious dance. I don't know where they got the idea of the clothes and the settings that they used at the ball. . . ." No one thought to question her about the Hollywood view of life, as shown upon the screen, even though she had worked at a studio for some months adapting *The Fountainhead* into a movie and then seeing it through production.)

The possibility of a future blacklist was first advanced by superpatriot Taylor, who was asked by counsel Robert Stripling how he would rid the industry of its Communists. "Well, sir," Taylor began, "if I were given the responsibility of getting rid of them, I would love nothing better than to fire every last one of them and never let them work in a studio or in Hollywood again. . . . I believe firmly that the producers, the heads of the studios in Hollywood, would be and are more than willing to do everything they can to rid Hollywood of Communists and fellow travelers. I think if given the tools with which to work—specifically, some sort of national legislation or an attitude on the part of the government as such which would provide them with the weapons for getting rid of these people—I have no doubt personally but what they would be done in very short order."

Screenwriter Fred Niblo, Jr., was among more than fifteen friendly volunteers that first week in the Washington hearing room. A close friend to Morrie Ryskind, the only spokesman on the inquisitory side with any grain of wit (he had co-authored *Of Thee I Sing*), Niblo soon would attempt to persuade the Screen Writers Guild to make a loyalty oath mandatory for new members as well as the Guild's executive board. His proposal would bring the meeting to a quick halt as scores of writers walked out, leaving the session without a quorum. Failing in this, he became an influential member of the Motion Picture Association for the Preservation of American Ideals, a group that was to be a clearinghouse for future motion picture production, granting clearance to Hollywood film workers, including all of his writing colleagues, who were "clean" or had purged themselves. A former West Pointer, he was to spend forty-five years in the film colony before his death in 1973. Perhaps it is not without significance that he was a nephew of George M. Cohan.

By the second week of the hearings, Hollywood was abroil with reaction. A plane-load of leading film stars flew in from the coast—Humphrey Bogart, his wife Lauren Bacall, John Garfield, and Errol Flynn were among them. It would seem that there were dissidents in Jack Warner's Burbank compound. This group called itself the Committee for the First Amendment, according to later testimony by actor Sterling Hayden, who was also aboard. The writers, the chief targets of the investigation, were going to stand on the First Amendment rather than the Fifth. The First Amendment guaranteed freedom of association, the right to belong to any group or party, whereas the Fifth simply was an umbrella under which any American could hide in order not to incriminate himself by his testimony.

Richard Nixon, who had been a quiet and unobtrusive member of the Committee during the first week, disappeared altogether the second week when word of the celebrated opposition broke. Even then, his politics were cautious; he only went in for the kill when he believed he would be unchallenged or meet a weakened or intimidated opposing force.

John Howard Lawson remembers a knock on his door early one October morning and going to answer in his bathrobe. The young man who handed him his subpoena commented on the handsome citrus trees surrounding his Valley home and left.

Lawson later was to be named a Communist by at least twenty-nine witnesses during the shameful period of recantation that went on before the Committee in the early 1950s after three years of militant blacklisting. He is an impressive man; broad-chested, with a jutting jaw and genial eyes that meet yours head on. He looks very much as you would imagine a leader of the IRA to look, defiant and amused by the follies of this world.

You could believe that he was a Communist and a dedicated one, but if you had been told that he was a vegetarian and that he was throwing up picket lines around all the meat markets, you could be sure that the boycott would be effective and the meat industry would call for his head. But he made no secret of his admiration for the Soviet Union, nor of his outrage against the filmmakers, who had abused the writer ever since Hollywood had become a film center.

Lawson and his wife had come to Hollywood in 1928 after a small group of other radical playwrights and he had formed a production group known as the New Playwrights (Elmer Rice was another member) and they had foundered. Thalberg, his first boss, did not look into the politics of the talent he hired any more than any other Hollywood chief. Lawson's most prestigious and far-out play, *Processional,* had excited enough comment to give him a certain power and influence in Hollywood in advance of his coming.

Lawson saw Irving as a man who cajoled and charmed his employees into doing far more for him than they ever would have done for, say, B. P. Schulberg. Lawson thought his employer had an "extraordinarily naive romanticism, an attitude that gave Metro its very nineteenth-century style in the late twenties just before sound came in."

His radical notions (one had Garbo in an offscreen voice speaking to her lover *over* a huge closeup of her—stream of consciousness as a way out of taking a chance on the world hearing Garbo's guttural accent) were largely unexplored by Metro and he was assigned conventional fare, "the meat and potatoes" programmers that were fed into the huge distribution process. He soon itched to get another play on Broadway, surprising and offending Thalberg. "You have a whole future here," he told Lawson, and one can hear echoes of his remarks to Charles MacArthur. "You have a great opportunity and you're just throwing it away." But he was given his freedom.

Lawson's play failed; his savings were soon depleted. He returned to Hollywood and Metro to help found the Screen Writers Guild for "by that time I was thoroughly disgusted with the position of the writer and the lack of creativity opportunity in Hollywood. Thalberg was away at the time (on that vacation with the MacArthurs). Louis B. Mayer was conspiring to get rid of Thalberg. But when Thalberg did get back, he was very bitter with me. He was sure that he could destroy it [the Guild]. . . . [It] was an open threat that writers would demand partial but more effective control of their material. . . ." And with Broadway's lack of response to his radical works, Lawson wanted to remain a dramatist. He and his family decided to remain in the film community. It was a fateful decision, as everybody knows, and one that would give the men within HUAC (House Un-American Activities Committee) a wedge, for everybody knew that Lawson was a gadfly, and, more to the point, a gadfly to reckon with.

Flown to Washington at government expense for his hearing, Lawson's testimony opened the second week (October 27th). He was called first and he petitioned for the right to make an opening statement. This was denied. He protested, of course. Warner, Mayer, and others had been allowed extensive opening remarks, but Chairman Thomas cut him off with a bang of the gavel. Apparently, Thomas had seen a copy, was outraged by its strong opposition to the Committee and said, "That statement is not pertinent to this inquiry." It was to become a rule of thumb that anything uttered by a witness that ran counter to the Committee's plan (to expose Communism in the movies) was excluded.

Chief inquisitor Stripling went next (after a brief background of Lawson's credits, etc.) to the big question that would always come: "Mr. Lawson, are you now or have you ever been a member of the Communist Party of the United

States?" Lawson became very agitated at this frontal assault. "In framing my answer to that question," he said, "I must emphasize the points that I have raised before. The question of Communism is no way related to this inquiry, which is an attempt to get control of the screen and to invade the basic rights of American citizens in all fields."

Then within moments, Lawson was the heretic that Thomas and his Congressional hugger-muggers knew him to be: "You are using the old technique, which was used in Hitler Germany, in order to create a scare here—" Blasphemy, according to the Congressmen and other "friendlies" gathered that morning, continued to pour from Lawson as Thomas pounded his gavel. ". . . In order that you can then smear the motion-picture industry, and you can proceed to the press, to any form of communication in this country. . . . The Bill of Rights was established precisely to prevent the operation of any committee which could invade the basic rights of Americans. Now if you want to know . . . (Angry voices of Committee members begin to rise) . . . about the perjury that has been committed here and the perjury that is planned. . . . You permit me and my attorneys to bring in here the witnesses that testified last week and you permit us to cross-examine these witnesses, and we will show up the whole tissue of lie. . . ." Chairman Thomas vigorously pounded his gavel and shouted: "We are going to get the answer to that question if we have to stay here for a week. Are you a member of the Communist Party, or have you ever been a member of the Communist Party?"

"It is unfortunate," Lawson said, and his tones now seemed pedagogical, "and tragic that I have to teach this committee the basic principles of American——." Lawson's lecture continued and Thomas asked security officers to "take this man away from the stand." There was both applause and boos as Lawson was removed from the room.

The Committee had advance information on Lawson, as they had on dozens of others. It was a fairly open secret in town that John Howard Lawson admired the Soviet Union and there were few writers within the Guild and without who did not think him a Communist. But nearly all of them closed ranks behind him in a solid wall of defense against this precursor of Senator McCarthy. It must be remembered that Martin Dies and J. Parnell Thomas caused as much grief, broke up as many families, sent as many to jail, as McCarthy ever did. The havoc they created still lives with us.

Lawson's film career ended that year with Susan Hayward's *Smash-Up: The Story of a Woman.* Donald Ogden Stewart, being a particular favorite of the Metro executives, lasted longer—until 1949 (the year his last Metro screenplay, *Edward, My Son,* was produced and released). Stewart said that was the year they began to close in on him. He is convinced that *they needed him* until then. Stewart was asked to clear himself and he didn't bother to do so.

Lawson's greatest power had been with the Guild, not with the studios. But Stewart had influence, first with Thalberg, then with Mannix and Stromberg and others. He was allowed, for instance, to retain some strong antifascist sentiment in *The Keeper of the Flame.* It is said that Louis B. Mayer walked out on it. The film's premise was that Fascism might come to America in the guise of patriotism. " . . . In this film, we exposed the technique of using labor unions, of using youth groups, of all of the things that Hitler had used, as possible in America. . . . It *did* work. It *did* tell the audience that there was this danger . . . because . . . it's awfully hard to go back to the thirties and realize that it wasn't just a strange feeling that we had . . . that they might just take over America."

Both Lawson and Stewart were *survivors.* Not only did they outlive their chief persecutor by many years (both are still alive—Lawson in his Hollywood area home and Stewart in his Hampstead Heath place in London), but they lived to see two of the Committee members, J. Parnell Thomas and Richard Nixon in far greater trouble than they ever knew. Thomas was to go into the Federal Penitentiary at Danbury, Connecticut, in 1951, for malfeasance in office (padding his Congressional payroll) and Nixon's Waterloo was Watergate.

Lawson still has his old radical vision. He is working on a vast literary project that "will be of value in the great task of using modern technology creatively and converting new forms of communication. I see the outlines of a vast new landscape of peoples' art. A multimedia reflection of human experience."

4.

One of the pictures the Committee was especially interested in was *Crossfire*, the stark portrait of a Jew-hater who kills a man simply because his name is "Samuels." This killer, played by Robert Ryan, in what remains one of the finest performances of his long career as a leading man, finally trips himself up through his rabid and psychotic hatred of all Jews.

There was no preachment, no dogma, injected into this tight script by John Paxton from Richard Brooks's book. Producer Adrian Scott had allowed America to see an Archie Bunker without the redeeming grace of buffoonery—a savage, outrageous brute of an American; one we all encounter some time if we live long enough and are unlucky enough. The film reputedly had cost only half a million dollars, and under Edward Dmytryk's tightly controlled direction, it never skipped a telling moment or a chance to grab at the guts. It was a persuasive portrait of an American to be ashamed of and the Committee proclaimed its displeasure to such a degree it cited two of the men involved (Scott and Dmytryk) for contempt of Congress, which sent both to jail for a year, and it got three of them (Scott, Dmytryk, and Paxton) onto the Blacklist, a compilation of persons who were unfriendly witnesses before the Committee or who were named as presumed Communists by friendly witnesses. That list was to hold in most cases for about fifteen years.

Anne Shirley, alias Dawn O'Day, had been in one form of show business or another literally all of her life. During the time of the Committee investigation, she was Mrs. Adrian Scott.

Unlike many of her peers who were "born in a trunk," Anne Shirley was not a burnt-out case. She was not on pep-up pills, downers; her neuroses were the ordinary ones. If she was onto anything it was *obedience.* Obedience had been ingrained in her by her mother from infancy. There was never any rebellion in Annie.

And she was too sweet for her own good, not sickeningly so, just too gentle for one of the toughest rackets in the world. And this was no mask she was holding up to hide her dislike of the "unnice" things in the movie business beyond number. Anne Shirley was the genuine article. Little Miss Anne of Green Gables stepping from the pages of a book and the character to the life.

She had been working in Los Angeles since 1922, when she was three years old, where she made her movie debut as a little boy, "Prince Carlos of Spain" in Pola Negri's *The Spanish Dancer.* She was never a child star, she went to early "cattle calls," but she was also remembered by such directors as Herbert Brenon and she would be called back. Her one distinction out of those childhood years was that she played eight stars as children (Miss Negri, in another movie, Barbara Stanwyck, Fay Wray, Jean Arthur, Myrna Loy, Madge Bellamy, Frances Dee, and Janet Gaynor). In the silent days, they believed in little prologues with the hero and heroine as children dropping portentous clues of the drama to come. She had an incredible collection of dolls—mementoes from those leading ladies.

By the time she was eighteen, she was a star on loan-out to Sam Goldwyn and her only complaint to him was that director King Vidor did not inform her each day whether she was performing well or not: she needed that pat on the head. Something was said to Vidor (the movie was *Stella Dallas*), and after that there was always a smile from that handsome gentleman and "You were very good!"

She worked with some important directors besides Vidor: F. W. Murnau, John Ford, Brenon, and William Wellman. She starred in Garson Kanin's first movie, *A Man to Remember*.

Anne Shirley became one of RKO's medium-weight stars, important enough to have billboards announcing her pictures splashed around the country but not important enough ever to be able to pick and choose her parts. When she met Adrian Scott in 1944 she was not really interested in matrimony—she had got out of a bad marriage with actor John Payne. But they liked each other at once. Adrian had much of Annie's sweetness and gentleness of spirit. Neither of them knew that what he needed at the time was a compatible tough lady who would go out and denounce Committees and stir up women's groups: make angry speeches at rallies.

Producer Adrian Scott cast actress Anne Shirley in one of the leading roles in a tough Raymond Chandler adaptation, *Murder, My Sweet.* She wanted the part of the hooker (labeled for the Code as the "second wife of the old man" just as the mistress in *Citizen Kane* would be), but Claire Trevor had done this kind of thing for more than two-thirds of her career and they cast the part to type. The film was a success; Adrian was given more authority by his boss, Dore Schary, who liked his creative approach to movie projects. Adrian and Shirley were married.

Their mutual idealism made things *seem* right for quite a

long time. They both ran counter to the more formidable Hollywood types; they were not venal; they climbed over no dead bodies to get movies or roles. And then suddenly the blue sky began falling.

Annie remembered that it began so innocuously, a little thing like a subpoena, but *everyone* was getting them. Then suddenly Adrian needed a lawyer. And Annie was out of it all. The investigators never bothered to call her just as they never called Alan Campbell. They knew better.

"Which friends stayed around?" she pondered. "Which didn't? Some became better friends, some parted forever. Trying to get an important lawyer. I remember that . . . that left me quite bewildered, because here were these liberal marvelous gentlemen and everyone wanted to help them and then they found the lawyer that they wanted. And he said he'd love to do it because he believed in the . . . I can't remember what he wanted. Was it $50,000 . . . $100,000. Rally round the money flag. . . . He and Eddy (Dmytryk) . . . it was good-bye, buddy, except nobody announced it. And you'd been told . . . they can't do that to you 'cause that's un-American and it's unfair and there's the Bill of Rights and the Constitution and . . . terrific! Except you're not working any more and you have to go to Washington."

With the Blacklist fully operative, it numbered several hundred and included dozens of writers, stars Karen Morley, Gale Sondergaard, Larry Parks, directors Lewis Milestone, Edward Dmytryk, Joseph Losey, and Jules Dassin. As the McCarthy era widened the scope of the Committee, it began creating film career dead-ends for John Garfield, Charles Laughton. The bravest of the studio heads was Harry Cohn, whose outrage was mentioned earlier, but Columbia eventually was forced into line. The most articulate "foe" of the Committee among the chiefs, Dore Schary, was pressured into surrender, as was Eric Johnston, who took over the reins of the Motion Picture Producers Authority from Will Hays.

Many fled to England, where jobs appeared to have been promised them in the prospering British film industry. But this must have riled British natives within the movies for jobs evaporated before contracts could be signed. For most, including Adrian Scott, England was—in those early months— a big let-down.

When Scott was convicted, the last appeal shot to hell by a change in the makeup of the United States Supreme Court (it no longer was dominated by liberals), Anne Shirley and Adrian parted. In militant circles, she was denounced. Among their close friends, their parting was understood. Annie Scott was a lady who had grown up before the camera, always under the protective eye of Mama. She had retired from films to become a housewife and helpmate to a talented young producer. Now she was tied to a man who spent most of his time in lawyer's offices or hearing rooms, moving from one country to another. They had no home, no income. She had none of the resources Adrian needed at the time and they both knew it. They were both victims of a time when a group of politicians attempted to put across one of the greatest frauds of this century—that American movies were riddled with Soviet propaganda.

5.

Abraham Polonsky, who had made such an impressive script of *Body and Soul*, was very possibly the most significant talent to emerge from the brief life of Enterprise Productions. In December 1948 the film that gave him a substantial niche in Hollywood, one to which he would return following the years of the Blacklist, was released. *Force of Evil*, like *Body and Soul*, dealt with the blight of human avarice. It was an area Polonsky (an East Side boy who had become a New York lawyer for a time) knew intimately.

The movie was directed by Polonsky as well as written by him in collaboration with Ira Wolfert, the author of the book on which it was based, *Tucker's People*. The film was not a success despite the presence once again of John Garfield and nearly unanimous raves. It was not, as *Gone with the Wind* had been and, latterly, *The Graduate*, a great audience picture. It cast a chill. It left you with a sense of despair because it was all so damned convincing.

But it was a *succès d'estime* of such proportions that Abe Polonsky had moved into the ranks of the Daniel Manns and just a notch or two below the Fred Zinnemanns. Then, within months, he was on the Blacklist and unemployable. Abraham Polonsky probably had the fastest rise and briefest career of any major figure in Hollywood since Jackie Coogan.

Under pseudonyms, he kept an income flowing in to keep to his family going. Back in New York, he wrote many of the half-hour TV melodramas called *Danger;* he did numerous *You Were There* episodes. His talent for re-creating reality was still being tapped. It wasn't until the 1960s that he was asked to rewrite *Madigan* for the movies and finally was able to write and direct *Tell Them Willie Boy Was Here*, which put him back where he was in late 1948.

Albert Maltz was sent to a Southern prison camp. He later spoke of it as having had "worse food but it didn't have bars and guards and so on. It just had signs that said 'Keep Inside.' . . . Most of the guys in my place were in for three or six months for making illegal liquor. . . . They assumed, most of them, that I was in for illegal liquor too and then if they asked me and I said, 'Contempt of Congress,' they'd say, 'What the hell is that?' and then I'd tell them and they'd say, 'Jesus Christ, what's this world coming to?' I set out from the beginning just to be myself and I found very quickly . . . that guys would approach me and say 'I can tell you've had some education. Would you help me write out my appeal for parole or my . . .'—that kind of thing. And I'd say 'Yeah.' . . . I remember a hillbilly came to me—and about 40 percent of the

camp was illiterate—and in prison in general, guys feel a
certain kinship to everyone else as against the administration
of those who put you in, provided you're not a son-of-a-bitch.
If a guy comes in who's a real bastard, prisons don't like him
any more than they'd like him on the block. And if you're all
right with them . . . For instance, in my camp I was a
medical orderly. And because of the fact that the orderly who
preceded me had not had any money, so he couldn't buy . . .
peanuts, cigarettes, that kind of thing, when guys came to him
for pills he would say 'Got a couple of cigarettes?' and he
wouldn't give them aspirin or things like that unless they
forked over. Well, I didn't do that kind of thing so that was a
big up for me, you see. . . . You were allowed to do writing,
but it had to be read by the superintendent of the camp and
passed. And if it was not passed, you couldn't take it
out. . . . Now it so happened that I got the idea for a novel
that I subsequently wrote, about prison, when I was in the
Washington jail. . . . But if I wrote about that while I was in
prison, they wouldn't let it out because that was one thing you
were forbidden to write about in your letters—all letters were
censored, of course. And you could not put anything about
camp conditions or what you lived in or what it was like. So,
wanting to write about the Washington jail was impossible.
. . . So I made some notes in prison about certain things
which passed the prison superintendent, but . . . I wrote
out . . . a tremendous amount, maybe fifty pages of notes on
conditions in the jail, food, what we got for every meal, of
people in the jail. And before we left there, which we stayed
in for two and a half weeks, I memorized all of those and tore
them up. And the minute I got to where I went, which was in
West Virginia, I wrote them all out again. And then I knew
them; then I memorized them again and I tore those up. So
when I got out, I put them down again and I had the definitive
material. . . . I wanted the meticulous detail."

After getting out of prison, Maltz and his family settled in

Hollywood for a time, where he wrote fiction, then moved on to Mexico. That stay drew out to eleven years.

Maltz, Scott, Lawson, and Dmytryk were among the Hollywood Ten who were tried and jailed of the original eighteen, the others being Herbert Biberman, Lester Cole, Dalton Trumbo, Samuel Ornitz, Ring Lardner, Jr., and Alvah Bessie. In his account of his involvement, Bessie would write in *Inquisition in Eden*: ". . . In my last interview before leaving Texarkana to reenter the *free* world, one of the prison officials said, 'Bessie, I've read your testimony and the others'; I've looked up the Supreme Court decision in similar cases and I've studied a lot of American history since you came here. And I want to tell you this: I understand you're some sort of radical—and I don't hold with such ideas—but from what I understand of the American democratic tradition, you are here on a bum rap.'"

6.

Sometime in 1948, the Screen Writers Guild held its first annual awards dinner at the Bel Air Hotel. The Guild itself had considered itself *Amicus curiae* of every member under attack by the Committee, but none of the defendants can recall either Latin legal word being very much in prominence. The survivors of the shipwreck, and they were in the majority, elected to behave on this occasion as though nothing were amiss.

Ben Hecht was a member in good standing of the Guild but an increasingly controversial figure on the stage of world politics. He had been boycotted in England and no film bearing his name could play there because of his flagrant attacks upon the British Empire's internment program for hopeful Israeli emigrants. He had helped pull together for this festive evening a first performance anywhere by the *Simfonietta*, an orchestral group consisting of Harry Kurnitz, William Wyler, Everett Freeman, and Hecht himself on fiddles; Harpo Marx on clarinet; Jesse Lasky on trumpet; Dwight Taylor on sax; Charlie Lederer on drums; Orson Welles on a primitive instrument he had invented himself which he called "the jawbone of an ass"; and two cuddly nineteen-year-old sisters on tuba. The group had rehearsed numerous evenings under George Stoll and Georges Antheill, and felt sufficiently professional to treat guest speaker Oscar Hammerstein II as well as Leonard Spiegelgass and other members assembled to John Philip Sousa's *The Stars and Stripes Forever* and *The Emperor's Waltz*.

They opened with the Sousa march and went resoundingly through the opening bars, which end, if I am not mistaken, in the clash of a cymbal. Charlie Lederer, not one of a race of giants, reached out to clang the cymbal and fell off his stool. The roar of laughter registered .6 on the University of California's seismograph.

And there were serious efforts by others, among them Billy Wilder, to shake the town out of its paralysis, for the Blacklist had unnerved everyone, was still going on, and threatened to destroy whatever creativity was left. Wilder today says that he was solidly behind the defendants in the trial of the Hollywood Ten. "If I hadn't been in the middle of getting a movie ready," he insists, "I would have flown to Washington with the Committee for the First Amendment." No one ever can fault Wilder's hindsight. As he himself says, "It's always twenty-twenty." But more believably, he remembers: "The whole thing was a tragicomedy. John Howard Lawson was one thing and we knew it and we also knew that there was no communistic dogma going into pictures."

"We've grown up politically. *Wages of Fear* and the films of Costa-Gavras are accepted and praised. I have read leftist stories in the *Los Angeles Times*."

But back in 1950 when he was shooting *Sunset Boulevard* at Paramount, a film which for a few weeks diverted the town's attention away from its political illness, he was his own boss and he did not have to take a loyalty oath. "I certainly sympathized with those who had to or could not do so for personal reasons." Politically, he was "clean" in any case. He never attended one of the meetings of the Anti-Nazi League. Having lost most of his family in the extermination centers of Europe, they didn't have a thing to tell him.

"Brackett and I," he remembers, "were determined to do a Hollywood picture. You think since you know it so well, it would be easy, but it's not. We originally wanted to do it with Mae West, but she refused to play an older woman. It ultimately was distilled into the drama of the silent star who cannot adjust to the change and is destroyed. Gloria Swanson, Mary Pickford and Pola Negri were all considered. And then we decided on Montgomery Clift for the writer. But he bowed out because, being the serious New York actor that he was, his audience, he felt, would never accept him making love to a woman thirty-five years his senior. William Holden was our emergency casting."

Norma Desmond, as played so convincingly by Gloria Swanson, has gone into Hollywood legend, so great is the status of this film. People will point out this house or that along Sunset Boulevard as the house "used in the movie." It has outgrossed both versions of *A Star Is Born* as the most popular film about Hollywood ever made. But when it was released there was a terrible furore, exactly as Billy had hoped there would be. Louis B. Mayer said that Wilder "should be thrown out of Hollywood for befouling the nest and biting the hand that fed him."

The unlikely opening, showing a corpse floating in a swimming pool while in a voice-over narration he tells us how he wound up there, was always in Wilder's mind in one form or another. Originally, the movie started out in the morgue with the dead Joe Gillis lying there along with six or eight other corpses, all under sheets. And then we stayed with Gillis's corpse as he began to tell the same story as the floating corpse. After being shot, this didn't look quite right to Wilder and he and Brackett rewrote the opening.

For those who might think otherwise, Joe Gillis's death and Norma Desmond's madness had nothing to do with the Retribution demanded by the Code for their having had an affair. But Wilder is often bemused by the Code's fantasies. "In a love scene, the man had to have one foot on the ground. Also, someone would come in with a tape measure to determine the depth of the cleavage of a woman's dress."

Walking around Paramount in those days, Wilder is said to have observed a belch of smoke coming from nearby RKO Studios and saying to someone, "What a horrible stink!" When his friend wondered what they were burning, Wilder allegedly replied, "Probably Eddie Dmytryk." Dmytryk was to go to prison within weeks and serve approximately nine months.

Quite another fate awaited director, Joseph Losey, black-listed because he was supposed to have helped suspected Communist Hanns Eisler, a composer friend of Bertolt Brecht, into this country and himself labeled a Communist during that bizarre parade of informers before the Committee in the years 1951–53, as motion picture unemployables sought to purge themselves. Losey would go into exile in England, where he would resume his career and watch it ascend to a level of prestige that few American directors enjoy—on a level with Antonioni, Chabrol, Bertolucci, Truffault, Fellini, Nichols, Bogdanovich, Reisz, Resnais, Bergman, Hitchcock, Polanski, Kubrick, Ray, Schlesinger, and Kurosawa.

Brecht, one of the world's most significant playwrights, was treated like some diseased parcel of immigrant flesh before the Committee, given what is known as "the third degree" by

Robert Stripling, most of it literary, having to do with his plots and what he was saying in his works. Then, as though in recompense for all this difficulty and embarrassment heaped upon him, he was dismissed with "words of approbation" from the chairman.

It was 1951 and his play *Galileo,* as translated and adapted by Charles Laughton in close collaboration with Brecht back in California, was about to open, but the climate in New York and elsewhere in the country under the windy blasts of Joe McCarthy was more than Brecht could bear and he left before the premiere.

Galileo came into New York for a limited run at the Maxine Elliott Theatre. Charles Laughton's bravery can hardly be underestimated. Even the audiences, and it was sold out most nights, had the feeling that their mere presence in that theater for that play was provocation for they knew not what sort of retribution. There were furtive glances as many hurried inside and some wondered if the FBI was taking photographs of the audience.

What they were seeing was Brecht and Laughton's careful reconstruction of a time and the trials of a man under the same kind of political pressures as those who had gone before the Committee. Galileo was ordered to recant his theory of the universe because it went against all current religious orthodoxy.

An Aside—Charles Laughton

As the sympathetic murderer in *Payment Deferred,* Charles Laughton first hit upon the role that suited him best—the life-abused or fierce individualist with a subtle strain of humanity showing through. The play had a long run in London, was produced in New York by Gilbert Miller, and brought Laughton a flood of Hollywood offers.

But he could not be bought easily. He never would be much

interested in money and he went through several fortunes. In fact, he never had entertained any notion of becoming a screen star. He knew he was not good-looking; in fact, he once told his wife, actress and comedienne Elsa Lanchester, that his face was like an elephant's behind. But once when Marlene Dietrich (on the next sound stage to his at Denham, England) was quoted in a London newspaper as saying "I would rather be kissed by Charles Laughton than by any leading man I can think of," he threw his hat into the air and celebrated with champagne with his wife, who had had the wisdom to pick out such a sensuous brute.

Paramount finally won him with a contract that gave him six months off every year. It allowed him to wait for the right part much of his career and even at less pay in some cases. This premise worked out so well for him that few actors ever have enjoyed a longer or more critically acclaimed life as a star. He and Elsa lived simply in London flats, a rustic cottage in Surrey that was their true home, and rented Mediterranean houses in Hollywood.

In his first American movie, he starred as a submarine captain (in an unnamed nation's fleet) stationed with his nymphomaniac wife (Tallulah Bankhead) in an African port. *The Devil and the Deep* (1932) featured Hollywood's two handsomest leading men as the wife's lovers: Gary Cooper and Cary Grant; but it was Laughton who riveted the audience's attention, despite Cooper's natural grace and timing before the camera. Laughton, as the cuckolded husband, was not interested in pity. He was nasty, vicious, his ego bleeding all over the screen.

Laughton had begun his screen career as an obstreperous character. He played a cabaret customer in the British-made *Piccadilly* (1929) who ruins dancer Gilda Gray's performance by loudly complaining about a dirty plate. It was a day's work, but the audience was aware of a new screen presence and a commanding one. For a number of years, even his fellow actors were in awe of him on the set. Marilyn Monroe was to liken the experience of playing in a vignette with him to "playing opposite God."

Charles Laughton had come out of Scarborough, England, an innkeeper's son, the least fair perhaps of that Fair town's lads to make a great success in the world, but he was catnip to the screen's sex queens. It was easy to believe that he had tumbled every last one of Henry VIII's wives in the hay when he played that monarch in the Korda film (1933). He had completed his role as Nero in Cecil B. De Mille's *The Sign of the Cross* that same year and there was some fear, especially in Laughton, that he was being type-cast to play the world's great just as George Arliss once had been.

Then *The Beachcomber* came along and shot this possibility to smithereens. "Ginger Ted," in this marvelous film made by Laughton-Pommer-Mayflower (the first instance of a major British star forming his own producing company), has lived on a South Sea island for more years than anyone can remember, taking his pleasure with the native girls, who don't care that he is unwashed and a heathen, whose best friend is a mongrel dog. Then a schoolmarmish type comes along, sister of a British missionary, and they are thrown together on a reef. She (Elsa Lanchester) is prepared to secure her virtue with a knife. She is shocked to learn that he hasn't the slightest interest. Laughton's role as "Ted" is remarkably similar in concept and performance to Humphrey Bogart's "Allnut" in the *The African Queen*, which was made by John Huston twenty years later.

Laughton's Henry VIII won him an Oscar and he got a nomination for his Captain Bligh in 1935. But his greatest moment came that first night in New York in 1951 when the inquisitory forces in the United States seemed to be running the country and he walked on stage at the Maxine Elliott Theatre as "Galileo," one of the great heretics of all time. Laughton had worked closely with Bertolt Brecht on the

English version of the play (and was given credit as a collaborator by Brecht). In the play, Galileo is urged to recant his heretical belief that the world is not the center of the universe (as the Church insisted!). Under the combined pressures of excommunication (which he doubtless can withstand) and execution (which he finds he cannot), Galileo finally caves in. The play really is about a man who has sold out and can't live with his conscience.

Galileo did not enjoy the success of Arthur Miller's *The Crucible*, which came two years later, probably because Miller's historical case was a more striking parallel to those few who stood up to McCarthy and Dies and Thomas (and usually wound up in prison for their bravery). Brecht was writing about the more human and less heroic man who was far more common in those nightmare years of the early fifties.

But Laughton's bravery in bringing in a play at such a time earned him a standing ovation when he appeared. (Senator Joe McCarthy already had made his Wheeling, West Virginia, speech: "I have here the names . . ."; and normally outspoken liberal Americans were looking over their shoulders before denouncing the incredible situation to their friends). Surely at that moment Laughton ranked with all legendary heroes. The justly celebrated Laughton will of iron was often called "pathological" by film reviewers but never had it been more in evidence or more cherished.

Then he and Elsa returned to their handsome airy flat on Gordon Square in London, where ten years earlier they had entertained Virginia Woolf, David Garnett, and Ruth Gordon. A few years later, he would play the lead in *I, Claudius,* a doom-ridden film project wrecked midstream by the hospitalization of its leading lady, Merle Oberon, whose face was horribly disfigured in an auto crash. Her face was saved but not the picture, which was shown in an hour-length version many years later as *The Epic That Never Was.*

Then there were a few colorful character parts and a long

cross-country tour doing Shaw's *Don Juan in Hell* in concert
form with Agnes Morehead and Charles Boyer. But he
obviously was under a strain. He tired easily, and in the
summer of 1962, he was laid up at Memorial Hospital in New
York followed by weeks in his bed at the Hotel St. Moritz.
Ruth Gordon remembered he was "thinner. And whiter."
Eyes deeper and very blue. He looked like one of his beloved
French Impressionist paintings. On the night table were twigs
from Central Park he had asked Elsa to pick. He wanted
something growing.

That December he was dead, at sixty-three, and he was,
like the Marilyn who likened him to God, irreplaceable.

In mid-1951, mystery writer Dashiell Hammett was sent to
jail. After repeated demands on the part of the government, he
had adamantly refused to reveal the sources of a fund set up to
pledge bail for four Communist officials, who then skipped
town, three of them remaining fugitives (they had been jailed
under the notorious Smith Act, which made it a crime to
belong to the Communist Party).

Hammett was then fifty-seven years old, in frail health, and
he went into a Kentucky prison camp and emerged six months
later altered in attitude and gait and totally withdrawn. He
went into isolation at the home of his old companion Lillian
Hellman from which he seldom ventured. Within ten years,
he was dead.

Hammett quietly but in forceful ways had remained at the
forefront of every significant liberal movement in the country
for more than twenty-five years. He and Dorothy Parker often
shared the same podium, but Mrs. Parker (and Lillian
Hellman) were questioned and excused. Miss Hellman even
was allowed to have a letter of explanation read at the time in
which she wrote the now-famous "I cannot and will not cut
my conscience to fit this year's fashions."

History for once was going to serve the people instead of the juggernaut reverse. The House Un-American Activities Committee's investigation of Hollywood and its hope of controlling the content of American movies through screening those who worked for Hollywood were to be dashed.

By 1948, it became essential for American film companies to begin tapping huge accumulations of frozen currency, there since the end of World War II. These collections were in England, France, Italy; in fact, in nearly every country on the Continent and several beyond. Anglo-American deals were worked out, Anglo-American-French deals; Italian-American; the combinations were as various as Sam Spiegel's names and fortunes and he was often in the middle of them. Hollywood was forced to become a part—through these financial pressures—of a world cinema. Control of such a sprawling industry would have taxed the resources of even the United Nations, much less a left-footed Congressional Committee.

Joseph Breen, administrating the Code, was shocked the following year to hear that Ingrid Bergman was about to divorce her husband, forsake her child, and marry Roberto Rossellini. Although the Blacklist was still in force, it was a relief to many that a star's morality was of more concern to the Hollywood Establishment than his or her politics.

Breen presumed to write Miss Bergman a letter:

> It goes without saying that these reports are the cause of great consternation among large numbers of our people who have come to look upon you as the *first lady* of the screen—both individually and artistically.
>
> On all hands, I hear nothing but expressions of the most profound shock that you have any such plans. . . . Such stories will not only *not* react favorably to your picture, but may very well *destroy your career as a motion picture artist.* They may result in the American public becoming so thoroughly outraged that your pictures will be ignored, and your box-office value ruined.

Miss Bergman sent Breen a reply from Stromboli, where she had set up housekeeping arrangements with Rosselini and was preparing for the birth of a daughter:

Stromboli

May 8, 1949

Dear Mr. Breen:

Since the arrival of your very kind letter I have made a statement. But so much harm is already made I believe no statement can cure it. I am deeply sorry to have hurt my friends involved in the pictures we have already made. I hope with all my heart they will not have to pay for my fault.
My sincere thanks for your concern and kindness.

Yours,

Ingrid Bergman

Miss Bergman survived the storm that swirled around her for three or four years, and from her courage stars ventured to enjoy their private lives, despite the public's continuing speculation about what they were doing. If anything, Miss Bergman's stand increased public curiosity in the celebrated for they afterward began to look upon stars as a breed apart—no longer gods to be emulated or worshipped.

7.

On April 25, 1951, director Edward Dmytryk, just out of prison and facing the certainty of never again working in Hollywood films, recanted everything in an appearance before the House Un-American Activities Committee, saying that the situation "has somewhat changed."

Dmytryk said that he thought that the Soviet Union and Red China supported the North Koreans in the Korean War. ". . . There is a Communist menace," he told the Committee,

". . . and the Communist Party in this country is a part of that menace." Apparently he believed that the circumstantial evidence against Alger Hiss, collected by Committee investigators and publicly charged as damning by no less than Richard Nixon, had led to a just verdict in Hiss's subsequent trial, or so he told the Committee. "I don't say," he testified, "all members of the Communist Party are guilty of treason, but I think a party that encourages them to act in this capacity is treasonable. For this reason I am willing to talk today." He further said that what the Hollywood Communists were after was money, prestige, and control of the content of pictures by taking over the guilds and unions. He then named six of the Screen Directors Guild and fourteen screenwriters as party members, not omitting John Howard Lawson. He attempted to minimize his own perfidy by saying something to the effect that he was performing a public service by turning in his friends. "I never heard of anybody informing on the Boy Scouts," he concluded.

Dmytryk was promptly reinstated as a director, but the idealism that had illuminated his earlier films and made them seem even better than they were, was gone. After three successful adaptations of best-selling novels: *The Caine Mutiny, Raintree County* and *The Young Lions*, his career began to falter. By the end of the 1950s and the beginning of the 1960s, he would be doing junk epics such the dreadful remake of *The Blue Angel*, and *A Walk on the Wild Side*, *The Carpetbaggers* and *Where Love Has Gone*. Quite literally, he had moved from his symbolic soapbox to soap opera.

8.

American films still have an identity in the world, but the Hollywood production has not. No one, even in America, cares any longer whether *Lady Sings the Blues*, a major international success, was shot on location in and around New

York or in Los Angeles, or whether *The Sting* was shot in its entirety on the back lot of Universal.

Lady Sings the Blues, the fictionalized screen biography of the blues and jazz singer Billie Holliday, was released in 1972 nearly forty years after the initial enforcement of the Code. It violates a number of the Code's original "don'ts," but in the 1960s, under the administration of Jack Valenti, the Motion Picture Producers organization inaugurated a rating system of the most sensible sort. The film starred Diana Ross as Billie Holliday in what was perhaps the most auspicious acting debut in contemporary American movies. She was on the screen nearly all of its length and director Sidney Furie was able to extract a variety of emotions and spiritual agonies of almost unbearable intensity. It carried an "R" rating, meaning *restricted to patrons 18 or older.* Anyone under that age had to be accompanied by an adult. There were numerous reasons for the film being given this rating rather than a PG (Parental Guidance advised) and there was no effort on the part of the producers to take out the vulgarisms or the graphic rape scene, showing in some detail what had been implied or left to the imagination in *Rasputin,* released exactly forty years earlier. The scene, tossed in by the screenwriters Terence McCoy and Chris Clark with Suzanne dePasse, informed us in harrowing detail that Billie Holliday had been violated by an aging drunk drifter when she was still a young girl. It was not a fact found in the book of the same title written by Bill Dufty with the cooperation of Billie herself and was one of several factors which led the author to ask that his name be deleted from the credits of the picture.

Interestingly, the rape does not appear in the British cut of the film, either deleted by the censors or to remove some playing time from this longish movie. The British version is superior to the American one, the rape scene seeming gratuitous in retrospect and actually slowing down the swift pace of the story.

The "X" rating, which officially excludes minors from attendance altogether, is a much-abused symbol, both by the industry, exhibitors, and the censors themselves. A recent Supreme Court ruling gave back to local censorship boards the right to require cuts in films as a condition of their being shown, presumably in the wake of the French-Italian production, Bernardo Bertolucci's *Last Tango in Paris* (1973). Because of the explicitness of its nude sex scenes and language, this film got into censorship trouble even in the native land of its producer (Alberto Grimaldi) and director (Bertolucci). It was banned in numerous cities in America and in all of certain states. In Milan, its makers and its stars (Marlon Brando and Maria Schneider) were tried on obscenity charges and convicted *in absentia.*

In actual fact, *Last Tango in Paris* is not an obscene film. It is a sex-obsessed film, but that is primarily because its central characters are. There is little doubt but that it would shock anyone ill-prepared for its visual and verbal assaults upon our assumedly civilized selves; its minor sadomasochistic variations—digit-anal contact and a prolonged and possibly sacrilegious act of sodomy ("Come on!" Paul ordered, as he forced himself into her, "Say it! Holy Family; the church of good citizens." There was a furor everywhere it was shown and moviehouse owners arrested in hundreds of communities around the world.

The story is much less complicated than Bertolucci's other films (*The Conformist, The Spider's Stratagem*) but equally as talky. Paul, essentially inarticulate, has spurts of talking far too much so that he begins to resemble, at least verbally, the girl's garrulous boyfriend, Tom, the incessant moviemaker. There are one or two other flaws. The kinky-haired girl is far too shallow to make us care very much whether or not anything happens to her, good or bad. It is not so much her background or what she says as the way she looks (pouty and constipated) and acts. When she finally shoots Paul at the end of the film, her desperation is no more deeply felt by the audience than her earlier piques and is more irritating than dramatic.

But Brando is a fascinating and compelling Paul from the moment he enters the flat that is for rent and encounters the girl. His wife is a recent suicide and the girl wants to get away from her wealthy family and her compulsive filmmaking fiancé (Jean-Pierre Léaud). Paul is the former manager of a seedy hotel who feels that he has driven his wife to kill herself because he has had a showdown with her over her more virile lover. Paul has become impotent with his wife, still is sexually troubled, and uses the vacant apartment as an emotional battleground on which to achieve a sexual hold upon the girl.

Since the entire point of the film is Paul's effort to prove himself a puissant lover again, to excise the sex acts would be to remove the vital elements of the movie. And besides, there are so many references to the act and its variations throughout and so little made of the background (the flat is barely furnished; a mattress is thrown on the floor), audiences would find a "purified" version meaningless.

Much more serious than the ruckus over *Last Tango in Paris* is the business of making X-rated movies for a specialized clientele addicted to hard-core pornography. These films are made in color on relatively low budgets with, in the main, human bodies cast rather than actors. Once every year or two, one of them will have an amusing premise (*Deep Throat* and *The Devil in Miss Jones*) that will attract a wider audience. But they have made tatters of the rating system. "X-Rated" more often than not no longer means "restricted to adults only." It means stag-film fare with almost endless shots of penises and vaginas and bobbing heads and bottoms. No one should deny an audience, if such is their pleasure, the right to see such monotony. But there are far too many towns and small cities in the Midwest, South, and Far West and even New England, where the only moviehouse in town is showing these films on an exclusive basis, denying the entire community the right to see *Sunday, Bloody Sunday, True Grit, Mean Streets, Badlands,* or even *Last Tango in Paris.*

Writers for other media are slightly intimidated by the screen. It has become too important for those not initiated into its cabalistic format to trifle with. It has come into its own as a significant art form and there are genuine efforts being made to preserve the works of its progenitors, particularly those made by The American Film Institute and Henri Langlois in France.

There are a number of former movie-goers who have been alienated by the freedom that has come to the screen since the rating system was begun. They speak of "garbage" and "filth." While their delicate sensibilities should not be dismissed (nearly all the films made by the Walt Disney company are free of "filth") let us be thankful that they no longer have the collective strength to band together into a Legion that can deprive us of the art of a performer or a movie they consider "pagan" or morally corruptive. Time has a way of delivering up the heads of tyrants even if it takes nearly half a century.

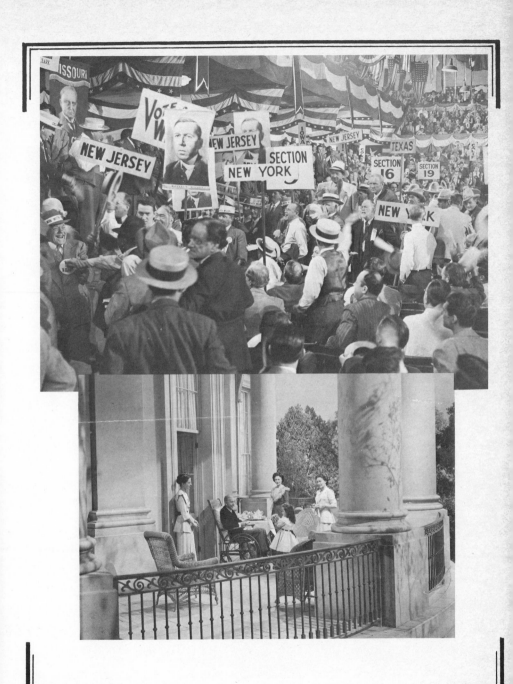

ABOVE: The Democratic convention, 1916, is re-created with near-documentary precision in Henry King's production of *Wilson* (1944) as supervised by Darryl F. Zanuck. Lamar Trotti's script was wordy, but then so was the President. A triumphant evocation of a rich moment in America's past. *(Author's collection)*
BELOW: An incapacitated President Wilson (Alexander Knox) enjoys a moment with a child on the White House terrace. With him are daughters Margaret (Ruth Ford) and Eleanor (Mary Anderson, far right) and wife Edith (Geraldine Fitzgerald), 1944. *(Author's collection)*

ABOVE: Fay Wray, *femme fatale* to oversized gorillas, married and divorced writers John Monk Saunders and Robert Riskin; she liked men of quiet mien and much talent. Circa 1931. *(Culver Pictures)* CENTER: Luise Rainer as *The Toy Wife* (1938) is still on the telephone. She won an Academy Award for her use of one in *The Great Ziegfeld*. *(Author's collection)* BELOW: Myrna Loy, a rare combination of wit and the exotic. Married to producer Arthur Hornblow, Jr., she was much admired by the writers' colony. *(Author's collection)*

ABOVE: Playwright Clifford Odets was something of a Don Juan. Here, he wines and dines Fay Wray at the Stork Club, circa 1940. *(Culver Pictures)* CENTER: Christopher Isherwood, the novelist and playwright, had seen much of the world by the time of his arrival in Hollywood. He has been "kept" by Sally Bowles for at least three decades and his movie scripts have been ways of keeping his hand in and refining his visual perceptions. 1946. *(Photo by William Caskey)* BELOW: Bette Davis probably the most popular dramatic actress of all time, was certainly *Queen of the Forties*. An overly mannered actress with perhaps half a dozen calculated tics going for her, she was acclaimed as the new Bernhardt or Duse by untold millions of fans. *(Culver Pictures)*

ABOVE: Aldous Huxley was a gifted man with an enormous curiosity. He became a canyon-dweller with wife Maria in the late 1930s, was burned out in an early sixties brushfire, and eventually died in California. Circa 1948. *(Photo by William Caskey)* CENTER: Charles Foster Kane as played by Orson Welles was much less gentle and human than the real-life William Randolph Hearst. But the Welles portrait was compelling and Dorothy Comingore was winsome as "the second wife." *(Culver Pictures)*   BELOW: Here, in a rare candid photo, are Hearst, Marion Davies, silent star Eleanor Boardman, and great Davies friend Charlie Chaplin as they watch an ice show. In the context of Mankiewicz's script, Marion, a truly gifted comedienne was seriously libeled, but Hearst chose not to sue. *(Courtesy Robert Board)*

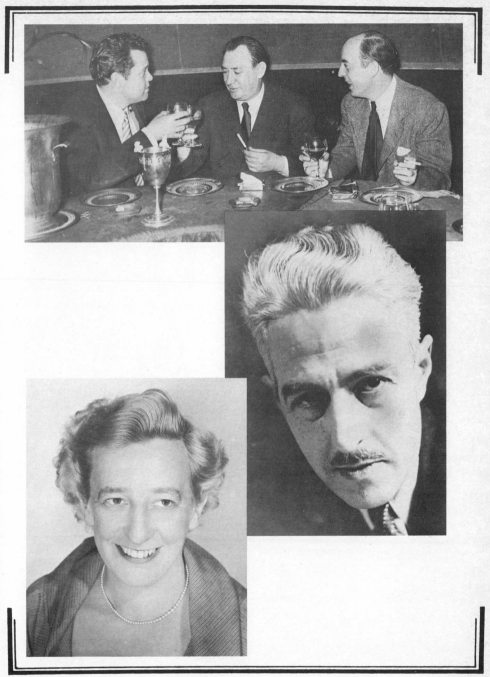

ABOVE: Orson Welles toasts a friend, Louis Philbert, at Maxim's in Paris as Charlie Lederer looks on. Circa 1947. *(Courtesy Charles Lederer)* CENTER: Detective novelist Dashiell Hammett was as fierce an individualist as his good friend, Miss Hellman. However, he went to jail for it. *(Culver Pictures)* BELOW: Lillian Hellman married another screenwriter, Arthur Kober, then divorced him and became Dashiell Hammett's companion. Samuel Goldwyn allowed Miss Hellman to work in films on her own terms, which was the way she worked and lived most successfully. *(Culver Pictures)*

"The Mighty One on a Little Outing as Met by Two Poets" (Nietzsche), a painting by George Grosz. *(Courtesy Arnott White)*

ABOVE: Veronica Lake needs both eyes for this seductive glance at Joel McCrea. *Sullivan's Travels*, 1941. *(Author's collection)* BELOW: In front of Veronica Lake, holding his hand to show how he wants his star framed, is Preston Sturges, who wrote and directed *Sullivan's Travels*, a Hollywood satire, 1941. Sturges was the most total and original filmmaker since D. W. Griffith, but, as with Griffith, the film community never fully accepted him. *(Author's collection)*

ABOVE: In *Hail the Conquering Hero*, Eddie Bracken is the army reject suddenly transformed by well-intentioned marines into the town hero. Even his ex-girlfriend comes rushing back when he is nominated for mayor. Mom (Georgia Caine) is willing to believe nearly everything, 1944. *(Author's collection)* BELOW LEFT: Playwright Harry Kurnitz had a nice contempt for his less literate Hollywood employers. *(Courtesy Charles Lederer)* BELOW RIGHT: German novelist Thomas Mann and his brother Heinrich were among the numerous literary exiles from Hitler's Europe who settled in Hollywood in the late thirties and early forties. *(Photo by Robert Disraeli)*

ABOVE: Hildy Johnson (Rosalind Russell), her fiancé, Bruce (Ralph Bellamy), and her skeptical boss and ex-husband Walter Burns (Cary Grant) enjoy an improbable lunch together in *His Girl Friday* (1940). *(Author's collection)* BELOW: Cary Grant broods over some changes in the script of *I Was a Male War Bride*, as director Howard Hawks and writer Charles Lederer keep their anxiety in hand with pipe and cigarette. Cameraman Gregg Toland waits for the word. 1948. *(Courtesy Charles Lederer)*

ABOVE: John Howard Lawson on a Sunday outing with his children Jeffrey Edmund and Susan Amanda at Del Rey, California, in November 1929. He had two decades of Hollywood success ahead of him before he collided with the inquisitors. *(Courtesy John Howard Lawson)* CENTER: On the eve of his departure for Hollywood, Abraham Polonsky relaxes in Briarcliff Manor, New York. *(Courtesy Abraham Polonsky)* BELOW: The second time around for Alan Campbell and Dorothy Parker, who remarried in 1950. Donald Ogden Stewart shares this rather pensive moment. *(Courtesy Beatrice Ames)*

ABOVE: The first writer among the blacklisted to return to a career in Hollywood was Dalton Trumbo, who is shown here with wife Cleo at their Valley ranch. *(Culver Pictures)* CENTER: John Garfield relaxes on the set of *Body and Soul* (1947). *(Author's collection)* BELOW: Writer-producer Dore Schary, whose take-over of production at Metro (after Mayer's forced retirement) was widely heralded as a portent of a new era in filmmaking; however, the new modesty did not become Metro-Goldwyn-Mayer. In the end Schary's plans were crippled by the Blacklist. Circa 1948. *(Culver Pictures)*

ABOVE: Charles Laughton in *The Private Life of Henry VIII*, which gave Alexander Korda of Great Britain his first great international success (1932). BELOW: "Ginger Ted" was the first drop-out dramatized on the screen. Charles Laughton as *The Beachcomber* was never finer than as this South Sea island recluse in the Maugham story produced by Laughton and Erich Pommer (1937). *(Author's collection)*

ABOVE: The Laughtons in their London flat on Gordon Square. *(By courtesy of* Women's Journal; © *Joan Woolacombe)* BELOW: Elsa Lanchester (Mrs. Charles Laughton) as Hendrickje Stoffels in *Rembrandt* (1937). Droll, sustaining, and gifted in her own right, she allowed Charles to take the most of the bows. *(Faber & Faber)*

ABOVE: Writer-producer Adrian Scott and wife Anne Shirley enjoy an evening at the theater. His ordeal in hearing rooms and courts was just ahead. Circa 1946. *(Author's collection)* CENTER: Albert Maltz in his study after his return from prison and exile. *(Courtesy Albert Maltz)* BELOW: Prisoner 3567 upon his jailing in July 1950. *(Courtesy Albert Maltz)*

Anna Magnani in Roberto Rossellini's *The Miracle,* a film that was proscribed by the Catholic Church and banned briefly in New York. Its premise was that a retarded shepherdess, having been raped, believed that she had conceived immaculately, that God had sent her a child. It stirred up the biggest public controversy over a movie since *The Birth of a Nation. (Author's collection)*

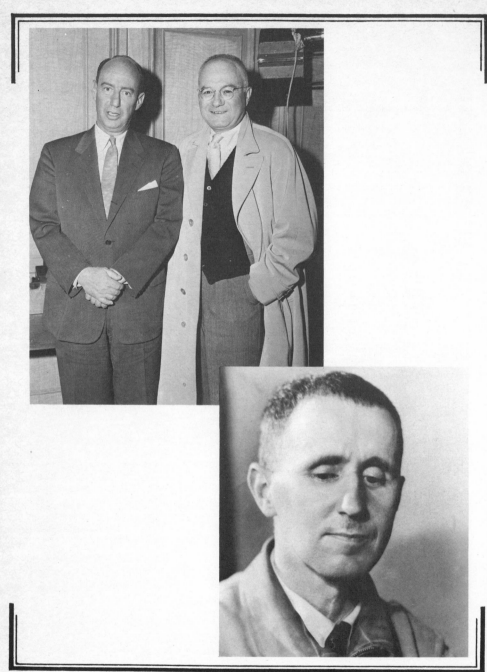

ABOVE: Allen Rivkin, veteran screenwriter and longtime officer in the Screen Writers' Guild, with Adlai E. Stevenson. 1951. *(Courtesy Allen Rivkin)* BELOW: Dramatist Bertolt Brecht lived in the Hollywood area until his life was disrupted by the harassment of Congressional committees. *(Culver Pictures)*

ABOVE: Billy Wilder, who learned his craft at the huge German UFA studios in the twenties, began as a writer, then became one of the most important writer-producer-directors of the forties. Here, he checks out a setup for *Love in the Afternoon*. *(Culver Pictures)* BELOW: In *Sunset Boulevard*, Norma Desmond (Gloria Swanson) celebrates New Year's Eve in her mansion with her kept young writer-friend Joe Gillis (William Holden). A small orchestra plays waltzes to the solitary couple. 1950. *(Author's collection)*

ABOVE: Marilyn Monroe was just becoming visible as the forties ended. Here she appears as vulnerable as a baby doe in the Bill Goetz mansion. *(Photo by Joshua Logan)* BELOW: Since the Hollywood film has disappeared as such, the new freedom is often far more human than anything that has come before. In Penelope Gilliatt's *Sunday, Bloody Sunday* (1971), an older man (Peter Finch) and a not-so-young woman (Glenda Jackson) attempt in separate struggles to hold a young man, but he eludes them. *(Culver Pictures)*

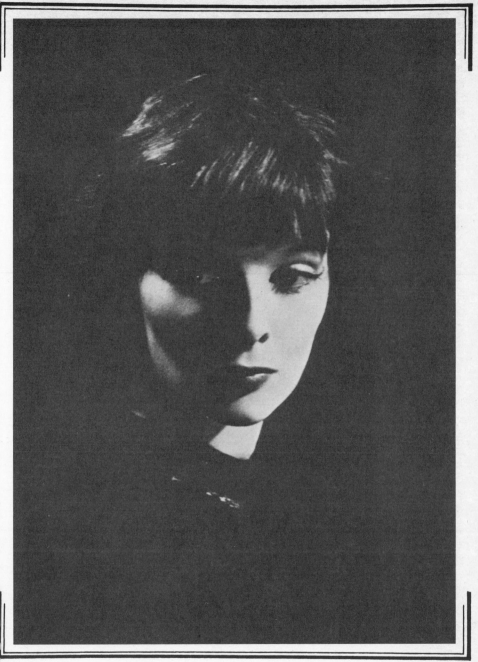

Hepburn, as much as anyone, represents that unique quality that set Hollywood films apart from those made anywhere else. Fickle moviegoers and her own individuality made success come hard for her. *(Photo by Cecil Beaton)*

EPILOGUE

In 1948, Charlie MacArthur wrote his last screen play to order (*Miss Lulu Belle* for Dorothy Lamour). Then he came back to Nyack a physical wreck, his spirit half destroyed. Wife Helen blamed Hollywood, asserting the place and the system had ravaged him.

It was not hyperbole. One ailment after another hobbled him, most of them traceable to prolonged abuse of the human body. But who is to say when the man within has reached his limits of tolerance and has to seek such succor as he can find?

Charlie M. was no longer fun to be around. Some found him an almost impossible guest and the invitations slackened. Ben Hecht saw him much less frequently; he found the suffering of those close to him nearly intolerable. Then Ludwig Bemelmans stepped into the breach and they embarked on a number of literary projects together. The old spark was not entirely dimmed. Charlie helped Bemelmans with the first draft and general hilarious direction of his book, *My War with the U.S.A.*

Then Charlie's eyesight began to go. A specialist found a cataract in one eye, a "sad condition" he termed it as it is impossible to fit cataract lenses when only one eye is involved. Anita Loos, always in the wings of the MacArthur household, offered to be Charlie's "seeing eye dog." Like Bemelmans, Anita fought to keep Charlie's interest in life at least on a low burner. She (or someone) got him involved in writing a play for Helen based on the life of Elsie de Wolfe (Lady Mendl). For a time it was called *Glory Be!* and there was the old elaborate packaging of theatrical yard-goods with discussion of casting, road tours and directors. But it was gift wrap around an empty package and Anita and Helen both guessed that Charlie knew that it was.

An old friend in Nassau, Victor Sassoon, offered his estate there for Charlie and Anita's use in completing the play.

Helen was invited to go along with son Jim. Charlie went out and bought a white linen suit and panama hat for the trip—more gift wrap. Just before departure time, Charlie told Helen that he wasn't going, that he wanted "the girls" to go on with Jim. "I'm tired of dames around all the time," he told her.

They went without him, Helen feeling uneasy about his need to be alone. Charlie lived just a month following their return.

Ben Hecht survived his old collaborator seven years. His screen work was in decline by then both in quality and demand. Something had gone out of him, as well. He wrote a magazine column and a number of articles on Hollywood. The venom in his attacks on the old town was there, but it was more cantankerous than caustic; he was a rebel who had lived beyond the revolution but was no longer young enough to help run the new order.

Alan Campbell died in his sleep in 1963 and Dorothy Parker stayed on in the small Hollywood house they had bought on Norma Place in West Hollywood. She told friends she wanted to sell the house and it was listed with a broker, but she resented that part of her own fame that brought out the gawkers, who had no serious intention of buying. Finally, with the broker screening out the literary landmark lookers, a buyer was found and she hurried back to New York, where the only friends who mattered to her any more lived—Lillian Hellman, Beatrice Ames, the Zero Mostels, George Oppenheimer, Wyatt Cooper, and perhaps half a dozen others.

She moved twice before settling into the Volney, a residential hotel on East 74th Street. Her sole live-in companion was one of the poodles, Trois, but called "Troy," so the "plebeians" who knew no French and who sometimes walked him for her could pronounce it.

She was frail (down to a little over eighty pounds) and

seeming to move from one melancholy into another. She thought humor was dead in the world and that was what had sustained her into an old age she never had wanted. She did occasional reviews for *Esquire* Magazine but these were infrequent, although they kept her on salary long after she had ceased to deliver.

It didn't matter that she had outlived all of her family. What did concern her and make her fret was that nearly all of her closest friends were gone.

About ten days before she died, she was having to rest a great deal, but she stubbornly resisted giving up her beloved Scotch or cigarettes. There is a touching photograph of her taken on a sofa with Troy under one arm. She is living in a haunted body, all sad incurious eyes and frail wrists, but the inevitable cigarette dangles loose from two fingers.

During one of her days in bed, she was attended by her intimate friend Beatrice Ames, who came daily and saw that she had something to eat and was the one person in the world who had never told her *not* to do something. Suddenly, her eyes appeared to be focusing on some remote corner of her past and she said, "I wonder why Ernest always hated me so." Bea Ames knew at that moment that Dorothy *had* heard a remark made by Hemingway over thirty years earlier in Paris, where, at a dinner party, he had stood and raised his glass, saying, "Now let's drink to Dorothy Parker. Nothing becomes her so much in life as her nearly leaving it." He was referring to one of Dorothy's suicide attempts, and there had been several in her life, but Bea Ames had never been sure Dorothy *really* had been listening. She had pretended not to be.

Then early in the morning on June 7, 1967, Bea Ames received a call from John at the desk of the Volney. He was near tears as he told her, "She's gone." Mrs. Ames's first response, perhaps to stave off the truth, was, "Don't tell me she's moved again." Only six weeks earlier, Dorothy had moved to a smaller apartment to save $25 a week and she said that she hated it. "No," he said, "she's left us."

Mrs. Ames hurried over by taxi, but not before phoning the hotel maid and asking her to go into Mrs. Parker's apartment and get Troy before the police arrived, avoiding having the dog impounded for a time as property of the deceased. By the time she got there, the police *had* arrived, but Troy was safely in another apartment.

Dorothy had a sheet covering her body and only her frail hands dangled by the sides of the bed. The police were searching her desk and bureau drawers for money and valuables to safeguard. They found stacks of unopened mail, many of the envelopes containing royalty checks and totaling thousands of dollars. They were puzzled but no one ever cleared the matter up for them—that Dorothy Parker may have been going blind and no longer could read her mail. With a fierce pride and resistance to physical deterioration to the end, she had told no one. Her black-rimmed glasses allowed her to move about, but she didn't open the stack of incoming books still flowing in to her, hopefully for a comment that might be used on a jacket or an ad.

Then Mrs. Ames picked up Troy, got into another taxi, and returned to her own apartment. Lillian Hellman took over at that point in her no-nonsense fashion, phoned *The Times*, arranged the time of the services next day, delivered a moving tribute to her late friend, and then flew off to Martha's Vineyard to mourn alone. That was something in Lillian that always had intimidated Dorothy—her terrifying efficiency and firm notion of how things must be done.

Dorothy Parker's estate, consisting mostly of literary works still in print, was willed to Martin Luther King, Jr., for his use in his lifetime and, upon his death, for his Foundation. Not surprisingly, it was administered by Lillian Hellman.

SELECTED FILMOGRAPHIES BY JOHN E. SCHULTHEISS

*Additional filmographies compiled by Richard Corliss wherever starred.
†Verified by screenwriter or other source.

ZOE AKINS

1930

Anybody's Woman, *co-scr.*, *dial.*
The Right to Love, *scr.*
Sarah and Son, *adapt.*, *dial.*

1931

Women Love Once, *scr.*
Girls About Town, *story*
Once a Lady, *co-scr.*, *adapt.*
Working Girls, *scr.*

1933

Christopher Strong, *scr.*

1934

Outcast Lady, *scr.*
No More Yesterdays, *co-scr.*

1937

Camille, *co-scr.*

1938

The Toy Wife, *scr.*
Zaza, *scr.*

1947

Desire Me, *co-scr.*

ERIC AMBLER

1946

The Way Ahead, *scr.*, *story, co-scr.*

1948

The Hangman's Noose (also known as October Man), *scr.*, *story, scr.*

1949

One Woman's Story, *scr.*

1951

Highly Dangerous, *scr.*, *story, scr.*

1952

The Magic Box, *scr.*
Encore (*Sequel to* Trio),
"Gigolo and Gigolette," *scr.*
"Winter Cruise," Arthur Mac Rae, *scr.*
"The Ant and the Grasshopper," *scr.*
"T.E.B. Clark," *scr.*
The Promotor, *scr.*

1953

Shoot First, *scr.*
The Cruel Sea, *scr.*

1955

The Purple Plain, *scr.*

1956

Lease of Life, *scr.*

1957

Battle Hell, *story, scr.*

1958

A Night to Remember, *scr.*

1959

The Wreck of the Mary Deare, *scr.*

MAXWELL ANDERSON

1930

All Quiet on the Western Front, *co-scr.*, *co-dial.*

1932

Rain, *scr.*
Washington Merry-Go-Round, *story*

1934

Death Takes a Holiday, *co-scr.*
We Live Again, *co-adapt.*

1935

So Red the Rose, *co-scr.*

1948

Joan of Arc, *co-scr., from his play,*
Joan of Lorraine

1957

The Wrong Man, *story, co-scr.*

━━━━━

S.N. BEHRMAN

1930

Liliom, *dial., co-scr. with Sonya
Levien*
Lightnin', *co-scr. and co-dial. with
Sonya Levien*

1931

Daddy Longlegs, *co-dial. with Sonya
Levien*
The Brat, *co-scr. with Sonya Levien
and co-dial. with Sonya Levien and
another writer*
Surrender, *co-scr. and co-dial. with
Sonya Levien*

1932

Rebecca of Sunnybrook Farm, *co-scr.
and co-dial. with Sonya Levien*
Tess of the Storm Country, *co-scr.
with Sonya Levien and another
writer*

1933

Brief Moment, *from his play* My Lips
Betray, *dial.*
Hallelujah, I'm a Bum, *scr.*
Queen Christina, *dial.*

1934

As Husbands Go, *co-scr. with Sonya
Levien*

1935

Anna Karenina, *co-scr. with Sonya
Levien*
A Tale of Two Cities, *co-scr.*

1937

Conquest, *co-scr. with Salka Viertel
and other writers*
Parnell, *co-scr.*

1938

The Cowboy and the Lady, *co-scr.
with Sonya Levien*

1940

No Time for Comedy, *from his play,*
Waterloo Bridge, *co-scr.*

1941

Two-Faced Woman, *co-scr. with Salka
Viertel and other writers*

1951

Quo Vadis, *co-scr. with Sonya Levien
and another writer*

1956

Gaby, *remake of* Waterloo Bridge

1958

Me and the Colonel, *adapt., co-scr.*

━━━━━

ROBERT BENCHLEY

1932

Sport Parade, *dial. (uncredited)*
Sky Devils, *co-dial. (uncredited)*

1934

The Gay Divorcee, *contrib. to dial.
(uncredited)*
How To Sleep, *story, scr.***

**Partial listing of his award-winning shorts; others included *No News Is Good News*
and *The Courtship of the Newt.*

1935

Murder on a Honeymoon, *co-scr.*

1940

Foreign Correspondent, *contrib. to scr.*

STEPHEN VINCENT BENÉT

1930

Abraham Lincoln, *co-continuity, co-dial., adapt.*

1941

All That Money Can Buy, *story, co-scr.* (*also known as* The Devil and Daniel Webster

Cheers for Miss Bishop, *adapt.*

SALLY BENSON

1943

Shadow of a Doubt, *co-scr.*

1946

Anna and the King of Siam, *co-scr.*

1949

Little Women, *contrib. to scr.*
Come to the Stable, *co-scr.*

1950

No Man of Her Own, *co-scr.*
Conspirator, *co-adapt., scr.*

1953

The Farmer Takes a Wife, *co-scr.*

1963

Summer Magic, *scr.*

1964

Viva Las Vegas, *ss., scr.*

1965

Signpost to Murder, *scr.*
Joy in the Morning, *co-scr.*

1966

The Singing Nun, *co-scr.*

GUY BOLTON

1925

Grounds for Divorce, *adapt.*

1929

The Love Doctor, *co-adapt., dial.*
The Love Parade, *libretto*

1931

Yellow Ticket, *co-dial.*
Delicious, *story, co-adapt.*
Ambassador Bill, *story, dial.*
Transatlantic, *story*
The Lady Refuses, *co-story*

1932

Devil's Lottery, *scr.*
Careless Lady, *scr.*
The Woman in Room 13, *scr.*
Almost Married, *co-scr.*
The Painted Woman, *co-scr.*

1933

Pleasure Cruise, *scr.*

1934

The Lady Is Willing, *sc.*
Ladies Should Listen, *adapt. from play by Bolton and Savoir*

1935

The Murder Man, *co-story*
Morals of Marcus, *co-adapt.*
Mister Hobo, *scr.*

1945

Weekend at the Waldorf, *adapt.*

1946

Till the Clouds Roll By, *ss.*

1948

Words and Music, *co-ss.*

===

CHARLES BRACKETT

1934

Enter Madame, *co-scr.*

1935

College Scandal, *co-scr.*
The Last Outpost, *co-scr.*
Without Regret, *co-scr.*

1936

Rose of the Rancho, *co-scr.*
Piccadilly Jim, *co-scr.*
Woman Trap, *story*
The Jungle Princess, *co-scr.*
(uncredited)

1937

Wild Money, *co-scr. (uncredited)*
Live, Love and Learn, *co-scr.*

1938

Bluebeard's Eighth Wife, *co-scr.*
with Billy Wilder

1939

What a Life, *co-scr. with Billy
Wilder*
Midnight, *co-scr. with Billy Wilder*
Ninotchka, *co-scr. with Billy Wilder
and Walter Reisch*

1940

Arise My Love, *co-scr. with Billy
Wilder*

1941

Hold Back the Dawn, *co-scr. with
Billy Wilder*

Ball of Fire, *co-scr. with Billy
Wilder*

1942

The Major and the Minor, *co-scr. with
Billy Wilder*

1943

Five Graves to Cairo, *co-scr. with
Billy Wilder, prod.*

1945

The Lost Weekend, *co-scr. with Billy
Wilder, prod.*

1946

To Each His Own, *story, co-scr., prod.*

1948

The Emperor Waltz, *co-story and
co-scr. with Billy Wilder, prod.*
A Foreign Affair, *co-scr. with
Richard Breen, prod.*
Miss Tatlock's Millions, *co-scr. with
Richard Breen, prod.*

1950

Sunset Boulevard, *co-scr. with Billy
Wilder and Donald Marshman, prod.*

1951

The Mating Season, *co-scr. with
Richard Breen and Walter Reisch,
prod.*
The Model and the Marriage Broker,
*co-scr. with Richard Breen and
Walter Reisch, prod.*

1953

Niagara, *co-story and co-scr. with
Richard Breen and Walter Reisch,
prod.*
Titanic, *co-story and co-scr. with
Richard Breen and Walter Reisch,
prod.*

1955

The Girl in the Red Velvet Swing, *co-story and co-scr. with Walter Reisch, prod.*

1956

Teenage Rebel, *co-scr. with Walter Reisch, prod.*

1959

Journey to the Center of the Earth, *co-scr. with Walter Reisch, prod.*

MILLEN BRAND

1947

The Snake Pit, *co-scr.*

BERTOLT BRECHT

1943

Hangmen Also Die, *co-ss., co-scr.*

LOUIS BROMFIELD

1940

Brigham Young—Frontiersman, *sc.*

HARRY BROWN

1945

The True Glory, *co-scr., co-story*

1947

The Other Love, *co-scr.*

1948

Arch of Triumph, *co-scr.*
Wake of the Red Witch, *co-scr.*

1949

Sands of Iwo Jima, *story, co-scr.*
Man on the Eiffel Tower, *scr.*

1950

Kiss Tomorrow Goodbye, *sc.*

1951

A Place in the Sun, *co-scr.*
Only the Valiant, *co-scr.*
Bugles in the Afternoon, *co-scr.*

1952

The Sniper, *scr.*
Eight Iron Men, *scr. from his play, A Sound of Hunting*

1953

All the Brothers Were Valiant, *scr.*

1955

Many Rivers to Cross, *co-scr.*
The Virgin Queen, *co-scr.*

1956

D-Day, the Sixth of June, *co-scr.*

1957

Between Heaven and Hell, *scr.*

1958

The Deep Six, *co-scr.*
The Fiend Who Walked the West, *co-scr.*

1960

Ocean's Eleven, *co-scr.*

SIDNEY BUCHMAN

1927

Matinee Ladies, *co-story*

1931

Daughter of the Dragon, *dial.*
Beloved Bachelor, *dial.*

1932

No One Man, *adapt., dial.*

Thunder Below, *adapt.*
The Sign of the Cross, *adapt., dial.*
If I Had a Million, *co-scr.*

1933

From Hell to Heaven, *co-scr.*
Right to Romance, *co-scr.*

1934

All of Me, *co-scr.*
Whom the Gods Destroy, *co-scr.*
His Greatest Gamble, *co-scr.*
Broadway Bill, *co-scr. (uncredited)*

1935

I'll Love You Always, *co-scr.*
Love Me Forever, *co-scr.*
She Married Her Boss, *scr.*

1936

The King Steps Out, *scr.*
Theodora Goes Wild, *scr.*
Adventure in Manhattan, *scr.*

1937

The Awful Truth, *co-scr. (uncredited)*
Lost Horizon, *co-scr. (uncredited)*

1938

Holiday, *co-scr.*

1939

Mr. Smith Goes to Washington,
scr.

1940

The Howards of Virginia, *scr.*

1941

Here Comes Mr. Jordan, *co-scr.*

1942

The Talk of the Town, *co-scr.*

1943

Sahara, *co-scr. (uncredited)*

1945

A Song To Remember, *scr., prod.*
Over 21, *scr., prod.*

1946

The Jolson Story, *co-story
(uncredited)*

1948

To the Ends of the Earth, *co-scr.
(uncredited)*

1949

Jolson Sings Again, *story, scr., prod.*

1951

Saturday's Hero, *co-scr.*

1961

The Mark, *co-scr.*

1963

Cleopatra, *co-scr.*

1966

The Group, *scr., prod.*

1972

La Maison sous les Arbres, *co-scr.*

W. R. BURNETT

1931

Finger Points, *co-story*

1932

Beast of the City, *story*
Scarface, *co-scr., co-dial.*

1941

The Get-Away, *co-scr.*
High Sierra, *co-scr. from his novel*

1942

This Gun for Hire, *co-scr.*
Wake Island, *co-story, co-scr.*

1943

Background to Danger, *scr.*
Crash Dive, *story*
Action in the North Atlantic
co-additional dial.

1945

San Antonio, *co-story, co scr.*

1946

Nobody Lives Forever, *scr. from his novel*

1948

Belle Starr's Daughter, *story, scr.*
Yellow Sky, *story*

1950

Vendetta, *scr.*

1954

Dangerous Mission, *co-scr.*

1955

Captain Lightfoot, *story, co-scr.*
I Died a Thousand Times, *scr. from his novel* High Sierra
Illegal, *co-scr.*

1956

Accused of Murder, *co-scr. from his novel* Vanity Row

1957

Short Cut to Hell, *from his scr.* This Gun for Hire

1960

September Story, *scr.*

1962

Sergeants Three, *story, scr.*

1963

The Great Escape, *co-scr.*

NIVEN BUSCH

1932

The Crowd Roars, *co-scr.*
Scarlet Dawn, *co-scr., co-dial.*
Miss Pinkerton, *co-scr., co-dial.*

1933

College Coach, *co-scr.*

1934

The Man with Two Faces, *co-scr.*
He Was Her Man, *co-scr.*
The Big Shakedown, *co-scr.*

1935

Three Kids and a Queen, *co-scr. (uncredited)*
Lady Tubbs, *co-scr. (uncredited)*

1939

Off the Record, *co-scr.*
Angels Wash Their Faces, *co-scr.*

1940

The Westerner, *co-scr.*

1941

Belle Starr, *story*

1946

The Postman Always Rings Twice, *co-scr.*

1947

Duel in the Sun, *from his novel*
Moss Rose, *scr.*
Pursued, *story, scr.*

1950

The Furies, *from his novel* The Capture, *scr.*

1951

Distant Drums, *story*

1953

The Man from the Alamo, *co-scr.*
The Moonlighter, *story, scr.*

1955

The Treasure of Pancho Villa, *scr.*

JAMES M. CAIN

1938

Algiers, *add. dial.*

1939

Stand up and Fight, *co-scr.*
When Tomorrow Comes, *story*

1944

Gipsy Wildcat, *co-scr.*

1949

Everybody Does It, *story*

ERSKINE CALDWELL
1943

Mission to Moscow, *contrib. to treatment*

ROBERT CARSON

1937

The Last Gangster, *co-ss.*
A Star Is Born, *co-ss., co-scr.*

1938

Men with Wings, *scr., ss.*

1939

Beau Geste, *scr.*

1940

The Light That Failed, *scr.*

1941

Western Union, *scr.*

1942

The Desperadoes, *scr.*
The Tuttles of Tahiti, *co-scr.*

1949

Once More, My Darling, *story, scr.*

1952

Just for You, *scr.*

1954

A Star Is Born *(remake)*, *co-ss., co-scr.*

1956

Bundle of Joy, *co-scr.*

1957

Action of the Tiger, *scr.*

RAYMOND CHANDLER

1944

Double Indemnity, *co-scr.*
And Now Tomorrow, *co-scr.*

1945

The Unseen, *co-scr.*

1946

The Blue Dahlia, *story, scr.*

1951

Strangers on a Train, *co-scr.*

MARC CONNELLY

1926

Exit Smiling, *story*

1933

Cradle Song, *scr.*

1936

Green Pastures, *scr., co-dir., from his play of same name*

1937

Captains Courageous, *co-scr.*

1940

Victory, *contrib. to scr. construction*

1942

I Married a Witch, *co-scr.*
Reunion in France, *co-scr.*

1944

The Impostor, *add'l. dial.*

1957

Crowded Paradise, *added scenes*

BARTLETT CORMACK

1928

The Racket, *adapt. from his* A Racket, *a play (1928)*

1929

Gentlemen of the Press, *scr.*
The Greene Murder Case, *dial.*
The Laughing Lady, *co-adapt.*
Woman Trap, *scr., dial.*

1930

The Benson Murder Case, *scr., dial.*
The Spoilers, *adapt., dial.*

1932

Is My Face Red?, *dial.*
Thirteen Women, *co-scr.*
The Phantom of Crestwood, *co-story, scr.*

1933

This Day and Age, *story*

1934

Four Frightened People, *co-scr.*
The Trumpet Blows, *scr.*
Cleopatra, *adapt.*

1935

Doubting Thomas, *adapt.*
Orchids to You, *co-scr.*

1936

Fury, *co-scr.*

1939

The Beachcomber, *scr.*

1941

Unholy Partners, *co-scr.*

NOEL COWARD

1933

Bitter Sweet, *scr., music, lyrics*

1943

In Which We Serve *(British), story, scr.*

1946

Brief Encounter *(British), adapt., co-prod.*

1947

This Happy Breed *(British), scr.*

1950

The Astonished Heart, *scr.*

MILDRED CRAM

1932

Sinners in the Sun, *story*

1935

Stars over Broadway, *story*

1939

Love Affair, *co-ss.*

1940

Beyond Tomorrow, *co-story*

1957

An Affair to Remember, *co-ss.*

═══════

RACHEL CROTHERS

1935

Splendor, *adapt., scr.*

═══════

RUSSEL CROUSE

1937

Mountain Music, *co-scr.*
Artists and Models, *co-contrib. to
scr., co-adapt.*

1938

Artists and Models Abroad, *co-ss.,
co-scr.*

1939

The Great Victor Herbert, *co-scr.*

1954

Woman's World, *co-add'l. dial.*

═══════

CLEMENCE DANE

1935

Anna Karenina, *co-scr.*
The Transatlantic Tunnel,
add'l., dial.

1936

The Amateur Gentleman,
co-scr., dial.

1937

Fire over England, *co-scr.*

1940

Sidewalks of London *(British), story,
scr.*

1946

Vacation from Marriage *(British), ss.,
co-scr.*

1949

Bride of Vengeance, *add'l. dial.*

═══════

DELMER DAVES*

1929

The Duke Steps Out, *adapt.*

1930

The Bishop Murder Case, *adapt.*

1931

Shipmates, *scr., co-adapt.,
co-dial.*

1932

Divorce in the Family,
scr., dial.

1933

Clear All the Wires, *adapt., scr.*

1934

No More Women, *co-story, co-scr.*
Dames, *co-story, scr.*
Flirtation Walk, *co-story, scr.*

1935

Stranded, *co-scr.*
Page Miss Glory, *co-scr.*
Shipmates Forever,
story, scr.

1936

The Petrified Forest, *co-scr.*

1937

The Go-Getter, *scr.*
Slim, *co-scr. (uncredited)*
The Singing Marine,
story, scr.

1938

She Married an Artist, *co-scr.*
Professor Beware, *scr.*

1939

Love Affair, *co-scr.*
$1,000 a Touchdown,
story, scr.

1940

The Farmer's Daughter, *story*
Safari, *scr.*

1941

The Unexpected Uncle, *co-scr.*
The Night of January 16th, *co-scr.*

1942

You Were Never Lovelier, *co-scr.*

1943

Stage Door Canteen, *story, scr.*
Destination Tokyo, *co-scr.*

1944

The Very Thought of You,
co-scr.
Hollywood Canteen,
story, scr.

1945

The Pride of the Marines

1947

The Red House, *scr.*
Dark Passage, *scr.*

1948

To the Victor, *scr.*

1949

Task Force, *story, scr.*

1951

Bird of Paradise,
story, scr.

1952

The Return of the Texan

1953

Treasure of the Golden Condor,
scr.
Never Let Me Go

1954

Drum Beat, *story,*
scr., prod.

1956

White Feather, *co-scr.*
Jubal, *co-scr.*
The Last Wagon, *co-scr.*

1957

An Affair to Remember, *remake of*
Love Affair, *co-scr.*
Kings Go Forth

1958

The Badlanders

1959

A Summer Place, *scr. prod.*

1961

Parrish, *scr., prod.*
Susan Slade, *scr., prod.*

1962

Rome Adventure, *scr., prod.*

1963

Spencer's Mountain,
scr., prod.

1964

Youngblood Hawks,
scr., prod.

1965

The Battle of the Villa Fiorita,
scr., prod.

VINA DELMAR

1930

A Soldier's Plaything, *story*

1933

Chance at Heaven, *story*

1934

Sadie McKee, *story*

1935

Hands Across the Table, *story*

1936

King of Burlesque, *story*

1937

Make Way for Tomorrow, *scr.*
The Awful Truth, *scr.*

———

JOHN DOS PASSOS

1936

The Devil Is a Woman, *adapt.*

———

PHILIP DUNNE*

1933

Student Tour, *co-scr.*

1934

The Count of Monte Cristo, *co-scr.*

1935

The Melody Lingers On, *co-scr.*
Under Pressure, *co-scr. (uncredited)*
Helldorado, *co-scr. (uncredited)*

1936

The Last of the Mohicans, *sc.*

1937

Lancer Spy, *scr.*
Suez, *co-scr.*
Breezing Home, *co-story*

1938

The Rains Came, *co-scr.*

1939

Swanee River, *co-scr.*
Stanley and Livingstone, *co-scr.*

1940

Johnny Apollo, *co-scr.*

1941

How Green Was My Valley,
scr.

1942

Son of Fury, *scr.*

1947

The Late George Apley, *scr.*
Forever Amber, *co-scr.*
The Ghost and Mrs. Muir, *scr.*

1948

The Luck of the Irish, *scr.*
Escape, *scr.*

1949

Pinky, *co-scr.*

1951

Anne of the Indies, *co-scr.*
David and Bathsheba, *story,
scr.*

1952

Lydia Bailey, *co-scr.*
Way of a Gaucho, *scr., prod.*

1953 ·

The Robe, *scr.*

1954

Demetrius and the Gladiators, *story,
scr.*

The Egyptian, *co-scr.*
The View from Pompey's Head, *scr.*,
prod.

1956

Hilda Crane, *scr.*

1957

Three Brave Men, *scr.*

1958

Ten North Frederick, *scr.*
Blue Denim, *co-scr.*

1965

The Agony and the Ecstasy, *scr.*

1966

Blindfold, *co-scr.*

* * *

GUY ENDORE

1935

Rumba, *co-story idea*
Mark of the Vampire, *co-scr.*
Mad Love, *adapt.*

1936

The Devil-Doll, *co-scr.*

1937

The League of Frightened Men,
co-scr.

1938

Carefree, *co-story idea*

1941

Lady from Louisiana, *co-scr.*

1944

Song of Russia, *co-story*

1945

G.I. Joe, *co-scr.*

1948

The Vicious Circle, *co-scr.*

1949

Johnny Allegro, *co-scr.*

1951

Tomorrow Is Another Day, *co-scr.*,
ss.
He Ran All the Way, *scr.*

* * *

JULIUS J. EPSTEIN*

1935

The Big Broadcast of 1936, *co-scr.*
(uncredited)
Living on Velvet, *co-story, co-scr.*
In Caliente, *co-scr.*
Broadway Gondolier, *co-scr.*
Little Big Shot, *co-scr.*
I Live for Love, *co-story, co-scr.*
Stars over Broadway, *co-scr.*

1936

Sons O'Guns, *co-scr.*

1937

Confession, *co-adapt., co-scr.*

1938

Secrets of an Actress, *co-story, co-scr.*
Four Daughters, *co-scr.*
There's That Woman Again, *co-scr.*
The Mad Miss Manton, *scr.*

1939

Daughters Courageous, *co-scr.*
Four Wives, *co-scr.*

1940

Saturday's Children, *co-scr.*
No Time for Comedy, *co-scr.*

1941

Strawberry Blonde, *co-scr.*
The Bride Came C.O.D., *co-scr.*
The Man Who Came to Dinner, *co-scr.*
Honeymoon for Three, *co-scr.*

1942

The Male Animal, *co-scr.*
Casablanca, *co-scr.*

1944

Mr. Skeffington, *co-prod., co-scr.*
Arsenic and Old Lace, *co-scr.*
One More Tomorrow, *co-additional dial.*

1948

Romance on the High Seas, *co-scr.*

1949

Chicken Every Sunday, *from his and Philip G. Epstein's stage adaptation of the novel by Rosemary Taylor*
My Foolish Heart, *co-scr.*

1950

Born Yesterday, *co-scr. (uncredited)*

1951

Take Care of My Little Girl, co-scr.

1953

Forever Female, *co-scr.*

1954

The Last Time I Saw Paris, *co-scr.*
Young at Heart, *co-scr.*

1955

The Tender Trap, *scr.*

1957

Kiss Them for Me, *scr.*

1958

The Brothers Karamazov, *co-adapt.*

1959

Take a Gaint Step, *co-scr. prod.*

1960

Tall Story, *scr.*

1961

Fanny, *scr.*

1963

The Light in the Piazza, *scr.*

1964

Send Me No Flowers, *scr.*

1965

Return from the Ashes, *scr.*

1966

Any Wednesday, *scr., prod.*

1973

Pete 'n' Tillie, *scr.*

===

WILLIAM FAULKNER

1933

Today We Live, *story and dial.*

1936

Road to Glory, *co-scr., co-ss.*
Banjo on My Knee, *co-scr. (uncredited)*

1937

Slave Ship, *add'l. dial.: reviews attrib. ss. to him*

1938

Submarine Patrol, *co-dial. (uncredited)*

1939

Gunga Din, *co-scr. (uncredited)*

1943

Drums Along the Mohawk, *co-scr. (uncredited)*
Air Force, *contrib. to scr. (uncredited)*
Northern Pursuit, *co-scr. (uncredited)*

1945

To Have and Have Not, *co-scr.*
Escape in the Desert, *co-scr. (uncredited)*
The Southerner, *co-scr. (uncredited)*

1946

The Big Sleep, *co-scr.*

1955

Land of the Pharaohs, *co-ss., co-scr.*

W. C. FIELDS*

1934

The Old-Fashioned Way, *story*
It's a Gift, *co-story*

1935

The Man on the Flying Trapeze, *co-story*

1939

You Can't Cheat an Honest Man, *story*

1940

My Little Chickadee, *co-story, co-scr.*
The Bank Dick, *story, scr.*

1941

Never Give a Sucker an Even Break, *story*

F. SCOTT FITZGERALD†

1923

Glimpses of the Moon, *titles*

1924

Grit, *scr.*

1927

Lipstick, *scr. (unproduced)*

1931

Red-Headed Woman, *scr.*

1938

A Yank at Oxford, *co-scr. (uncredited)*
Three Comrades, *co-scr.*
Infidelity, *scr. (unproduced)*
Marie Antoinette, *contrib. to scr. (uncredited)*

1939

The Women, *co-scr. (uncredited)*
Gone with the Wind, *contrib. to scr. (uncredited)*
Winter Carnival, *contrib. to treatment. (uncredited)*
Air Raid, *contrib. to scr. (uncredited)*
Open That Door *(based on novel* Bull by the Horns*)*
Everything Happens at Night *contrib. to scr. (uncredited)*

1940

Raffles, *contrib. to scr. (uncredited)*
Cosmopolitan, *scr. (based on his story,* Babylon Revisited, *unproduced)*
Brooklyn Bridge, *contrib. unknown (unproduced)*
The Light of Heart, *scr. adapted from Emlyn William's play (unproduced in this form)*

†Verified by the Fitzgerald-Hemingway Annuals.

1943

Madame Curie, *contrib. to scr.*
(uncredited)

=======

COREY FORD

1929

The Sophomore, *story*

1932

The Sport Parade, *co-scr.*
The Half-Naked Truth, *co-scr.*

1933

Her Bodyguard, *story*

1939

Remember, *co-scr., co-ss.*
Topper Takes A Trip, *co-scr.*
Zenobia, *scr.*

=======

CARL FOREMAN*

1941

Spooks Run Wild, *co-scr.*
Bowery Blitzkieg, *co-scr.*

1942

Rhythm Parade, *co-story, co-scr.*

1945

Dakota, *story*

1948

So This Is New York, *co-scr.*

1949

Champion, *scr.*
Home of the Brave, *scr.*
The Clay Pigeon, *scr.*

1950

The Men, *scr.*

Young Man with a Horn, *co-scr.*
Cyrano de Bergerac, *scr.*

1952

High Noon, *scr.*

1957

The Bridge on the River Kwai, *scr.*,
(uncredited)

1958

The Key, *scr., prod.*

1961

The Guns of Navarone, *scr., prod.*

1963

The Victors, *scr., prod.*

1969

Mackenna's Gold, *scr., prod.*

1972

Young Winston, *scr.*

=======

GENE FOWLER

1932

Union Depot, *co-story*
Roadhouse Murder, *additional dial.*
State's Attorney, *co-scr., co-dial.*
What Price Hollywood?, *co-adapt.*

1933

The Way to Love, *co-scr.*

1934

The Mighty Barnum, *scr.*

1935

Call of the Wild, *co-scr.*

1936

Professional Soldier, *co-scr.*

Career Woman, *story*
White Fang, *co-scr.*
Half Angel, *co-scr.*

1937

Ali Baba Goes to Town, *co-ss.*
Love Under Fire, *co-scr.*
Nancy Steele Is Missing, *co-scr.*

1940

Earl Of Chicago, *co-ss.*

1941

Billy the Kid, *scr.*

1949

Big Jack, *co-scr.*

═══════

ROSE FRANKEN

1934

Elinor Norton, *co-scr.*

1935

Alias Mary Dow, *co-scr.*

1936

Beloved Enemy, *co-scr.*
Next Time We Love, *contrib. to scr.*

1939

Made for Each Other, *story idea*

1946

Claudia and David, *co-scr.*
The Secret Heart, *co-adapt.*, *co-ss.*
from her Holiday *(play) and*
"Twenty-two" *(short story)*

═══════

JULES FURTHMAN*

1915

Steady Company, *story*

Bound on the Wheel, *story*
Mountain Justice, *story*
Chasing the Limited, *story*
Quits, *story*

1918

The Camouflage Kiss, *story,*
co-screenplay (as Stephen Fox)
More Trouble, *screenplay*
Japanese Nightingale, *screenplay*
All The World to Nothing, *screenplay*
(as Stephen Fox)
Mantle of Charity, *screenplay (as*
Stephen Fox)
Hobbs in a Hurry, *screenplay (as*
Stephen Fox)
Wives and Other Wives, *scr., story*
(as Stephen Fox)
When a Man Rides Alone,
scr., story
(as Stephen Fox)

1919

Where the West Begins, *scr., story*
(as Stephen Fox)
Brass Buttons, *scr., story (as*
Stephen Fox)
Some Liar, *scr. (as Stephen Fox)*
A Sporting Chance, *story (as Stephen*
Fox)
This Hero Stuff, *story (as Stephen*
Fox)
Six Feet Four, *scr. (as Stephen Fox)*
Victory, *scr. (as Stephen Fox)*

1920

The Valley of Tomorrow, *story (as*
Stephen Fox)
Treasure Island, *scr. (as Stephen Fox)*
Would You Forget? *scr., story*
Leave It to Me, *scr.*
The Twins of Suffering Creek, *scr.*
White Circle, *co-adapt.*
The Man Who Dared, *scr., story*
The Skywayman, *scr., story*

The Great Redeemer, *co-adapt.*
The Texan, *co-scr.*
Iron Rider, *scr.*
Land of Jazz, *scr., co-story, dir.*

1921

The Cheater Reformed, *co-scr., story*
The Big Punch, *scr., story*
The Blushing Bride, *story, scr., dir.*
Colorado Pluck, *scr., dir.*
High Gear Jeffrey, *story, scr.*
Singing River, *scr.*
The Last Trail, *co-scr.*
The Roof Tree, *scr.*

1922

Gleam O'Dawn, *scr.*
The Ragged Heiress, *story, scr.*
Arabian Love, *story, scr.*
The Yellow Stain, *story, scr.*
Strange Idols, *scr.*
Calvert's Valley, *scr.*
The Love Gambler, *scr.*
A California Romance, *story*
Pawn Ticket 210, *scr.*

1923

Lovebound, *co-scr.*
St. Elmo, *scr.*
North of the Hudson Bay, *story, scr.*
The Acquittal, *scr.*
Condemned, *story, scr.*

1924

Try and Get It, *scr.*
Call of the Mate, *story, scr.*

1925

Sackcloth and Scarlet, *co-scr.*
Any Woman, *co-scr.*
Before Midnight, *story, scr.*
Big Pal, *story, scr.*

1926

The Wise Guy, *story*
You'd Be Surprised, *story, scr.*

1927

Hotel Imperial, *scr.*
Casey at the Bat, *scr.*
Underworld, *scr. by Charles (and Jules?) Furthman*
Fashions for Women, *co-adapt.*
Barbed Wire, *co-scr., adapt.*
The Way of All Flesh, *scr.*
City Gone Wild, *scr., co-story*

1928

The Dragnet, *co-scr., adapt.*
The Docks of New York, *scr.*

1929

Abie's Irish Rose, *scr.*
The Case of Lena Smith, *scr.*
Thunderbolt, *scr., co-story*
New York Nights, *scr.*

1930

Common Clay, *scr., dial.*
Renegades, *adapt., continuity, dial.*
Morocco, *scr., dial.*

1931

Body and Soul, *scr.*
Merely Mary Ann, *scr.*
Yellow Ticket, *scr.*
Over The Hill, *co-scr.*

1932

Shanghai Express, *scr.*
Blonde Venus, *co-scr., co-story*

1933

Girl in 419, *story*
Bombshell, *co-scr.*

1935

China Seas, *co-scr.*
Mutiny on the Bounty, *co-scr.*

1936

Come and Get It!, *co-scr.*

1938

Spawn of the North, *co-scr.*

1939

Only Angels Have Wings, *scr.*

1940

The Way of All Flesh, *co-story*

1941

The Shanghai Gesture, *collaborated on adaptation*

1943

The Outlaw, *scr.*

1944

To Have and Have Not, *co-scr.*

1946

The Big Sleep, *co-scr.*

1947

Moss Rose, *co-scr.*
Nightmare Alley, *scr.*

1950

Pretty Baby, *co-story*

1951

Peking Express, *adapt.*

1957

Jet Pilot, *story, scr., prod.*

1959

Rio Bravo, *co-scr.*

══════

PAUL GALLICO

1936

Wedding Present, *scr., ss.*

1942

Pride of the Yankees, *ss.*

1952

Assignment—Paris, *co-ss.*

1953

Lili, *ss.*

1958

Bitter Victory, adapt.

══════

ELINOR GLYN

1921

The Great Moment, *story*

1922

The World's a Stage, *story*

1924

His Hour, *supv. scen.*
How to Educate a Wife, *story*
Three Weeks, *scen. from her novel (1907)*

1925

Man and Maid, *scen. from her novel (1922)*
The Only Thing, *pers. supv., story, adapt.*

1926

Love's Blindness, *pers. supv., adapt. from her novel (1925)*

1927

It, *adapt. from her short story (1927)*
Ritzy, *story*

1928

Three Week-Ends, *story*

1929

The Man and the Moment, *story*

1930

Such Men Are Dangerous, *story*

FRANCES GOODRICH AND ALBERT HACKETT

1933

The Secret of Madame Blanche, *adapt.*
Penthouse, *adapt.*

1934

Fugitive Lovers, *co-scr.*
The Thin Man, *scr.*
Hide-Out, *scr.*

1935

Naughty Marietta, *co-scr.*
Ah, Wilderness!, *adapt., scr.*

1936

Rose Marie, *co-scr.*
After the Thin Man, *scr.*
Small Town Girl, *add. scenes*

1937

The Firefly, *co-scr.*

1939

Society Lawyer, *(remake of Penthouse)*
Another Thin Man, *scr.*

1944

Lady in the Dark, *scr.*
The Hitler Gang, *story, scr.*

1946

The Virginian, *co-scr.*
It's a Wonderful Life, *co-scr.*

1948

The Pirate, *scr.*
Easter Parade, *story, co-scr.*

1950

Father of the Bride, *scr.*

1951

Father's Little Dividend, *story*
Too Young To Kiss, *scr.*

1953

Give a Girl a Break, *scr.*

1954

The Long Long Trailer, *scr.*
Seven Brides for Seven Brothers, *co-scr.*

1956

Gaby, *co-scr.*

1958

A Certain Smile, *scr.*

1959

The Diary of Anne Frank, *scr. from their play*

1962

Five-Finger Exercise, *scr.*

PAUL GREEN

1932

Cabin in the Cotton, *scr.*

1933

State Fair, *co-scr.*
Voltaire, *co-scr.*
Dr. Bull, *scr.*

A. B. GUTHRIE, JR.

1953

Shane, *scr.*

1955

The Kentuckian, *scr.*

DASHIELL HAMMETT

1931

City Streets, *story*

1935

Mister Dynamite, *story*

1937

After the Thin Man, *story*

1939

Another Thin Man, *ss.*

1943

Watch on the Rhine, *scr.*

MOSS HART

1932

Flesh, *dial.*

1933

The Masquerader, *dial.*

1935

The Broadway Melody of 1936, *story*

1936

Frankie and Johnnie, *scr.*

1944

Winged Victory, *scr., from his play*

1947

Gentlemen's Agreement, *scr.*

1952

Hans Christian Andersen, *scr.*

1954

A Star Is Born, *scr.*

Prince of Players, *scr.*

BEN HECHT

1927

Underworld, *story*

1928

The Big Noise, *co-scr.*

1929

Unholy Night, *story*
The Great Gabbo, *story*

1930

Roadhouse Nights, *story*

1931

Unholy Garden, *co-scr.*

1932

Scarface, *story*
Back Street, *co-scr. (uncredited)*

1933

Hallelujah, I'm a Bum, *story*
Topaze, *scr.*
Turn Back the Clock, *co-story, co-scr.*
Design for Living, *scr.*
Queen Christina, *co-scr. (uncredited)*

1934

Upperworld, *story*
The Twentieth Century, *co-scr.*
Crime Without Passion, *co-dir.,
co-story, co-scr.*
Viva Villa!, *scr.*

1935

Once in a Blue Moon, *co-dir.,
co-story, co-scr.*
The Scoundrel, *co-dir., co-scr.*
Barbary Coast, *co-story, co-scr.*

1936

Soak the Rich, *co-dir., co-scr.*

1937

Nothing Sacred, *scr.*
The Hurricane, *co-scr. (uncredited)*

1938

The Goldwyn Follies, *story, scr.*

1939

Let Freedom Ring, *story, scr.*
It's a Wonderful World, *scr., co-story*
Lady of the Tropics, *story, scr.*
Gunga Din, *co-scr.*
Wuthering Heights, *co-scr.*
Gone with the Wind, *co-scr.*
(uncredited)

1940

His Girl Friday, *co-author of
original play* The Front Page
Angels over Broadway, *co-dir.,
story, scr.*
Foreign Correspondent, *co-story,
co-scr. (uncredited)*
Comrade X, *co-scr.*
The Shop Around the Corner,
co-scr. (uncredited)

1941

Lydia, *co-scr.*
Tales of Manhattan, *co-story, co-scr.*
The Black Swan, *co-scr.*
China Girl, *prod., scr.*
Roxie Hart, *co-scr. (uncredited)*

1943

The Outlaw, *story (uncredited)*

1945

Spellbound, *scr.*

1946

Spectre of the Rose, *co-dir., scr.*

Notorious, *story, scr.*
Gilda, *co-scr. (uncredited)*

1947

Her Husband's Affairs, *co-story,
co-scr.*
Kiss of Death, *co-scr.*
Ride the Pink Horse, *co-scr.*
Dishonored Lady, *co-scr. (uncredited)*
The Paradine Case, *co-scr.*
(uncredited)

1948

The Miracle of the Bells, *co-scr.*
Rope, *co-scr. (uncredited)*

1949

Whirlpool, *co-scr.*
Love Happy, *co-scr. (uncredited)*

1950

Where The Sidewalk Ends, *scr.*

1951

The Thing, *co-scr. (uncredited)*

1952

Actors and Sin, *dir., prod., scr.*
Monkey Business, *co-scr.*

1953

Roman Holiday, *co-scr. (uncredited)*

1955

Ulysses, *co-scr.*
The Indian Fighter, *co-scr.*
The Court-Martial of Billy Mitchell,
courtroom scenes (uncredited)

1956

Miracle in the Rain, *scr.*
The Iron Petticoat, *story, scr.*

1957

Legend of the Lost, *story, scr.*
A Farewell to Arms, *scr.*

1964

Circus World, *co-scr.*

LILLIAN HELLMAN

1935

The Dark Angel, *co-scr.*

1936

These Three, *scr. from her play* The Children's Hour

1937

Dead End, *scr.*

1941

The Little Foxes, *scr., from her play*

1943

Watch on the Rhine, *scenes, add'l. dial. from her play*
The North Star, *scr., ss.*

1946

The Searching Wind, *scr. from her play*

1961

The Children's Hour, *story, adapt., from her play*

1966

The Chase, *scr.*

ERNEST HEMINGWAY

1937

The Spanish Earth, *(Documentary), story, scr., narration*

1958

The Old Man and the Sea, *contrib. to scr. (uncredited)*

JAMES HILTON

1936

Camille, *co-scr.*

1939

We Are Not Alone, *story, co-scr. from his novel*

1942

The Tuttles of Tahiti, *adapt.*
Mrs. Miniver, *co-scr.*

1944

Forever and a Day, *co-scr.*

SAMUEL HOFFENSTEIN

1931

An American Tragedy, *scr.*

1932

Dr. Jekyll and Mr. Hyde, *co-scr.*
Sinners in the Sun, *co-scr.*
Love Me Tonight, *co-scr.*
The Miracle Man, *co-dial.*

1933

The Song of Songs, *co-scr.*
White Woman, *co-scr.*

1934

Wharf Angel, *co-scr.*
All Men Are Enemies, *co-scr., co-dial.*
Change of Heart, *add'l dial.*
The Fountain, *dial.*
The Gay Divorcee, *musical adapt.*

1935

Enchanted April, *co-scr.*
Paris in Spring, *co-scr.*

1937

Conquest, *co-scr.*

1938

The Great Waltz, *co-scr.*

1939

Bridal Suite, *scr.*

1941

Lydia, *co-scr.*
That Night in Rio, *additional dial.*

1942

The Loves of Edgar Allan Poe,
co-scr., co-ss.
Tales of Manhattan, *co-scr., co-ss.*

1943

Flesh and Fantasy, *co-scr.*
Phantom of the Opera, *co-scr.*

1944

His Butler's Sister, *co-scr., co-ss.*
Laura, *co-scr.*

1946

Sentimental Journey, *co-scr.*
Cluny Brown, *co-scr.*

1948

Give My Regards to Broadway,
co-scr.

═══════

SIDNEY HOWARD

1929

Bulldog Drummond, *co-scen., scr.,
dial.*
Condemned, *scr., dial.*

1930

A Lady to Love, *scen., dial. from*

his play They Knew What They
Wanted
Raffles, *scr.*
One Heavenly Night, *adapt.*

1931

Arrowsmith, *adapt.*

1932

The Greeks Had a Word for It,
adapt.

1936

Dodsworth, *scr.*

1939

Raffles, *co-scr.*
Gone with the Wind, *scr.*

═══════

JOHN HUSTON
(from Romano Tozzi's
*John Huston: A Pictorial
Treasury of His Films*)

1931

A House Divided, *dial.*

1932

Law and Order, *co-scr., co-dial.*
Murders in the Rue Morgue, *dial.*

1938

The Amazing Doctor Clitterhouse,
co-scr.
Jezebel, *co-scr.*

1939

Juarez, *co-scr.*

1940

Dr. Ehrlich's Magic Bullet,
co-story, co-scr.

1941

Sergeant York, *co-scr.*
High Sierra, *co-scr.*
The Maltese Falcon, *scr., dir.*

1942

In This Our Life, *co-scr., dir.*

1943

Report from the Aleutians, *scr.,
narrator, dir.*

1944

The Battle of San Pietro, *scr.,
narrator, dir.*

1945

Let There Be Light, *scr., dir.*

1946

Three Strangers, *co-scr.*
The Stranger, *co-adapt., dial.*

1948

The Treasure of the Sierra Madre,
scr., dir.
Key Largo, *co-scr., dir.*

1949

We Were Strangers, *co-scr., dir.*

1950

The Asphalt Jungle, *co-scr., dir.*

1951

The Red Badge of Courage,
co-scr., dir.

1952

The African Queen, *co-scr., dir.*

1954

Beat the Devil, *co-scr., dir.*

1956

Moby Dick, *co-scr., dir., prod.*

1957

Heaven Knows, Mr. Allison,
co-scr., dir.

1964

The Night of the Iguana,
co-scr., dir.

1970

The Kremlin Letter, *co-scr., dir.*

ALDOUS HUXLEY

1940

Pride and Prejudice, *co-scr.*

1944

Jane Eyre, *co-scr.*

1947

A Woman's Vengeance, *story, scr.
from his story* "The Gioconda Smile"

CHRISTOPHER ISHERWOOD

1934

Little Friend, *co-scen., co-dial.
(his novel* Prater Violet *was based
on the filming of this)*

1941

Rage in Heaven, *co-scr.*

1944

Forever and a Day, *co-scr.*

1945

Up at the Villa, *scr. from a
S. Maugham story (unproduced)*

1949

Adventure in Baltimore, *co-ss.*
The Great Sinner, *co-scr. (based on Dostoievski's* The Gambler*)*

1956

Diane, *ss., scr.*

1957

The Wayfarer, *scr.*

1958

Jean Christophe, *scr. (unproduced)*

1965

The Loved One, *co-scr.*

1966

Reflections in a Golden Eye, *scr. (unproduced by Tony Richardson)*

1967

I, Claudius, *co-scr. (unproduced by Tony Richardson)*

1968

The Sailor from Gibraltar, *(British), co-scr.*

1973

Frankenstein, the True Story, *co-scr.*

===

TALBOT JENNINGS

1935

Mutiny on the Bounty, *co-scr.*

1936

Romeo and Juliet, *scr.*

1937

The Good Earth, *co-scr.*

1938

Spawn of the North, *co-scr.*

1939

Rulers of the Sea, *co-ss., co-scr.*

1940

Northwest Passage, *co-scr.*
Edison, the Man, *co-scr.*

1941

So Ends Our Night, *scr.*

1944

Frenchman's Creek, *scr.*

1946

Anna and the King of Siam, *co-scr.*

1950

The Black Rose, *scr.*

1951

Across the Wide Missouri, *co-ss., scr.*

1953

Knights of the Round Table, *co-scr.*

1955

Escape to Burma, *co-scr.*
Untamed, *co-scr., co-adapt.*
Pearl of the South Pacific, *add'l. dial.*

1957

Gunsight Ridge, *co-ss., co-scr.*

1959

The Naked Maja *(Italian-American), co-ss.*

1965

The Sons of Katie Elder, *story*

========

NUNNALLY JOHNSON

1927

Rough House Rosie

1933

A Bedtime Story, *co-adapt.*
Momma Loves Poppa, *scr.*

1934

The House of Rothschild, *scr.*
Bulldog Drummond Strikes Back, *scr.*
Moulin Rouge, *scr.*
Kid Millions, *author*

1935

The Man Who Broke the Bank at Monte Carlo, *scr., prod.*
Thanks a Million, *scr.*
Baby-Face Harrington, *scr. with Edwin W. Knopf*

1936

The Prisoner of Shark Island, *story, scr.*
Banjo on My Knee, *scr.*

1939

Jesse James, *story, scr., assoc. prod.*
Rose of Washington Square, *scr., prod.*
Wife, Husband and Friend, *scr., prod.*

1940

The Grapes of Wrath, *scr., assoc. prod.*
Chad Hanna, *scr., assoc. prod.*

1941

Tobacco Road, *scr.*

1942

Roxie Hart, *scr., prod.*
The Pied Piper, *scr., prod.*
Life Begins at 8:30, *scr., prod.*

1943

The Moon Is Down, *scr., prod.*
Holy Matrimony, *scr., prod.*

1944

The Woman in the Window, *scr., prod.*
Casanova Brown, *scr., prod.*
Keys of the Kingdom, *co-scr.*

1945

Along Came Jones, *scr.*

1946

The Dark Mirror, *scr., prod.*

1948

Mr. Peabody and the Mermaid, *scr., prod.*

1949

Everybody Does It, *scr., prod., remake of* Wife, Husband and Friend

1950

Three Came Home, *scr., prod.*
The Mudlark, *scr., prod.*

1951

The Desert Fox, *scr., prod.*
The Long Dark Hall, *scr.*

1952

Phone Call from a Stranger, *scr., prod.*

We're Not Married, *scr., prod.*
My Cousin Rachel, *scr., prod.*
O. Henry's Full House:
    "Ransom of Red Chief"
    episode, scr.

1953

How To Marry a Millionaire, *scr.,*
    prod.

1954

Night People, *scr., prod.*
Black Widow, *scr., prod.*

1955

How To Be Very Very Popular,
    scr., prod.

1956

The Man in the Gray Flannel Suit,
    scr.

1957

The True Story of Jesse James,
    remake of Jesse James
Oh, Men! Oh, Women,
    scr. (uncredited)
The Three Faces of Eve,
    scr., prod.

1959

The Man Who Understood
    Women, *scr., prod.*

1960

The Angel Wore Red, *scr.*
Flaming Star, *co-scr.*

1962

Mr. Hobbs Takes a Vacation,
    scr.

1963

Take Her, She's Mine, *scr.*

1964

The World of Henry Orient,
    co-scr.

1967

The Dirty Dozen, *co-scr.*

══════

GARSON KANIN*

1942

Woman of the Year, *idea (uncredited)*

1943

The More the Merrier, *story, co-scr.*
    (uncredited)

1945

The True Glory, *co-compilation*

1946

From This Day Forward, *adapt.*

1948

A Double Life, *co-story, co-scr.*

1949

Adam's Rib, *co-story, co-scr.*

1950

Born Yesterday, *from his play*

1951

The Marrying Kind, *co-story, co-scr.*

1952

Pat and Mike, *co-story, co-scr.*

1954

It Should Happen to You,
    story, scr.

1956

The Girl Can't Help It, *from his*
    short story Do Re Mi

1960

The Rat Race, *scr., from his play*

1961

The Right Approach, *from his play*
The Live Wire

1969

Where It's At, *scr. from his novel*
Some Kind of a Nut, *story, scr.*

===

GEORGE S. KAUFMAN

1933

Roman Scandals, *co-story*

1935

A Night at The Opera, *co-scr.*

===

SIDNEY KINGSLEY

1948

Homecoming, *ss.*

===

ARTHUR KOBER

1932

Make Me a Star, *co-scr.*
Guilty As Hell, *co-scr.*
Hat Check Girl, *co-scr.*
Me and My Gal, *scr.*

1933

Broadway Bad, *co-scr.*
Infernal Machine, *scr.*
Bondage, *co-scr.*
It's Great to Be Alive, *dial.*
Headline Shooter, *add'l. dial.*
Mama Loves Papa, *co-scr.*
Meet the Baron, *co-dial.*

1934

Palooka, *co-scr.*
Hollywood Party, *co-story, co-scr.*

1935

The Great Hotel Murder, *scr.*
Calm Yourself, *scr.*
Ginger, *story, scr.*

1936

Early to Bed, *scr.*
Big Broadcast of 1937, *co-ss.*

1938

Having Wonderful Time, *scr.*

1941

The Little Foxes, *add'l. dial.,
scenes*

1943

Wintertime, *ss.*

1944

In the Meantime, Darling, *co-ss.,
co-scr.*

1945

Don Juan Quilligan, *co-scr.*

1949

My Own True Love, *adapt.*

===

HOWARD KOCH*

1940

The Sea Hawk, *co-story, co-scr.*
The Letter, *scr.*
Virginia City, *co-story (uncredited)*

1941

Shining Victory, *co-scr.*
Sergeant York, *co-scr.*

1942

In This Our Life, *scr.*
Casablanca, *co-scr.*

1943

Mission to Moscow, *scr.*

1944

In Our Time, *co-story, co-scr.*

1945

Rhapsody in Blue, *scr.*

1946

Three Strangers, *co-story, co-scr.*

1948

Letter from an Unknown
Woman, *scr.*

1950

No Sad Songs for Me, *scr.*

1951

The Thirteenth Letter, *scr.*

1961

The Greengage Summer
(Loss of Innocence),
scr.

1962

The War Lover, *scr.*

1967

The Fox, *co-scr.*

NORMAN KRASNA

1932

Hollywood Speaks, *story, co-scr.,
co-dial.*
That's My Boy, *scr.*

1933

Parole Girl, *story, adapt., dial.*
So This Is Africa, *story, adapt.*
Love, Honor and Oh, Baby!,
co-adapt.
Meet the Baron, *co-story.*

1934

The Richest Girl in the World, *story,
adapt., scr.*
Romance in Manhattan, *co-story.*

1935

Four Hours to Kill, *scr., from his
play* Small Miracle
Hands across the Table, *co-scr.*

1936

Wife versus Secretary, *co-scr.*
Fury, *story.*

1937

The King and the Chorus Girl,
co-story, co-scr.
As Good As Married, *story.*
The Big City, *story, prod.*

1938

The First Hundred Years, *story, prod.*
You and Me, *story, adapt.*

1939

Bachelor Mother, *scr.*

1940

It's a Date, *scr.*

1941

The Devil and Miss Jones, *story,
scr., co-prod.*
Mr. and Mrs. Smith, *story, scr.*
The Flame of New Orleans, *story, scr.*
It Started with Eve, *co-scr.*

1943

Princess O'Rourke, *story, scr.*

1944

Bride by Mistake, *story.*
Practically Yours, *story, scr.*

1950

The Big Hangover, *story, scr., prod.*

1956

The Ambassador's Daughter, *scr.,
prod.*
Bundle of Joy, *co-scr., remake of*
Bachelor Mother

1958

Indiscreet, *scr., from his play*
Kind Sir

1960

Who Was That Lady?, *prod., scr.
from his play* Who Was That Lady
I Saw You With?
Let's Make Love, *story, scr.*

HARRY KURNITZ

1938

Fast Company, *co-scr.*

1939

Fast and Furious, *scr.*

1941

Shadow of the Thin Man, *scr.,
story*

1942

They Got Me Covered, *scr.*

1944

The Heavenly Body, *adapt.*

See Here, Private Hargrove,
scr.
(from the book by Marion Hargrove)
The Thin Man Goes Home,
co-story

1945

What Next, Corporal Hargrove?,
scr., story

1947

Something in the Wind, *co-scr.*
The Web, *story*

1948

One Touch of Venus,
co-scr.
*(based on the musical by Ogden
Nash and S. J. Perelman)*
A Kiss in the Dark, *scr.*

1949

The Adventures of Don Juan,
co-scr.
My Dream Is Yours, *co-scr.*
The Inspector General, *co-scr.*

1950

Pretty Baby, *co-scr.*

1951

Of Men and Music, *film concert*

1953

Tonight We Sing, *co-scr.*
Melba, *scr.*

1954

The Man Between, *scr.*

1955

Land of the Pharaohs, *co-scr.*

1956

The Happy Road, *co-scr.*

1957

Witness for the Prosecution, *co-scr.*

1958

The Girl on the Subway, *co-scr.*

1962

My Geisha, *story, scr.*

1963

Sunday in New York, *scr. from his play*

1964

I'd Rather Be Rich, *co-scr., remake of* It Started With Eve

HAROLD LAMB

1935

The Crusades, *co-scr.*

1937

The Plainsmen, *co-scr.*

1938

The Buccaneer, *co-scr.*

1951

The Golden Horde, *story*

RING LARDNER, JR.

1937

A Star Is Born, *junior writer*

1942

Woman of the Year, *co-scr.*

1947

Forever Amber, *co-scr.*

1969

M*A*S*H

ARTHUR LAURENTS

1948

Rope, *scr.*
The Snake Pit, *co-scr. (uncredited)*

1949

Home of the Brave, *co-scr. from his play* Anna Lucasta
Caught, *scr.*

1956

Anastasia, *scr.*

1958

Bonjour Tristesse, *scr.*

1973

The Way We Were, *co-scr. from his novel*

EMMET LAVERY

1942

Army Surgeon, *co-scr.*
Hitler's Children, *scr.*

1943

Behind the Rising Sun, *scr., ss.*

1944

Forever and a Day, *co-scr.*

1946

A Night in Paradise, *adapt.*

1950

Guilty of Treason, *scr.*
Magnificent Yankee, *scr.*

1953

Bright Road, *scr.*

1955

The Court Martial of Billy Mitchell,
co-scr., *co-ss.*

======

JOHN HOWARD LAWSON

1928

Dream of Love, *co-titl.*

1929

Dynamite, *co-dial.*
The Pagan, *titl.*

1930

Our Blushing Brides, *co-cont.*, *co-dial.*
The Sea Bat, *co-scr.*, *co-dial.*
The Ship from Shanghai, *scr.*

1931

Bachelor Apartment, *story.*

1933

Goodbye Love, *co-scr.*, *co-dial.*

1934

Success at Any Price, *co-scr.*, *from his
play*
Treasure Island, *contrib. to treat.
(uncredited)*

1935

Party Wire, *co-scr.*

1938

Blockade, *scr.*, *ss.*
Algiers, *scr.*

1939

They Shall Have Music, *co-scr.*

1940

Earthbound, *co-scr.*
Four Sons, *scr.*

1943

Action in the North Atlantic, *scr.*
Sahara, *scr.*

1945

Counterattack, *scr.*

1947

Smash-Up—The Story of a
Woman, *scr.*

======

CHARLES LEDERER

1931

The Front Page, *co-dial.*

1932

Cock of the Air, *dial.*, *co-story,
co-scr.*
Frankie and Johnny, *scr. (uncredited)*

1933

Topaze, *co-scr. (uncredited)*

1935

Baby-Face Harrington, *add'l. dial.*

1937

Double Or Nothing, *co-scr.*
Mountain Music, *co-scr.*

1939

Broadway Serenade, *scr.*
Within the Law, *scr.*

1940

His Girl Friday, *scr.*
Comrade X, *co-scr.*
I Love You Again, *co-scr.*

1941

Love Crazy, *co-scr.*

1943

Slightly Dangerous, *scr.*
The Youngest Profession, *co-scr.*
The Outlaw, *story (uncredited)*

1947

Kiss of Death, *co-scr. with Ben Hecht*
Ride the Pink Horse, *co-scr. with Ben Hecht*
Her Husband's Affairs, *co-story and co-scr. with Ben Hecht*

1949

I Was a Male War Bride, *co-scr.*
Red, Hot and Blue, *story*

1950

Wabash Avenue, *co-story, co-scr.*

1951

The Thing, *scr.*
On the Loose, *scr. (uncredited)*

1952

Fearless Fagan, *scr.*
Monkey Business, *co-scr. with Ben Hecht and I. A. L. Diamond*

1953

Gentlemen Prefer Blondes, *scr.*

1955

Kismet, *co-scr. from his and Luther Davis' Broadway musical adaptation of Edward Knoblock's play*

1956

Gaby, *co-scr.*

1957

The Spirit of St. Louis, *adapt.*

Tip on a Dead Jockey, *scr.*

1958

The Fiend Who Walked the West, *remake of* Kiss of Death

1959

Can-Can, *co-scr.*
Never Steal Anything Small, *story, scr., dir.*
It Started with a Kiss, *scr.*

1960

Ocean's Eleven, *co-scr.*

1962

Follow That Dream, *scr.*
Mutiny on the Bounty, *scr.*

1964

A Global Affair, *co-scr.*

SONYA LEVIEN

1919

Who Will Marry Me, *story*

1922

First Love, *story*
The Top of New York, *story*
Pink Gods, *co-scr.*

1923

The Snow Bride, *co-story, scr.*
The Evicters, *co-scr.*

1926

The Love Toy, *scr.*

1928

A Ship Comes In, *co-scr.*
Power of the Press, *co-scr.*

1929

Younger Generation, *scr.*

Trial Marriage, *story, scr.*
Behind That Curtain, *co-scr.*
(*uncredited*)
Lucky Star, *scr.*
They Had to See Paris, *scr.*
South Sea Rose, *scr.*
Frozen Justice, *scr.*

1930

Son o' My Heart, *co-scr.*
Lightnin', *co-scr. and co-dial. with*
S. N. Behrman
So This Is London, *co-scr.*
(*uncredited*)
Liliom, *co-scr. with S. N. Behrman*
The Brat, *co-scr. and co-dial. with*
S. N. Behrman
Surrender, *co-scr. and co-dial.*
with S. N. Behrman
Delicious, *co-scr.*
Daddy Longlegs, *scr., co-dial.*
with S. N. Behrman

1932

She Wanted a Millionaire, *story*
After Tomorrow, *scr., dial.*
Rebecca of Sunnybrook Farm, *co-scr.*
and co-dial. with S. N. Behrman
Tess of the Storm Country, *co-scr.*
with S. N. Behrman and others

1933

State Fair, *co-scr.*
Cavalcade, *co-adapt.*
Warrior's Husband, *co-adapt.*
Berkeley Square, *co-adapt.*
Mr. Skitch, *co-adapt., co-dial.*

1934

As Husbands Go, *co-scr. with S. N.*
Behrman
Change of Heart, *co-scr.*
The White Parade, *co-scr.*

1935

Here's to Romance, *co-story*

Navy Wife, *scr.*

1936

The Country Doctor, *scr.*
Reunion, *co-scr.*

1938

In Old Chicago, *co-scr.*
Kidnapped, *co-scr.*
Four Men and a Prayer, *co-scr.*
The Cowboy and the Lady, *co-scr.*
with S. N. Behrman

1939

Drums Along the Mohawk, *co-scr.*
The Hunchback of Notre Dame,
co-scr.

1941

Ziegfield Girls, *co-scr.*

1943

The Amazing Mrs. Holliday, *story*

1945

The Valley of Decision, *co-scr.*
Rhapsody in Blue, *story.*
State Fair, *remake from her co-scr.*

1946

The Green Years, *co-scr.*

1947

Cass Timberlane, *co-adapt.*

1948

Three Darling Daughters, *co-scr.*

1951

The Great Caruso, *co-scr. with*
William Ludwig

1952

The Merry Widow, *co-scr. with*
William Ludwig

1954

The Student Prince, *co-scr. with William Ludwig*

1955

Hit the Deck, *co-scr. with William Ludwig*
Interrupted Melody, *co-story, co-scr. with William Ludwig*
Oklahoma!, *co-scr. with William Ludwig*

1956

Bhowani Junction, *co-scr.*

1957

Jeanne Eagles, *co-scr.*

1960

Pepe, *story*

1962

State Fair, *remake from her co-scr.*

HOWARD LINDSAY

1936

Swing Time, *co-scr.*

1937

Artists and Models, *co-contrib. to scr., dial.*

1938

Artists and Models Abroad, *co-scr., co-ss.*

1954

Woman's World, *co-adapt.*

STEPHEN LONGSTREET

1944

The Impostor, *adapt.*

1945

Uncle Harry, *scr.*

1946

The Jolson Story, *scr., ss.*
Stallion Road, *story, scr. from his novel*

1948

Silver River, *story, co-scr. from his novel*

1956

The First Traveling Saleslady, *co-scr., co-ss.*

1957

Untamed Youth, *ss.*
The Helen Morgan Story, *co-scr., co-ss.*

1963

Rider on a Dead Horse, *scr.*

FREDERICK LONSDALE

1931

Devil To Pay, *dial., scr.*

1932

Lovers Courageous, *story*

1934

The Private Life of Don Juan, *co-story, co-dial.*

1937

Angel, *contrib. to scr. construc.*

1944

Forever and a Day, *co-scr.*

ANITA LOOS*

1912

The New York Hat

1913

The Power of the Camera
A Horse on Bill
A Hicksville Epicure
Highbrow Love
Unlucky Jim
A Hicksville Romance
A Fallen Hero
A Cure for Suffragettes
The Path of True Love
The Suicide Pact
Bink Runs Away
How the Day Was Saved
The Wedding Gown
Yiddish Love
His Awful Vengeance
Pa Says
The Widow's Kid
His Hoodoo
The Lady in Black

1914

False Colors
Billy's Rival
When the Roads Part
A Bunch of Flowers
Gentleman Or Thief
The Road to Plaindale
The Wallflower
When a Woman Guides
Fall of Hicksville's Finest
For Her Father's Sin
All for Mabel
The Fatal Dress Suit
The Meal Ticket
The Saving Presence
A Corner in Hqts
Only a Burglar's Bride
Izzy and His Rival
The Million-Dollar Bride
The Suffering of Susan
A Flurry in Art

1915

Sympathy Sal
The Cost of a Bargain
The Female Villain
Mixed Values
Pennington's Choice, *scr.*

1916

Macbeth, *titles*
A Corner in Cotton, *story, scr.*
Wild Girl of the Sierras, *co-story, co-scr.*
Calico Vampire
French Milliner
The Wharf Rat, *story, scr.*
Stranded, *story, scr.*
The Social Secretary, *co-story, co-scr.*
His Picture in the Papers, *story, scr.*
The Half-Breed, *scr.*
Manhattan Madness
The Matrimaniac, *co-scr.*
Intolerance, *titles*

1917

The Americano, *story, scr.*
In Again, Out Again, *co-story, co-scr.*
Wild and Woolly, *story, scr.*
Reaching for the Moon, *co-story, co-scr.*

1918

Let's Get a Divorce, *co-scr.*
Hit-the-Trail Holiday, *co-scr.*
Come on In, *co-scr.*
Good-Bye Bill, *co-scr.*

1920

Two Weeks, *co-scr.*
In Search of a Sinner, *co-story, co-scr.*
The Love Expert, *co-story, co-scr.*
The Perfect Woman, *co-story, co-scr.*
The Branded Woman, *co-scr.*

1921

Dangerous Business, *co-story, co-scr.*
Mama's Affair, *co-scr.*
Woman's Place, *co-story, co-scr.*

1922

Red-Hot Romance, *co-story, co-scr.*
Polly of the Follies, *co-story, co-scr.*

1923

Dulcy, *co-scr.*

1924

Three Miles Out, *co-scr.*

1925

Learning to Love, *co-story, co-scr.*

1926

The Whole Town's Talking, *from the play by Emerson and Loos*

1927

Stranded, *from her story*
Publicity Madness, *from a story by Loos*

1928

Gentlemen Prefer Blondes, *co-scr. from her novel, titles by Loos and Herman J. Mankiewicz*

1929

The Fall of Eve, *co-story*

1931

The Struggle, *co-story, co-scr., co-dial.*
Ex-Bad Boy, *from the play* The Whole Town's Talking *by Loos and Emerson*

1932

Red-Headed Woman, *scr.*

1933

Hold Your Man, *co-scr.*
Midnight Mary, *story*
The Barbarian, *co-scr.*

1934

Social Register, *from the play by Emerson and Loos*
The Girl from Missouri, *co-scr.*
Biography of a Bachelor Girl, *co-story, co-scr.*

1935

Riffraff, *co-scr.*

1936

San Francisco, *scr.*

1937

Mama Steps Out, *scr.*

1939

The Women, *co-scr.*

1940

Susan and God, *scr.*

1941

They Met in Bombay, *co-scr.*
When Ladies Meet, *co-scr.*
Blossoms in the Dust, *scr.*

1942

I Married an Angel, *scr.*

1953

Gentlemen Prefer Blondes, *from the play by Joseph Fields and Loos*

1955

Gentlemen Marry Brunettes, *co-scr., from her novel*

CHARLES MacARTHUR

1930

The Girl Said No, *dial.*
Billy the Kid, *add'l. dial.*
Way for a Sailor, *co-scr., add'l. dial.*

1931

The Sin of Madelon Claudet, *add'l. scenes and dial. (uncredited)*
Paid, *co-scr. dial.*
The Unholy Garden, *co-story, co-scr., co-dial. with Ben Hecht*
The New Adventures of Get-Rich-Quick Wallingford, *scr., dial.*

1932

Rasputin and the Empress, *story, sc.*

1934

Twentieth Century, *co-scr. from his, Ben Hecht's and Charles Milholland's play*
Crime Without Passion, *co-story, co-scr., co-prod. with Ben Hecht*

1935

Once in a Blue Moon, *co-story, co-scr., co-prod. with Ben Hecht*
The Scoundrel, *co-scr., co-prod. with Ben Hecht*
Barbary Coast, *co-story, co-scr. with Ben Hecht*

1936

Soak the Rich, *co-scr., co-prod. with Ben Hecht, from his and Ben Hecht's play*

1939

Gunga Din, *co-scr. with Ben Hecht,*
Joel Sayre and Fred Guial
Wuthering Heights, *co-scr. with Ben Hecht*

1940

I Take This Woman, *story*

1947

The Senator Was Indiscreet, *scr.*

1948

Lulu Belle, *co-scr. from his and Edward Sheldon's play*

JOHN LEE MAHIN

1932

Red Dust, *co-scr.*
The Beast of the City, *co-scr.*
Scarface, *co-scr.*

1933

Hell Below, *co-dial.*
Eskimo, *co-scr.*

1934

Treasure Island, *co-scr.*
Chained, *co-scr.*

1935

Naughty Marietta, *co-scr.*

1936

Wife vs. Secretary, *co-scr.*
The Devil Is a Sissy, *co-scr.*

1937

Captains Courageous, *co-scr.*

1938

Boom Town, *scr.*

1941

Dr. Jekyll and Mr. Hyde, *co-scr.*

1942

Tortilla Flat, *co-scr.*

1943

The Adventures of Tartu, *scr.*

1952

My Son John, *scr.*
Showboat, *co-scr.*

1954

Elephant Walk, *scr.*

1956

The Bad Seed, *co-scr.*

1957

Heaven Knows, Mr. Allison, *co-scr.*

1959

The Horse Soldiers, *co-scr.*,
co-prod.

═══════

ALBERT MALTZ

1942

This Gun for Hire, *co-scr.*

1943

Destination Tokyo, *co-scr.*

1945

The House I Live In, *scr.*
Pride of the Marines, *scr.*

1946

Cloak and Dagger, *co-scr.*

1948

The Naked City, *co-scr.*

1970

Two Mules for Sister Sara, *scr.*

1971

The Beguiled, *co-scr. (uncredited)*

═══════

HERMAN J. MANKIEWICZ

1926

Stranded in Paris, *scr.*

1927

Fashions for Women, *co-adapt.*
A Gentleman of Paris, *titl.*
Figures Don't Lie, *titl.*
The Spotlight, *titl.*
The City Gone Wild, *titl.*
The Gay Defender, *co-titl.*
Honeymoon Hate, *co-titl.*

1928

Two Flaming Youths, *titl.*
Gentlemen Prefer Blondes, *co-titl.*
The Last Command, *titl.*
Love and Learn, *titl.*
A Night of Mystery, *titl.*
Abie's Irish Rose, *co-scr.*
Something Always Happens, *titl.*
His Tiger Lady, *titl.*
The Dragnet, *titl.*
The Magnificent Flirt, *titl.*
The Big Killing, *titl.*
The Water Hole, *titl.*
The Mating Call, *titl.*
Avalanche, *co-scr., titl.*
The Barker, *titl.*
Three Week Ends, *co-titl.*
What a Night!, *titl.*

1929

Marquis Preferred, *titl.*
The Dummy, *scr., dial.*
The Canary Murder Case, *titl.*
The Man I Love, *story, dial.*
Thunderbolt, *dial.*
Men Are Like That, *co-scr., dial.*

The Love Doctor, *titl.*
The Mighty, *titl.*

1930

The Vagabond King, *scr., dial.*
Honey, *scr., dial.*
Ladies Love Brutes, *co-scr., co-dial.*
True to the Navy, *dial.*
Love Among the Millionaires, *dial.*
The Royal Family of Broadway,
  co-scr.

1931

Ladies' Man, *scr., dial.*
Man of the World, *story, scr.*

1932

Dancers in the Dark, *co-scr.*
Girl Crazy, *co-scr., dial.*
The Lost Squadron, *co-dial.*

1933

Meet the Baron, *co-story.*
Dinner at Eight, *co-scr.*
Another Language, *co-scr.*

1934

The Show-off, *scr.*
Stamboul Quest, *scr.*

1935

After Office Hours, *scr.*
Escapade, *scr.*
It's in the Air,
  co-scr. (uncredited)

1937

The Emperor's Candlesticks,
  co-scr. (uncredited)
My Dear Miss Aldrich, *story, scr.*
John Meade's Woman, *co-scr.*

1939

It's a Wonderful World, *co-story*

1941

Citizen Kane, *story, co-scr.*
Rise and Shine, *scr.*
Keeping Company, *story*

1942

The Pride of the Yankees, *co-scr.*

1943

Stand by for Action, *co-scr.*

1944

Christmas Holiday, *scr.*

1945

The Spanish Main, *co-scr.*

1949

A Woman's Secret, *scr.*

1952

The Pride of St. Louis, *scr.*
Mankiewicz also co-scripted (without credit) and produced the following films:

1930

Laughter

1931

Monkey Business

1932

Horse Feathers
Million Dollar Legs

JOSEPH L. MANKIEWICZ*

1929

The Dummy, *titl.*
Close Harmony, *titl.*
The Studio Murder Mystery, *titl.*
The Man I Love, *titl.*
River of Romance, *titl.*

The Mysterious Dr. Fu Manchu, *titl.*
The Saturday Night Kid, *co-dial.*
   (uncredited)
Fast Company, *dial.*

1930

Slightly Scarlet, *co-scr., co-dial.*
Paramount on Parade, *co-scr.*
   (uncredited, for Jack Oakie
    sequence)
The Social Lion, *co-scr., dial.*
Sap from Syracuse, *co-scr.*
   (uncredited)
Only Saps Work, *co-scr.*
The Gang Buster, *dial.*

1931

Finn and Hattie, *dial.*
June Moon, *co-scr., co-dial.*
   Skippy, *co-scr.*
Dude Ranch, *co-scr. (uncredited)*
Forbidden Adventure, *co-scr.*
Touchdown, *co-scr. (uncredited)*
Sooky, *co-scr.*

1932

This Reckless Age, *scr.*
   Sky Bride, *co-scr.*
Million Dollar Legs, *story, co-scr.*
If I Had a Million, *co-scr.*
   (for Jack Oakie sequence)

1933

Diplomaniacs, *story, co-scr.*
Emergency Call, *co-scr.*
Too Much Harmony, *scr.*
Alice in Wonderland, *scr.*

1934

Manhattan Melodrama, *co-scr.*
Our Daily Bread, *dial.*
Forsaking All Others, *scr.*

1935

I Live My Live, scr.

1944

The Keys of the Kingdom, *co-scr.,*
prod.

1946

Dragonwyck, *scr.*

1947

Somewhere in the Night, *co-scr.*

1949

A Letter to Three Wives, *scr.*

1950

No Way Out, *co-scr.*
All About Eve, *scr.*

1951

People Will Talk, *scr.*

1953

Julius Caesar, *adapt., scr.*

1954

The Barefoot Contessa, *story, scr.*

1955

Guys and Dolls, *scr.*

1957

The Quiet American, *scr.*

1963

Cleopatra, *co-scr.*

1967

The Honey Pot, *scr.*
*Mankiewicz contributed to but did not
sign the screenplays of the following
films, which he produced:*

1936

Three Godfathers
Fury

The Gorgeous Hussy
Love on the Run

1937

The Bride Wore Red
Double Wedding
Mannequin

1938

Three Comrades
The Shining Hour
A Christmas Carol

1939

The Adventures of Huckleberry Finn

1940

Strange Cargo
The Philadelphia Story

1941

The Wild Man of Borneo
The Feminine Touch

1942

Woman of the Year
Reunion
and he contributed to but did not sign the scripts of the following films, which he also directed:

1947

The Late George Apley
The Ghost and Mrs. Muir
Escape

1952

Five Fingers

1959

Suddenly Last Summer

1970

There Was a Crooked Man

1973

Sleuth

═══════

FRANCES MARION*

1915

A Daughter of the Sea, *story, scr.*
Camille, *scr.*

1916

The Foundling, *story, scr.*
The Yellow Passport, *co-scr.*
Then I'll Come Back to You, *scr.*
The Social Highwayman, *scr.*
The Feast of Life, *story, scr.*
Tangled Fates, *scr.*
The Battle of Hearts, *story*
La Vie de Bohème, *scr.*
The Crucial Test, *story, scr.*
A Woman's Way, *scr.*
The Summer Girl, *scr.*
Friday the 13th, *scr.*
The Revolt, *scr.*
The Hidden Scar, *scr.*
The Gilded Cage, *scr.*
Bought and Paid For, *scr.*
All Man, *scr.*
The Rise of Susan, *story, scr.*
On Dangerous Ground, *scr.*

1917

A Woman Alone, *scr.*
Tillie Wakes Up, *scr.*
The Hungry Heart, *scr.*
A Square Deal, *scr.*
A Girl's Folly, *co-story, co-scr.*
The Web of Desire, *scr.*
Poor Little Rich Girl, *scr.*
As Man Made Her, *scr.*
The Social Leper, *scr.*
Forget-Me-Not, *story, scr.*
Darkest Russia, *scr.*
The Crimson Dove, *story, scr.*

The Stolen Paradise, *story, scr.*
The Divorce Game, *scr.*
The Beloved Adventuress, *story,*
scr.
The Amazons, *scr.*
Rebecca of Sunnybrook Farm, *scr.*
A Little Princess, *scr.*

1918

Stella Maris, *scr.*
Amarilly of Clothes-Line Alley,
scr.
M'Liss, *scr.*
How Could You, Jean?, *scr.*
The City of Dim Faces, *story,*
scr.
Johanna Enlists, *scr.*
He Comes up Smiling, *scr.*
The Temple of Dusk, *story, scr.*
The Goat, *story, scr.*

1919

Captin Kidd, Jr., *scr.*
The Misleading Widow, *scr.*
Anne of Green Gables, *scr.*
A Regular Girl, *story, scr.*

1920

The Cinema Murder, *scr.*
Pollyanna, *scr.*
Humoresque, *scr.*
The Flapper, *story, scr.*
The Restless Sex, *scr.*
The World and His Wife, *scr.*

1921

The Love Light, *story, scr.*
Straight Is the Way, *scr.*

1922

Just Around the Corner, *adapt.,*
scr.
Back Pay, *scr.*
The Primitive Lover, *scr.*
Sonny, *co-adapt., scr.*

East Is West, *adapt., scr.*
The Eternal Flame, *adapt., scr.*
The Toll of the Sea, *story, scr.*
Minnie, *titles*

1923

The Voice from the Minaret,
adapt., scr.
The Famous Mrs. Fair, *adapt., scr.*
The Nth Commandment, *scr.*
Within the Law, *adapt., scr.*
The Love Piker, *scr.*
Potash and Perlmutter, *scr.*
The French Doll, *adapt., scr.*

1924

The Song of Love, *adapt., scr.*
Through the Dark, *scr.*
Abraham Lincoln, *story, scr.*
Secrets, *adapt., scr.*
Cytherea, *adapt., scr.*
Tarnish, *scr.*
In Hollywood with Potash and
Perlmutter, *adapt., scr.*
Sundown, *co-scr.*

1925

A Thief in Paradise, *adapt., scr.*
The Lady, *scr.*
The Flaming Forties, *scr.*
His Supreme Moment, *adapt., scr.*
Zander the Great, *adapt., co-scr.*
Lightnin', *scr.*
Graustark, *adapt., scr.*
The Dark Angel, *scr.*
Lazy Bones, *scr.*
Thank You, *scr.*
Simon the Jester, *adapt., scr.,*
prod.
Stella Dallas, *adapt., scr.*

1926

The First Year, *scr.*
Partners Again—Potash and
Perlmutter, *adapt., scr.*

Paris at Midnight, *adapt., scr.,*
  prod.
The Son of the Sheik, *adapt.,*
  co-scr.
The Scarlet Letter, *adapt.,*
  titles, scr.
The Winning of Barbara Worth,
  adapt., scr.

1927

The Red Mill, *adapt., scr.*
The Callahans, and the Murphys,
  scr.
Madame Pompadour, *scr.*
Love, *continuity, scr.*

1928

Bringing up Father, *cont., scr.*
The Cossacks, *adapt., cont., scr.*
Excess Baggage, *cont., scr.*
The Wind, *scr.*
The Awakening, *story, scr.*
The Masks of the Devil, *cont.,*
  scr.

1929

Their Own Desire, *scr.*

1930

Anna Christie, *scr.*
The Rogue Song, *co-scr.*
The Big House, *story, scr., dial.*
Let Us Be Gay, *cont., scr., dial.*
Good News, *scr.*
Min and Bill, *co-dial., co-scr.*
Wu Li Chang, *scr.*

1931

The Secret Six, *story, scr.*
The Champ, *story, scr.*

1932

Emma, *story*
Blondie of the Follies, *story*
Cynara, *co-scr.*

1933

Secrets, *scr.*
Peg o' My Heart, *adapt.*
Dinner at Eight, *co-scr.*
The Prizefighter and the Lady,
  story
Going Hollywood, *story*

1935

Riffraff, *story, co-scr.*

1937

Camille, *co-scr.*
Love from a Stranger, *scr.*
Knight Without Armor, *adapt.*

1940

Green Hell, *story, scr.*

1945

Molly and Me, *story*

1953

The Clown, *story*

DON MARQUIS

1936

Captain January, *contrib. to scr.*

SOMERSET MAUGHAM

1922

The Ordeal, *story*

EDWIN JUSTUS MAYER

1927

Women Love Diamonds, *titl.*
The Love Mart, *titl.*
The Devil Dancer, *titl.*
Husbands for Rent, *story*

1928

Blue Danube, *co-titl.*
Midnight Madness, *titl.*
The Whip Woman, *titl.*
Man-Made Woman, *titl.*
Sal of Singapore, *titl.*
Ned McCobb's Daughter, *titl.*
The Divine Lady, *co-titl.*
Unholy Night, *scr.*
Loves of Casanova, *titl.*

1930

Not So Dumb, *dial.*
Redemption, *dial.*
In Gay Madrid, *co-scr., co-dial.*
The Lady of Scandal, *dial.*
Our Blushing Brides, *co-dial.*
Romance, *co-scr., co-dial.*
Never the Twain Shall Meet, *scr., dial.*
Phantom of Paris, *co-dial.*

1932

Merrily We Go to Hell, *scr., dial.*
Wild Girl, *co-scr., co-dial.*

1933

Tonight Is Ours, *scr., dial.*

1934

I Am Suzanne, *co-scr.*
Thirty Day Princess, *co-scr.*
Here Is My Heart, *co-scr.*

1935

So Red the Rose, *co-scr.*

1936

Give Us This Night, *co-scr.*
Desire, *co-scr.*
'Til We Meet Again, *co-scr.*
Wives Never Know, *co-scr.*
(uncredited)

1938

The Buccaneer, *co-scr.*

1939

Exile Express, *story*
Midnight, *co-story*
Rio, *co-scr.*

1941

Underground, *co-story*
They Met in Bombay, *co-scr.*

1942

To Be Or Not To Be, *scr.*

1945

A Royal Scandal, *scr.*
Masquerade in Mexico, *remake of Midnight*

1958

The Buccaneer, *co-scr., remake of the 1938 film*

JANE MURFIN

1919

The Right To Lie, *scr.*
Marie, Ltd., *scr.*

1921

The Silent Call, *prod., scr.*

1922

Brawn of the North, *prod., scr.*

1924

Flapper Wives, *scr.*
The Love Master, *prod., scr.*

1925

White Fang, *prod., scr.*

1926

The Savage, *scr.*
Meet the Prince, *scr.*

1927

Notorious Lady, *scr.*
The Prince of Headwaiters, *scr.*

1929

Half Marriage, *scr.*
Street Girl, *scr.*
Seven Keys to Baldpate, *scr.*

1930

Dance Hall, *co-scr., co-dial.*
Runaway Bridge, *scr., dial.*
Lawful Larceny, *scr., dial.*
The Pay Off, *scr., dial.*
Leathernecking, *co-scr.*

1931

Too Many Cooks, *scr.*
White Shoulders, *adapt.*
Friends and Lovers, *co-scr.*

1932

Way Back Home, *story, scr., dial.*
Young Bride, *co-dial.*
What Price Hollywood, *co-dial.*
Rockabye, *co-scr.*

1933

Our Betters, *adapt.*
The Silver Cord, *adapt.*
Double Harness, *adapt.*
Ann Vickers, *adapt.*
After Tonight, *story, adapt.*

1934

Crime Doctor, *scr.*
Spitfire, *co-scr.*
This Man Is Mine, *scr.*
The Life of Vergie Winters, *scr.*
The Fountain, *co-scr.*

Romance in Manhattan, *co-scr.*
Little Minister, *co-scr.*

1935

Roberta, *co-scr.*
Alice Adams, *co-scr.*

1936

Come and Get It, *co-scr.*
That Girl from Paris, *story*

1937

I'll Take Romance, *co-scr.*

1938

The Shining Hour, *co-scr.*

1939

Stand Up and Fight, *co-scr.*
The Women, *co-scr.*

1940

Pride and Prejudice, *co-scr.*

1941

Andy Hardy's Private Secretary,
co-scr.

1944

Dragon Seed, *co-scr.*

═══════

ROBERT NATHAN

1944

The White Cliffs of Dover, *add'l.
poetry*

1945

The Clock, *co-scr.*

1948

Tenth Avenue Angel, *contrib. to scr.
(uncredited)*

1950

Pagan Love Song, *co-scr.*

DUDLEY NICHOLS*

1930

Men Without Women, *scr.*
On the Level, *scr.*
Born Reckless, *scr.*
One Mad Kiss, *scr.*
A Devil with Women, *co-scr.*

1931

Seas Beneath, *scr.*
Not Exactly Gentlemen, *co-scr.*
Hush Money, *dial.*
Skyline, *co-scr.*

1932

This Sporting Age, *scr.*

1933

Pilgrimage, *dial.*
Robbers Roos, *scr.*
The Man Who Dared, *co-scr.*
Hot Pepper, *from his story*

1934

You Can't Buy Everything, *co-story*
Hold That Girl, *co-scr., co-story*
The Lost Patrol, *co-scr.*
Wild Gold, *co-story*
Call It Luck, *co-scr., co-story*
Judge Priest, *co-scr.*

1935

Mystery Woman, *co-story*
The Informer, *scr.*
The Arizonian, *story, scr.*
The Crusades, *co-scr.*
Steamboat 'Round the Bend, *co-scr.*
The Three Musketeers, *scr.*

1936

Mary of Scotland, *scr.*
The Plough and the Stars, *scr.*

1937

The Toast of New York, *co-scr.*
The Hurricane, *co-scr.*

1938

Bringing up Baby, *co-scr.*
Carefree, *co-story, co-adapt.*

1939

Stagecoach, *scr.*
The 400 Million, *commentary*

1940

The Long Voyage Home, *scr.*

1941

Man Hunt, *scr.*
Swamp Water, *scr.*

1943

This Land Is Mine, *story, scr.*
Air Force, *story, scr.*
For Whom the Bell Tolls, *scr.*
Government Girl, *scr., dir.*

1944

It Happened Tomorrow, *co-scr.*
The Sign of the Cross, *prologue for re-release*

1945

And Then There Were None, *scr.*
The Bells of St. Mary's, *scr.*
Scarlet Street, *scr.*

1946

Sister Kenny, *co-scr., dir.*

1947

The Fugitive, *scr.*

Mourning Becomes Electra, *scr.,*
dir.

1949

Pinky, *co-scr.*

1951

Rawhide, *story, scr.*

1952

Return of the Texan, *scr.*
The Big Sky, *scr.*

1954

Prince Valiant, *scr.*

1956

Run for the Sun, *co-scr.*

1957

The Tin Star, *scr.*

1959

The Hangman, *scr.*

1960

Heller in Pink Tights, *co-scr.*

═══════

CLIFFORD ODETS

1936

The General Died at Dawn, *scr.*

1944

None But the Lonely Heart, *scr.,*
dir.

1946

Deadline at Dawn, *scr.*
Humoresque, *co-scr.*

1957

Sweet Smell of Success, *co-scr.*

1960

The Story on Page One, *scr., ss.,*
dir.

1961

Wild in the Country, *scr.*

═══════

JOHN O'HARA

1940

He Married His Wife, *co-scr.*
I Was an Adventuress, *co-scr.*

1942

Moontide, *scr.*

1956

The Best Things in Life Are Free,
story.

═══════

GEORGE OPPENHEIMER

1933

Roman Scandals, *add'l. dial. and*
material

1935

Rendezvous, *co-scr.*
No More Ladies, *contrib. to dial.*

1936

Libeled Lady, *co-scr.*
We Went to College, *co-ss.*

1937

Man-Proof, *co-scr.*
I'll Take Romance, *co-scr.*
London by Night, *scr.*
Married Before Breakfast, *co-scr.*
A Day at the Races, *co-scr.*
The Last of Mrs. Cheyney, *adapt.*

1938

Paradise for Three, *co-scr.*
A Yank at Oxford, *co-scr.*
The Crowd Roars, *co-scr.*
Three Loves Has Nancy, *co-scr.*

1940

Broadway Melody of 1940, *co-scr.*
I Love You Again, *co-scr.*

1941

The Feminine Touch, *co-scr., co-ss.*
Two Faced Woman, *co-scr., co-ss.*

1942

A Yank at Eton, *co-scr., ss.*
The War Against Mrs. Hadley, *scr., ss.*
Pacific Rendezvous, *co-scr.*

1943

Slightly Dangerous, *co-scr.*
The Youngest Profession, *co-scr.*

1947

Killer McCoy, *co-ss.*

1949

The Adventures of Don Juan, *co-scr.*

1950

Born To Be Bad, *add'l. dial.*
Perfect Strangers, *adapt.*

1952

Anything Can Happen, *co-scr.*

1953

Tonight We Sing, *co-scr.*
Decameron Nights, *scr.*

=====

SAMUEL ORNITZ

1929

The Case of Lena Smith, *story*

1930

Sins of the Children, *adapt.*

1932

Hell's Highway, *co-story, co-ss.*
Secrets of the French Police, *scr., from his* The Lost Empress
Men of America, *co-scr.*

1933

One Man's Journey, *co-scr.*

1934

The Man Who Reclaimed His Head, *co-scr.*

1936

Follow Your Heart, *co-scr.*
Fatal Lady, *scr.*

1937

Two Wise Maids, *scr.*
Portia on Trial, *scr.*
It Could Happen To You, *co-scr.*
The Hit Parade, *co-scr.*
A Doctor's Diary, *co-ss.*

1938

Little Orphan Annie, *co-scr., co-ss.*
Army Girl, *co-scr.*
King of the Newsboys, *co-ss.*

1940

Miracle on Main Street, *co-ss.*
Three Faces West, *co-scr., co-ss.*

1944

They Live in Fear, *co-scr.*
Little Devils, *scr.*

1945

Circumstantial Evidence, *adapt.*

PAUL OSBORN

1938

The Young in Heart, *scr.*

1942

Mrs. Miniver, *contrib. to scr.*
(uncredited)

1943

Madame Curie, *co-scr.*

1944

Cry Havoc, *scr.*

1946

The Yearling, *scr.*

1948

The Homecoming, *scr.*
Portrait of Jennie, *co-scr.*

1952

Invitation, *scr.*

1955

East of Eden, *scr.*

1957

Sayonara, *scr.*

1958

South Pacific, *scr.*

1960

Wild River, *scr.*

DOROTHY PARKER

1934

Here Is My Heart, *contrib. to dial.*
(uncredited)
One Hour Late, *contrib. to dial.*
(uncredited)

1935

Mary Burns, *fugitive, contrib. to*
dial. (uncredited)
Hands Across the Table, *contrib. to*
scr. construc. (uncredited)
The Big Broadcast of 1936, *co-lyrics*
(uncredited)
Paris in Spring, *contrib. to treat.*
(uncredited)

1936

Suzy, *co-scr.*
Three Married Men, *co-scr.*
The Moon's Our Home,
co-add'l. dial.
Lady Be Careful, *co-scr.*

1937

A Star Is Born, *co-scr.*

1938

Trade Winds, *co-scr.*
Sweethearts, *co-scr.*

1941

The Little Foxes, *add'l. scenes and*
dial.
Weekend for Three, *co-scr.*

1942

Saboteur, *co-ss., co-scr.*

1947

Smash-Up—The Story
of a Woman,
co-ss.

1949

The Fan, *co-scr.*

JOHN PATRICK

1936

15 Maiden Lane, *co-scr.*
36 Hours To Kill, *co-scr.*

High Tension, *co-scr.*
Educating Father, *co-scr., co-ss.*

1937

The Holy Terror, *co-scr., co-ss.*
Big Town Girl, *co-scr.*
Dangerously Yours, *co-scr., co-ss.*
Look Out, Mr. Moto, *co-scr.*
Born Reckless, *co-scr.*
Sing and Be Happy, *co-scr., co-ss.*
One Mile from Heaven, *co-scr.*
Midnight Taxi, *co-scr.*
Time out for Romance, *co-scr.*

1938

International Settlement, *co-scr.*
Up the River, *co-scr.*
Five of a Kind, *co-scr., co-ss.*
The Battle of Broadway,
    co-scr.

1948

Enchantment, *scr.*

1953

The President's Lady, *scr.*

1954

Three Coins in the Fountain, *scr.*

1955

Love Is a Many-Splendored
    Thing, *scr.*

1956

High Society, *scr.*
The Teahouse of the August
    Moon, *scr. from his play*

1957

Les Girls, *scr.*

1958

Some Came Running, *co-scr.*

1960

The World of Suzie Wong, *scr.*

1962

Gigot, *scr.*

1963

The Main Attraction, *scr., ss., prod.*

1968

The Shoes of the Fisherman, *co-scr.*

=======

ELLIOT PAUL

1941

A Woman's Face, *co-scr.*

1945

Rhapsody in Blue, *co-scr.*
It's a Pleasure, *co-scr., co-ss.*
Guest in the House, *add'l. dial.*
    (uncredited)

1947

New Orleans, *co-scr., co-ss.*

1953

My Heart Goes Crazy, *co-scr.*

=======

JOHN PAXTON*

1944

My Pal Wolf, *co-scr.*

1945

Murder My Sweet, *scr.*

1946

Cornered, *scr.*
Crack-Up, *co-scr.*

1947

Crossfire, *scr.*
So Well Remembered, *scr.*

1949

Rope of Sand, *add'l. dial.*

1950

Of Men and Music, *co-story, co-scr.*

1951

Fourteen Hours, *scr.*

1953

The Wild One, *scr.*

1955

Prize of Gold, *co-scr.*

1956

The Cobweb, *scr.*
Interpol (Pickup Alley), *scr.*

1959

How to Murder a Rich Uncle, *scr.,
prod.*
On the Beach, *scr.*

1971

Kotch, *scr.*

———

S. J. PERELMAN

1932

Hold 'Em Jail, *co-scr.*
Horse Feathers, *co-story*

1933

Sitting Pretty, *co-scr.*

1935

The Big Broadcast of 1936, *contrib.
to treat. (uncredited)*

1936

Florida Special, *co-scr.*
Early to Bed, *contrib. to scr.
(uncredited)*

1939

Boy Trouble, *co-scr.*
Ambush, *co-scr.*

1940

The Golden Fleecing, *co-scr.*

1956

Around the World in 80 Days, *co-scr.*

———

J. B. PRIESTLY

1939

Jamaica Inn, *dial.*

1950

Last Holiday, *scr., ss. co-prod.*

———

ABRAHAM POLONSKY

1947

Golden Earrings, *co-scr.*
Body and Soul, *story, scr.*

1948

Force of Evil, *co-scr.*

1951

I Can Get It for You Wholesale, *scr.*

1968

Madigan, *co-scr.*

1969

Tell Them Willie Boy Is Here, *scr.*

1972

Mario and the Magician, *scr. (in preparation)*
The Ramayana, *co-scr.*

1973

Childhood's End, *co-scr. (in preparation)*

=====

AYN RAND

1945

Love Letters, *scr.*
You Came Along, *co-scr.*

1949

The Fountainhead, *story, scr., from her novel*

=====

SAMSON RAPHAELSON

1927

The Jazz Singer, *from his play*

1930

Boudoir Diplomat, *co-scr. (uncredited)*

1931

The Smiling Lieutenant, *co-scr., co-dial.*
Magnificent Lie, *scr., co-dial.*

1932

One Hour with You, *scr.*
Broken Lullaby, *co-scr.*
Trouble in Paradise, *scr.*

1934

The Merry Widow, *co-scr.*
Caravan, *scr.*
Servant's Entrance, *scr.*

1935

Ladies Love Danger, *co-scr.*
Dressed To Thrill, *scr.*

1937

The Last of Mrs. Cheyney, *co-scr.*
Angel, *scr.*

1940

The Shop Around The Corner, *scr.*

1941

Suspicion, *co-scr.*

1943

Heaven Can Wait, *scr.*
Without Love, *co-scr. (uncredited)*

1947

Green Dolphin Street, *scr.*

1948

That Lady in Ermine, *story, scr.*
In the Good Old Summertime, *musical remake of* The Shop Around the Corner

1953

Main Street to Broadway, *scr.*

=====

QUENTIN REYNOLDS

1948

Miracle of the Bells, *co-scr.*

=====

ELMER RICE

1922

Doubling for Romeo, *story*
Rent Free, *adapt.*

1933

Counsellor at Law, *scr.*, *from his play*

1942

Holiday Inn, *adapt.*

LYNN RIGGS

1934

Stingaree, *adapt.*

1936

The Garden of Allah, *co-scr.*

1942

Destination Unknown, *co-scr.*
Madame Spy, *co-scr.*
Sherlock Holmes and the Voice of Terror, *scr.*
Sherlock Holmes in Washington, *co-scr.*

ROBERT RISKIN

1931

Men in Her Life, *dial.*, *co-scr.*
Plantinum Blonde, *dial.*

1932

Three Wise Girls, *dial.*
Big Timer, *dial.*
American Madness, *story*, *scr.*, *dial.*
Nightclub Lady, *scr.*, *dial.*
Virtue, *scr.*
Shopworn, *co-dial.*

1933

Ann Carver's Profession, *adapt.*
from his story Rules for Wives
Lady for a Day, *adapt.*

1934

It Happened One Night, *scr.*
Broadway Bill, *co-scr.*

1935

Carnival, *scr.*
The Whole Town's Talking, *co-scr.*

1936

Mr. Deeds Goes to Town, *scr.*

1937

When You're in Love, *scr.*
Lost Horizon, *scr.*

1938

You Can't Take It with You, *scr.*

1941

Meet John Doe, *scr.*

1944

The Thin Man Goes Home, *co-story*, *co-scr.*

1947

Magic Town, *co-story*, *scr.*, *prod.*

1950

Mister, *scr.*
Riding High, *remake of* Broadway Bill

1951

Half Angel, *scr.*
Here Comes the Groom, *co-story*

1956

You Can't Run Away from It, *remake of* It Happened One Night

1961

Pocketful of Miracles, *remake of* Lady for a Day

ALLEN RIVKIN

1932

Is My Face Red?, *story*
70,000 Witnesses, co-dial.
Madison Square Garden, co-scr.

1933

Melody Cruise, *co-add. dial.*
Dancing Lady, *co-scr.*

1935

Our Little Girl, *co-scr.*

1937

This Is My Affair, *co-story*
& co-scr.
Love under Fire, *co-scr.*

1940

Typhoon, *scr.*

1942

Joe Smith, American, *scr.*
Sunday Punch, *co-scr.*

1947

The Farmer's Daughter,
co-scr.

1953

Battle Circus, *co-story*

1955

Timberjack, *scr.*
The Eternal Sea, *scr.*
Road to Denver, *scr.*

DAMON RUNYON

1934

A Very Honorable Guy, *story*

1936

Professional Soldier, *story*

MORRIE RYSKIND

1929

The Coconuts, *scr. from his and*
George S. Kaufman's play

1930

Animal Crackers, *co-scr., co-dial.*
from his and George S. Kaufman's
play

1931

Palmy Days, *co-scr., co-dial.*

1935

A Night at the Opera,
co-scr. from his and George S. Kaufman's
play
Ceiling Zero, *co-scr.*
(uncredited)

1936

My Man Godfrey, *co-scr.*
Rhythm on the Range, *co-adapt.*

1937

Stage Door, *co-scr.*

1938

Room Service, *scr.*
There's Always a Woman, *co-scr.*

1939

Man About Town, *scr.*

1941

Penny Serenade, *scr.*

1943

Claudia, *scr.*

1945

Where Do We Go from Here?,
co-story

1946

Heart Beat, *adapt.*

======

WILLIAM SAROYAN

1943

The Human Comedy, *ss.*

======

JOHN MONK SAUNDERS

1928

The Docks of New York, *story*
Legion of the Condemned,
co-scen.

1929

She Goes to War, *dial., titl.*
Wings, *story*

1931

The Last Flight, *scr., from his
novel* Single Lady
Finger Points, *co-ss., dial.*

1933

The Eagle and the Hawk, *story*
Ace of Aces, *scr., from his story,*
The Bird of Prey

1935

Devil Dogs of the Air, *scr.*
West Point of the Air, *co-story*
I Found Stella Parrish, *story*

1938

A Yank at Oxford, *story idea*

CHARLES SCHNEE*

1947

I Walk Alone, *scr.*

1948

They Drive By Night (The
Twisted Road), *scr.*
Red River, *co-scr.*

1949

Scene of the Crime, *scr.*
Easy Living, *scr.*

1950

Paid in Full, *co-scr.*
The Next Voice You Hear, *scr.*
The Furies, *scr.*
Right Cross, *story, scr.*

1951

Bannerline, *scr.*
Westward the Women, *scr.*

1952

When in Rome, *co-scr.*
The Bad and the Beautiful, *scr.*

1960

Butterfield 8, *co-scr.*
The Crowded Sky, *scr.*

1962

Two Weeks in Another Town,
scr.

======

BUDD SCHULBERG

1938

Little Orphan Annie, *co-scr.*

1939

Winter Carnival, *ss., co-scr.*

1941

Weekend for Three, *story*

1943

City Without Men, *co-ss.*
Government Girl, *adapt.*

1954

On the Waterfront, *scr., ss.*

1957

A Face in the Crowd, *story, scr.*

1958

Wind Across the Everglades, *scr.,
ss.*

GEORGE BERNARD SHAW

1938

Pygmalion, *scr., from his play*

1941

Major Barbara, *scr., from his play*

1946

Caesar and Cleopatra, *scr., from his
play*

IRWIN SHAW

1936

The Big Game, *co-scr.*

1942

The Talk of the Town, *co-scr.*
The Hard Way, *co-scr.*
Commandos Strike at Dawn, *scr.*

1949

Take One False Step, *story, scr.
from David and Irwin Shaw's story*
Night Call
Easy Living, *story*

1951

I Want You, *scr.*

1953

Act of Love, *scr.*

1955

Ulysses, *co-scr.*

1957

Fire Down Below, *scr.*

1958

Desire under the Elms, *scr.*
This Angry Age, *co-scr.*

1961

The Big Gamble, *scr., ss.*

1963

In the French Style, *story, scr.
from his two stories*, In the
French Style *and* A Year to
Learn the Language

1968

Survival 1967, *scr., ss.*

R. C. SHERRIFF

1932

The Old Dark House, *dial.*

1933

Invisible Man, *adapt.*

1934

One More River, *scr.*

1937

The Road Back, *co-scr.*

1939

Four Feathers, *co-scr.*
Goodbye Mr. Chips, *co-scr.*

1941

That Hamilton Woman, *co-scr.*

1942

This Above All, *scr.*
Stand By for Action, *co-adapt.*

1943

Forever and a Day, *co-scr.*

1947

Odd Man Out, *co-scr.*

1949

Quartet, *co-scr.*

1950

Trio, *co-scr.*

1951

No Highway in the Sky, *co-scr.*

1955

The Night My Number
Came Up, *scr.*
The Dam Busters, *scr.*

1956

Storm over the Nile, *scr.*

=====

ROBERT E. SHERWOOD

1926

The Lucky Lady, *co-scr.*

1931

The Age for Love, *dial.*
Around the World in
80 Minutes with
Douglas Fairbanks, *dial.*

1932

Cock of the Air, *co-story, co-scr.*
Rasputin and the Empress, *co-scr.*
(uncredited)

1933

Roman Scandals, *co-story*

1935

The Scarlet Pimpernel, *co-scr.*

1936

The Ghost Goes West, *scr.*
Rembrandt, *co-scr. (uncredited)*

1937

Thunder in the City, *co-story, co-scr.*
Tovarish, *scr. (English version)*

1938

The Adventures of Marco Polo, *scr.*
The Divorce of Lady X, *co-scr.*
Idiot's Delight, *scr. from his play*
Marie Antoinette, *co-scr.*
(uncredited)

1940

Over the Moon, *co-story*
Rebecca, *co-scr.*
Abe Lincoln in Illinois, *scr. from his play*

1946

The Best Years of Our Lives, *scr.*

1947

The Bishop's Wife, *co-scr.*

1953

Man on a Tightrope, *scr.*
Main Street to Broadway, *story*

=====

SAMUEL AND BELLA SPEWACK

The following were authored by Samuel Spewack alone:

1931

Terror by Night, *story, scr.*

Secret Witness, *scr. from his novel*
Murder in the Gilded Cage
*The following were co-authored with his
wife, Bella Spewack:*

1933

Private Jones, *co-adapt.*
Clear All Wires, *co-adapt., co-dial.,
from his and Bella Spewack's play*
The Nuisance, *co-adapt., co-dial.*
Should Ladies Behave?, *co-scr.*

1934

The Cat and the Fiddle, *co-scr.*
The Gay Bride, *co-scr.*

1935

Rendezvous, *co-adapt.*

1937

Walter Wanger's Vogues of 1938,
co-scr., co-ss.

1938

Boy Meets Girl, *co-scr., from his
and Bella Spewack's play*
The Chaser, *co-scr.*
Three Loves Has Nancy, *co-scr.*

1940

My Favorite Wife, *co-scr., co-ss.*

1945

Weekend at the Waldorf, *co-scr.*

=====

LAURENCE STALLINGS

1925

The Big Parade, *story*

1926

Old Ironsides, *story*

1928

Show People, *co-treatment*

1929

Marianne, *story*

1930

Billy the Kid, *dial.*
Way for a Sailor, *co-scr., co-dial.*

1933

Fast Workers, *dial.*
Big Executive, *scr.*

1935

After Office Hours, *co-story*
So Red the Rose, *co-scr.*

1938

Too Hot To Handle, *co-scr.*

1939

Stand up and Fight,
add'l. dial.

1940

Northwest Passage, *co-scr.*
Man from Dakota, *scr.*

1942

Jungle Book, *scr.*

1945

Salome, Where She Danced, *scr.*

1947

Christmas, *co-story, scr.*

1948

A Miracle Can Happen *or* On Our
Merry Way, *co-scr.*

1949

Three Godfathers, *co-scr.*
She Wore a Yellow Ribbon, *co-scr.*

1954

The Sun Shines Bright, *scr.*

JOHN STEINBECK

1941

The Forgotten Village *(documentary)*,
story, *scr.*

1944

Lifeboat, *ss.*

1945

Medal for Benny, *co-ss.*

1948

The Pearl, *story, co-scr., from his
novel*

1949

The Red Pony, *story, scr., from his
story*

1952

Viva Zapata, *story, scr.*

====

DONALD OGDEN STEWART

1926

Brown of Harvard, *adapt.*

1930

Laughter, *dial.*
Finn and Hattie, *(orig. book* Mr.
and Mrs. Haddock Abroad*)*

1931

Tarnished Lady, *scr.*
Rebound, *dial. and play basis*

1932

Smilin' Through, *co-dial.*

1933

White Sister, *scr.*
Going Hollywood, *scr.*
Another Language, *co-dial.*

Dinner at Eight, *add'l. dial.*

1934

The Barretts of Wimpole Street,
co-scr.

1935

No More Ladies, *co-scr.*

1936

Romeo and Juliet, *rewriting scenes
(uncredited)*

1937

The Prisoner of Zenda, *co-scr.*

1938

Holiday, *co-scr.*
Marie Antoinette, *co-scr.*

1939

Love Affair, *co-scr.*

1940

Night of Nights, *story, scr.*
The Philadelphia Story, *scr.*
Kitty Foyle, *co-scr.*

1941

That Uncertain Feeling, *scr.*
A Woman's Face, *co-scr.*
Smilin' Through, *co-scr.*

1942

Tales of Manhattan, *co-scr.*
Keeper of the Flame, *scr.*

1943

Forever and a Day, *co-scr.*

1945

Without Love, *scr.*

1947

Life with Father, *scr.*
Cass Timberlane, *scr.*

1949

Edward, My Son, *scr.*

1952

Europa 51 (The Greatest Love), *dial.*
for English-language dubbed version

1953

Melba, *add'l. dial.*

1955

Escapade, *scr.*

1960

Moment of Danger, *co-scr. (uncredited)*

=====

JO SWERLING

1930

Ladies of Leisure, *scr., dial.*
Around the Corner, *story, scr.*
Sisters, *scr., dial.*
Hell's Island, *scr.*
Ladies Must Play, *dial.*
Rain Or Shine, *co-scr., co-dial.*
Madonna of the Streets, *scr., dial.*

1931

Last Parade, *scr.*
Dirigible, *co-scr., dial.*
Ten Cents a Dance, *story, scr., dial.*
Good Bad Girl, *scr., dial.*
Platinum Blonde, *co-scr.*
Miracle Woman, *co-scr., dial.*
The Deceiver, *dial.*

1932

Forbidden, *scr., dial.*
Shopworn, *co-dial.*
Love Affair, *co-scr., dial.*
Behind the Mask, *story, co-scr., dial.*
Attorney for Defense, *scr., dial.*
Hollywood Speaks, *co-scr., co-dial.*

War Correspondent, *scr., dial.*
Washington Merry-Go-Round, *scr., dial.*
Man Against Woman, *scr.*

1933

The Circus Queen Murder, *adapt.*
Below the Sea, *story, adapt., dial.*
The Woman I Stole, *adapt.*
As the Devil Commands, *adapt.*
The Wrecker, *adapt., dial.*
East of Fifth Avenue, *adapt.*
Man's Castle, *adapt.*

1934

No Greater Glory, *scr.*
Once to Every Woman, *scr.*
Sisters Under the Skin, *scr.*
The Defense Rests, *story, scr.*
Lady by Choice, *scr.*

1935

The Whole Town's Talking, *co-scr.*
Love Me Forever, *co-scr.*

1936

The Music Goes 'Round, *scr.*
Pennies from Heaven, *scr.*

1937

Double Wedding, *scr.*

1938

Dr. Rhythm, *co-scr.*
I Am the Law, *scr.*

1939

Made for Each Other, *story, scr.*
The Real Glory, *co-scr.*

1940

The Westerner, *co-scr.*

1941

Blood and Sand, *scr.*
New York Town, *story, co-scr.*
Confirm Or Deny, *scr.*

1942

The Pride of the Yankees,
co-scr.

1943

Crash Dive, *scr.*
A Lady Takes a Chance, *story*

1944

Lifeboat, *scr.*
Leave Her to Heaven, *scr.*

1946

It's a Wonderful Life, *co-scr.*
(uncredited)

1953

Thunder in the East, *scr.*

1961

King of the Roaring 20's—The
Story Of Arnold Rothstein, *scr.*

═══════

IRVING STONE

1946

Magnificent Doll, *scr., ss.*

═══════

PRESTON STURGES

1930

The Big Pond, *co-dial.*
Fast and Loose, *dial.*

1933

The Power and the Glory, *story, scr.*

1934

Thirty Day Princess, *co-scr.*
We Live Again, *co-scr.*
Imitation of Life, *co-scr.,*
(uncredited)

1935

The Good Fairy, *scr.*
Diamond Jim, *co-scr.*

1936

Next Time We Love, *co-scr.*
(uncredited)

1937

Hotel Haywire, *story, scr.*
Easy Living, *scr.*

1938

Port of Seven Seas, *scr.*
If I Were King, *scr.*

1939

Never Say Die, *co-scr. with Don*
Hartman and Frank Butler

1940

Remember the Night, *story, scr.*
The Great McGinty, *story, scr.*
Christmas in July, *story, scr.*

1941

The Lady Eve, *scr.*
Sullivan's Travels, *story, scr.*

1942

The Palm Beach Story, *story, scr.*

1944

The Miracle of Morgan's Creek,
story, scr.
Hail the Conquering Hero, *story, scr.*
The Great Moment, *scr.*

1947

I'll Be Yours, *from his scr.* The
Good Fairy
Mad Wednesday (The Sin of Har-
old Diddlebock), *story, scr.*

1948

Unfaithfully Yours, *story, scr.*
1949
The Beautiful Blonde from Bashful
Bend, *scr.*

1956

The Birds and the Bees, *scr. from*
The Lady Eve

1957

Les Carnets Du Major Thompson
(The French They Are a Funny
Race), *scr.*

1958

Rock-a-Bye Baby, *scr., remake of*
The Miracle of Morgan's Creek

DWIGHT TAYLOR

1932

Are You Listening?, *adapt.*

1933

Today We Live, *co-scr.*
If I Were Free, *scr.*

1934

Long, Lost Father, *scr.*
Lady by Choice, *story*

1935

Top Hat, *story, co-scr.*

1936

Follow the Fleet, *co-scr.*

1937

The Awful Truth, *adapt., contrib.
to scr.*
Head Over Heels in Love, *co-adapt.*

1939

When Tomorrow Comes, *scr.*
East Side of Heaven, *contrib. to
scr. construc. (uncredited)*

1940

The Amazing Mr. Williams, *co-scr.*
Rhythm on the River, *scr.*

1941

Kiss the Boys Goodbye, *co-scr.*
Hot Spot, *scr.*

1942

Nightmare, *scr.*

1945

Conflict, *co-scr.*
The Thin Man Goes Home,
co-scr.

1947

The Foxes of Harrow, *co-contrib. to
dial. (uncredited)*

1952

Something To Live For, *scr., ss.*
We're Not Married, *adapt.*

1953

Pickup on South Street, *ss.*
Vicki, *scr.*

1955

Special Delivery, *co-scr.*

1957

Boy on a Dolphin, *co-scr.*

LAMAR TROTTI

1933

The Man Who Dared, *co-story &
co-scr.*

1934

You Can't Buy Everything,
co-story
Hold That Girl, *co-story &
co-scr.*
Wild Gold, *co-story*
Call It Luck, *co-scr.*
Judge Priest, *co-scr.*
Bachelor of Arts, *scr.*

1935

Life Begins at 40, *co-scr.*
Steamboat 'Round the Bend,
co-scr.
This Is the Life, *co-scr.*

1936

The Country Beyond, *co-scr.*
The First Baby, *story & scr.*
Ramona, *scr.*
Pepper, *story & scr.*
Career Woman, *scr.*
Can This Be Dixie?, *co-story
& scr.*

1937

Slave Ship, *co-scr.*
This Is My Affair, *co-story
& co-scr.*
Wife, Doctor and Nurse,
co-story & co-scr.

1938

In Old Chicago, *co-scr.*
The Baroness and the Butler,
co-scr.
Alexander's Ragtime Band,
co-story & co-scr.

Kentucky, *co-scr.*
Gateway, *scr.*

1939

The Story of
Alexander Graham Bell,
scr.
Young Mr. Lincoln, *story & scr.*
Drums Along the Mohawk,
co-scr.

1940

Brigham Young, *scr.*
Hudson's Bay, *story & scr.*

1941

Belle Starr, *scr.*

1942

To the Shores of Tripoli, *scr.*
Tales of Manhattan,
co-story & co-scr.
Thunder Birds, *scr.*

1943

The Immortal Sergeant, *scr.*
The Ox-Bow Incident, *scr.*
Guadalcanal Diary, *scr.*

1944

Wilson, *story & scr.*

1945

A Bell for Adano, *co-scr.*

1946

The Razor's Edge, *scr.*

1947

Captain from Castile, *scr.*
Mother Wore Tights, *scr.*

1948

The Walls of Jericho, *scr.*

When My Baby Smiles at Me, *scr.*
Yellow Sky, *scr.*

1949

You're My Everything, *co-scr.*

1950

Cheaper by the Dozen, *scr.*
My Blue Heaven, *co-scr.*
American Guerilla in the
Philippines, *scr.*
I'd Climb the Highest Mountain,
scr.

1952

With a Song in My Heart,
story & scr.
O'Henry's Full House, *co-story*
& co-scr.
Stars and Stripes Forever, *scr.*

1954

There's No Business Like
Show Business, *story*

=====

DALTON TRUMBO*

1936

Road Gang, *scr.*
Love Begins at 20, *co-scr.*
Tugboat Princess, *co-story*

1937

Devil's Playground, *co-scr.*
That Man's Here Again,
co-adapt.

1938

Fugitive for a Night, *scr.*
A Man To Remember, *scr.*

1939

The Flying Irishman, *co-story, co-scr.*
Sorority House, *scr.*
The Kid from Kokomo, *story*
Five Came Back, *co-scr.*

Heaven with a Barbed Wire Fence,
story, co-scr.
Career, *scr.*

1940

Half a Sinner, *story*
A Bill of Divorcement, *scr.*
Kitty Foyle, *scr.*
Curtain Call, *story, scr.*
The Lone Wolf Strikes, *story*
We Who Are Young, *story, scr.*

1941

You Belong to Me, *story*
Accent on Love, *story*

1942

The Remarkable Andrew, *scr.,*
from his novel

1943

Tender Comrade, *story, scr.*
A Guy Named Joe, *scr.*

1944

Thirty Seconds over Tokyo, *scr.*

1945

Our Vines Have Tender Grapes,
scr.
Jealousy, *story*

1950

Emergency Wedding, *story, from*
You Belong to Me

1951

The Prowler, *co-scr. (uncredited)*
The Brave Bulls, *co-scr. (uncredited)*

1954

Carnival Story, *co-story (as Marcel*
Klauber)

1956

The Boss, *co-story, co-scr.*
(Uncredited)

1957

The Green-Eyed Blonde, *story, scr.*
(*as Sally Stubblefield*)
The Abominable Snowman, *co-scr.*
(*uncredited*)
The Brave One, *story (as Robert Rich)*

1958

Cowboy, *co-scr. (uncredited)*

1959

Last Train from Gun Hill, *story (as
Les Crutchfield)*

1960

Spartacus, *scr.*
Exodus, *scr.*

1961

The Last Sunset, *scr.*

1962

Lonely Are the Brave, *scr.*

1965

The Sandpiper, *co-scr.*

1966

Hawaii, *co-scr.*

1968

The Fixer, *scr.*

1971

The Horsemen, *scr.*
Johnny Got His Gun,
scr., dir.

———

ERNST VAJDA

1926

The Crown of Lies, *story*
The Cat's Pajamas, *story*
You Never Know Women,
story

1927

Service for Ladies, *story*
Serenade, *story, scr.*

1928

A Night of Mystery, *adapt., scr.*
His Tiger Lady, *adapt., scr.*
Loves of an Actress, *story*
Manhattan Cowboy, *co-scr.*
His Private Life, *co-story*
Manhattan Cocktail, *story*

1929

Innocents of Paris, *adapt., dial.,
co-scr.*
The Love Parade, *adapt.*
Marquis Preferred, *co-scr.*

1930

Such Men Are Dangerous, *adapt.,
dial., scr.*
Monte Carlo, *scr.*

1931

Son of India, *scr., co-dial. with
Claudine West*
The Guardsman, *co-scr. and
co-dial.
with Claudine West*
Tonight Or Never, *scr.*
The Smilin' Lieutenant, *co-scr.,
co-dial.*

1932

Smilin' Through, *co-scr.*
Broken Lullaby (The Man I
Killed), *co-scr., co-dial.*
Payment Deferred, *co-scr. with
Claudine West*

1933

Reunion in Vienna, *co-scr. with
Claudine West*

1934

The Merry Widow, *co-scr.*
The Barretts of Wimpole Street,
co-scr.

1936

A Woman Rebels, *co-scr.*

1937

Personal Property, *co-scr.*
The Great Garrick, *story, scr.*

1938

Marie Antoinette, *co-scr. with
Claudine West*
Dramatic School, *co-scr.*

1940

He Stayed for Breakfast, *co-scr.*

1941

They Dare Not Love, *co-scr.*
The Chocolate Soldier, *remake of*
The Guardsman

JOHN VAN DRUTEN

1935

The King of Paris, *adapt.*

1936

I Loved a Soldier, *co-scr.*

1937

Parnell, *co-scr.*
Night Must Fall, *scr.*

1939

Raffles, *co-scr.*

1940

Lucky Partners, *co-scr.*

1941

My Life with Caroline, *co-scr.*

1943

Old Acquaintances, *co-scr., from
his play*
Johnny Come Lately, *scr.*

1944

Forever and a Day, *co-scr.*
Gaslight, *co-scr.*

1948

Voice of the Turtle, *scr., from his
play*

HUGH WALPOLE

1935

David Copperfield, *adapt.*
Vanessa, Her Love Story, *co-scr.,
from his book*

1936

Little Lord Fauntleroy, *scr.*

(LT. COM.) FRANK WEAD

1929

Flying Fleet, *co-story*

1931

Dirigible, *story*
Shipmates, *co-scr.*
Hell Divers, *story*

1932

Air Mail, *co-story, co-scr., dial.*
All American, *co-scr., dial.*

1933

Midshipman Jack, *co-story, scr.,
dial.*

1934

Fugitive Lovers, *co-story*
I'll Tell the World, *co-story*

1935

West Point of the Air, *co-scr.*
Murder in the Fleet, *co-scr.*
Ceiling Zero, *scr. from his play*
Storm over the Andes, *co-scr.*
The Great Impersonation, *co-scr.*

1936

China Clipper, *story, scr.*

1937

Sea Devils, *co-story, co-scr.*
Submarine D-1, *story, co-scr.*

1938

Test Pilot, *story*
The Citadel, *co-scr.*
A Yank at Oxford, *co-scr. (uncredited)*

1939

Tailspin, *story, scr.*
20,000 Men a Year, *story*

1940

Sailor's Lady, *story*
Moon over Burma, *co-scr.*

1941

International Squadron, *from his play and screenplay* Ceiling Zero
Dive Bomber, *story, co-scr.*
I Wanted Wings, *co-story*

1943

Destroyer, *story, co-scr.*

1945

They Were Expendable, *scr.*

1946

The Hoodlum Saint, *co-story*

1947

The Beginning of the End, *scr.*
Blaze of Noon, *co-scr.*

1957

The Wings of Eagles, *from the biography* Wings of Men *by him, and his novels, plays, screenplays and life*

MAE WEST*

1933

She Done Him Wrong, *from her play* Diamond Lil
I'm No Angel, *co-story*

1934

Belle of the Nineties, *story, scr.*

1935

Goin' to Town, *scr.*

1936

Klondike Annie, *scr., dial., from her play*
Go West Young Man, *scr.*

1937

Every Day's a Holiday, *story, scr.*

1940

My Little Chickadee, *co-story, co-scr.*

1970

Myra Breckinridge, *her own dialogue (uncredited)*

NATHANAEL WEST

1936

Ticket to Paradise, *co-scr.*
Follow Your Heart, *co-scr.*
The President's Mystery, *co-scr.*

1937

Rhythm in the Clouds, *adapt.*
It Could Happen to You, *ss., co-scr.*

Jim Hanvey, Detective, *contrib. to
scr. (uncredited)*

1938

Born To Be Wild, *ss., scr.* Gangs
of New York, *co-scr. (uncredited)*.
Orphans of the Street, *contrib. to
scr. (uncredited)*

1939

I Stole a Million, *scr.*
Five Came Back, *co-scr.*
Spirit of Culver, *co-scr.*

1940

Men Against the Sky, *scr.*
Let's Make Music, *ss., scr.*
Stranger on the Third Floor, *contrib.
to scr. (uncredited)*

=======

BILLY WILDER*

1929

Menschen am Sonntag, *co-scr.*

1930

Seitensprunge, *story*

1931

Der Falsche Ehemann, *co-scr.*
Emil und die Detektive, *scr.*
Ihre Hoheit Befiehlt, *co-scr.*
Der Mann, der Seinen Mörder
Sucht, *co-scr.*

1932

Das Blaue vom Himmel, *co-scr.*
Ein Blonder Traum, *co-scr.*
Es War Einmal ein Walzer, *scr.*
Scampolo, ein Kind der Strasse,
co-scr.

1933

Madame Wunscht Keine Kinder,
co-scr.

Adorable, *remake of* Ihre Hoheit
Befiehlt
Was Frauen Traumen, *co-scr.*
Mauvaise Graine, *story*

1934

Music in the Air, *co-scr.*
One Exciting Adventure, *co-story*

1935

Lottery Lover, *co-scr.*

1937

Champagne Waltz, *co-story*

1938

Bluebeard's Eighth Wife, *co-scr.*

1939

What a Life, *co-scr.*
Midnight, *co-scr.*
Ninotchka, *co-scr.*

1940

Arise My Love, *co-scr.*
Rhythm on the River, *co-story*

1941

Hold Back the Dawn, *co-scr.*
Ball of Fire, *co-story, co-scr.*

1942

The Major and the Minor, *co-scr.*

1943

Five Graves to Cairo, *co-scr.*

1944

Double Indemnity, *co-scr.*

1945

The Lost Weekend, *co-scr.*

1948

The Emperor Waltz, *co-story, co-scr.*
A Foreign Affair, *co-scr.*

A Song Is Born, *remake of* Ball of Fire

1950

Sunset Boulevard, *co-scr.*

1951

Ace in the Hole (The Big Carnival), *co-story, co-scr.*

1953

Stalag 17, *co-scr.*

1954

Sabrina, *co-scr.*

1955

The Seven-Year Itch, *co-scr.*

1957

The Spirit of St. Louis, *co-scr.*
Love in the Afternoon, *co-scr.*

1958

Witness for the Prosecution, *co-scr.*

1959

Some Like It Hot, *co-scr.*

1960

The Apartment, *co-story, co-scr.*

1961

One, Two, Three, *co-scr.*

1963

Irma La Douce, *co-scr.*

1964

Kiss Me, Stupid, *co-scr.*

1966

The Fortune Cookie, *co-story, co-scr.*

1970

The Private Life Of Sherlock Holmes, *co-story, co-scr.*

1973

Amelia, *co-scr.*

1974

The Front Page, *co-scr.*

THORNTON WILDER

1935

The Dark Angel, *contrib. to scr. (uncredited)*

1940

Our Town, *co-scr., from his play*

1943

Shadow of a Doubt, *co-scr.*

P. (Pelham) G. (Grenville) WODEHOUSE

1928

OK, Kay!, *titl., from his and Guy Bolton's* Oh Kay! *(1926)*

1930

Those Three French Girls, *dial.*

1937

Damsel in Distress, *co-story, co-scr.*

PHILIP YORDAN*

1942

Syncopation, *co-scr.*

1943

The Unknown Guest, *story, scr.*

1944

Johnny Doesn't Live Here
Anymore, *co-scr.*

1945

Dillinger, *story, scr.*
The Woman Who Came Back,
*"from a
short story by John Kafka, as
suggested by Philip Yordan"*

1946

The Chase, *scr.*
Whistle Stop, *scr.*
Suspense, *story, scr.*

1948

Bad Men of Tombstone, *co-scr.*

1949

House of Strangers, *scr.*
Anna Lucasta, *co-scr., from his play*
The Black Book (Reign of Terror),
co-story, co-scr.

1950

Edge of Doom, *scr.*

1951

Detective Story, *co-scr.*
Drums in the Deep South, *co-scr.*

1952

Maru Maru, *co-story*
Mutiny, *co-scr.*

1953

Houdini, *scr.*
Blowing Wild, *story, scr.*

1954

The Naked Jungle, *co-scr.*
Johnny Guitar, *scr.*

Broken Lance, *remake of* House of
Strangers
Man Crazy, *co-story, co-scr., co-prod.*

1955

Conquest of Space, *co-adapt.*
The Man from Laramie, *co-scr.*
The Last Frontier, *co-scr.*
The Big Combo, *story, scr.*

1956

The Harder They Fall, *scr., prod.*
Joe Macbeth, *scr.*

1957

Four Boys and a Gun, *co-scr.*
Men in War, *scr.*
Gun Glory, *from his novel* Man of
the West

1957

No Down Payment, *scr.*
Street of Sinners, *scr.*

1958

The Bravados, *scr.*
God's Little Acre, *scr.*
Island Women, *scr.*
The Fiend Who Walked the West,
co-scr.
Anna Lucasta, *scr., from his play*

1959

Day of the Outlaw, *scr.*

1960

The Bramble Bush, *co-scr.*
Studs Lonigan, *prod., scr.*

1961

King of Kings, *scr.*
El Cid, *co-scr.*

1963

The Day of the Triffids, *executive prod., scr.*
55 Days at Peking, *co-story, co-scr.*

1964

The Fall of the Roman Empire, *co-scr.*

Battle of the Bulge, *co-story, co-scr., co-prod.*

1969

The Royal Hunt of the Sun, *scr.*

BIBLIOGRAPHY

Agee, James. *Agee on Film,* Volume I. New York: Grosset & Dunlap, 1967

Amory, Cleveland and Bradlee, Frederic, Editors. *Vanity Fair: A Cavalcade of the 1920s and 1930s.* New York: Viking, 1960

Atkinson, Brooks. *Broadway.* New York: Macmillan, 1970

Baker, Carlos. *Ernest Hemingway: A Life Story.* New York: Scribner, 1969

Baxter, John. *Hollywood in the Thirties.* New York: A. S. Barnes, 1968

Bazin, André. *What Is Cinema?,* Volume II. Berkeley: University of California Press, 1971

Behlmer, Rudy. *Memo from David O. Selznick.* New York: Viking, 1972

Benchley, Nathaniel. *Robert Benchley.* New York: McGraw-Hill, 1955

Bentley, Eric. *Thirty Years of Treason: Excerpts from Hearings before the House Committee on Un-American Activities, 1938–1968.* New York: Viking, 1971

Bessie, Alvah, *Inquisition in Eden.* New York: Macmillan, 1965

Blum, Daniel. *A Pictorial History of the Talkies.* New York: Putnam, 1958 and revised 1968

Bogdanovich, Peter. *Fritz Lang in America.* New York: Praeger, 1970.

Brown, John Mason. *Dramatis Personae.* New York: Viking, 1963
    The Worlds of Robert E. Sherwood: Mirror to His Times. New
    York: Harper & Row, 1965
    Ordeal of a Playwright. New York: Harper & Row, 1972

Brownlow, Kevin. *The Parade's Gone By . . .* New York: Knopf,
    1968

Bruccoli, Matthew J. and Clark, C. E. Frazer, Jr., Editors. *Fitzger-
    ald-Hemingway Annuals, 1969–72.* Washington, D.C.: NCR/
    Microcard Editions

Burnett, Whit. *This Is My Best.* New York: Dial, 1942

Capra, Frank. *The Name Above the Title: An Autobiography.* New
    York: Macmillan, 1971

Case, Frank. *Tales of a Wayward Inn.* New York: Stokes, 1938

Chaplin, Charles. *My Autobiography.* New York: Simon & Schuster,
    1964

Cogley, John. *Report on Blacklisting,* Parts I and II. New York: The
    Fund for the Republic, 1956

Cook, Fred J. *The Nightmare Decade: The Life and Times of Senator Joe
    McCarthy.* New York: Random House, 1971

Cooke, Alistair. *Garbo and the Night Watchmen.* New York:
    McGraw-Hill, 1971

Corliss, Richard. *The Hollywood Screenwriters.* New York: Discus/
    Avon, 1972

Coward, Noel, *Future Indefinite.* New York: Doubleday, 1954

Crawford, Joan. *A Portrait of Joan* (with Jane Kesner Ardmore).
    New York: Doubleday, 1962

Crowther, Bosley. *Hollywood Rajah: The Life and Times of Louis B.
    Mayer.* New York: Holt, Rinehart & Winston, 1960

Davis, Bette. *The Lonely Life.* New York: Putnam, 1962

de Acosta, Mercedes. *Here Lies the Heart.* New York: Reynal &
    Company, 1960

Esslin, Martin. *Brecht: The Man and His Work.* Garden City: Anchor
    Books, 1961

Everson, William K. *The Films of Laurel and Hardy.* Secaucus:
    Citadel, 1972

Ewen, Frederic. *Bertolt Brecht: His Life, His Art, and His Times.* New York: Citadel, 1967

Farmer, Frances. *Will There Really Be a Morning?* New York: Putnam, 1972

Farr, Finis. *O'Hara: A Biography.* Boston: Little, Brown, 1973

Ferber, Edna. *A Peculiar Treasure: An Autobiography.* New York: Doubleday, 1939

Filmlexicon degli Autori e delle Opere. Edizioni di Bianco e Nero. Roma, 1959

Fitzgerald, F. Scott. *The Stories of F. Scott Fitzgerald.* New York: Scribners, 1951
The Crack-Up: Edited by Edmund Wilson. New York: New Directions, 1945
The Portable F. Scott Fitzgerald. New York: Viking, 1945
The Great Gatsby. New York: Scribners, 1925
The Last Tycoon. New York: Scribners, 1941

Flanagan, Hallie *Arena.* New York: Duell, Sloan & Pearce, 1940

Fowler, Gene and Meredyth, Bess. *The Mighty Barnum: A Screen Play.* New York: Covici-Friede, 1934

Fowler, Gene. *Good Night, Sweet Prince: The Life and Times of John Barrymore.* New York: Viking, 1944

Fredrik, Nathalie. *Hollywood and the Academy Awards.* Beverly Hills: Hollywood Awards Publications, 1970

Froug, William. *The Screenwriter Looks at the Screenwriter.* New York: Macmillan, 1972

Gassner, John and Nichols, Dudley. *Best Film Plays, 1943–44.* New York: Crown, 1945

Gassner, John and Quinn, Edward. *The Reader's Encyclopedia of World Drama.* New York: Crowell, 1969

Geduld, Harry M. and Gottesman, Ronald. *Sergei Eisenstein and Upton Sinclair: The Making and Unmaking of* Qué Viva Mexico! Bloomington: Indiana University Press, 1970

Gelb, Arthur and Gelb, Barbara. *O'Neill.* New York: Harper & Row, 1960.

Gill, Brendan and Zerbe, Jerome. *Happy Times.* New York: Harcourt, Brace, Jovanovich, 1973

Glyn, Anthony. *Elinor Glyn.* New York: Doubleday, 1955

Gordon, Ruth. *Myself Among Others.* New York: Atheneum, 1971

Gow, Gordon. *Hollywood in the Fifties.* New York: A. S. Barnes, 1971

Graham, Sheilah. *A State of Heat,* New York: Grosset & Dunlap, 1972
Beloved Infidel: The Education of a Woman (with Gerold Frank). New York: Henry Holt and Company, Inc., 1959
The Garden of Allah. New York: Crown, 1970

Gussow, Mel. *Don't Say Yes Until I Finish Talking: A Biography of Darryl F. Zanuck.* New York: Doubleday, 1971

Halliwell, Leslie. *The Filmgoer's Companion,* 3rd Edition, Revised. New York: Hill and Wang, 1970

Hayden, Sterling. *Wanderer.* New York: Knopf, 1963

Hayes, Helen. *On Reflection* (with Sanford Dody). New York: M. Evans, 1968

Hays, Will H., *The Memoirs of Will H. Hays.* New York: Doubleday, 1955

Hecht, Ben. *A Child of the Century.* New York: Simon & Schuster, 1954
Spectre of the Rose, unpublished (later filmed)

Hellman, Lillian. *An Unfinished Woman: A Memoir.* Boston: Little, Brown, 1969
Pentimento: A Book of Portraits. Boston: Little, Brown, 1973
The Collected Plays. Boston: Little, Brown, 1972

Henderson, Robert M., *D. W. Griffith: His Life and Work.* New York: Oxford University Press, 1970

Higham, Charles and Greenberg, Joel. *The Celluloid Muse: Hollywood Directors Speak.* Chicago: Henry Regnery Company, 1969
Hollywood in the Forties. New York: A. S. Barnes, 1968

Houston, Penelope. *The Contemporary Cinema.* Middlesex, England: Penquin, 1963

Huxley, Aldous. *After Many a Summer Dies the Swan.* New York: Harper, 1939

Huxley, Laura Archera. *This Timeless Moment: A Personal View of Aldous Huxley.* New York: Farrar, Straus & Giroux, 1968

Jablonski, Edward and Stewart, Lawrence D. *The Gershwin Years.* New York: Doubleday, 1958

Kahn, Gordon. *Hollywood on Trial: The Story of the Ten Who Were Indicted.* New York: Boni & Gaer, 1948

Knef, Hildegard. *The Gift Horse.* New York: McGraw-Hill, 1971

Knight, Arthur and Elisofon, Eliot. *The Hollywood Style.* New York: Macmillan, 1969

Keats, John. *You Might as Well Live: The Life and Times of Dorothy Parker.* New York: Simon & Schuster, 1970

Lake, Veronica. *Veronica* (with Donald Bain). London: W. H. Allen & Co., Ltd., 1969

Lambert, Gavin. *On Cukor.* New York: Putnam, 1972. *GWTW: The Making of Gone With the Wind.* Boston: Atlantic Monthly Press, Little, Brown, 1973

Lanchester, Elsa. *Charles Laughton and I.* London: Faber and Faber, 1938

Latham, Aaron. *Crazy Sundays: F. Scott Fitzgerald in Hollywood.* New York: Viking, 1971

Lawson, John Howard. *Film: The Creative Process.* New York: Hill and Wang, 1964

Loos, Anita. *A Girl Like I.* New York: Random House, 1966

Madsen, Axel, *Billy Wilder.* Bloomington: Indiana University Press, 1969
William Wyler. New York: Crowell, 1973

Martin, Jay. *Nathanael West: The Art of His Life.* New York: Farrar, Strauss & Giroux, 1970

Martin, Olga J., *Hollywood's Movie Commandments.* New York: Arno Press and *The New York Times,* 1970

Marx, Harpo, *Harpo Speaks!* (with Rowland Barber) New York: Bernard Geis, 1961

Mayfield, Sara. *The Constant Circle: H. L. Mencken and His Friends.* New York: Delacorte Press, 1968

Exiles from Paradise: Zelda and Scott Fitzgerald. New York: Delacorte Press, 1971

Michael, Paul. *The American Movies: A Pictorial Encyclopedia.* New York: Garland Books, 1969*

Milford, Nancy. *Zelda.* New York: Harper & Row, 1970

Mizener, Arthur. *The Far Side of Paradise: A Biography of F. Scott Fitzgerald.* Boston: Houghton, Mifflin Company, 1951

Nathan, George Jean. *Passing Judgments.* New York: Knopf, 1938
The Morning After the First Night. New York: Knopf, 1954

Oppenheimer, George. *The View from the Sixties: Memories of a Spent Life.* New York: McKay, 1966

Paris Review Interviews. *Writers at Work,* Third Series. New York: Viking, 1967

Parker, Dorothy. *The Portable Dorothy Parker.* New York: Viking, 1944
Constant Reader. New York: Viking, 1970
Here Lies. New York: Viking, 1939
Enough Rope. New York: Boni and Liveright, 1927

Phelps, Robert and Deane, Peter. *The Literary Life: A Scrapbook Almanac of the Anglo-American Literary Scene from 1900 to 1950.* London: Chatto and Windus, 1969

Phillips, Cabell. *From the Crash to the Blitz, 1929–39.* New York: Macmillan, 1969

Powdermaker, Hortense. *Hollywood: The Dream Factory.* Boston: Little, Brown, 1950

Reed, Rex. *Conversations in the Raw.* New York: World, 1969

Rice, Elmer. *Minority Report: An Autobiography.* New York: Simon & Schuster, 1963

Rosten Leo. *Hollywood: The Movie Colony, The Movie Makers.* New York: Harcourt, Brace and Company, 1941

Samuels, Charles Thomas. *Encountering Directors.* New York: Capricorn, 1972

Schary, Dore. *Case History of a Movie.* New York: Random House, 1950

*Published originally as *The American Movies Reference Book: The Sound Era.* Englewood Cliffs, N.J.: Prentice-Hall

Schorer, Mark. *Sinclair Lewis: An American Life.* New York: McGraw-Hill, 1961

Schulberg, Budd. *What Makes Sammy Run?* New York: Random House, 1941
The Disenchanted. New York: Random House, 1950

Shirer, William L. *The Rise and Fall of the Third Reich.* New York: Simon & Schuster, 1960

Sennett, Ted. *Warner Brothers Presents.* New York: Castle Books, 1971

Smith, Grover. *Letters of Aldous Huxley.* New York: Harper & Row, 1969

Stephenson, Ralph and Debrix, J. R. *The Cinema as Art.* Middlesex, England: Penguin, 1965

Symons, Julian. *The 30's.* London: Cresset Press, 1960

Terkel, Studs. *Hard Times.* New York: Pantheon Books, 1970

Thomas, Bob. *King Cohn: The Life and Times of Harry Cohn.* New York: Putnam, 1967
Thalberg. New York: Doubleday, 1969

Time-Life Book Staff. *This Fabulous Century, 1930–40, 1940–50.* New York: Time-Life Books, 1969

Time-Life Book Staff, John Dille, Editor. *Time Capsules, 1932.* New York: Time-Life Books, 1967

Tozzi, Romano. *John Huston: A Pictorial Treasury of His Films.* New York: Crescent Books Division, Crown, 1971

Trumbo, Dalton. *Additional Dialogue.* New York: M. Evans, 1970.
The Time of the Toad. New York: Harper & Row, 1972

Turnbull, Andrew. *The Letters of F. Scott Fitzgerald.* New York: Bantam Books, 1973
Scott Fitzgerald. New York: Scribner, 1960

Tyler, Parker. *Classics of the Foreign Film.* New York: Citadel, 1962

Ursini, James. *The Fabulous Life and Times of Preston Sturges: An American Dreamer.* New York: Curtis Books, 1973

van Passen, Pierre. *Days of Our Years.* New York: Hillman-Curl, Inc., 1939

Vaughn, Robert. *Only Victims: A Study of Show Business Blacklisting.* New York: Putnam, 1972

Viertel, Salka. *The Kindness of Strangers.* New York: Holt, Rinehart and Winston, 1969

Vizzard Jack, *See No Evil: Life Inside a Hollywood Censor.* New York: Simon & Schuster, 1970

von Sternberg, Josef. *Fun in a Chinese Laundry: An Autobiography.* New York: Macmillan, 1965

Vogue Magazine (and Viking Press). *The World in Vogue.* New York: Viking, 1963

Warner, Jack. *My First Hundred Years in Hollywood.* New York: Random House, 1965

Weinberg, Herman G. *The Lubitsch Touch.* New York: Dutton, 1968

West, Nathanael. *The Day of the Locust.* New York: Random House, 1939

Williams, Henry Lionel and Williams, Ottalie K. *Great Houses of America.* New York: Putnam, 1966

Wilk, Max. *The Wit and Wisdom of Hollywood.* New York: Atheneum, 1971

Wilson, Arthur. *The Warner Brothers Golden Anniversary Book* (with a critical essay by Arthur Knight). New York: Dell/Film and Venture, 1973

Wood, Tom. *The Bright Side of Billy Wilder, Primarily.* New York: Doubleday, 1970

Zierold, Norman. *The Moguls.* New York: Coward-McCann, 1969

NOTES ON SOURCES

The Epigraph is from a speech by Posthumus in Shakespeare's *Cymbeline*, Act V, Scene 5.

Front quotation: "They are gone . . ." from an article by Ben Hecht, "If Hollywood Is Dead or Perhaps the Following," *Playboy* Magazine, November, 1960, courtesy John E. Schultheiss collection.

Part One: Requiem

1

p. 5   "Blithe and handsome Dorothy Mackaill . . .": Interview, Dorothy Mackaill and FLG, September 27, 1970.

p. 6   Comparisons with Sammy Glick based upon Budd Schulberg's *What Makes Sammy Run?* (Random House, New York, 1941).

2

p. 8   Col. Charles E. Lindbergh's Hollywood reception: *Marion Davies* by Fred Lawrence Guiles (McGraw-Hill, New York, 1972, pp. 197–198.

p. 9   Footnote; "*A Lost Lady* was bought . . .": Letter from William A. Koshland to author dated September 23, 1974.

p. 10   " . . . That is, indeed, an accurate description," etc.: *Pentimento* by Lillian Hellman (Little, Brown; Boston, 1973), p. 65.

"In 1934, John O'Hara . . .": *O'Hara* by Finis Farr (Little, Brown; Boston, 1973), p. 169.

p. 11   Background on John O'Hara in Hollywood drawn from *O'Hara* by Finis Farr (Little, Brown; Boston, 1973), p. 174.

Footnote on Frances Marion: Interview, Frances Marion and FLG, October 21, 1969.

p. 12   Description of Broadway during the Depression derived from *From the Crash to the Blitz* by Cabell Phillips (Macmillan, New York, 1969), p. 365.

p. 00   Eugene O'Neill in California taken from *O'Neill* by Arthur and Barbara Gelb (Dell edition, New York, 1965), p. 465, rev. ed., 1974 (Harper & Row original publishers).

p. 13   "The country was divided into large regional areas," etc.: *Minority Report* by Elmer Rice (Simon and Schuster, New York, 1963), pp. 352–354.

"One of the most exciting groups . . .": *Ibid.*, p. 355.

p. 14   "By 1930, the Germans were aware that dramatist Bertolt

Brecht . . .": *Bertolt Brecht: His Life, His Art and His Times* by
Frederic Ewen (Citadel Press, New York, 1967), pp. 196–203.

Inset quotation: "Rushing out of the subway stations," etc.:
Ibid., pp. 201–202.

p. 16 "Christopher Isherwood began going to the movies at
around ten years . . .": Interview, Christopher Isherwood and
FLG, October 29, 1973.

"But this admiration was not always returned . . .": Interview, Nunnally Johnson and FLG, November 5, 1973.

3

p. 17   "Writers were often thought to be amusing companions,"
etc.: Interview, George Oppenheimer and FLG, February 28, 1973.

". . . the Samuel Goldwyns' formal very British dinners
. . .": Interview, Charles Lederer and FLG, July 4, 1973.

". . . the informal gatherings of Salka Viertel," etc.: Interview, Christopher Isherwood and FLG, November 3, 1973.

". . . Anita Loos's Sunday brunches in Santa Monica,"
etc.: Interview, Anita Loos and FLG, October 6, 1973.

p. 18   Inset quotation: "When the *City of Angels* roared into the
station . . .": *The Constant Circle: H. L. Mencken and His Friends* by
Sara Mayfield (Delacorte Press, New York, 1968, pp. 107–108.

Inset quotation: "She was all out to improve herself":
Interview, Dorothy Parker and Wyatt Cooper, 1963, used by
permission of Mr. Cooper.

"During that last year or so of her life," etc.: *Ibid.*

p. 20   Inset quotation: "I think almost every writer who ever
worked with him wrote his best," etc.: Samson Raphaelson, as
quoted in *The Lubitsch Touch* by Herman G. Weinberg (Dutton,
New York, 1968), p. 204.

p. 21   "Catherine Gibbs Francis was the perfect Lubitsch heroine," etc.: Interview, Beatrice Ames and FLG, March 8, 1974.

pp. 22–23 Will H. Hays's goal in "self-censorship" is derived
from *The Memoirs of Will H. Hays* (Doubleday, 1955), p. 433.

p. 23   ". . . His screen version of Noel Coward's *Design for
Living* (1933) was the first major casualty," etc.: inference drawn
from Ben Hecht's article "If Hollywood Is Dead or Perhaps the
Following," *Playboy* Magazine, November, 1960, courtesy John E.
Schultheiss collection.

Footnote on *Design for Living* is based upon review of

movie in *The New York Times* by Mordaunt Hall, November 23, 1933.

Footnote on Will Rogers derived from interview, Anne Shirley Lederer and FLG, March 28, 1974. (Anne Shirley co-starred with Rogers in his final film, released posthumously.)

4

p. 24   Mlle. Perrier story by Aldous Huxley as recounted to author by Charles Lederer, November 1, 1973.

p. 26   "If you were a Metro star, director, producer or writer," etc.: Interviews with Frances Marion, Eleanor Boardman, George Oppenheimer, and Ann Shirley Lederer.

p. 27   Inset quotation: "never played any politics . . .": *On Cukor* by Gavin Lambert (Capricorn Books, New York, 1973), p. 80.

p. 28   Inset quotation (Sir Edward Shortt): "I cannot believe that any *single* film," etc.: *Hollywood's Movie Commandments* by Olga J. Martin (Arno Press/*New York Times*, New York, 1970), p. 66.

p. 29   "Samuel Goldwyn believed almost to the end of his long career," etc.: Interview, Charles Lederer and FLG, June 21, 1973.

"Sometimes, a large literary reputation could excuse . . .": Information drawn from interview, Dorothy Parker and Wyatt Cooper, 1963.

5

p. 30   ". . . emboldened them to consider hiring George Bernard Shaw," etc.: *The Moguls* by Norman Zierold (Coward-McCann, New York, 1969), p. 128.

"Soon after World War I, a number of important authors," etc.: *The Parade's Gone By . . .* by Kevin Brownlow (Knopf, New York, 1969), p. 276; and *A Peculiar Treasure* by Edna Ferber (Doubleday, New York, 1939), p. 262.

". . . the necessity for action wherever possible; a flowing movement," etc.: Interview, Nunnally Johnson and FLG, November 5, 1973.

"An exception was Mrs. Glyn," etc.: *Elinor Glyn* by Anthony Glyn (Doubleday, New York, 1955), pp. 285–286.

p. 31   "Maeterlinck came and went very quickly," etc.: Interview, George Oppenheimer and FLG, May 18, 1973.

p. 32   Inset quotation: "It's really almost impossible," etc.: Interview, Christopher Isherwood and FLG, November 3, 1973.

p. 34   "Dorothy Parker was once seen weeping openly," etc.: Interview, George Oppenheimer and FLG, February 28, 1973.

". . . it was the rivalry among themselves," etc.: Interviews, George Oppenheimer and FLG, February 28, 1973; John Howard Lawson and FLG, May 16, 1972; and "Writing for the Movies" by Donald Ogden Stewart in *Focus on Film*, No. 5, Winter, 1970.

p. 35   "The tag . . . which you like," etc. A letter to Anita Loos dated July 4, 1947, *Letters of Aldous Huxley* edited by Grover Smith (Harper & Row, New York, 1969, p. 572.

". . . it was the expressionistic play *Processional*," etc.: description of play drawn from *Broadway* by Brooks Atkinson (Macmillan, 1970), p. 287.

p. 36   "Also, he was wary of Hollywood moguls," etc. Interview, John Howard Lawson and FLG, May 16, 1972.

". . . the Screen Playwrights, with four rightist scenarists on the prowl," etc.: Interviews, John Howard Lawson, as above; George Oppenheimer, May 18, 1973; and Frances Goodrich and Albert Hackett, November 25, 1973; all with FLG.

p. 37   Footnote on Mahin: Interview, Charles Lederer and FLG, July 3, 1973.

"Even the rather liberal George Oppenheimer," etc.: Interview, George Oppenheimer and FLG, May 18, 1973.

". . . The hardest-won recognition of all," etc.: Interview, John Howard Lawson and FLG, May 16, 1972.

p. 38   "Isherwood lived a little apart from the mainstream," etc.: Interview, Christopher Isherwood and FLG, November 3, 1973.

"Thornton Wilder, on his way to dinner," etc.: Interview, Helen Hayes and FLG, November 3, 1973.

p. 39   "Jack Warner . . . recalls buying Raymond Chandler's thriller, *The Big Sleep*," etc.: *My First Hundred Years in Hollywood* by Jack Warner (Random House, New York, 1965), pp. 309–310.

p. 40   ". . . as his peculiar 'goofiness' when drunk began to isolate him from the writers' colony,": Interview, Charles Lederer and FLG, November 8, 1973.

". . . she was rarely omitted from any guest list," etc.: Interview, Charles Lederer and FLG, June 21, 1973.

"Both of these writers had been drinking their way," etc.: Interview, Wyatt Cooper and FLG, November 28, 1973.

". . . although Scott entertained a notion for a long time," etc.: Based upon a letter from Fitzgerald to his daughter, July, 1937, from *The Letters of F. Scott Fitzgerald*, edited by Andrew Turnbull (Bantam edition, New York, 1971), p. 17 (Scribner original publisher, 1963).

"Mrs. Parker, who knew him from back East, thought Fitzgerald more interesting," etc.: Interview, Dorothy Parker and Wyatt Cooper, 1963.

6

p. 41 "In 1927, John Considine of United Artists offered him an assignment," etc.: *The Far Side of Paradise: A Biography of F. Scott Fitzgerald*, by Arthur Mizener (Houghton Mifflin, Boston, 1951), p. 203.

p. 42 Footnote on Lois Moran obtaining screen test for Fitzgerald derived from *Zelda* by Nancy Milford (Harper & Row, New York, 1970), p. 129; Hemingway doing the voice-over narration for *The Spanish Earth: Ernest Hemingway: A Life Story* by Carlos Baker (Scribner, New York, 1969), p. 315.

". . . one of the screen's perennial Vassar girls.": the *Detroit Times*, October 29, 1931.

References to Lois Moran in *The Road to Mandalay* drawn from review in *Mid-Week Pictorial*, July 8, 1926.

"Scott's friendship with Lois Moran," etc.: Conversation with Eleanor Boardman (and FLG), the summer of 1970.

"In a letter apparently intended for Zelda," etc.: *Zelda*, p. 181.

"Zelda had an electric presence and a heightened sense of life that was an oddness," etc.: Inference drawn from *Zelda*, pp. 53–54.

p. 43 "Scott was to call it that . . .": Letter from Scott to Dr. Mildred Squires, *Ibid.*, p. 222.

"Miss Moran had studied ballet in Paris," etc.: *Filmlexicon degli Autorie e delle Opere*, Edizioni di Bianco e Nero, Roma, 1959.

". . . once back in France," etc. Letter, Eleanor Boardman d'Arrast to FLG, March 3, 1974.

"By 1931, Zelda already was alienated from Scott," etc.: *Zelda*, p. 158.

"There was certainly a case to be made by her supporters," etc.: *Exiles from Paradise* by Sara Mayfield (Delacorte Press, New York), p. 183.

"... as would Lois Moran; in 1931," etc.: Review in the *Detroit Times*, October 29, 1931.

"... formed an alliance against," etc.: Interview, George Oppenheimer and FLG, February 28, 1973.

"*The Redheaded Woman* was not going well ...": *Looking Back on Fitzgerald* by Andrew Turnbull, Arthur Mizener and Sheilah Graham, *Famous Writers Magazine*, Winter, 1963, pp. 16–51.

p. 44 "But neither could she forget that in the late twenties," etc.: Conversation with Anita Loos, 1970.

Inset quotation: "I ran afoul of a bastard named de Sano," etc.: Same letter to Scottie Fitzgerald as one mentioned on p. 40, *The Letters of F. Scott Fitzgerald*, p. 17 (Bantam edition).

p. 45 "... Sheilah Graham, who was also his salvation," etc.: Interviews, George Oppenheimer and FLG, May 18, 1973, and Professor Matthew Bruccoli and FLG, January 18, 1974.

"He was able to shed some of his sense of insecurity," etc.: *The Far Side of Paradise*, pp. 222–223.

"But it was possible for Charlie Lederer," etc.: Interview, Charles Lederer and FLG, November 1, 1973.

"A genius at procrastination ...": Interview, Helen Hayes and FLG, November 3, 1973.

p. 46 "There was 'bad blood' between David O. Selznick and MacArthur," etc. *Ibid.*

p. 47 "During a collaboration of Charlie Lederer and Ben Hecht ...": Interview, Charles Lederer and FLG, June 21, 1973.

7

p. 48 "The Algonquin had been for many years," etc.: *Tales of a Wayward Inn* by Frank Case (Stokes, New York, 1938); and *On Reflection* by Helen Hayes (M. Evans, New York, 1968), pp. 149–151.

p. 49 "Harpo Marx, an occasional guest, recalls ...": *Harpo Speaks* (with Rowland Barber) (Bernard Geis, New York, 1961), pp. 197–199.

"Edna Ferber called their influence 'tonic,'" etc.: *A Peculiar Treasure*, pp. 292–293.

p. 51 "... Scott Fitzgerald said that others do," etc.: *On Reflection*, p. 162.

"... the woman to whom Charlie was gallant ...": *Ibid.*, p. 162.

"Helen Hayes MacArthur already had become . . .": *Ibid.*, p. 175.

p. 52 ". . . he and Helen were married that same year . . .": "Charlie," an article condensed from *A Gift of Joy* by Helen Hayes with Lewis Funke (M. Evans, New York, 1965) in *The Reader's Digest*, November, 1965.

". . . Charlie and director King Vidor became tennis partners . . .": Interview, Helen Hayes and FLG, November 3, 1973.

". . . there was that nut, John Gilbert," etc.: *Ibid.*

p. 54 ". . . Friends told Charlie *everything*," etc.: Interview, Miss Hayes.

". . . He [Thalberg] once told screen writer Allen Rivkin," etc.: Interview, Allen Rivkin and FLG, June 19, 1973.

p. 55 "So it is not surprising that Irving Thalberg," etc.: Interview, Miss Hayes.

"A bit earlier, producer Walter Wanger had told her . . .": *Ibid.*

p. 56 "*The New York Times* echoed the general feeling . . .": Mordaunt Hall's review of *The Sin of Madelon Claudet*, *The New York Times* , November 8, 1931.

". . . That preview night, his wife declined to see her own picture," etc.: Interview, Miss Hayes.

p. 57 "He had tailored his revision to his wife's talents . . .": *Ibid.*

8

p. 58 "Sally Rand, performing with her fans . . .": *New York Daily News*, October 1, 1933.

"On March 10, 1933, at five-thirty in the afternoon, the four Marx brothers . . .": Conversation with Charles Lederer, April, 1974.

p. 59 "Goldwyn hired 'household words' . . .": Interview, George Oppenheimer and FLG, May 18, 1973.

p. 60 "Bartering began . . .": Interview, Billy Wilder and FLG, April 19, 1974.

p. 61 "When Capra told Cohn the film would cost . . .": *The Name above the Title* by Frank Capra (Macmillan, New York, 1971), p. 191.

p. 62 Inset quotation, *Ibid.*, pp. 192–193.

p. 64 "Capra lost three nights of sleep . . .": *Ibid.*, p. 200.

9

p. 64 "Sometime in the fall of 1933, Charlie MacArthur . . .":
Interview, Miss Hayes.

"When Helen was about to give birth to Mary . . .": *On Reflection*, p. 174.

p. 65 "Helen was rushed to the pier . . .": *Thalberg*, by Bob Thomas (Doubleday, New York, 1969), p. 241.

"He had been asked, ordered finally, to make something fresh . . .": Interview, Miss Hayes.

"Only the year before—or perhaps a year and a half . . .": *Ibid.*

p. 67 "One rumor, persistent in Hollywood after his departure . . .": Letter from Sam Marx in Writers' Guild of America, West *News Letter*, April, 1973.

"Ben Hecht and others believed that a discarded mistress . . .": Article by Ben Hecht, "If Hollywood Is Dead or Perhaps the Following," *Playboy* Magazine, November, 1960, courtesy John E. Schultheiss collection.

p. 68 "Thalberg, according to Salka Viertel's memoirs . . .": *The Kindness of Strangers*, by Salka Viertel (Holt, Rinehart and Winston, New York, 1969), p. 173.

10

p. 70 ". . . it was about 9,000 feet of film extracted by," etc.: *Sergei Eisenstein and Upton Sinclair: The Making and Unmaking of* Que Viva Mexico! by Harry M. Geduld and Ronald Gottesman (Indiana University Press, Bloomington, 1970), pp. 357 and 371.

". . . 'the Mexican Picture Trust' set up and managed by Mary Craig," etc.: *Ibid.*, pp. 102–107.

". . . and the Sinclairs were alarmed by its 'lack of a story'": *Ibid.*, pp. 32–33.

"Eisenstein stated then that it was his plan . . .": *Ibid.*, p. xxvii.

p. 71 "Stalin believed he was 'a deserter' . . .": *Ibid.*, p. 212.

p. 72 ". . . attended services at Aimee Semple McPherson's," etc.: *The Kindness of Strangers* by Salka Viertel (Holt, Rinehart and Winston, New York, 1969), p. 145.

". . . Marie Seton noted that Mexico had interested Eisenstein," etc.: *Sergei Eisenstein and Upton Sinclair*, pp. 3–5.

Inset quotation, ". . . In Mexico, death is no longer," etc.: *Ibid.*, p. 5.

Inset quotation, "Death. Skulls of people . . .": *Ibid.*, p. xxvii.

p. 73 "Sinclair planned a picnic lunch . . .": *The Kindness of Strangers*, pp. 143–144.

p. 74 "Sinclair, ten months into the film . . .": *Sergei Eisenstein and Upton Sinclair*, pp. 199–200.

Inset quotation, "Dear Zalka!" (letter dated January 27, 1932): *The Kindness of Strangers*, pp. 155–157.

p. 76 "Seeing that the impasse with the Sinclairs . . .": *Ibid.*, p. 159.

"When the abortion, *Thunder Over Mexico*, opened . . .": Review by Richard Watts, Jr., *New York Herald Tribune*, October 1, 1933.

p. 77 "In a letter to a friend." etc.: *Sergei Eisenstein and Upton Sinclair*, pp. 404–405.

"The Sinclairs even tried to sell bullfighting footage . . .": *Ibid.*, p. 361.

p. 78 "Around 1955, Jay Leyda . . .": *Ibid.*, pp. 424–425.

"Richard Watts, Jr., called Sinclair a 'despoiler,'" etc.: Review, *New York Herald Tribune*, October 1, 1933.

12

p. 85 ". . . she didn't have the wherewithal to buy her own lunch," etc.: Interview, Dorothy Parker and Wyatt Cooper.

"She dismissed the Roundtable Group . . .": *Ibid.*

"George Oppenheimer loaned them his home . . .": Interiew, George Oppenheimer and FLG, February 28, 1973.

p. 86 "Dorothy would sit nearby, often knitting . . .": Interview, Wyatt Cooper and FLG, November 28, 1973.

"He told me that he used to affect a cane and spats," etc.: Interview, Dorothy Parker and Wyatt Cooper.

"George Oppenheimer was to advance them the money," etc.: Interview, George Oppenheimer and FLG.

p. 87 "Dorothy despised her mother-in-law and her 'little ways' . . .": Interview, Dorothy Parker and Wyatt Cooper, 1963.

"She said her older sister . . .": *Ibid.*

"Her politics did not come . . .": Interview, Beatrice Ames and FLG, March 8, 1974.

p. 88 ". . . she and Alan threw a huge buffet dinner in their new mansion for the Scottsboro Boys," etc.: *Ibid.*

p. 89   "Her last public appearance . . .": Interview, Wyatt Cooper and FLG, November 28, 1973.

p. 90   "She gave Alan the back of her hand . . .": *You Might As Well Live: The Life and Times of Dorothy Parker* by John Keats (Simon and Schuster, New York, 1970), pp. 249 and 267.

". . . And what did you do for Jesus today?," etc.: Interview, Dorothy Parker and Wyatt Cooper, 1963.

13

Inset quotation: "There came a period in the early thirties . . .": *My First Hundred Years in Hollywood* by Jack Warner (Random House, New York, 1965), p. 218.

"It was one of the more degrading spectacles . . .": *Only Victims* by Robert Vaughn (Putnam, New York, 1972), p. 77.

". . . as was the case with the poignant Ann Dvorak," etc.: *My First Hundred Years in Hollywood*, p. 277.

pp. 93–96   Background and reviews on Anna Sten are drawn from *Cinema Arts* Magazine, July, 1937, and the *New York Herald Tribune*, February 2, 1934.

Part Two: Rebellion and Retreat

p. 98   "The First Defector (1919)": *D. W. Griffith: His Life and Work* by Robert M. Henderson (Oxford University Press, New York, 1972), pp. 205–206.

1

p. 100   "It was tough-minded, self-confident Joseph L. Mankiewicz . . .": Interview, Joseph L. Mankiewicz and FLG, May 1, 1974.

"When Irving Thalberg's health began to wane . . .": *Ibid.*

p. 101   "Joan Crawford said that Joe took the suds . . .": *Joan Crawford: an Autobiography* (with Jane Jesner Ardmore) (Paperback Library, New York, 1964), p. 85 (Doubleday, original publisher, 1962).

"He rose from a lowly title writer . . .": Interview, Joseph L. Mankiewicz and FLG, May 1, 1974.

p. 102 "His titles—*Three Sinners* . . .": *Memo from David O. Selznick* edited by Rudy Behlmer (Viking, New York, 1972), p. 20.

"Garbo's contract in the early 30's . . .": *Ibid.*, p. 97.

p. 103 "Mankiewicz had to learn to live with getting 'frozen out' . . .": Interview, Joseph L. Mankiewicz and FLG.

". . . Zanuck (who had no subtlety at all"), etc.: *Ibid.*

". . . Myron, who promptly would 'stick him,'" etc.: *Memo from Selznick*, p. 335.

2

p. 103 "Following an elevator incident . . .": Interview, Charles Lederer and FLG, June 21, 1973.

p. 104 ". . . with just four stars (George Arliss, etc.)": *Don't Say Yes Until I Finish Talking* by Mel Gussow (Pocket Books edition, New York, 1972), p. 56 (Doubleday, original publisher, 1971).

"Johnson's byline at the time . . .": Interview, Nunnally Johnson and FLG, November 5, 1973.

pp. 105–106 Inset quotation: "Mr. Darryl Zanuck, the producer . . .": *The Mighty Barnum: A Screenplay*, by Gene Fowler and Bess Meredyth (Covici, Friede, New York, 1934), Foreword, pp. xii–xiv.

3

p. 109 Footnote: "The Production of *Rasputin*, etc." : Interview, Ann Shirley Lederer, March 28, 1974.

p. 110 ". . . and turned out at least half a dozen first acts, etc.": *A Child of the Century* by Ben Hecht (Signet edition, New York, 1955), p. 364 (Simon and Schuster, original publisher, 1954).

p. 111 Inset quotation: "I do not mean . . . writers or directors, etc.": *Ibid.*, pp. 438–439.

p. 113 "Ben was careful in setting down . . . the names, etc.": "Elegy for Wonderland," article by Ben Hecht, *Esquire* Magazine, March, 1959 (courtesy, John E. Schultheiss collection).

p. 114 Inset quotation: "Two generations of Americans . . .": *A Child of the Century*, pp. 437–438.

p. 115 Inset quotation: "Out of these grass roots . . .": *The Memoirs of Will H. Hays*, p. 433.

p. 116 "Hays got together a group of 'experts,' etc.": *Ibid.*, pp. 439, 440.

Inset quotation: "A matter that came in for a lot of discussion . . .": *Ibid.*, p. 442.

p. 117   "So the Codemakers went for *Romance*. . . .": *Ibid*.
        Inset quotation: "The Movement was like an avenging
fire, etc.": *Ibid*., p. 451.
    p. 118   "Billy Wilder was to say . . .": Interview, Billy Wilder
and FLG, April 19, 1974.
        "On one of their first evenings, the Hechts . . .":
Interview, Helen Hayes and FLG, November 3, 1973.

4

    p. 122   "He returned from a vacation in Italy in July, 1936
. . .": *The New York Times*, July 7, 1936.
    p. 123   Inset quotation: "Standing on a set . . .": *A Child of the
Century* by Ben Hecht, p. 451.

5

    p. 124   ". . . especially since Helen Hayes, etc.": *Future Indefi-
nite* by Noel Coward (Doubleday, New York, 1954), p. 206.
        "The film writers . . . were off to Charleston, etc.":
"Miracle in Astoria," article by Katharine Best, *Stage* Magazine,
March, 1935, courtesy John E. Schultheiss collection.
    p. 125   ". . . and crept out two years later in a remote Boston
theater, etc.": Review of *Once in a Blue Moon* by Howard Barnes,
New York Herald Tribune, December 2, 1936.
        "The credo of the film was spoken, etc.": Quotation taken
from review of *Soak the Rich* by Frank S. Nugent, *The New York
Times*, February 5, 1936.
    p. 126   ". . . needs a spanking, etc.": *Ibid*.
        "Then word came to them that their samaritan . . .":
Interview, Charles Lederer and FLG, November 8, 1973.
    p. 128   ". . . both Hecht and MacArthur were pinning their
hopes," etc.: Interview, Helen Hayes and FLG.
        "Rose Hecht was in Europe . . .": Interview, Charles
Lederer and FLG, November 8, 1973.

6

    p. 128   "When I am doing something commercial . . .": Early
draft of *The Specter of the Rose* by Ben Hecht.

p. 129 "*Dodsworth* was called *Infidelity* . . .": *Filmlexicon degli Autori e delle Opere.*

p. 130 "Samuel Goldwyn's production of *The Hurricane* . . .": Interview, Charles Lederer and FLG, July 4, 1973.

"*The Times* called special-effects man . . .": Review of *The Hurricane* by Frank S. Nugent, *The New York Times*, November 10, 1937.

Part Three: Fitzgerald Returns: Dorothy Parker Goes to the Front

1

p. 135 "In May of 1936, European newspapers . . .": *Days of Our Years* by Pierre van Passen (Hillman-Curl, New York, 1939), p. 421.

". . . with Generalísimo Franco as his country's 'Saviour', etc.": *Ibid.*, pp. 433–434.

"The Nazis were already well into the Civil War . . .": *Ibid.*, p. 446.

p. 136 "Donald Ogden Stewart, who had become exceedingly valuable . . .": Interview, Beatrice Ames and FLG, March 8, 1974.

p. 137 "Mrs. Parker called Benchley 'Fred' . . .": *Ibid.*

"Beatrice Ames, divorced over thirty-five years . . .": Interview, Beatrice Ames and FLG, March 8, 1974.

p. 138 "(Kyle Crichton was called a Communist . . .)": *O'Hara* by Finis Farr, p. 170.

p. 139 "Biberman was . . . a director of considerable daring, etc.'": *Herbert Biberman: Artist and Man*, article by Gale Sondergaard Biberman, *American Dialog Magazine*, Winter, 1972.

Inset quotation: "The story that the film throws . . .": *The Morning After the First Night*, by George Jean Nathan (Knopf, New York, 1938), pp. 226–227.

p. 140 "On Labor Day weekend, the Thalbergs . . .": *Thalberg* by Bob Thomas (Doubleday, New York, 1969), p. 316.

"Back East, Charlie MacArthur was alone . . .": Interview, Helen Hayes and FLG.

2

p. 143   "The following year, British author Graham Greene
. . .": *The Literary Life* by Robert Phelps and Peter Deane (Chatto
and Windus, London, 1969), p. 166.

p. 144   "*New York Times* critic Frank Nugent warned . . .":
Review of *Wee Willie Winkie, The New York Times*, July 24, 1937.

3

p. 146   ". . . producer Sol Wurtzel, who supervised, etc.": Conversation with Charles Lederer, November 1, 1973.

"One of the first titles Selznick appended . . .": *Memo
from Selznick*, p. 108.

"In 1937, in a memo to his long-time aide . . .": *Ibid.*, pp.
108, 109.

4

p. 148   "The third Hollywood venture . . .": *The Letters of F.
Scott Fitzgerald*, letter to his daughter, July, 1937, p. 17.

"There are clauses in the contract . . .": *Ibid.*, letter to
Max Perkins, before July 19, 1937, pp. 278–279.

p. 149   "Helen Hayes MacArthur brought Scottie . . .":
Interview, Helen Hayes and FLG.

"Late in July, Marc Connelly invited Sheilah Graham
. . .": *Beloved Infidel* by Sheilah Graham and Gerold Frank (Bantam
edition, New York, 1959), p. 132 (Holt, original publisher, 1959).

5

p. 149   "At Helen Hayes's suggestion . . .": Interview, Helen
Hayes and FLG.

"I stared at the telegram . . .": *Beloved Infidel*, p. 136.

"But Scott would come . . . and we'd all go out . . .":
Interview, Helen Hayes and FLG.

p. 150   "Early on, Sheilah noticed that the more literate . . .":
Beloved Infidel, p. 133.

"When she [Sheilah] discovered what a strong bond
. . .": Conversation with Gerold Frank, March 20, 1973.

p. 151   "Dorothy Parker and too many of Scott's other friends
. . .": Interview, Dorothy Parker and Wyatt Cooper, 1963.

"That obsessional regard for appetizing fare . . .": *Beloved Infidel*, p. 41.

"Scott, the terrible puritan, was hopelessly involved . . .": *Ibid.*, p. 193.

Footnote, "I liked Quentin and his close friend, John McClain, etc.": *A State of Heat*, by Sheilah Graham (Grosset & Dunlap, New York, 1972), p. 115.

"But she . . . had enrolled in Scott's 'College of One,' etc.": *Beloved Infidel*, p. 198.

p. 152 "In novelist Anthony Powell's words . . .": *Hollywood Canteen: A Memoir of Scott Fitzgerald in 1937* by Anthony Powell, published in the *Fitzgerald-Hemingway Annual*, 1971 edition, and first published in the *London Times* (*The Times* Saturday Review), Microcard Editions, Washington, 1971, p. 71.

"Before Irving Thalberg's death . . .": *Crazy Sundays: F. Scott Fitzgerald in Hollywood* by Aaron Latham (Viking, New York, 1971), pp. 71–73.

pp. 153–154 ". . . an example of Scott's dialogue, etc.": *A Yank at Oxford* by F. Scott Fitzgerald, original manuscript, Loew's Inc., courtesy Professor Matthew Bruccoli.

p. 154 "George Oppenheimer who was one of the writers . . .": Interview, George Oppenheimer and FLG, February 28, 1973.

p. 155 "Daughter Scottie was 'having the time of her young life . . .'": *The Letters of F. Scott Fitzgerald*, letter to Max Perkins dated before August 24, 1937, p. 279.

"Only the year before . . .": drawn from *The Crack-Up* (New Directions, New York, 1956).

p. 157 "When he went on his first alcoholic binge . . .": *Beloved Infidel*, pp. 151–152.

p. 158 "Fitzgerald's screenplay was brilliant . . .": Conversation with Matthew Bruccoli, January 18, 1974.

"Later he would do the same thing . . .": Interview, Joseph L. Mankiewicz and FLG, May 1, 1974.

"Scott wrote Mankiewicz . . .": *The Letters of F. Scott Fitzgerald*, letter to Joseph L. Mankiewicz dated January 20, 1938, pp. 570–571.

p. 159 ". . . [Mankiewicz] had, like Isherwood, lived part of the twenties . . .": Interview, Joseph L. Mankiewicz and FLG.

"Prior to the film's release . . .": *Crazy Sundays*, pp. 145–146.

6

p. 160   ". . . in the company of Lillian Hellman.": *Pentimento* by Lillian Hellman (Little, Brown, Boston, 1973), p. 102.

"Dorothy had bought herself . . .": *New York Post*, August 19, 1937, p. 11.

"Alan made her nervous . . .": *Pentimento*, p. 102.

p. 161   "Lillian had gone into partnership . . .": *Ernest Hemingway: A Life Story* by Carlos Baker (Scribner, New York, 1969), p. 300.

"Lillian got bored with the Campbells' "fancy friends' . . .": *Pentimento*, pp. 103–104.

p. 162   ". . . but Lillian stayed on in Europe, etc.": *The Little War* by Lillian Hellman, part of a diary published in *This Is My Best* edited by Whit Burnett (Dial, New York, 1942), pp. 989–996.

p. 163   ". . . she wrote several dispatches for *The New Masses*, etc.": *You Might As Well Live: The Life and Times of Dorothy Parker* by John Keats (Simon and Schuster, New York, 1970), p. 223.

"In her story on the Spanish Civil War . . .": *Soldiers of the Republic*, a story by Dorothy Parker, *The Portable Dorothy Parker* (Viking, New York, 1944), p. 165.

p. 164   Footnote, "In Spain, there was specific name-calling . . .": *Days of Our Years*, pp. 448–449.

p. 165   "On May 15, 1938, he [Wanger] sent a wire . . .": *New York World Telegram*, May 16, 1938.

"Wanger told reporters . . .": *Ibid.*

7

p. 167   "In a letter to Max Perkins . . .": *The Letters of F. Scott Fitzgerald*, pp. 280–281.

"While Scott's obsession with good breeding . . .": based upon reading the screenplay *Infidelity* by F. Scott Fitzgerald as published in *Esquire* Magazine, December, 1973.

pp. 168–177   *Ibid.*

p. 170   "On May 10, 1938, he sent Stromberg . . .": *New Treatment and End of Infidelity* by F. Scott Fitzgerald, courtesy Professor Matthew Bruccoli.

p. 171   "In one of them, he writes . . ." *Six Previously Unpublished Fitzgerald Letters to Hunt Stromberg* with an introduction by R. L. Samsell, letter dated April 12, 1938, published in *The Fitzgerald-*

Hemingway Annual, 1972, edited by Matthew J. Bruccoli and C. E. Frazer Clark, Jr., Microcard Editions, Washington, 1972, p. 14.

"... he rested for a few days, etc.": *Beloved Infidel*, p. 201.

p. 172 "He was instructed not to add ...": *Crazy Sundays*, pp. 214–215.

"Sheilah came home to find them ...": *Beloved Infidel*, pp. 223–224.

"... hard enough to make her ears ring, etc.": *Ibid.*, pp. 224–225.

p. 173 "In Cuba, Fitzgerald attempted ...": *The Far Side of Paradise* by Arthur Mizener (Houghton Mifflin, Boston, 1951), p. 283.

"Scott dismissed Ober ...": *Ibid.*, p. 285.

p. 174 "He wrote his daughter ...": *The Letters of F. Scott Fitzgerald*, letter to Frances Scott Ftizgerald dated October 31, 1939, p. 62.

"Six thousand words into the work ...": *The Far Side of Paradise*, p. 287.

"Help again came from Hollywood ...": *Ibid.*, pp. 289–290.

"... listening to crickets, etc.": *Beloved Infidel*, p. 235.

p. 175 "... Scott wrote that he was 'coming out of hibernation', etc.": Interview, Beatrice Ames and FLG, March 8, 1974.

"Dorothy and Alan had found ...": *Ibid.*

p. 176 "In Andrew Turnbull's phrase ...": *Scott Fitzgerald* by Andrew Turnbull (Scribner, New York, 1962).

"He wonders how Ernest (Hemingway) feels about things ...": *The Letters of F. Scott Fitzgerald*, letter to Max Perkins dated June 6, 1940, pp. 294–295.

p. 177 "Except for a dinner ...": Interview, Wells Root and FLG, April 3, 1974.

"Fitzgerald had set it 'safely in a period' ...": Notes for *The Last Tycoon*, edited by Edmund Wilson (Scribner, New York, 1941), p. 141.

"Christmas week, Scott felt well enough ...": *Beloved Infidel*, p. 248.

"He spoke with Sheilah ...": *Ibid.*, p. 250.

p. 178 "Sheilah saw 'out of the corner of my eye' ...": *Ibid.*, p. 251.

"Fitzgerald was laid out ...": *The Far Side of Paradise*, p. 298.

8

p. 180 "Back in the Spring of 1937 . . .": *Letters of Aldous Huxley*, letter to Julian Huxley dated May 7, 1937, p. 421.

". . . very extraordinary place, etc.": *Ibid.*, letter to Julian dated June 3, 1937, p. 421.

". . . he received an inquiry from a Los Angeles bookseller, etc.": *Ibid.*, letter to Jacob I. Zietlin dated July 12, 1937, p. 423.

"In the fall, Huxley wrote a first draft . . .": *Ibid.*, footnote, p. 423.

p. 181 ". . . the old John Jacob Astor estate, etc.": *Ibid.*, letter to Harold Raymond dated December 15, 1937, p. 429.

". . . as man becomes more promiscuous, etc.": *Ibid.*, letter to J. B. Priestley dated December 17, 1937, p. 430.

"In the Arizona desert . . .": *Ibid.*, footnote, p. 433.

". . . in Hollywood exactly one block south of where Scott, etc.": Interview, Christopher Isherwood and FLG, November 3, 1973.

"In July, Huxley was put under contract . . .": *Letters of Aldous Huxley*, letter to Julian Huxley dated July 22, 1938, p. 435.

"'I shall enjoy doing the job' . . .": *Ibid.*

p. 182 "Garbo had become friendly . . .": Interview, Christopher Isherwood and FLG, October 29, 1973.

9

p. 182 "Goldwyn had sent a background unit . . .": Interview, Geraldine Fitzgerald and FLG, March 1, 1974.

"Goldwyn was unhappy about his [Olivier's] 'unusual face'.": *Ibid.*

10

p. 183 "In 1939, after a world tour . . .": Interview, Christopher Isherwood and FLG, November 3, 1973.

p. 185 "Charlie Lederer's 'spoof' of the Russians', etc.": Conversation with Charles Lederer, June 21, 1973.

"Thoeren himself deserves a mention . . .": Interview, Charles Lederer and FLG, October 31, 1973.

pp. 186–188 Background on William Randolph Hearst drawn from *Citizen Hearst* by W. A. Swanberg (Scribner, New York, 1961), and *Marion Davies* by FLG.

p. 187   "At least a dozen Americans of great wealth . . .": *Great Houses of America* by Henry Lionel Williams and Ottalie Williams (Putnam, New York, 1966).

p. 188   "Aldous Huxley even used . . .": *Letters of Aldous Huxley*, letter to Harold Raymond dated August 20, 1939, p. 446.

"Herman Mankiewicz was bolder . . .": Interview, Mrs. Herman Mankiewicz and FLG, July, 1970.

p. 189   "And there were subtler forms of abuse . . .": *Ibid.*

Part Four: Of Idiot's Delight and Related Matters

1

p. 193   "Charlie Lederer . . . described Sherwood, etc.": Interview, Charles Lederer and FLG, June 21, 1973.

Footnote: "His collaborator . . .": *Ibid.*

Critical reaction in London to *Acropolis*: *The Worlds of Robert E. Sherwood: Mirror to His Times* by John Mason Brown (Harper & Row, New York, 1965).

". . . which was to lead to a nasty divorce, etc.": *Ibid.*, p. 286.

p. 194   Description of Sherwood's politics: *Ibid.* and Volume II, *The Ordeal of a Playwright: Robert E. Sherwood and the Challenge of War* (Harper & Row, New York, 1970).

p. 195   ". . . it was not considered good form, etc." Interview, Charles Lederer and FLG, July 3, 1973.

Inset quotation: ". . . he dined with such friends, etc.": *The Worlds of Robert E. Sherwood*, p. 345.

". . . to read his script of *Idiot's Delight*, etc.": *Ibid.*, p. 346.

p. 196   "Sherwood suddenly asked . . .": Interview, Charles Lederer and FLG, July 3, 1973.

p. 199   Selznick selecting writer for *Rebecca*: *Memo from Selznick*, p. 274.

Inset quotation: "I had pretty well decided . . .": *Ibid.*, p. 282.

2

p. 201   "Hawks was an excellent critic . . .": Interview, Charles Lederer and FLG, March 30, 1974.

pp. 201–205 Comparison of early draft with final production drawn from screening of film after reading an early draft of *His Girl Friday* by Charles Lederer, unpublished.

pp. 205–209 Charles Lederer's beginnings as a screenwriter: Interview, Charles Lederer and FLG, July 2, 1972.

p. 210 "Equally playful but more energetic . . .": *The Fabulous Life and Times of Preston Sturges: An American Dream* by James Ursini (Curtis, New York, 1973).

p. 211 "They could not have been more unlike . . .": Conversation with Veronica Lake, London, July 15, 1969, and *Veronica* by Veronica Lake (with Donald Bain) (W. H. Allen, London, 1969).

p. 212 "'a true canvas of the suffering . . .'": *The Fabulous Life and Times of Preston Sturges*, p. 90.

pp. 213–215 *An Aside—Veronica Lake*: Conversation with Veronica Lake.

3

p. 215 "René Clair . . .": *Agee on Film*, Volume I (Grosset & Dunlap, New York, 1967), p. 343.

p. 216 Footnote, "*Hail the Conquering Hero* is a nearly pure . . .": Interview, Charles Lederer and FLG, June 21, 1973.

p. 217 "Oppenheimer had been surprised . . .": *The View from the Sixties: Memories of a Spent Life* by George Oppenheimer (McKay, New York, 1966), p. 172.

5

p. 219 Inset quotation: "For some time, I had been mulling over . . .": Preface to *Wilson* by Darryl F. Zanuck in *Best Film Plays, 1943–44*, edited by John Gassner and Dudley Nichols (Crown, New York, 1945), p. 1.

p. 220 Footnote on Samuel Gompers from *Who Was Who in America* (Marquis, Chicago).

"Trotti turned out to be . . .": *Don't Say Yes Until I Finish Talking* by Mel Gussow, p. 64.

p. 221 Inset quotation: "I saw how destructive . . .": Preface to *Wilson*, pp. 1 and 2.

p. 222 "We had learned . . .": *Ibid.*, p. 2.

". . . to make its point, a picture must be, etc., *Ibid.*, p. 4.

p. 223 "A prime example is the scene in the railway . . .": *Wilson*, a screenplay by Lamar Trotti as published in *Best Film Plays, 1943–44*.

pp. 225–231 *An Aside—Geraldine Fitzgerald:* Interview, Geraldine Fitzgerald and FLG, March 1, 1974, and Interview, Charles Lederer and FLG, June 21, 1973.

6

p. 233 "Sturges only made one film for Hughes . . .": *The Fabulous Life and Times of Preston Sturges*, p. 171.

Part Five: Fear and Dissolution

p. 236 "How do you protect . . .": *Thirty Years of Treason: Excerpts from Hearings before the House Committee on Un-American Activities, 1938–1968*, edited by Eric Bentley (Viking, New York, 1971, p. 248.

1

p.237 *The Spectre of the Rose* scenario is by Ben Hecht, unpublished.

p. 239–241 Background on Hecht's role in the Irgun from interview, Charles Lederer and FLG, July 6, 1973.

p. 240 "'I am like the buffalo hunter' . . .": *Ibid.*

2

p. 242 "Their studio was new and fairly audacious . . .": Interview, Abraham Polonsky and FLG, March 23, 1974.

p. 243–244 *An Aside—John Garfield:* Conversation with John Garfield, Aversa, Italy, 1945.

p. 245 "Then suddenly, after weeks of inquisitory sessions . . .": *Ibid.*

p. 246 ". . . he was dead, etc.": John Garfield's obituary, *The New York Times*, May 22, 1952.

3

p. 246 "Abraham Polonsky, who talks freely . . .": Interview, Abraham Polonsky and FLG.

pp. 247–248 John Howard Lawson's interrogation and indictment: Interview, John Howard Lawson and FLG, May 16, 1972.

p. 248 Inset quotation: "Today, when the American screen

. . .": *Film: The Creative Process* by John Howard Lawson (Hill and Wang, New York, 1964), p. 67.

"Miss Rand was a Russian ex-patriate . . .": *Only Victims: A Study of Show Business Blacklisting* by Robert Vaughn (Putnam, New York, 1972), p. 90.

p. 249   "You paint a very dismal picture . . .": *Ibid.*, p. 91.

p. 251   ". . . if I were given the responsibility of getting rid, etc.": *Ibid.*, p. 79.

"Screenwriter Fred Niblo, Jr. . . .": Obituary, Fred Niblo, Jr., *The New York Times*, February 22, 1973.

p. 252   "John Howard Lawson remembers a knock . . .": Interview, John Howard Lawson and FLG, May 16, 1972.

pp. 253–254   Background on Lawson in Hollywood: *Ibid.*

p. 254   "Mr. Lawson, are you now, or have you ever been . . .": *Only Victims*, pp. 93–94.

p. 256   "But Stewart had influence . . .": Interview, Donald Ogden Stewart and Max Wilk, Oral History Project, American Film Institute, Louis B. Mayer Foundation, London, December 8, 13, and 20, 1971.

4

pp. 258–261   "Anne Shirley, alias Dawn O'Day, had been . . .": Interview, Anne Shirley Lederer and FLG, March 28, 1974.

5

p. 262   "Under pseudonyms, he kept an income . . .": Interview, Abraham Polonsky and FLG, March 23, 1974.

pp. 262–264   "Albert Maltz was sent to a southern prison camp . . .": Interview, Albert Maltz and FLG, May 19, 1972.

p. 264   Inset quotation: ". . . in my last interview before leaving, etc.": *Inquisition in Eden*, by Alvah Bessie (Macmillan, New York, 1965), p. 267.

6

p. 264   "Sometime in 1948 . . .": Interview, Allen Rivkin and FLG, May, 1973, and conversation with Charles Lederer, March 28, 1974.

pp. 265–266   "If I hadn't been in the middle of getting a movie . . .": Interview, Billy Wilder and FLG, April 19, 1974.

p. 267 "Walking around Paramount in those days . . .": *The Bright Side of Billy Wilder, Primarily* by Tom Wood (Doubleday, New York, 1970), pp. 3–4.

"Brecht . . . was treated like some diseased parcel, etc.": *Bertolt Brecht: His Life, His Art and His Times* by Frederic Ewen, pp. 497–509.

p. 268 "But he could not be bought easily . . .": *Charles Laughton and I* by Elsa Lanchester (Faber and Faber, London, 1938), p. 95.

p. 269 "But once when Marlene . . .": *Ibid.*, p. 222.

"Laughton had begun his screen career . . .": *Ibid.*, p. 94.

p. 272 "Ruth Gordon remembered he was . . .": *Myself Among Others* by Ruth Gordon (Atheneum, New York, 1971), p. 74.

"In mid-1951, mystery writer Dashiell Hammett was sent to jail . . .": *New York Post*, July 23–26, 1951 ("The Strange Case of Dashiell Hammett").

p. 273 Joseph Breen letter to Ingrid Bergman: *See No Evil* by Jack Vizzard (Simon and Schuster, New York, 1970), pp. 146–147.

p. 274 Miss Bergman's reply: *Ibid.*, p. 148.

"On April 25, 1951, director Edward Dmytryk . . .": *Only Victims*, pp. 144–145.

(continued from page iv)

INDEX

ABOUT THE AUTHOR

Fred Lawrence Guiles first became known outside New York theatrical circles with his biography of Marilyn Monroe, *Norma Jean*, which has been translated into nine languages, and has sold over a million copies in all editions. Mr. Guiles is also the author of the definitive biography *Marion Davies*, and is at work on a forthcoming biography of Stan Laurel. The author of several screenplays, he completed the screen version of *Norma Jean*. Mr. Guiles divides his time between a rambling Dutchess County home, a Brooklyn apartment, and Beverly Hills, California.